**DOCTOR WHO**

**365 DAYS** OF
MEMORABLE MOMENTS
AND IMPOSSIBLE
THINGS

JUSTIN RICHARDS

1 3 5 7 9 10 8 6 4 2

BBC Books, an imprint of Ebury Publishing
20 Vauxhall Bridge Road,
London SW1V 2SA

BBC Books is part of the Penguin Random House group of companies whose
addresses can be found at global.penguinrandomhouse.com

 Penguin
Random House
UK

This book is published to accompany the television series entitled *Doctor Who*,
broadcast on BBC One. *Doctor Who* is a BBC Wales production.
Executive producers: Steven Moffat and Brian Minchin

Commissioning editor: Albert DePetrillo
Editor: Charlotte Macdonald
Illustrations: Freakhouse Graphics
Production: Alex Goddard
Copyeditor: Steve Tribe
Jacket design: Two Associates

With thanks to Andrew Pixley

First published by BBC Books in 2016

www.eburypublishing.co.uk

A CIP catalogue record for this book is available from the British Library

ISBN 9781785940262

Typeset in India by Thomson Digital Pvt Ltd, Noida, Delhi
Printed and bound in Great Britain by Clays Ltd, St Ives PLC

Penguin Random House is committed to a sustainable future for our business,
our readers and our planet. This book is made from Forest Stewardship
Council® certified paper.

MIX
Paper from
responsible sources
FSC
www.fsc.org    FSC® C018179

# CONTENTS

# ABOUT THIS BOOK

Let's make one thing quite clear: this is not the sort of book you read from cover to cover, beginning to end. Well, you might. But you probably shouldn't. It is a book to be dipped into, a book in which you can discover things in random order. In fact, if you did read it from start to finish, you would find that the sequence of main topics covered seems rather strange.

That's because the topics are – as far as possible – tied to the dates and events that happened on those days. So the Third Doctor is discussed on 3 January, as that is when his first episode was transmitted. But the First Doctor didn't appear until 23 November – so we don't cover him until much later.

So far as possible the main topic for each day is in some way related to something that happened on that day. But not always. There are some topics we wanted to cover which don't really relate to a specific date. And there are some dates on which nothing much actually happened – or if it did, it's already covered on another more appropriate day.

But for each and every day, we do cover one topic from the worlds of *Doctor Who* in detail while we also provide a list of things that happened on this day. That list contains fictional and actual historical events (shown in bold type) from the Doctor Who narrative, as well as production events that are worthy of note. It also lists every episode that received its first UK transmission on that day (up to the end of 2015). Some other broadcasts – notable repeats, or showings on a different day on BBC Wales, for example – are also listed. As a convention, we refer to 'classic' *Doctor Who* – from 1963 to 1989 – as having 'seasons', while the current version of *Doctor Who* has series. So the first season featured the First Doctor and ran from *An Unearthly Child* in 1963 to *The Reign of Terror* in 1964. But the first series featured the Ninth Doctor and ran from *Rose* to *The Parting of the Ways* in 2005.

One last thing – the cover of this book lies. It says '365 days', but in fact we've included 29 February, so there are 366. This seems only fair as things happened on that day in the *Doctor Who* universe. But let's not dwell on that – when the Doctor is involved things can get quite wibbly-wobbly and timey-wimey enough, thank you.

# 1 JANUARY

# Who is the Doctor?

Although we have followed his adventures through space and time for over fifty years, the Doctor remains an enigma. We do know that he is a Time Lord from the planet Gallifrey. For all their great powers, his fellow Time Lords did nothing but observe, whereas the Doctor wanted to experience the wonders of the universe. So he stole a TARDIS and ventured out to explore the universe at first hand. Since then, he has come to realise that there is evil that must be fought. When his body wears out or is damaged he can change his form, regenerating into a new person – who looks and behaves quite differently but retains the same basic underlying character.

Apart from this we know almost nothing about him. We don't even know his name.

But we do know that the Doctor is a man of knowledge and wisdom. The limits of his abilities and talents, if indeed there are any, are unknown and unknowable.

He walks for ever in eternity. And he walks alone, lost in his own wanderlust and rocked between boundless enthusiasm and numbing ennui. Companions may come and go, but he is rarely very close to any of them. The only *real* feeling we can be sure that the Doctor demonstrates at all is his utter abhorrence of evil.

**1966** The TARDIS lands in Trafalgar Square during the new year celebrations as depicted in the First Doctor episode *Volcano*.

**1966** *Volcano* – the eighth episode of *The Daleks' Master Plan* – is broadcast.

**1972** *Day of the Daleks* Episode 1 opens Season 9, and sees the Daleks return for the first time since 1967's *The Evil of the Daleks*.

**1977** Leela is introduced in Part 1 of *The Face of Evil*.

**2000** The events of the *Doctor Who* TV movie conclude on this day.

**2007** A 60-minute pilot episode for *The Sarah Jane Adventures* titled *Invasion of the Bane* is broadcast.

**2010** *The End of Time, Part Two* is David Tennant's last episode as the Doctor. It is also the last episode on which Russell T Davies and Julie Gardner are Executive Producers.

# 2 JANUARY

## The Arrival of the Master

First introduced in *Terror of the Autons* (1971), the Master is a renegade Time Lord like the Doctor. In *The Sea Devils* (1972), the Doctor tells Jo: 'He used to be a friend of mine once. A very good friend. In fact you might almost say that we were at school together.' They might be at opposite ends of the moral spectrum, but the Doctor and the Master each have an empathy with the other.

Why or when the Master left his people is never stated, and in *The Deadly Assassin* (1976) we discover that he has destroyed all traces of his existence. He has also plundered the Time Lord files for information that might be of use to him.

The Master is charming yet ruthless, suave but evil. Whatever form he is in – as the saturnine opponent of the Third Doctor, the decaying husk of *The Deadly Assassin* and *The Keeper of Traken* (1981), the later more antagonistic regeneration, masquerading as Harold Saxon, or even in female form as 'Missy' – one thing about the Master remains indisputable: he is hungry for power. Whether it be power over the individuals he hypnotises, or dominion over the Universe itself, this never falters and is tempered only by a black sense of humour and a passion for destruction.

**1948** Deborah Watling, who played the Second Doctor's companion Victoria Waterfield, was born.

**1965** Vicki joins the Doctor, Ian and Barbara in the first episode of *The Rescue*, titled *The Powerful Enemy*. It is Dennis Spooner's first episode as Story Editor.

**1971** *Terror of the Autons* Episode 1 opens Season 8 and introduces Jo Grant, Captain Mike Yates, and the Master.

# 3 JANUARY

# Meet the Third Doctor

Exiled to twentieth-century Earth by the Time Lords, the Third Doctor represented a return to the more overtly authoritarian figure after the apparent muddling through of his predecessor. He became an intellectual man of action that his colleagues in UNIT respected and his companions looked up to. Despite his two hearts, his historical anecdotes, and his Venusian Aikido, his enforced alliance with UNIT brought the Doctor down to Earth in more ways than one.

Although he initially resents his situation, his relationship with his assistant Jo Grant softens the Doctor. By the time he meets Sarah Jane Smith in *The Time Warrior* (1973–1974), the Doctor has come to appreciate his almost revered position within UNIT. And beneath the sometimes crusty, arrogant exterior, the Doctor still retains the same depth of compassion and contempt for oppression and injustice. He is a man who feels things deeply – be it the loss of a friend as he drains his champagne at the close of *The Green Death* (1973) and slips quietly away from Jo's engagement party, or the remorse at having had to trick Omega in *The Three Doctors* (1972–1973).

**1970** Episode 1 of *Spearhead from Space* is the first episode to star Jon Pertwee as the Doctor, and opens Season 7. Liz Shaw is also introduced, as are the Autons and the Nestene Consciousness. It is the first episode made in colour, and shot entirely on film rather than predominantly on videotape.

**1976** *The Brain of Morbius* Part 1 introduces the Sisterhood of Karn.

**1980** *Warriors' Gate* Part 1

**1983** Omega returns (although his identity is kept secret for a while) in Part 1 of *Arc of Infinity* which opens Season 20. The future Sixth Doctor Colin Baker plays Commander Maxil – responsible for 'executing' his predecessor in this story.

# 4 JANUARY

## Meet the Fifth Doctor

One of the most 'human' of Doctors, the Fifth Doctor was apparently younger than his predecessors. He was also more affected by the regeneration process, needing to spend time in the TARDIS Zero Room in order to recover from the process.

Rather than a father figure, he was more of an older brother to his companions, and his affection for them was obvious. The Doctor's grief at the death of Adric in *Earthshock* (1982), or after Tegan leaves following the harrowing events of *Resurrection of the Daleks* (1984) is as poignant and as deep as his sadness when Nyssa decides to stay on Terminus.

But despite his apparent youth, the Doctor demonstrates again and again a depth of wisdom and experience that is at odds with his appearance. As Sharaz Jek tells him in *The Caves of Androzani* (1984), 'You have the mouth of a prattling jackanapes but your eyes, they tell a different story...'

The Fifth Doctor is also perhaps the most selfless of the Doctor's incarnations. Ultimately, he sacrifices his own life to save Peri – a young woman he barely knows.

**1964** *The Escape* – the third episode of *The Daleks*

**1969** *The Krotons* Episode 2

**1975** *Robot* Part 2

**1982** *Castrovalva* Part 1 is first episode to star Peter Davison as the Doctor and opens Season 19. It is the first episode not to debut on a Saturday. The story is script edited by Eric Saward.

**1989** *The Greatest Show in the Galaxy* Part 4 closes Season 25.

# 5 JANUARY

## When is a Police Box not a Police Box?

A TARDIS has the ability to change its appearance to blend in with the surroundings when it materialises in a new location. Only the exterior of the TARDIS exists as a real space-time event, but mapped onto one of the interior continua – so it can be changed into any shape as the outer-plasmic shell is driven by the Chameleon Circuit. But while both the Master's and the Meddling Monk's TARDISes do indeed change to fit in with their surroundings, the Chameleon Circuit in the Doctor's TARDIS is faulty.

When we first see the TARDIS, it is disguised as a police telephone box, in keeping with the era and location in which it arrives – although why a police box would be located in a junkyard is debateable. But when it leaves the junkyard at Totter's Lane, the Doctor is surprised that it doesn't change to fit in with the desolate landscape in which it then appears.

The Doctor has made several attempts to fix the Chameleon Circuit. He enlisted the help of the Logopolitans and their skill with Block Transfer Computation in *Logopolis* (1981). In *Attack of the Cybermen* (1985), the Doctor does manage to get the TARDIS to change – ironically on a return visit to the same junkyard in Totter's Lane. But the fix is only temporary and by the end of the story the TARDIS is once again stuck in its familiar police box form. That said, in *Vengeance on Varos* (1985) Peri does remark that the TARDIS materialised as a pyramid on the frozen plains of Ewa Nine…

ON THIS DAY

**1974** *The Time Warrior* Part 4

**1980** *The Horns of Nimon* Part 3

**1982** *Castrovalva* Part 2

**1983** *Arc of Infinity* Part 2

**1984** Both the Silurians and the Sea Devils return in *Warriors of the Deep* Part 1, which opens Season 21.

**1985** *Attack of the Cybermen* Part 1 opens Season 22. It is the first planned 45-minute episode, although the previous year's *Resurrection of the Daleks* had been edited from four 25-minute episodes into two 50-minute episodes to accommodate BBC One's coverage of the Winter Olympics.

# 6 JANUARY

## The Time Lords Send Three Doctors to Stop Omega

Omega was the solar engineer who provided the power source that gave the Time Lords time travel. But he was lost in the supernova created when he used a remote stellar manipulator (sometimes called 'the Hand of Omega') to detonate a star. Trapped inside a black hole, he created a world of antimatter by the sheer force of his will. This world reflected his mood – thunder rolled when he was angry. But although he could create whatever he wanted in this world, he could not escape from it, as to leave meant his will would no longer hold it together. Omega wore a mask to combat the corrosive effect of the singularity beam, but beneath the mask he no longer existed – having already corroded away so that only his will survived.

Determined to take his revenge on the Time Lords, who he believed had abandoned him, Omega drained away their energy, threatening their ability to travel in time. It took the combined efforts of the first three incarnations of the Doctor to stop Omega.

But although his antimatter world is destroyed in *The Three Doctors* (1972–1973), Omega returns in *Arc of Infinity* (1983), attempting to create a body for himself in the real universe based on the Fifth Doctor's form.

ON THIS DAY

**1968** *The Enemy of the World* Episode 3

**1973** *The Three Doctors* Episode 2

**1979** *The Power of Kroll* Part 3

**1984** *Warriors of the Deep* Part 2

# 7 JANUARY

# The Quest is the Quest

Although the Time Lords adopted a strict policy of not interfering in the affairs of other worlds and races, they were not always so distant and uninvolved.

It was at least partly what happened on the planet Minyos that led to this Time Lord policy of non-intervention. The Minyans thought of the Time Lords as gods, which was flattering, so the Time Lords gave them medical help, better communications and scientific aid. But rather than showing gratitude, the Minyans expelled the Time Lords at gunpoint. As the Fourth Doctor says: 'Then they went to war with each other, learned how to split the atom, discovered the toothbrush, and finally split the planet…'

The Doctor and Leela encounter the last of the Minyans on their ship the R1C, 100,000 years later on the other side of the universe in *Underworld* (1978). These Minyans maintain that 'the Quest is the Quest'. That quest is a seemingly never-ending mission to locate another Minyan ship, the P7E, which carries a race bank from which the Minyan race can be reborn.

**1967** *The Highlanders* Episode 4

**1978** *Underworld* Part 1 is Anthony Read's first episode as Script Editor.

**2014** Peter Capaldi's first full day of shooting for his debut story as the Twelfth Doctor – *Deep Breath*

## 8 JANUARY

# A Very Different Sort of Companion

Leela is a warrior of the tribe of Sevateem, which, although they do not know it, is descended from a human Survey Team. Leela is a huntress, a creature of instinct and intuition and, with typical impulsiveness, she runs into the TARDIS and dematerialises it at the end of *The Face of Evil* (1977). While she never loses her simplistic view of life, Leela does begin to understand the distinction between technology and magic as she travels with the Fourth Doctor.

She also gains more of an appreciation of the value of life. When she first meets the Doctor, Leela is happy to use her Janis thorns to paralyse and kill enemy Sevateem, or hatch-wielding Chinese servants of Weng-Chiang. But as he grows to value Leela's friendship and help, so the Doctor tries to 'educate' her.

Certainly, Leela learns. By the time she leaves the Doctor to stay on Gallifrey with Commander Andred in *The Invasion of Time* (1978), Leela has at least begun to fit into more advanced society. That said, she never loses her warrior instincts and outlook.

Although she is obviously deeply fond of the Doctor as well as seeing him as her mentor, Leela's closest relationship is perhaps with K-9. It is Leela who urges the Doctor to take K-9 in the TARDIS in *The Invisible Enemy* (1977), and K-9 in return decides to stay with Leela on Gallifrey.

ON THIS DAY

**1908** William Hartnell, who played the First Doctor, was born.

**1966** *Golden Death* – the ninth episode of *The Daleks' Master Plan*

**1972** *Day of the Daleks* Episode 2

**1977** *The Face of Evil* Part 2

# 9 JANUARY

## Jo Grant is the Doctor's New Assistant

Introduced in *Terror of the Autons* (1971), Josephine Grant joins UNIT against the Brigadier's wishes and at the insistence of her uncle – a high-ranking official in the UN. The Brigadier in turn passes her on to the Third Doctor, to serve as his new assistant.

Jo tells the Doctor that she is a fully qualified agent, but since she also tells him she took an A level in General Science, only to point out later that 'I didn't say I passed', this may be an exaggeration. Jo is certainly enthusiastic. She may start as 'clumsy' and 'ham-fisted' as the Doctor puts it, but her failures and mistakes only make her more determined to succeed. Very quickly, the Doctor and the Brigadier come to realise what an asset she really is.

Investigating mysterious deaths in Llanfairfach, Jo meets Professor Cliff Jones, who she admits to the Doctor 'reminds me of a sort of younger you'. When she agrees to marry Cliff, Captain Yates is disappointed and saddened, yet he is able to put a brave face on things and join in the celebratory party. But the Doctor is devastated. He downs his champagne in a single swallow, then leaves, alone, to drive off into the sunset.

**1324** Marco Polo, who met the First Doctor, dies in Venice. (He actually died some time between the sunsets of 8 and 9 January.)

**1913** Future US President Richard Milhous Nixon was born.

**1964** *Desperate Measures* – the second episode of *The Rescue*

**1971** *Terror of the Autons* Episode 2

## 10 JANUARY

# A Rebel Time Lord Cheats Death

Morbius was a Time Lord who, like the Doctor, opposed their policy of non-intervention. But Morbius's opposition was far more extreme than the Doctor's suggestion that the Time Lords should use their powers to help those in need. As President of the High Council, Morbius decided the Time Lords should be great rulers. When the other members of the High Council opposed his plans, Morbius raised an army of mercenaries. The Doctor describes Morbius as 'a war criminal. A ruthless dictator but with millions of fanatical followers and admirers.'

Morbius offered his mercenaries the precious Elixir of Life, guarded by the Sisterhood of Karn. The planet Karn became the centre of the battlefield where Morbius and his army was finally defeated. He was captured and sentenced to death, his body placed in a dispersal chamber and atomised to the nine corners of the universe.

But one of Morbius's followers, a brilliant surgeon named Mehendri Solon, somehow managed to save the brain of Morbius and kept it alive in a tank of colloidal nutrients. Hidden away on Karn, he worked secretly to create a new body for Morbius, using the more 'suitable' parts of the bodies of life forms killed when their spaceships crashed on the planet. When the Doctor and Sarah arrived on Karn in *The Brain of Morbius* (1976) – perhaps directed there by the Time Lords – all that Solon now needed for the body he had built was a head. And it looked as if the Doctor's would do very well…

**1970** *Spearhead from Space* Episode 2

**1976** *The Brain of Morbius* Part 2

**1980** *Warriors' Gate* Part 2

# 11 JANUARY

# The HADS Saves the TARDIS from Destruction

The TARDIS is an incredibly powerful machine. It is also able to defend itself against attack. Over the centuries, many life forms have tried to destroy the TARDIS, without success. Even more have tried to get inside – again, finding it impossible without the Doctor's help.

One of the TARDIS's defence mechanisms is the Hostile Action Displacement System, or 'HADS' for short. This has only been seen in action twice – in *The Krotons* (1968–1969) and *Cold War* (2013). This may be because, like so many of the TARDIS systems, the HADS doesn't always work. Or it may be because the Doctor rarely remembers to turn it on.

If it is set and functioning properly, the HADS detects when the TARDIS is in danger – for example when a Kroton tries to disperse it. It then dematerialises the TARDIS, taking it out of danger, rematerialising it a short while later in a safe location nearby. Although in *Cold War*, the HADS apparently rematerialises the TARDIS on the other side of planet Earth.

This is different from the Hostile Action Dispersal System, which the Twelfth Doctor uses in *The Witch's Familiar* (2015). That redistributes the TARDIS until the Doctor can reassemble the real-time envelope exterior.

ON THIS DAY

**1964** *The Ambush* – the fourth episode of *The Daleks* – is the first episode in which the Dalek planet Skaro is named, and also the first episode in which the Daleks use the word 'Exterminate'.

**1969** The TARDIS uses its Hostile Action Displacement System (HADS) to escape trouble in Episode 3 of *The Krotons*.

**1975** *Robot* Part 3.

**1982** *Castrovalva* Part 3.

**1983** *Arc of Infinity* Part 3.

**1995** Peter Pratt, who played the Master in *The Deadly Assassin*, died.

# 12 JANUARY

## 'If Nothing Else, I'm Sure It's Good for My Teeth'

All the incarnations of the Doctor have worn distinctive clothing – some more distinctive and eccentric than others. The Third Doctor is well known for his flamboyant smoking jackets and capes; the Fourth for his wide-brimmed hat and long scarf. The Sixth Doctor's multicoloured attire and cat emblems are perhaps the most extravagant of the Doctor's outfits.

The Fifth Doctor chose to wear cricketing whites, with the addition of a stick of celery attached to his lapel. He picks up the celery, apparently on a whim, during his first story *Castrovalva* (1982) and pins it to his coat with no explanation. The fact that this celery is presumably illusory, just like the rest of the unreal town of Castrovalva may explain why it seems not to wilt over the course of his adventures.

It is not until his final story – *The Caves of Androzani* (1984) – that the Doctor explains why the celery is important to him. He tells Peri that he is allergic to certain gases in the Praxis range of the spectrum. If any of these gases are present, the celery turns purple, providing an early warning mechanism. When Peri asks him what he does then, the Doctor tells her: 'I eat the celery. If nothing else, I'm sure it's good for my teeth.' But he may not be as flippant as he seems, as the Doctor places the celery under Peri's nose to revive her when she is delirious with spectrox toxaemia, explaining that it is a powerful restorative to the superior olfactory senses of a Time Lord.

**1974** The first episode of *Invasion of the Dinosaurs* is titled simply *Invasion* on screen to keep secret the fact that it features dinosaurs. But the ploy is rather undermined by *Radio Times*, which accompanies the episode listing with an illustration of the Doctor being attacked by a pterodactyl.

**1976 Crime novelist Agatha Christie died.**

**1980** The final episode of *The Horns of Nimon* closes Season 17, as the story that was planned to follow it – *Shada* – was not completed due to industrial action at the BBC. It is the last broadcast episode to be script edited by Douglas Adams and produced by Graham Williams.

**1982** *Castrovalva* Part 4

**1983** *Arc of Infinity* Part 4

**1984** *Warriors of the Deep* Part 3

**1985** *Attack of the Cybermen* Part 2

## 13 JANUARY

# Kroll Poses a Huge Threat

Kroll was the name given to a huge giant squid by the Swampies – the original inhabitants of Delta Magna, who worshipped Kroll as a god. When humans colonised Delta Magna, they shipped the Swampies to the planet's third moon – a wet, swampy place with almost constant rain storms. At least one giant squid was taken to the Third Moon of Delta Magna along with the Swampies.

The Fifth Segment of the Key to Time was disguised as the Swampie High Priest's 'symbol of power'. When a giant squid attacked the temple, eating both the High Priest and the Symbol of Power, the segment of the Key to Time caused the creature to grow to enormous size. Kroll's central mass is a quarter of a mile across and 140 feet high. It has been sleeping, producing methane that, by the time the Doctor and Romana arrive in *The Power of Kroll* (1979), the humans now collect and refine. This work – the sound of the orbit shots and the rise in lake temperature from the refinery's heat exchangers – has awakened Kroll.

The creature hunts by detecting surface vibrations. It is predominantly vegetarian but has learned that anything that moves is edible. When the Doctor uses the core of the Key to Time to retrieve the Fifth Segment, Kroll undergoes cellular regeneration to become hundreds of baby giant squids.

**1968** *The Enemy of the World* Episode 4

**1973** *The Three Doctors* Episode 3

**1979** *The Power of Kroll* Part 4

**1984** *Warriors of the Deep* Part 4

# 14 JANUARY

## Visiting Mythical Atlantis

**1967** *The Underwater Menace* Episode 1

**1978** *Underworld* Part 2

Atlantis is a legend, first mentioned by the ancient Greek philosopher Plato. It is a mythical island which was destroyed when it fell out of favour with the gods and sank into the sea.

The Second Doctor, together with Ben, Polly and Jamie, visited Atlantis in *The Underwater Menace* (1967), after it had sunk beneath the water. In this Atlantis, humans converted into 'Fish People' harvest the plankton-based food the civilisation needs to survive. Professor Zaroff claims to have a plan to raise Atlantis above the sea, but in fact he is planning to drain the sea into the centre of the Earth and destroy the planet. The Doctor defeats Zaroff by flooding Atlantis, drowning Zaroff.

In *The Dæmons* (1971), Azal implies that Atlantis was an experiment that the Dæmons destroyed when they deemed it a failure.

The Third Doctor and Jo travelled 4,000 years back in time to Atlantis in *The Time Monster* (1972). Here the Master plotted with Queen Galleia to usurp the throne from her husband King Dalios. The Master also wanted to control Kronos, one of the powerful Chronovores – creatures that exist outside space-time and can consume time itself. The Doctor describes the Chronovores as 'time-eaters, who will swallow a life as quickly as a boa-constrictor can swallow a rabbit, fur and all'.

# 15 JANUARY

# When Things Get Timey-Wimey

First mentioned in *Day of the Daleks* (1972), the Blinovitch Limitation Effect offers an explanation for certain constraints on time travel. According to some accounts it is named after Aaron Blinovitch, who formulated his theory in 1928.

At its most basic, the Blinovitch Limitation Effect seems to prevent individuals from crossing their own time streams and changing their own past history – which would create a paradox. If the two people were to meet – as two versions of Brigadier Lethbridge-Stewart do in *Mawdryn Undead* (1983) – this would short out the time differential.

The First Law of Time also prevents people from meeting themselves, but can be suspended by the Time Lords – for example to bring the first three incarnations of the Doctor together to oppose Omega in *The Three Doctors* (1972–1973).

In *Day of the Daleks*, resistance fighters from a future Earth where the Daleks have invaded plan to go back in time (using stolen Dalek time technology) and kill Sir Reginald Styles, who they blame for creating the circumstances that allowed the Daleks to invade. But having failed to kill him on 12 September, the Doctor says that they cannot simply return to the same day and try again. Because of the Blinovitch Limitation Effect their two time periods are now linked.

**1936** Richard Franklin, who played Captain Mike Yates in the Third Doctor's era, was born.

**1965** The first *Doctor Who* episode, *An Unearthly Child*, is screened in Australia by ABC TV.

**1966** *Escape Switch* – the tenth episode of *The Daleks' Master Plan*

**1972** *Day of the Daleks* Episode 3

**1974** *Invasion of the Dinosaurs* Part 1 is first shown on BBC Wales.

**1977** *The Face of Evil* Part 3

**1996** Shooting starts in Vancouver (doubling for San Francisco) on the TV movie *Doctor Who*, starring Paul McGann as the Eighth Doctor.

# 16 JANUARY

# A UNIT Officer and Future Traitor

Mike Yates does not appear in *Doctor Who* until the Nestenes try to invade for a second time in *Terror of the Autons* (1971), although the Doctor says that Captain Yates was responsible for 'clearing up the mess' after the failed Nestene invasion attempt of *Spearhead from Space* (1970).

Although he is outranked by other UNIT officers who appear from time to time – for example Major Cosworth in *The Mind of Evil* (1971) – Captain Yates is swiftly established as the Brigadier's right-hand man. He and the Doctor share a mutual respect, and Mike Yates is evidently very fond of Jo Grant – hiding his sadness and disappointment when she gets engaged to Professor Jones in *The Green Death* (1973).

But he is also an idealist. And it is misplaced idealism that causes Yates to side with the instigators of Operation Golden Age in *Invasion of the Dinosaurs* (1974), betraying his friends and colleagues at UNIT. When the crisis is over, the Brigadier arranges for Yates to be allowed to resign quietly. But this is not the end of Mike Yates's association with the Doctor and UNIT as he discovers the link between K'Anpo's meditation centre and the giant spiders of Metebelis Three in *Planet of the Spiders* (1974).

**1965** *The Slave Traders* – the first episode of *The Romans*

**1971** *Terror of the Autons* Episode 3

**1979** Peter Butterworth, who played the Meddling Monk in *The Time Meddler* (1965) and *The Daleks' Master Plan* (1965–1966), died.

## 17 JANUARY

# The Nestenes Come to Colonise Earth

The Third Doctor describes the Nestene Consciousness as 'a ruthlessly aggressive intelligent alien life form'. It is able to imbue any plastic item with a portion of its intelligence and consciousness. The Nestenes have been colonising worlds for a thousand million years by the time they decide to colonise Earth in *Spearhead from Space* (1970). The Nestene Consciousness is a collective brain and nervous system. If it is killed then all the Nestene plastic on Earth in effect 'dies' as the life force that powers the plastic is withdrawn.

Since the Great Time War, when its food stock planets were destroyed, the Nestene Consciousness has mutated from a disembodied, mutually telepathic intelligence into a living plastic desperate to find further food stocks from which to renew itself.

The principal weapons of the Nestene Consciousness are the Autons – plastic humanoid figures. They may be perfect duplicates that replace real people, or crude

approximations perhaps disguised as shop dummies. The name 'Auton' is derived from 'Auto Plastics' – the factory where the first Autons are created in *Spearhead from Space*.

As well as the Autons, the Nestene Consciousness has also animated other plastic artefacts. These include daffodils that spit a suffocating film over their victim's nose and mouth, a collapsing sofa, a wheelie bin that swallows Mickey Smith, a phone cable that attempts to throttle the Third Doctor, and a grotesque novelty troll doll…

**1970** *Spearhead from Space* Episode 3

**1974** Target Books follows up on the success of reissuing three *Doctor Who* novelisations first published in the mid 1960s with the publication of its first new *Doctor Who* novelisations. These are the first two stories to feature the Third Doctor: *Spearhead from Space* is published as *Doctor Who and the Auton Invasion* (adapted from Robert Holmes's script by Terrance Dicks), and *The Silurians* becomes *Doctor Who and the Cave Monsters* (by the story's original scriptwriter Malcolm Hulke).

**1976** *The Brain of Morbius* Part 3

**1980** *Warriors' Gate* Part 3

## 18 JANUARY

# Ian and Barbara Infiltrate the Dalek City

When the Doctor first encounters the Daleks it is within their City on the desolate planet Skaro. The Dalek City lies in a desert area, close to the Petrified Jungle. From the rear, the City is protected by the natural barrier of a range of mountains and the Lake of Mutations. It is through the swamps around the lake and the caves in the mountains that the First Doctor's companions Ian and Barbara together with a group of Thals set off to try to enter the Dalek City in the fifth episode of *The Daleks* (1963–1964).

The City is constructed mostly of metal, with low, angled, arched doorways high enough for the Daleks to pass through but which taller humans have to stoop to navigate. The Daleks themselves in their first story are unable to move outside the City. They draw power from the metal floors in the form of static electricity – a weakness that allows the Doctor and his friends to immobilise a Dalek by pushing it onto an insulating Thal cape, so they can escape from their cell.

The Second Doctor returns to the Dalek City in *The Evil of the Daleks* (1967). Not only have the Daleks been redesigned by now – with energy-storing slats around their midsections to enable them to move beyond their City's limits – but so has the City. It is far more open, with taller, wider doorways and latticework walls. At its heart is the huge, immobile Emperor Dalek. The Doctor, Jamie and Victoria escape in the TARDIS as the Dalek City burns following the Dalek Civil War instigated by the Doctor.

In *Destiny of the Daleks* (1979), it is implied that the Dalek City is built over the ruins of the original Kaled

ON THIS DAY

**1964** *The Expedition* – the fifth episode of *The Daleks*

**1969** *The Krotons* Episode 4

**1975** *Robot* Part 4. It is Barry Letts's last episode as Producer.

**1982** *Four to Doomsday* Part 1. The story is script edited by Antony Root.

**1983** *Snakedance* Part 1

Bunker where Davros created the Daleks in *Genesis of the Daleks* (1975). The Twelfth Doctor, together with Clara Oswald and Missy, also visits the Dalek City – or a new version of it – in *The Magician's Apprentice* and *The Witch's Familiar* (2015).

## 19 JANUARY

# The Doctor and Peri Arrive on Varos

The planet Varos is in the constellation of Cetes. It is the only known source of the rare ore Zeiton-7, which the Sixth Doctor needs to re-energise the TARDIS's Transitional Elements and realign the Transpower System. Over two hundred years before the Doctor and Peri arrive on Varos in *Vengeance on Varos* (1985), the planet was a prison colony for the criminally insane. Now the descendants of the officer elite still hold power.

The Governor of Varos is selected from the twelve senior officers, who put their names forward for one to be chosen at random. The Governor is held to account by the people, who can vote for him to be executed if they disagree with his policies. The idea is that a man in fear of his life will find solutions to Varos's problems. The flaw in this theory is that there are no popular solutions, and all are put to the vote.

Torture and execution are carried out in the Punishment Dome. The whole dome is covered by cameras, and Varos sells recordings of what happens in the Punishment Dome as well as broadcasting events to the populace to divert any questions or thoughts of discontent and revolution.

**1974** *Invasion of the Dinosaurs* Part 2

**1980** The first episode of *Shada* was due to be transmitted on this day. Sadly, the story was never completed due to industrial action at the BBC. The material that was completed is available on DVD, and the story has been adapted for audio by Big Finish Productions. A novel of the story, adapted by Gareth Roberts from Douglas Adams's original scripts, is available from BBC Books.

**1982** *Four to Doomsday* Part 2

**1983** *Snakedance* Part 2

**1984** *The Awakening* Part 1

**1985** *Vengeance on Varos* Part 1

## 20 JANUARY

# The Doctor's Exile Comes to an End

At the end of *The War Games* (1969), the Second Doctor was forced to call for help from the Time Lords to return thousands of stranded human soldiers to their rightful places in history. He hoped to escape before the Time Lords arrived, but they captured him and put him on trial for breaking their cardinal law of not interfering in the affairs of others.

The Doctor put up a spirited defence, pointing out that there is evil in the universe that must be fought, and accusing his fellow Time Lords of failing to use their great powers to help those in need. Despite accepting this in principle, his people found him guilty. He was sentenced to have his appearance changed, and, having noted his particular interest in Earth, they exiled him there in the late twentieth century.

Whether by accident or design, the Doctor's arrival coincided with the first invasion attempt by the Nestenes, and soon the Third Doctor was working with UNIT as their scientific adviser. During his exile, the Time Lords did occasionally allow the Doctor to travel in the TARDIS and perform errands for them. They sent him to prevent the Master taking control of the Doomsday Weapon, to sort out problems on the planet Peladon, and to deliver information to the planet Solos. It was only after the Doctor defeated the threat posed by Omega in *The Three Doctors* (1972–1973) that the Time Lords lifted his exile and he was free once again to travel through space and time.

ON THIS DAY

**1934** Tom Baker, who played the Fourth Doctor, was born.

**1968** *The Enemy of the World* Episode 5

**1969 Richard Nixon becomes US President.**

**1973** The Time Lords finally lift the Doctor's exile to Earth at the end of Episode 4 of *The Three Doctors*

**1974** *Invasion of the Dinosaurs* Part 2 is first shown on BBC Wales.

**1979** *The Armageddon Factor* Part 1

**1984** *The Awakening* Part 2

**1996** *The Ghosts of N-Space*, an original *Doctor Who* radio drama featuring the Third Doctor, begins on BBC Radio 2.

## 21 JANUARY

# Myths and Legends – Fiction or Reality?

**1967** *The Underwater Menace* Episode 2

**1978** *Underworld* Part 3

In *Underworld* (1978), the Fourth Doctor suggests that 'perhaps those myths are not just old stories of the past, but prophecies of the future'.

As well as visiting Atlantis in both *The Underwater Menace* (1967) and *The Time Monster* (1972), the First Doctor found himself embroiled in the siege of Troy in *The Myth Makers* (1965) – forced by Agamemnon and Odysseus to devise a way to capture the city…

The Doctor has also been involved in situations similar to ancient legends, but in the far future. In *Underworld*, the Fourth Doctor and Leela help the crew of the Minyan ship *R1C* led by Jackson on a quest to find another ship the *P7E*. It is a quest very similar to that undertaken by Jason on the *Argosy*.

In *The Horns of Nimon* (1979–1980), the Fourth Doctor and Romana meet the Nimon – creatures very similar to the legendary Minotaur. The first Nimon they encounter lives inside a futuristic labyrinth where the walls shift position, and demands tribute in the form of human sacrifices. The Eleventh Doctor meets another Minotaur-like creature in *The God Complex* (2011). In *Battlefield* (1989), it is implied that in some other dimension the Doctor is himself the wizard Merlin.

So it seems the Doctor may be right – myths and legends may well be more than just distorted stories of past events…

## 22 JANUARY

# Servants of the Daleks

The Ogrons are tall ape-like creatures that live in scattered communities on one of the barren outer planets on the remote fringes of the galaxy. They worship and fear a large, shapeless monster that also lives on the planet. Because of their great strength, mindless obedience, and inherent stupidity, the Ogrons have been used as mercenaries by various other life forms – most notably, the Daleks. If they have a weakness, apart from their lack of intelligence, it is that a blow to the top of the head can render them unconscious.

The Ogrons have been used for centuries by the Daleks as mercenaries. The Daleks rule them through fear, and use the Ogrons for security tasks and menial work which require little or no intelligence. In *Day of the Daleks* (1972), the Daleks used Ogrons as security troops to keep the human population of the conquered Earth under control after their invasion in the twenty-second century. Human traitors were used in positions that required more intelligence, but the Ogrons remained loyal directly to the Daleks.

In *Frontier in Space* (1973), the Master also used the Ogrons – possibly at the insistence of the Daleks as he was himself working for them – to provoke a war between the empires of Earth and Draconia. Certainly, the Master found it frustrating working with such stupid creatures.

**1901 Queen Victoria died.**

**1940** John Hurt, who played the War Doctor in 2013's *The Name of the Doctor* and *The Day of the Doctor* as well as the minisode *The Night of the Doctor*, was born.

**1966** *The Abandoned Planet* – the eleventh episode of *The Daleks' Master Plan*

**1972** *Day of the Daleks* Episode 4

**1977** *The Face of Evil* Part 4

## 23 JANUARY

# Nero Gets the Wrong Idea

One of the many historical events the Doctor has been involved in is the Great Fire of Rome. In *The Romans* (1965), the First Doctor inadvertently gives Emperor Nero the idea of burning down the city when he accidently sets fire to Nero's plans for a new Rome.

Nero, who first appears in the second episode of *The Romans*, is grotesque and spoilt. He is used to getting everything he wants, be it a gladiator fight or the Doctor's companion Barbara. And he doesn't care who suffers in the process. He takes pleasure in humiliating his personal slave Tigilinus – eventually allowing him to drink poison. Equally casually, Nero kills a guard after an escape at the amphitheatre simply because 'he didn't fight hard enough'. When the Doctor, disguised as the lyre player Maximus Pettulian, gets too much applause for his performance, Nero decides to have 'Pettulian' killed in the arena.

Vain and arrogant, Nero wonders whether to call his new city: 'Neropolis, Nero Caesum, or just plain Nero?' He is exhilarated by the idea of burning down Rome itself simply to get his own way and prove a point to the Senate.

**1965** *All Roads Lead to Rome* – the second episode of *The Romans*

**1971** *Terror of the Autons* Episode 4

# 24 JANUARY

## Romana Leaves the Doctor

When she first meets the Fourth Doctor in *The Ribos Operation* (1978), Romanadvoratrelundar is nearly 140, and has recently graduated from the Time Lord Academy with a Triple First. Inexperienced, but academically brilliant, she is sent by the White Guardian (disguised as the Time Lord President) to help the Doctor in his quest to find the six segments of the Key to Time.

The Doctor is not immediately welcoming, fearing she's going to be more trouble than she's worth, but Romana refuses to be intimidated by him. Although she remains aloof, she learns quickly and the Doctor soon comes to realise her value both as an accomplice in his quest and also as a friend.

Why Romana regenerates in *Destiny of the Daleks* (1979), taking on the form of Princess Astra of Atrios, is not clear. But perhaps it is a way of leaving behind the academic naivety and acknowledging that in the Doctor's company she has become, literally, a different person.

Romana's new personality retains the brilliant technical expertise and analytical ability of the original, but is less serious and 'cold'. Romana remains almost the Doctor's equal, gaining in confidence and aptitude as she acquires more experience.

It is Romana's decision to leave the Doctor at the end of *Warriors' Gate* (1981). Partly this is because Romana wants to strike out on her own. But she is also expected to return to Gallifrey, and after travelling with the Doctor her horizons have broadened and she no longer believes herself capable of fitting back into Time Lord society.

ON THIS DAY

**1965** Winston Churchill died.

**1970** *Spearhead from Space* Episode 4

**1976** *The Brain of Morbius* Part 4

**1981** Romana and K-9 leave to stay in E-Space at the end of Part 4 of *Warriors' Gate*.

# 25 JANUARY

## The Ice Warriors Take Over T-Mat

Possibly short for 'transmission of matter', a transmat system instantly transports life forms and artefacts from one location to another. The transmission starts and ends at a transmat station or receptor. The Doctor has used transmat systems on numerous occasions – for example on Space Station Nerva in *The Ark in Space* (1975) and, earlier in its history, in *Revenge of the Cybermen* (1975). The Sontarans set up a transmat system between their ship and the Rattigan Academy in *The Sontaran Stratagem* and *The Poison Sky* (2008).

In *The Seeds of Death* (1969), the Second Doctor comes across a precursor of transmat called Travelmat Relay – or T-Mat for short. According to the publicity material: 'Travelmat is the ultimate form of travel. Control centre of the present system is the Moon, serving receptions at all major cities on Earth. Travelmat provides an instantaneous means of public travel, transports raw materials and vital food supplies to all parts of the world. Travelmat supersedes all conventional forms of transport. Using the principle of dematerialisation at the point of departure, and rematerialisation at the point of arrival in special cubicles, departure and arrival are almost instantaneous. Although the system is still in its early stages, it is completely automated and fool proof against power failure.'

It is not, however, proof against sabotage by the Ice Warriors who use the T-Mat system as an integral part of their plan to transport deadly Martian seed pods to Earth…

**ON THIS DAY**

**1964** *The Ordeal* – the sixth episode of *The Daleks*

**1969** *The Seeds of Death* Episode 1

**1975** *The Ark in Space* Part 1. It is Philip Hinchcliffe's first episode as Producer.

**1982** *Four to Doomsday* Part 3

**1983** *Snakedance* Part 3

# 26 JANUARY

# The Doctor Gets the Better of Sil

The Sixth Doctor and Peri first meet Sil – a sycophantic and repugnant slug-like creature – in *Vengeance on Varos* (1985). Sil is sent to the planet Varos to negotiate the yearly Zeiton-7 price-review for Galatron Mining prior to a new contract. Galatron has been buying from Varos – and exploiting its people – for centuries. With a penchant for marsh minnows, and needing to be moisturised constantly in Varos's atmosphere, Sil's eccentric speech patterns are due to a fault in his language transposer.

Sil is a Mentor, from the planet Thoros-Beta, with its pink water and pale green sky. The Mentors are led by Lord Kiv and driven by the desire to make money. The Mentors have enslaved the Alphans – the humanoid inhabitants of Thoros-Alpha. In *The Trial of a Time Lord* (1986), the Doctor and Peri trace a high-tech weapon to Thoros-Beta, where they discover human scientist Crozier is experimenting on the Alphans to find a way of saving Lord Kiv as his brain grows too large for his body.

## 27 JANUARY

# The Shadow Awaits the Doctor

While the Fourth Doctor, Romana and K-9 are sent by the White Guardian to locate the various Segments of the Key to Time, the Black Guardian also sends his own agent to track down the Key – the cadaverous Shadow.

The Shadow's plan is to locate the final, Sixth Segment of the Key, and wait for the Doctor to bring the other Segments to him when seeking the Sixth – as he does in *The Armageddon Factor* (1979). To entrap the Doctor, the Shadow has had Drax – another renegade Time Lord and former school friend of the Doctor – build the supercomputer Mentalis to run the Zeon war against neighbouring planet Atrios. By ending the war the Shadow creates a situation where Mentalis will self-destruct, destroying both Atrios and Zeos, rather than allow the Marshal of Atrios to destroy it – the Armageddon Factor. This situation forces the Doctor to use the Key to Time to create a time loop so the countdown will never reach zero.

The Shadow, aided by his dark, gaunt, cloaked creatures referred to as Mutes, does not seek power, but glories in destruction. He sees the war between Atrios and Zeos as a 'rehearsal' for the time when he and the Black Guardian have the Key to Time, and will set the entire universe at war with itself.

ON THIS DAY

**1968** The Doctor himself appears in a specially scripted trailer following the last episode of *The Enemy of the World*, to warn viewers that the Yeti are returning in the next story – *The Web of Fear*. *The Enemy of the World* Episode 6 is Peter Bryant's last episode as Story Editor.

**1973** *Carnival of Monsters* Episode 1

**1974** *Invasion of the Dinosaurs* Part 3 is first shown on BBC Wales.

**1979** *The Armageddon Factor* Part 2

**1984** *Frontios* Part 2

## 28 JANUARY

# Would You Care for a Jelly Baby?

**1967** *The Underwater Menace* Episode 3

**1978** *Underworld* Part 4

Although jelly babies are associated most with the Fourth Doctor, he was not the first incarnation of the Doctor with a taste for the sweets. In *The Three Doctors* (1972–1973), for example, the Second Doctor offers Sergeant Benton and the Brigadier a jelly baby as they take shelter in the TARDIS from Omega's antimatter creature. The Fifth, Sixth, Eighth, Eleventh and Twelfth Doctors have also offered jelly babies on occasion – as has the Master to his wife in *The Sound of Drums* (2007).

Originally called 'Unclaimed Babies', the sweets were invented in 1864. In 1918, Bassett's marketed them as 'Peace Babies' to mark the end of the Great War. The term 'Jelly Babies' was not used until the sweets were relaunched in 1953.

Whether the Doctor is aware of the history of the sweets is unknown. But he can be rather inaccurate in the use of the term 'jelly baby'. In both *Image of the Fendahl* (1977) and *The Sun Makers* (1977) he offers a 'jelly baby' that is actually a liquorice allsort. (When asked about this at the time, *Doctor Who*'s Producer Graham Williams claimed it was a deliberate ploy by the Doctor to confuse his enemies.)

# 29 JANUARY

# The Death of Sara Kingdom

Featuring in *Mission to the Unknown* (1965) and *The Daleks' Master Plan* (1965–1966), the SSS is an Earth-based security service in the year 4000 AD. The initials SSS may stand for *Space Security Service* as stated on agent Marc Cory's ID, or for *Special Security Service* – which is how Cory later identifies himself. SSS agents are licensed to kill, and have the authority to enlist the aid of any persons, civil or military.

Sara Kingdom of the SSS was a loyal agent of Mavic Chen, Guardian of the Solar System, unaware that Chen was working with the Daleks. She was tricked by Chen into killing her brother, agent Bret Vyon, and as a result was initially unwilling to accept the First Doctor's assertion that Chen was a traitor. However, once she had been convinced, Sara helped the Doctor and Steven to destroy the Daleks – even at the cost of her own life. She aged to death on the planet Kembel when the Daleks' Time Destructor was activated.

After her death, the Doctor claims that the one thing Sara lived for was to see the total destruction of the Daleks. He knows that without her help it would not have been achieved.

**1966** Sara Kingdom is killed in the final episode of *The Daleks' Master Plan*, titled *The Destruction of Time.*

**1972** The Ice Warriors return and the Doctor travels to the planet Peladon for the first time in Episode 1 of *The Curse of Peladon.*

**1977** *The Robots of Death* Part 1

## 30 JANUARY

# Winston Churchill Delays the Doctor

Winston Spencer Churchill (1874–1965) is best known as the British Prime Minister who led the Allies to victory in the Second World War. When the Doctor first met Winston Churchill is unknown. But in *Victory of the Daleks* (2010), Churchill is able to contact the Eleventh Doctor when he is concerned about Professor Bracewell's new weapons – the Ironsides. The Doctor knows immediately that the Ironsides have not been developed by Bracewell but are in fact Daleks. They have set a trap for the Doctor – needing his testimony that they are indeed Daleks in order to trigger the creation of the New Dalek Paradigm…

Later, in *The Pandorica Opens* (2010), Churchill tries to contact the Doctor to discuss a painting by Vincent van Gogh that shows the TARDIS exploding. But instead he gets in touch with River Song.

In the alternative timeline depicted in *The Wedding of River Song* (2011), Churchill was the Holy Roman Emperor, and one of the few people to realise that time had 'stuck' at two minutes past 5 p.m. on 22 April 2011. He enlisted the help of the Eleventh Doctor – a soothsayer imprisoned in the Tower of London – to explain the paradox…

**1965** *Conspiracy* – the third episode of *The Romans* – is screened later than scheduled because of the state funeral of Winston Churchill.

**1971** *The Mind of Evil* Episode 1

## 31 JANUARY

# The Silurians Appear to Reclaim Their Planet

Millions of years ago, the Earth was inhabited by intelligent reptiles. When a colony of the creatures hidden beneath Wenley Moor awakes from hibernation in *The Silurians* (1970), they believe the Earth is still their planet. 'We were here before Man. We ruled this world millions of years ago,' the Silurian Leader claims. But 'a small planet was approaching the world. We calculated that it would draw off our atmosphere, destroying all life.' To avoid the catastrophe, the Silurians built huge hibernation chambers, where they slept through the crisis. They would be awakened when the atmosphere returned.

But as the atmosphere was never actually drawn away, the Silurians in this base and the others were not revived and continued in hibernation while Man evolved and became dominant. Now they have been disturbed by the work of the Wenley

Moor Research Establishment – an atomic research centre built into the caves.

In later stories it becomes clear that there are several different species of intelligent reptile in hibernation – the Silurians of *The Hungry Earth* and *Cold Blood* (2010), for example, are very different. Also, as the Doctor points out, the term 'Silurian' is a misnomer – he suggests 'Eocene' as an alternative. The creatures have also been referred to as Earth Reptiles, *Homo reptilia*, and by various other names. An aquatic species was nicknamed 'Sea Devils' in *The Sea Devils* (1972) although by the time they reappear alongside the Silurians in *Warriors of the Deep* (1984) the term seems to be accepted by the creatures themselves.

**1970** The Silurians are introduced in Episode 1 of *The Silurians*. It is actually titled *Doctor Who and the Silurians* on screen, which is the only time 'Doctor Who' has appeared in the series as part of the story title, with the exceptions of the fifth episode of *The Chase* (1965), which is titled *The Death of Doctor Who*, and the TV movie, which is simply titled *Doctor Who*. The Doctor's yellow vintage car Bessie is introduced in this episode, which is also Barry Letts's first episode as Producer.

**1975** *The Seeds of Doom* Part 1

**1981** *The Keeper of Traken* Part 1 introduces Nyssa. Geoffrey Beevers – the husband of Caroline John who played the Third Doctor's companion Liz Shaw – plays the Master.

FEBRUARY

# 1 FEBRUARY

## Happy Birthday to Jackie Tyler

Jacqueline Andrea Suzette Prentice is the mother of Rose Tyler – friend and companion of the Ninth and Tenth Doctors. Jackie married Peter Alan Tyler, who was killed in a hit-and-run accident on Jordan Road on 7 November 1987, leaving a widowed Jackie and their baby daughter Rose – events depicted in *Father's Day* (2005).

Jackie is as much a friend to Rose as a mother, though she is understandably protective and concerned for her daughter. Garrulous and outgoing, Jackie knows almost everyone on the Powell Estate where she and Rose live, and is forever on the phone or gossiping.

Though initially taken with the Doctor, her attitude to him changes as she discovers how he is affecting Rose. Once Rose returns after being missing for a year, Jackie is more sure than ever that the Doctor is a bad influence. Faced with the choice of saving the world at the possible cost of Rose's life, Jackie urges the Doctor to keep Rose safe – no matter what the consequence for herself. By *The Parting of the Ways* (2005) she is resigned to the fact that Rose's place is with the Doctor.

**1946** Elisabeth Sladen, who played the Fourth Doctor's companion Sarah Jane Smith, was born.

**1964** *The Rescue* – the seventh episode of *The Daleks*

**1967** Jackie Tyler was born. Her 40th birthday party (albeit on a parallel version of Earth) is shown in *Rise of the Cybermen* (2006).

**1969** *The Seeds of Death* Episode 2

**1975** *The Ark in Space* Part 2

**1982** *Kinda* Part 1. The story is script edited by Eric Saward.

**1983** Turlough first appears in Part 1 of *Mawdryn Undead*. Brigadier Lethbridge-Stewart also returns, as does the Black Guardian.

**2007** The events of the Tenth Doctor story *Rise of the Cybermen/ The Age of Steel* take place.

## 2 FEBRUARY

# Enter the Rani

The Rani is a renegade Time Lord but, unlike the Doctor or the Master, she is entirely amoral. A brilliant chemist as well as being adept in other areas of science, she was exiled by the Time Lords after she experimented on mice and turned them into monsters. The mice ate the Time Lord President's cat and also took a chunk out of him. In the Doctor's opinion, the Time Lords should never have exiled the Rani, but instead locked her in a padded cell. Ruler of planets such as Miasimia Goria and later Lakertya, she sees their inhabitants merely as subjects for her experiments.

When the Sixth Doctor and Peri encounter the Rani (together with the Master) in *The Mark of the Rani* (1985), her plan is to use fluid extracted from human brains to keep her own alien subjects on Miasimia Goria placid. She has been coming to Earth for centuries, using various times as cover including: the Trojan Wars, the Dark Ages, the American War of Independence and – as seen in this story – the Luddite riots.

When the Seventh Doctor and Mel later encounter the Rani in *Time and the Rani* (1987), she is kidnapping geniuses from throughout history and planning to use their combined talents to create a Time Manipulator. The fact that the people of Lakertya, the planet on which she is based, will be destroyed she sees merely as a side effect.

**1974** *Invasion of the Dinosaurs* Part 4

**1982** *Kinda* Part 2

**1983** *Mawdryn Undead* Part 2

**1984** *Frontios* Part 3

**1985** *The Mark of the Rani* Part 1 introduces the Rani.

## 3 FEBRUARY

# The Great Intelligence Traps the Doctor

The Second Doctor first encountered the disembodied Great Intelligence in the Himalayan mountains of Tibet in *The Abominable Snowmen* (1967). The Intelligence had possessed the Doctor's old friend Padmasambhava, the Master of Det-Sen Monastery. It used robot Yeti as its servants in a plan to assume corporeal form and take over the world.

Although the Doctor defeated the Intelligence, it returned – setting a trap for the Doctor in *The Web of Fear* (1968) in the London Underground system. Again, it used robot Yeti as its servants. The Doctor and his companions Jamie and Victoria – with help from Professor Travers, who they had met in Tibet, and a British army contingent led by Colonel Lethbridge-Stewart – were once again able to defeat the Intelligence, cutting off its contact with Earth.

When the Eleventh Doctor met the Great Intelligence in *The Snowmen* (2012), it had possessed Doctor Simeon. The snowmen it used as servants were not robot Yeti, but creatures of actual snow and ice. The Great Intelligence and its other servants – the Whisper Men – continued to pursue the Doctor in *The Bells of Saint John* (2013) and *The Name of the Doctor* (2013). The Great Intelligence planned to travel back through the Doctor's past history and unravel the whole of the Doctor's lives. It was only the intervention of Clara Oswald that finally defeated its plans…

ON THIS DAY

**1968** *The Web of Fear* Episode 1. It is Derrick Sherwin's first episode as Story Editor.

**1973** *Carnival of Monsters* Part 2

**1974** *Invasion of the Dinosaurs* Part 4 is first shown on BBC Wales.

**1979** *The Armageddon Factor* Part 3

**1984** *Frontios* Part 4

## 4 FEBRUARY

# Gallifrey's Head of Security

The Castellan is the Time Lord responsible for the security of the Capitol on Gallifrey. He is also in charge of the Chancellery Guard – their commander, reporting to the Castellan.

In *The Deadly Assassin* (1976), Castellan Spandrell is at first wary of the Fourth Doctor, believing that he has assassinated the President. But the Doctor is able to persuade Spandrell that he has been framed for the murder, and the two work together to unmask the true assassin.

When the Doctor assumes the role of President of the High Council of Time Lords in *The Invasion of Time* (1978), his Castellan is named Kelner. Apparently subservient, Kelner is a political animal – always manoeuvring for his own advancement. He has no hesitation in helping first the Vardans when they invade Gallifrey, and then the Sontarans.

It is the (unnamed) Castellan in *Arc of Infinity* (1983) who is responsible for the execution of the Fifth Doctor – carried out by Commander Maxil (coincidentally played by Colin Baker, who would soon become the Doctor himself). This same Castellan is later framed by President Borusa for reactivating the Death Zone on Gallifrey in *The Five Doctors* (1983). He is subsequently shot while allegedly attempting to escape.

**1919** Peter Butterworth, who played the Meddling Monk in *The Time Meddler* (1965) and *The Daleks' Master Plan* (1965–1966), was born.

**1967** *The Underwater Menace* Episode 4

**1978** *The Invasion of Time* Part 1

# 5 FEBRUARY

## The Aristocracy of Mars

If the formidable Ice Warriors are the troops of the Martian army, the so-called Ice Lords (they are never actually named as such on screen) are the officer class and aristocracy. Whereas the Ice Warriors are heavily armoured with their reptilian shells, the Ice Lords do not wear the heavy body armour. They also have a sleeker, more streamlined helmet, and some wear a cape.

The Second Doctor first encounters an Ice Lord in *The Seeds of Death* (1969). Lord Slaar leads the Martian attack on the moonbase, and is responsible for sending deadly Martian seed pods to Earth using T-Mat. He answers to the Grand Marshal.

In *The Curse of Peladon* (1972), the Third Doctor is sent to the planet Peladon by the Time Lords to ensure its entry into the Galactic Federation. Here the Doctor and Jo Grant met Lord Izlyr – the Federation's Martian delegate. Although the Doctor knows the Martians as 'a savage and warlike race', Izlyr explains that 'now we reject violence, except in self-defence'. He does however admit that 'unfortunately, in order to preserve peace, it is necessary to survive'.

When the Doctor returns to Peladon fifty years later in *The Monster of Peladon* (1974), a faction of Ice Warriors has chosen to return to 'the good old days of death or glory'. This faction is led by Lord Azaxyr.

ON THIS DAY

**1966** *War of God* – the first episode of *The Massacre*

**1972** *The Curse of Peladon* Episode 2

**1977** *The Robots of Death* Part 2

# 6 FEBRUARY

# Corporal Bell Keeps UNIT Running

Brigadier Lethbridge-Stewart's long-suffering personal assistant at UNIT, Corporal Bell is responsible for running the administrative side of UNIT HQ. She also handles the Brigadier's personal communications taking phone and radio messages, as well as organising transport, and – when asked – providing coffee.

Unlike the other UNIT 'regulars' – Sergeant Benton and Captain Yates – Corporal Bell appears in only two stories. In *The Mind of Evil* (1971) she is responsible for liaising with Captain Yates over the disposal of the Thunderbolt nerve gas missile. Her call sign – or the call sign of UNIT HQ – is 'Jupiter'.

In *The Claws of Axos* (1971), Corporal Bell takes messages from the UNIT RADAR station tracking Axos as it approaches Earth. She also relays information from the Met Office about the freak weather conditions on the South East coast of England where Axos lands.

**1965** The final episode of *The Romans*, titled *Inferno*, is Mervyn Pinfield's last episode as Associate Producer.

**1971** *The Mind of Evil* Episode 2

## 7 FEBRUARY

# The Krynoid Threatens to Start a Plant Rebellion

The Krynoid is a form of intelligent plant life that feeds on animals. On planets where the Krynoid takes hold, animal life becomes extinct. The Krynoid can infect animal life with its spores, causing the 'host' creature to mutate into a Krynoid which retains some of that host's knowledge, memory and intelligence. The Krynoid is also able to transfer some of its power to the local vegetation, making ordinary plant life hostile and deadly to animals.

No one knows for sure how the Krynoid plant pods travel through space to other planets. One theory is that the Krynoid planet of origin is volcanic and the pods are shot out (usually in pairs) by the eruptions.

When shown a photograph of a Krynoid pod discovered in Antarctica in *The Seeds of Doom* (1976), the Fourth Doctor immediately realises the danger. Two pods have been buried in the ice for about 20,000 years, but the scientists are sure they are still alive and put one under ultraviolet light. The pod opens and a shoot emerges which attacks one of the scientists.

While the resulting Krynoid creature is destroyed, plant-obsessed millionaire Harrison Chase acquires the second Krynoid pod. He has it brought back to his stately home in England where he hopes to nurture the Krynoid and allow plants to take over the world...

**1812** Charles Dickens was born.

**1965** The *Sunday Mirror* publishes the first in-depth *Doctor Who*-related interview with William Hartnell who played the First Doctor.

**1970** *The Silurians* Episode 2

**1975** *The Seeds of Doom* Part 2

**1981** *The Keeper of Traken* Part 2

**1984** Location shooting starts on Colin Baker's first story as the Sixth Doctor – *The Twin Dilemma*.

# 8 FEBRUARY

## The Doctor's Oldest Friend

TARDIS is an acronym, standing for 'Time And Relative Dimension In Space'. Outwardly a police telephone box of a type common in London in the early 1960s, the TARDIS is an unbelievably advanced vehicle that travels through time and space. It is also dimensionally transcendental – meaning it is bigger inside than out. It dematerialises from a location, and reappears at its destination – which could be absolutely anywhere, at any point in the past, the present, or the future.

The TARDIS contains everything necessary to support and sustain its crew and passengers from bedrooms to food machines to clothing. The main Control Room, like other areas within the TARDIS, can change in appearance, and there is at least one 'secondary' Control Room. Quite how large the TARDIS actually is has never been defined – the Doctor himself tells Sarah Jane Smith: 'There are no measurements in infinity.'

Although its origins – like the Doctor's own – are initially a mystery, over time we learn that the TARDIS is a Type 40 TT Capsule built by the Time Lords of Gallifrey. There is a suggestion that the TARDIS is female – certainly it takes on a female form in *The Doctor's Wife* (2011) – and that it is alive, having a symbiotic relationship with the Doctor...

**1964** The first episode of *The Edge of Destruction*, also titled *The Edge of Destruction*

**1969** *The Seeds of Death* Episode 3

**1974** Jon Pertwee, the Third Doctor, announces that he is leaving *Doctor Who*.

**1975** *The Ark in Space* Part 3

**1982** *Kinda* Part 3

**1983** *Mawdryn Undead* Part 3

**1984** *Resurrection of the Daleks* Part 1 is the first 'regular' episode not to run to 25 minutes. The story is run in two double-length episodes to accommodate the BBC's coverage of the Winter Olympics.

# 9 FEBRUARY

## Turlough Joins the TARDIS

A political exile from the planet Trion, Vislor Turlough is in effect held prisoner as a pupil at a public school on Earth when he meets the Fifth Doctor in *Mawdryn Undead* (1983). To escape his exile, he agrees to work for the Black Guardian – who wants Turlough to kill the Doctor…

But Turlough is no cold-blooded murderer. He is more amoral than immoral, albeit with a strong sense of self-preservation. Ultimately, having grown to like and respect the Doctor, Turlough rejects the Guardian's mission, even turning down riches beyond imagining.

Turlough seeks initially to return home to his own world, but ever the opportunist, he comes to recognise that travel with the Doctor offers him a unique chance to experience the universe in a way few can enjoy.

It is not until *Planet of Fire* (1984) that the Doctor finally discovers Turlough's true origins. Turlough learns that prisoners like himself are no longer persecuted by the authorities on Trion. While he is sorry to be leaving the Doctor, Turlough realises that his dreams of returning back home can now become real. An emissary of Trion agrees to transport him back to his home planet.

ON THIS DAY

**1969** Patrick Troughton announces he is retiring from the title role of *Doctor Who*.

**1974** *Invasion of the Dinosaurs* Part 5

**1982** *Kinda* Part 4

**1983** *Mawdryn Undead* Part 4

**1985** *The Mark of the Rani* Part 2

## 10 FEBRUARY

# The Third Doctor's Futuristic New Car

Although never named in the series' narrative, the Whomobile is the name generally given to the Third Doctor's futuristic silver car first seen in *Invasion of the Dinosaurs* (1974) and used again in *Planet of the Spiders* (1974). A low, two-seater with the registration number WVO2M, the Whomobile appears to be a hovercraft. Initially fitted with a low windscreen and open-topped, for its appearance in *Planet of the Spiders*, the Whomobile is fitted with a fully enclosed top canopy.

As is revealed in *Planet of the Spiders*, it is also capable of flight. The Doctor and Sarah take to the air to chase Lupton – who has

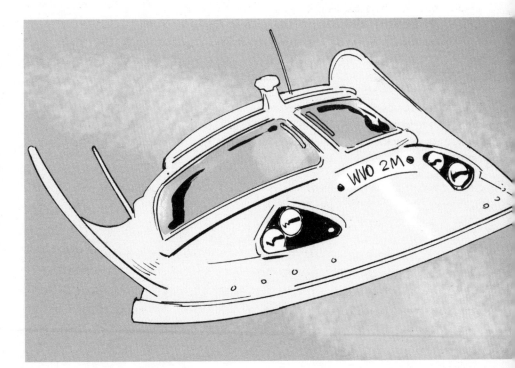

stolen a powerful blue crystal the Doctor found on the planet Metebelis Three, initially making his escape in the Whomobile. The policeman who spots the Brigadier in the Doctor's yellow vintage car Bessie chasing Lupton in the Whomobile estimates they are travelling at ninety miles per hour.

Owned by Third Doctor actor Jon Pertwee himself, the actual vehicle was apparently capable of a top speed of 105 mph, and is legally roadworthy, classed as an 'invalid tricycle'.

**1939** Peter Purves, who played the First Doctor's companion Steven Taylor, was born.

**1968** *The Web of Fear* Episode 2

**1973** *Carnival of Monsters* Episode 3

**1974** *Invasion of the Dinosaurs* Part 5 is first shown on BBC Wales.

**1979** *The Armageddon Factor* Part 4

## 11 FEBRUARY

# Defenders of Gallifrey

The main security force in the Capitol of Gallifrey, the Chancellery Guards wear distinctive red uniforms and helmets, with white decoration and a cape. Each has a communicator screen on the wrist of his glove, and the guards are generally armed with patrol stasers.

For the most part, the duties of the Chancellery guard are ceremonial. But when the Fourth Doctor returned to Gallifrey in *The Deadly Assassin* (1976), it was the Chancellery Guards led by Commander Hilred who were despatched to intercept the TARDIS and apprehend the Doctor.

It is also the Chancellery Guards, led by Commander Andred, who stand against first the Vardans and later the Sontarans in *The Invasion of Time* (1978). Andred is impressed with K-9, but even more taken with Leela – who remains on Gallifrey after the Sontarans have been defeated so as to be with Andred. K-9 also stays with them, although whether Andred makes good on his promise to make the robot dog a sergeant is unknown.

ON THIS DAY

**1967** *The Moonbase* Episode 1 features the first return of the Cybermen, now redesigned and much closer in appearance to the form they will take from now on.

**1978** *The Invasion of Time* Part 2

## 12 FEBRUARY

# Robots Cannot Harm Humans... Or Can They?

ON THIS DAY

**1966** *The Sea Beggar* – the second episode of *The Massacre*

**1972** *The Curse of Peladon* Episode 3

**1977** *The Robots of Death* Part 3

In *The Robots of Death* (1977), the Fourth Doctor and Leela find themselves on a huge Sandminer on a distant planet. Although there is a small human crew, the Sandminer is operated mainly by robots. The robots are stylised humanoids, identified by type and number, and programmed to obey the human crew. Each Voc-class robot has over a million multi-level constrainers which prevent it from being able to harm humans. But, as the Doctor and Leela discover, someone has learned how to override these constraints.

The robots are controlled by a Super Voc – on the Sandminer this is SV7. Silver in colour, it controls the other robots, acting as their coordinator and relaying all commands. The golden Voc-class robots, all numbered with a V prefix (for example V7 and V16) are intelligent with a degree of self-control. They can speak, and have a level of initiative. The dark-coloured Dum robots, however, are single-function robots used for simple labour tasks. They are all numbered, with a D prefix (for example, D33) and cannot speak. An exception is D84 – a more sophisticated robot (possibly another Super Voc) operating 'under cover' for the controlling company.

Some people – including crew member Poul, another company agent – suffer from Grimwade's Syndrome, also called robophobia, which is an unreasoning fear of robots.

## 13 FEBRUARY

# The TARDIS Lands on Vortis

**1965** The first episode of *The Web Planet*, also titled *The Web Planet*

**1971** *The Mind of Evil* Episode 3

The barren planet Vortis is in the Isop Galaxy. The surface is rich in mica, with pools of deadly acid, and the planet has a thin atmosphere. It has several moons (one named Tarun), attracted by the same force as draws the TARDIS here in *The Web Planet* (1965) – the Animus.

The Animus is a tentacled creature, something between octopus and spider, that lives at the centre of a giant web-city called the Carsenome. It can control anyone who comes into contact with gold, as well as the native Zarbi. The Zarbi are a giant cross between ants and beetles, controlled by the power of the Animus. The Animus also controls the larvae guns – grub-like creatures, with an armoured shell and many thin legs, like a woodlouse. Their long proboscis can fire a bolt of energy, powerful enough to kill.

The other native life form on Vortis was the Menoptra. Like giant butterflies, the Menoptra are the intelligent natives of Vortis. They were driven from their home world by the Animus and fled to a nearby moon before massing their invasion force on the nearby planet Pictos. Returning to Vortis, the Menoptra plan to destroy the Animus with an Isoptope – a living cell destructor, intended to reverse the Carsenome's growth process.

A stunted version of the Menoptra, the Optera, live underground. Their wings have withered and they do not remember that they were once Menoptra, who they now regard as their gods.

# 14 FEBRUARY

# Romance for Valentine's Day

While the Doctor rarely travels alone, and has made many friends over the centuries, he has rarely become romantically involved. But there have been exceptions. The First Doctor travelled with Susan Foreman – his granddaughter. Unless this is merely a term of affection, or an imprecise translation of a Gallifreyan term, this suggests that the Doctor has had children of his own, which is confirmed in later stories such as *Fear Her*. In *The Aztecs* (1964), the Doctor forms a friendship with the Aztec lady Cameca, and accidentally becomes engaged to her. It is clear that the Doctor has become very close to some of his companions – most notably Rose Tyler.

The relationship between the Doctor's companions has varied from the antagonistic – for example between Tegan and Adric – to the possibly romantic. Certainly the First Doctor's companions Ian Chesterton and Barbara Wright, and the Fourth Doctor's Sarah Jane Smith and Harry Sullivan – and others – were very close friends. Amy Pond and Rory Williams, of course, were married.

But it is only in *Human Nature* and *The Family of Blood* (2007), when the Doctor becomes human for a while, that we see him actually and undeniably in love. When 'John Smith' becomes the Doctor again, it is perhaps his relationship with Joan Redfern that is his greatest loss…

**1970** *The Silurians* Episode 3

**1975** *The Seeds of Doom* Part 3

**1981** *The Keeper of Traken* Part 3

**1983** *Terminus* Part 1 premieres in Wales – a day before the rest of the UK.

# 15 FEBRUARY

## The Fast Return Switch Nearly Destroys the TARDIS

The Fast Return switch is a control on the main TARDIS console that sends the TARDIS back through time, possibly retracing its previous journey. The First Doctor used it when leaving Skaro after his first encounter with the Daleks in the hope of returning Ian and Barbara to twentieth-century Earth. But, as the events of *The Edge of Destruction* (1964) show, the TARDIS malfunctions. The Fast Return switch gets stuck – potentially sending the TARDIS back to the creation of the universe, and its own destruction.

As the switch is not actually faulty, the TARDIS Fault Locator does not register the problem. But the TARDIS does try to warn the Doctor and his companions. Clocks apparently melt, the doors open while in flight, parts of the console become electrified, and the TARDIS scanner shows a progression of images tracing its past journeys…

Although he initially suspects Ian and Barbara of sabotaging the TARDIS, with their help the Doctor eventually works out where the problem lies. The spring inside the Fast Return switch has become dislocated, and so the switch has in effect remained pressed down. Once the Doctor releases the switch, the TARDIS returns to normal.

ON THIS DAY

**1964** *The Brink of Disaster* – the second episode of *The Edge of Destruction*

**1969** *The Seeds of Death* Episode 4

**1975** *The Ark in Space* Part 4

**1982** *The Visitation* Part 1. The story is script edited by Antony Root.

**1983** *Terminus* Part 1

**1984** Tegan leaves at the end of *Resurrection of the Daleks* Part 2.

# 16 FEBRUARY

# The Doctor Meets Death and the Terileptils

The Terileptils are bipedal reptilian creatures with a pronounced aesthetic sense. They banish their criminals to the planet Raaga where they are put to work in the tinclavic mines. It is a group of escaped criminals that the Fifth Doctor encounters close to London in 1666 in *The Visitation* (1982) after their ship crashes having been damaged in an asteroid storm. The Terileptils use a soliton gas generator to provide an atmosphere more suitable for Terileptil lungs, although they can survive in Earth's own atmosphere for a considerable time.

The Terileptils can control human minds using special polygrite bracelets with built in power-packs. The bracelets pulse as the power flows through them. They also use aesthetically designed androids to carry out menial tasks. The android the renegade Terileptils bring to Earth is also armed – able to fire energy bolts from its hand. With a specially designed 'skull' mask and equipped with a cloak and scythe, the Terileptils also use it to scare the superstitious villagers into thinking Death walks among them.

Unable to return home, since they are fugitives from the law, the Terileptils intend to take over Earth. They are infecting rats with a genetically engineered version of bubonic plague and plan to release them to wipe out humanity.

ON THIS DAY

**1964** Christopher Eccleston, who played the Ninth Doctor, was born.

**1974** *Invasion of the Dinosaurs* Part 6

**1982** *The Visitation* Part 2

**1983** *Terminus* Part 2

**1985** Patrick Troughton and Frazer Hines return as the Second Doctor and Jamie in Part 1 of *The Two Doctors*.

## 17 FEBRUARY

# Alastair Gordon Lethbridge-Stewart Makes His First Appearance

When he is first introduced in *The Web of Fear* (1968), Lethbridge-Stewart is a Colonel sent in to take charge of the 'Fortress' base in the London Underground after the death of Colonel Pemberton, who has been killed by the Yeti. Although they are initially wary of each other, the Second Doctor and Lethbridge-Stewart come to trust and respect one another. Already there is evidence of the characteristics that will endear the Brigadier (as he becomes) to the Doctor. Not afraid to lead his men by example, or to take risks, he displays a dislike of inaction.

A straightforward career soldier, Lethbridge-Stewart initially finds it hard to accept robot Yeti and the Great Intelligence. But promoted to Brigadier and placed in charge of the newly formed UNIT in *The Invasion* (1968), he takes such matters in his stride. Perhaps the hardest things he has to accept are to do with the face-changing, time-travelling Doctor rather than the alien menaces he battles against. But above all the Brigadier is as calm in a crisis as he is when all is running smoothly.

Following his time with UNIT, the Brigadier retires and becomes a Maths teacher – to the surprise of the Fifth Doctor in *Mawdryn Undead* (1983). But when the need arises, Lethbridge-Stewart is brought out of retirement to help UNIT combat mysterious and alien menaces, for example in *Battlefield* (1989).

**1968** Colonel (later Brigadier) Lethbridge-Stewart appears fully for the first time in Episode 3 of *The Web of Fear*.

**1973** *Carnival of Monsters* Episode 4

**1974** *Invasion of the Dinosaurs* Part 6 is first shown on BBC Wales.

**1979** *The Armageddon Factor* Part 5

## 18 FEBRUARY

# The Vardans Invade Gallifrey

The Vardans are life forms that can travel along any form of broadcast wavelength and materialise at the end of it. The Vardans can even travel through the TARDIS scanner. They are actually humanoid in shape, but until they properly materialise they appear as shimmering silver forms. K-9 detects the coordinates of their source planet as vector 3 0 5 2 alpha 7, 14th span.

The Vardans are telepathic, able to read thoughts (and even encephalographic patterns). Because of this the Fourth Doctor has to shield his thoughts when he meets them in *The Invasion of Time* (1978). In order to foil their planned invasion of Gallifrey, the Doctor pretends to be their accomplice. He claims the Presidency of the Time Lords – having accidentally been elected to the post in *The Deadly Assassin* (1976) – and allows the Vardans to break through Gallifrey's defences.

But this is a ruse so that the Doctor can get K-9 to use modulation rejection to eject the Vardans from Gallifrey. He then plans to time loop their planet. However, what the Doctor has not realised is that the Vardans are themselves working for another enemy of his – the Sontarans…

ON THIS DAY

**1967** *The Moonbase* Episode 2

**1978** *The Invasion of Time* Part 3

**1993** Jacqueline Hill, who played the First Doctor's companion Barbara Wright, died.

## 19 FEBRUARY

# The Doctor Solves the Problems of Peladon

The Third Doctor first visited the planet Peladon in *The Curse of Peladon* (1972), when it was applying to join the Galactic Federation. Peladon is a medieval society with little technology, ruled by King Peladon of Peladon (though he is yet to be crowned) from the storm-swept Citadel of Peladon – a remote castle built into the side of a mountain.

The Peladonians (sometimes called 'Pels') worship Aggedor – the royal beast, now extinct. On his first visit the Doctor meets the High Priest of the Temple of Aggedor, Hepesh, as well as Peladon's Chancellor, Torbis. Hepesh in particular is wary of joining the Federation – and as the Doctor discovers will go to great lengths to prevent it…

By the time he returns some fifty years later in *The Monster of Peladon* (1974), these two roles seem to have been combined into one as Ortron is both High Priest and Chancellor to the new queen, King Peladon's daughter, Thalira.

The Doctor's second visit is during a time of unrest. Many do not yet see any benefit from joining the Federation. The spirit of Aggedor has been seen, and the miners are close to revolt. The fact that the Federation is itself now at war with the forces of Galaxy Five adds to the tension. When Federation security forces arrive – a group of Ice Warriors led by Lord Azaxyr – the situation deteriorates. But as the Doctor discovers, not everything is as it seems…

**ON THIS DAY**

**1966** *Priest of Death* – the third episode of *The Massacre*. It is Donald Tosh's last episode as Story Editor.

**1972** *The Curse of Peladon* Episode 4

**1977** *The Robots of Death* Part 4

## 20 FEBRUARY

# The Doctor is Forced to Face His Worst Fears

**1965** *The Zarbi* – the second episode of *The Web Planet*

**1971** *The Mind of Evil* Episode 4

The Keller Machine is hailed as a revolutionary new way of rehabilitating hardened criminals. When the Third Doctor and Jo Grant attend a demonstration in *The Mind of Evil* (1971), they are told that its inventor, Professor Emil Keller, discovered that antisocial behaviour was governed by certain negative or evil impulses. The Keller Machine apparently extracts these impulses and leaves a rational, well-balanced individual. It is said to have been used very successfully in Switzerland, where 112 cases have been processed so far. But in the demonstration when a criminal named Barnham is processed, the Doctor realises that the Machine has over-reacted and extracted *all* the negative particles – leaving Barnham childlike and naïve.

The Doctor soon discovers that Keller is in fact the Master. Inside the Machine is a slimy brain-like creature, with an eye that feeds on the evil of the mind. It can instil in its victims visions of their greatest fear – visions so real that they can kill…

The first victim of the Keller Machine is Arthur Linwood, a medical student who suffers from a fear of rats. From the state of his body, it seems that he was attacked by a horde of the creatures. Professor Kettering, afraid of water, 'drowns' in the Process Room at Stangmoor Prison, his lungs found to be full of water.

When he is exposed to the Keller Machine, the Doctor sees images of fire, as well as of past enemies including the Daleks and Cybermen. Interestingly, when the Master is attacked by his own machine his greatest fear appears to be the Doctor.

## 21 FEBRUARY

# A Vintage Transport of Delight

In *Spearhead from Space* (1970), the Third Doctor escapes from hospital in a stolen vintage car. At the end of the story, one of the conditions he gives the Brigadier for working for UNIT is that he can have a similar car. That car, a bright yellow Edwardian roadster named Bessie, is introduced in the following story, *The Silurians* (1970).

She may appear old, but Bessie is fitted with some very modern gadgets and technology. In *The Ambassadors of* Death (1970), General Carrington and his associate Grey get stuck to Bessie when the Doctor presses a switch marked 'Anti-theft Device'. In *The Dæmons* (1971), the Doctor uses a remote control device to control Bessie's movement, horn and lights. He uses the remote-controlled Bessie to prove to the villagers of Devil's End that he is a wizard, and later to bring back the Master when he tries to escape.

In *The Mutants* (1972), the Doctor is interrupted by a message from the Time Lords while making a minimum-inertia super-drive for Bessie. By *The Time Monster* (1972), he has it working, using the 'Super Drive' to get to Wootton (72 miles away) in less than an hour along country roads. Bessie's brakes, he tells Jo, 'work by the absorption of inertia'.

With the Doctor gradually cutting his ties with UNIT, the Fourth Doctor's introductory story *Robot* (1974–1975) was the last time Bessie appeared until *Battlefield* (1989), apart from accompanying the Third Doctor in *The Five Doctors* (1983). The Brigadier tells the Seventh Doctor that he had Bessie 'mothballed' when the Doctor 'last went on his travels'. She now has a longer bonnet and her number plate has changed from WHO 1 to WHO 7.

**1970** *The Silurians* Episode 4

**1975** *The Seeds of Doom* Part 4

**1981** The Master regenerates at the end of Part 4 of *The Keeper of Traken*, taking the body of Nyssa's father Tremas. The role will be played by Anthony Ainley (who also played Tremas) for the rest of the classic series.

## 22 FEBRUARY

# The Doctor Meets Marco Polo at the Roof of the World

Born in 1254, Marco Polo was an Italian merchant and traveller. Although he was by no means the first European to travel to China, his account of his journeys – *The Travels of Marco Polo* (first published in around 1300) – was the first detailed description of the country, and effectively introduced many Europeans to Central Asia and China.

Leaving his home of Venice in 1271, Marco Polo spent three and a half years travelling with his father and uncle to Peking, arriving at Kublai Khan's court aged 21. On his 25th birthday, Marco Polo was given an appointment in the Khan's service and travelled throughout the Khan's domain and beyond…

When the First Doctor and his companions meet him in 1289 on the Pamir Plateau in *Marco Polo* (1964), the traveller is returning across the Gobi Desert to Peking, determined to gain permission from the Khan to return home to Venice. He tells the Doctor that he has not seen his home for eighteen years. 'Two years ago,' he explains, 'my father, my uncle and I asked the Khan for permission to go home. He refused.' Now Marco Polo plans to offer the Khan 'a gift so magnificent that he will not be able to refuse me.' Unfortunately for the Doctor, that gift is the TARDIS…

ON THIS DAY

**1964** The opening episode of *Marco Polo*, titled *The Roof of the World*, is the first to earn a *Radio Times* cover.

**1969** *The Seeds of Death* Episode 5

**1975** *The Sontaran Experiment* Part 1

**1982** *The Visitation* Part 3

**1983** *Terminus* Part 3

**2011** Nicholas Courtney, who played Brigadier Lethbridge-Stewart, died.

## 23 FEBRUARY

# Nyssa Leaves the TARDIS

When the Fourth Doctor and Adric first meet Nyssa on her home world of Traken, her widowed father Tremas has recently married Kassia. But during the course of *The Keeper of Traken* (1981), Kassia is possessed and then killed by the Master, who then kills Nyssa's father and takes his body for his own.

In the following story, *Logopolis* (1981), Nyssa sees the entropy cloud released by the Master's interference on Logopolis destroy her home world. Orphaned and alone in the universe, she has little choice but to join the Doctor on his travels.

Although she later tells the Doctor that she has 'enjoyed every moment' of her time in the TARDIS, during that time she witnesses the Doctor's regeneration, and the death of Adric. In *Arc of Infinity* (1983), the Doctor's apparent execution by his own people reduces her to tears.

Constantly frustrated at the lack of opportunity to put her considerable technical skills to good use, Nyssa feels for the most part under-employed on the TARDIS. She is not one to complain, however, always putting others before herself, perhaps because she has lost so much.

But when she sees an opportunity to put her skills to good use helping others, she takes it – staying on Terminus to help refine and improve the process for treating the victims of Lazar's disease.

ON THIS DAY

**1974** *Death to the Daleks* Part 1

**1982** *The Visitation* Part 4

**1983** Nyssa leaves at the end of the final episode of *Terminus*.

**1984** Peri's first episode is *Planet of Fire* Part 1.

**1985** *The Two Doctors* Part 2

**1985** A short scene featuring Colin Baker as the Sixth Doctor, called *A Fix With Sontarans*, is broadcast.

## 24 FEBRUARY

# The Dalek Wars

Exactly how many Dalek Wars there have been, how long they lasted or when they were fought is unknown. In *Mission to the Unknown* (1965) and *The Daleks' Master Plan* (1965–1966), both set around the year 4000 AD, the security force SSS seem largely concerned with opposing the Daleks. In *Death to the Daleks* (1974), Lieutenant Peter Hamilton of the Marine Space Corps says that his father was killed in the last Dalek War.

Steven Taylor tells the First Doctor and his companions in *The Chase* (1965) that the planet Mechanus was never colonised as Earth 'got involved in interplanetary wars'. He assumes that the planet was forgotten, despite being made ready for colonists by the robotic Mechonoids. He does not say if these wars were against the Daleks, but it seems quite likely that they were.

In *Bad Wolf* (2005),Captain Jack Harkness recognises the ships of the Dalek fleet, although he says they vanished. Up until now, the Doctor believed they were destroyed in the Great Time War between the Daleks and the Time Lords. But the Daleks, it seems, are not so easy to destroy. They have invaded Earth on several occasions – in *The Dalek Invasion of Earth* (1964), in *Day of the Daleks* (1972) where they manipulated history to invade again, and also in *The Stolen Earth* (2008). Whatever the future holds for the human race, the Daleks are out there waiting…

**1968** *The Web of Fear* Episode 4

**1973** *Frontier in Space* Episode 1

**1974** *Death to the Daleks* Part 1 is first shown on BBC Wales.

**1979** *The Armageddon Factor* Part 6 is Mary Tamm's last episode playing Romana, and closes Season 16. It is also Anthony Read's final episode as Script Editor.

**1984** *Planet of Fire* Part 2

## 25 FEBRUARY

# The Sontarans Invade Gallifrey

The troll-like Sontarans come from the high-gravity planet Sontar, and reproduce by cloning – at a rate of a million every four minutes in great muster parades. They are all identical in appearance. A brutal race of cloned warriors, the Sontarans are dedicated to warfare and have been at war with the Rutans for thousands of years.

Despite their ruthlessness, the Sontarans have a keen sense of honour. They even see their greatest weakness as a strength – a Sontaran can only be stunned by a blow to the probic vent. Since the probic vent is a small hole at the back of the neck, this means that the Sontarans must always face their enemies.

Although he had heard of them before, the Third Doctor first met a Sontaran in *The Time Warrior* (1973–1974) when he encountered Commander Linx whose ship had crashed in medieval England. In *The Sontaran Experiment* (1975), the Fourth Doctor took on Field-Major Styre, sent to make an assessment of the human race. He encountered the Sontarans again when they invaded Gallifrey in *The Invasion of Time* (1978). The Sixth and Second Doctors both encountered Group Marshal Stike, who attempted to learn the secrets of time travel in *The Two Doctors* (1985). The Tenth Doctor foiled the Sontaran attempt to turn Earth into a clone world in *The Sontaran Stratagem* and *The Poison Sky* (2008).

No less warlike and aggressive, but a friend of the Doctor is the Sontaran Strax, who works as 'manservant' to the Silurian Madame Vastra in Victorian London.

**1967** *The Moonbase* Episode 3

**1978** The Sontarans make a surprise appearance at the end of Part 4 of *The Invasion of Time*.

## 26 FEBRUARY

# The Sea Devils Rise from Beneath the Waves

The amphibious species of ancient reptiles related to the Silurians were named 'Sea Devils' by Clark, a man traumatised by encountering them on an abandoned sea fort in *The Sea Devils* (1972). The Third Doctor tells Jo that compared with the Silurians, the Sea Devils are 'a different species, completely adapted to life under water'.

Like the Silurians, they have been in hibernation for millions of years, woken by work being carried out on the sea fort to turn it into a SONAR testing station. They still regard Earth as their own planet, and plan to take it back from the upstart apes that now control the world. With the help of the Master, they plan to revive the Sea Devils and Silurians hibernating in other bases all round the world and wage war against mankind…

In *Warriors of the Deep* (1984), the Fifth Doctor is caught up in a combined attack by Silurians and Sea Devils on the underwater military installation Sea Base Four. The Silurians command a detachment of Sea Devil warriors, wearing Samurai-type armour. They also use a Myrka – a huge, aggressive quadrupedal reptile. It is a bio-engineered creature capable of electrifying its victims. But the Doctor realises that it is susceptible to exposure to certain wavelengths of light and kills it with an ultra-violet converter.

ON THIS DAY

**1966** Dodo – Dorothea Chaplet – enters the TARDIS believing it to be a real police box at the end of the final episode of *The Massacre*, titled *Bell of Doom*. It is Gerry Davis's first episode as Story Editor.

**1972** The Sea Devils first appear in Episode 1 of *The Sea Devils*.

**1977** *The Talons of Weng-Chiang* Part 1

## 27 FEBRUARY

# A Darker Side of the Doctor

The Dream Lord that the Eleventh Doctor, Amy and Rory encounter in *Amy's Choice* (2010) didn't really exist. But even so, he almost killed them by putting them inside dreams where they could end up dead. They had to distinguish between realities – deciding which was the dream and which was real…

In one 'reality', the TARDIS froze in the light of a 'cold star'. In another, the Doctor and his friends were attacked in Amy and Rory's home village by Eknodines – a proud and ancient race that inhabit and control other people's bodies. They are visible only as an eye on a stalk in the possessed person's mouth.

In fact, both these realities were dreams. The Dream Lord himself, while looking like an ordinary man, was actually a speck of psychic pollen from the Candle Meadows of Karass don Slava that fell into the TARDIS Time Rotor. A mind parasite, it fed on the darkness in the Doctor's mind to create the Dream Lord as he was perceived by the Doctor, Amy and Rory.

**ON THIS DAY**

**1965** *Escape to Danger* – the third episode of *The Web Planet*.

**1971** *The Mind of Evil* Episode 5

## 28 FEBRUARY

# Tegan Joins the TARDIS

An impulsive, self-confident Australian, Tegan Jovanka describes herself at one point as 'a mouth on legs'. She is on her way to her first day at work as an air stewardess when she finds the TARDIS in *Logopolis* (1981). She realises at once that it is a vehicle, but is unprepared for the journey to Logopolis. However, she implicitly trusts the Fourth Doctor, and soon forms a friendship with the quieter and more level-headed Nyssa. Her relationship with Adric is more volatile, although she is deeply distressed by his death in *Earthshock* (1982).

Tegan is initially keen to get back to Heathrow and her job – losing her temper with the Fifth Doctor in *The Visitation* (1982) when he arrives several hundred years too early. But when she is left there at the end of *Time-Flight* (1982), she seems genuinely sad, and wastes no time re-joining the Doctor and Nyssa when they meet again in *Arc of Infinity* (1983).

But Tegan's time with the Doctor does have its darker moments – not least Adric's death. It is Tegan who is possessed by the Mara in *Kinda* (1982). The Mara plays on the 'darker' characteristics of Tegan, and the experiences deeply unsettle her – particularly when she is again possessed in *Snakedance* (1983).

Seeing the deaths of so many people in *Resurrection of the Daleks* (1984) finally convinces Tegan that travelling with the Doctor is becoming more of an ordeal than a pleasure, and so she leaves. The Doctor is sad to see her go – Tegan and the Fifth Doctor enjoyed a love-hate relationship in which frequent arguments and apparent abrasiveness masked a deeper affection and respect.

ON THIS DAY

**1970** *The Silurians* Episode 5

**1975** *The Seeds of Doom* Part 5

**1981** *Logopolis* Part 1

**1981 The Doctor takes measurements of a real police box in *Logopolis*. Tegan's Aunt Vanessa is killed by the Master, and Tegan first enters the TARDIS.**

**1981 The events of the Fifth Doctor story *Four to Doomsday* take place.**

## 29 FEBRUARY

# The Doctor is Forced to Give the TARDIS Key to Marco Polo

**1964** *The Singing Sands* – the second episode of *Marco Polo*

The TARDIS is protected by a double-curtain trimonic barrier, which can be opened with a cipher-indent key. For most of the time, the TARDIS key looks just like a standard 'Yale' type key. Its shape is presumably affected by the Chameleon Circuit and in-keeping with the police box appearance of the TARDIS's outer plasmic shell. But for a while the Third and Fourth Doctors and also the Seventh and Eighth Doctors used a key shaped similar to the 'spade' symbol in a pack of playing cards.

Although the Doctor has given keys to various of his companions, he evidently has the ability to decide who can successfully use them. In *Spearhead from Space* (1970), for example, the Brigadier is unable to open the TARDIS using the Third Doctor's own key. Also, as a precaution, the Eighth Doctor keeps a spare key in a cubby hole hidden above the door in the TV movie *Doctor Who* (1996), while, in *Dark Water* (2014), the Twelfth Doctor has seven keys hidden around the TARDIS. This precaution may be a result of the events of *Marco Polo* (1964) in which the First Doctor is forced to give the only TARDIS key to Marco Polo – telling him he will not be able to use it to open the TARDIS. The Doctor does, however, confess to Ian that he has managed to make a second one. By the next story, *The Keys of Marinus* (1964), Susan has her own key again – the Doctor having destroyed her previous key sabotaging Dalek equipment in *The Daleks* (1963–1964).

In *The Daleks*, Susan tells Ian and Barbara that the whole TARDIS lock comes away from the door. She says that as a defence mechanism there are twenty-one different holes inside the lock. 'There's one right place and twenty wrong ones. If you make a mistake, the whole inside of the lock will melt.'

# 1 MARCH

# Peri's Holiday to Lanzarote Takes Her Further than She Expected

Perpugilliam Brown – Peri for short – is an American botany student holidaying in Lanzarote when she becomes involved in the Doctor's adventures. Although she is comfortable with the Fifth Doctor, once he regenerates – having sacrificed his fifth life for her – Peri is left feeling frightened and alienated by his new persona.

She does come to appreciate the new Sixth Doctor, but her relationship with him is more abrasive. The two frequently swap personal insults or tease each other about anything from usage of slang words to each other's weight. Peri is not someone who allows bad feelings to fester – she will always vocalise what's bothering her. She complains that she would be happier if the Doctor arranged purposeful travel rather than just aimless wandering through time and space, and it seems probable that it is a desire to broaden her mind rather than personal fondness that is key to her continuing to accompany the Doctor.

But after the events of *Revelation of the Daleks* (1985), Peri and the Doctor seem to mellow in their attitude towards each other. The Doctor is quietly understanding of her pain when she believes her world to have been entirely destroyed. But ironically, this new-found affection has little chance to flourish.

ON THIS DAY

**1918** Roger Delgado, who played the Master throughout the Third Doctor's era, was born.

**1969** *The Seeds of Death* Episode 6

**1975** *The Sontaran Experiment* Part 2

**1982** *Black Orchid* Part 1. The story is script edited by Eric Saward.

**1983** *Enlightenment* Part 1

**1984** *Planet of Fire* Part 3

 Peri parts company with the Doctor on Thoros-Beta. But exactly how they part is unclear due to distortions in the Matrix's representation of events in *The Trial of a Time Lord* (1986). Initially it seems she is killed. But later Time Lord testimony reports she in fact married the warlord King Yrcanos.

# 2 MARCH

# The Doctor is Almost Sacrificed to a City

Exxilon is a desolate wasteland of a planet. It is also a source of parrinium – an extremely rare chemical found in minute quantities on Earth which can cure and give immunity to a plague ravaging the outer planets of Earth's Empire. When the Third Doctor and Sarah Jane Smith arrive on Exxilon in *Death to the Daleks* (1974), the TARDIS mysteriously drained of power, they find both humans and Daleks have come to find the precious chemical.

The source of the power drain affecting not only the TARDIS but also human and Dalek technology (and weaponry) is a huge city – not unlike a massive step-pyramid – built by the advanced ancestors of the now primitive humanoid Exxilons. The Doctor describes the City as 'one of the seven hundred wonders of the Universe'. Only the Exxilon High Priests are allowed near it – anyone else found there is sacrificed, as the Doctor and Sarah discover.

The Exxilon Bellal tells the Doctor: 'Exxilon had grown old before life had even begun on other planets... Using all their knowledge [our ancestors] built a city that would last through all of time… They used their sciences to make the city into a living thing. It could protect itself, repair itself, maintain itself. They even gave it a brain… It then had no need of those who had made it. Our people had created a monster. They tried to destroy it; instead it destroyed them and drove out the survivors.'

While the Doctor is able to engineer a 'nervous breakdown' that destroys the City's brain, the Daleks destroy the beacon on top of the structure that drains power from the atmosphere.

**1968** *The Web of Fear* Episode 5

**1974** *Death to the Daleks* Part 2

**1982** *Black Orchid* Part 2

**1983** *Enlightenment* Part 2

**1984** Turlough leaves at the end of the last episode of *Planet of Fire*. The robot Kamelion is also destroyed in this episode.

**1985** *The Two Doctors* Part 3

## 3 MARCH

# The Master Tracks Down the Doomsday Weapon

In the twenty-fifth century, the planet Uxarieus is home to a human colony, a few birds and insects, and the native 'Primitives'. But centuries earlier a great civilisation flourished there. By genetic engineering they developed a super-race, which itself created a 'Doomsday Weapon'. The weapon, fortunately, was never used. As the Third Doctor realises when he and Jo Grant travel to the planet in *Colony in Space* (1971), 'the super-race became priests of a lunatic religion worshipping machines instead of gods'.

But the Master has learned of the Doomsday Weapon from stolen Time Lord files. Realising this, the Time Lords send the Doctor from his exile on Earth to prevent the Master from getting hold of the weapon – which destroys suns by making them explode. The Crab Nebula was the result of the super-race that developed it testing the weapon.

With the unscrupulous Interplanetary Mining Corporation trying to force out the colonists so that they can mine the planet for its rich deposits of duralinium, the Master poses as an Adjudicator sent from Earth to sort out the dispute. He finds the weapon, protected by a Guardian descended from its original creators. The Guardian tells the Master and the Doctor that once the Doomsday Weapon was built, 'our race began to decay. The radiation from the weapon's power source poisoned the soil of our planet…'

On the Guardian's instructions, the Doctor sets the weapon to self-destruct, but the Master escapes.

**1215** The shape-changing robot Kamelion arrives at Fitzwilliam Castle disguised as King John.

**1973** *Frontier in Space* Episode 2

**1974** *Death to the Daleks* Part 2 is first shown on BBC Wales.

**2472** The events of the Third Doctor story *Colony in Space* take place between 3 and 5 March.

## 4 MARCH

# The Doctor Learns the Secrets of the Demat Gun

The Demat Gun is an ancient and terrible Time Lord Weapon that dematerialises its target. The Fourth Doctor calls it 'the ultimate weapon', and knowledge of it has been hidden.

When the Sontarans invade Gallifrey in *The Invasion of Time* (1978), the Fourth Doctor has his friend Rodan build the Demat Gun under hypnosis while instructed by K-9 in the TARDIS laboratory. But even after it has been built, the question remains of how to arm it.

The Doctor realises that the arming mechanism is the Great Key. One of the commitments a President makes at inauguration is to 'seek to find the Great Key of Rassilon'. The Doctor realises that, rather than being merely a myth, the Great Key was given to the Time Lord Chancellor so that no President could wield absolute power.

Hundreds of keys hang on the wall behind Chancellor Borusa's desk – posing the question, which of these, if any, is the Great Key. In fact, the Great Key is the key to a drawer of the Chancellor's chest. Once he has the Great Key, the Doctor – the first President since Rassilon to hold the Great Key – is able to use it to arm the Demat Gun. He then uses the weapon to destroy the Sontaran Commander Storr.

ON THIS DAY

**1967** The first optical effect used in *Doctor Who* is seen as the Cybermen fire a laser cannon at the Moonbase in Episode 4 of *The Moonbase*. We also get our first glimpse of a Macra – just the claw – on the TARDIS scanner at the end of the episode.

**1215** The events of *The King's Demons* take place.

**1972** *The Sea Devils* Episode 2

**1978** *The Invasion of Time* Part 5

**2472** The events of the Third Doctor story *Colony in Space* take place between 3 and 5 March.

# 5 MARCH

# Dodo Makes Her First Trip in the TARDIS

Dorothea Chaplet, or Dodo for short, is a young orphan. Her mother died while Dodo was still at school, and she now lives with her great aunt. She may be a Cockney (her accent varies), and her grandfather was French. This leads the First Doctor to speculate that she may be descended from Anne Chaplette whom Steven was friends with in *The Massacre* (1966), although this is unlikely as Anne Chaplette's children would almost certainly have taken their father's surname.

Walking into the TARDIS believing it to be a real police box, Dodo takes the notion of travelling through time and space in the TARDIS in her stride. Steven sums her up when he says in *The Savages* (1966): 'If it isn't allowed, Dodo would be the first in the queue.'

The First Doctor seems close to Dodo, especially after Steven has left. As soon as he first sees her, he remarks to Steven that she reminds him of his granddaughter, Susan. But in *The War Machines* (1966), she is taken over by the computer WOTAN and conditioned to betray the Doctor. After the Doctor is able to break Dodo's conditioning, he sends her to the country to recuperate. She does not return, but sends a message – and her TARDIS key – back with Polly and Ben to say she has decided to stay on Earth. The Doctor is deeply disappointed not only that she decides to stay behind, but also that she does not tell him in person.

ON THIS DAY

**1966** *The Steel Sky* – the first episode of *The Ark* – is Dodo's first full episode.

**1977** *The Talons of Weng-Chiang* Part 2

**2005** Rose Tyler first meets the Ninth Doctor.

**2005** Clara Oswald's mother Ellie died, according to her gravestone seen in *The Rings of Akhaten*.

**2472** The events of the Third Doctor story *Colony in Space* take place between 3 and 5 March.

6 MARCH

# Rose Tyler Faces an Alien Invasion

Rose Tyler is just an ordinary 19-year-old girl working in a department store until she meets the Ninth Doctor in *Rose* (2005). Rose lives at home in a flat on the Powell Estate with her mother, Jackie. Her father, Peter Tyler, was killed in a hit-and-run car accident in 1987, when Rose was a baby. Now her life is routine – get up, go to work, maybe meet her boyfriend Mickey for lunch, back to work then home again.

She left school without doing A levels, but Rose is intelligent and quick-thinking. On their first meeting, she impresses the Doctor with her logical thought and deduction about the Autons that attack her – even though her guess that they may be students dressed up is more mundane and less dangerous than the truth.

After travelling with the Doctor, Rose is mortified to realise on her return in *Aliens of London* (2005) that she has been missing for a whole year. She enjoys her time back with her friends and family on the estate, but has no qualms about setting off with the Doctor again after the Slitheen have been defeated. In *The Parting of the Ways* (2005) she will risk anything to get back to the Doctor and save him.

Her friendship with the Tenth Doctor becomes even closer, and – when they are separated and find themselves in different universes in *Doomsday* (2006) – Rose confesses she loves him. It is apparent that the Doctor

also feels deeply for her. Reunited briefly in *The Stolen Earth / Journey's End* (2008), Rose returns to the parallel world that is her new home not with the Doctor, but with a copy of him created out of a biological metacrisis – perhaps the next best thing…

**1965** *Crater of Needles* – the fourth episode of *The Web Planet*

**1971** *The Mind of Evil* Episode 6

**1975** The last episode of *The Seeds of Doom* closes Season 13.

**2005** The Nestene Consciousness activates its shop dummy Autons to attack in *Rose*.

**2006** The Doctor brings Rose back for *Aliens of London / World War Three* – a year late!

# 7 MARCH

# The Doctor Travels to Logopolis

In *Logopolis* (1981), the Fourth Doctor takes the TARDIS to the brain-like city of Logopolis in the hope of repairing the TARDIS's Chameleon Circuit using the Logopolitans' knowledge of Block Transfer Computation. The Logopolitans, who intone numbers and calculations like components of an organic computer, are led by the Monitor. He explains that they are a people 'driven not by individual need, but by mathematical necessity'.

The Monitor also reveals that Logopolis is actually the 'keystone' of the universe – it is the Logopolitans' constant calculations that hold the fabric of the universe together. In any closed system, like the universe, entropy increases and the universe long ago passed the point of total collapse. But the Logopolitans have opened the system by creating Charged Vacuum Emboitments (CVEs) – voids into other universes. This allows more energy to flow into the universe and stave off the advance of entropy. But the solution depends upon the Logopolitans' continual endeavours while they search for a more permanent solution. When the Master interferes, Logopolis dies, and the voids start to close.

Block Transfer Computation is a way of modelling space-time events through pure calculation. The Logopolitans intone their computations as the calculations would change the nature of any machine they were calculated on – their manipulation of numbers directly changes the physical world, and only the living brain is immune. Using the technique,

the Logopolitans have created a duplicate of the
Pharos Project that exists on Earth. When Logopolis
is destroyed, the Doctor and the Master run the
Logopolitan program on the real Pharos computer to
keep the CVEs open and stable.

# 8 MARCH

# Davros Creates the Daleks

The Time Lords foresee a time when the Daleks will become the dominant creature in the universe. So in *Genesis of the Daleks* (1975) they send the Fourth Doctor back to the Daleks' very beginnings, at the end of a thousand-year war between the Thals and the Kaleds on the planet Skaro. His mission is either to avert their creation, or to affect their genetic development so they evolve into less aggressive beings. Failing that, he may be able to discover some inherent weakness in the Daleks. According to some sources, it is this action that triggers the start of the Great Time War.

Davros is a crippled Kaled scientist, kept alive in a mobile life-support system that resembles the lower half of a Dalek. Realising the cycle of mutation started by chemical and biological weapons used in the war could not be halted, Davros designed a travel machine and life-support system for the creature his race would mutate into – calling it a Dalek. Davros also changed the genetic make-up of the Dalek creatures so they would be superior – increasing their aggression and removing the conscience so they would one day rule supreme.

Although he was apparently destroyed by his own creations, Davros survived, and the Doctor has encountered him on several occasions. The Fourth Doctor is on Skaro when the Daleks return for Davros to help in their war against the Movellans in *Destiny of the Daleks* (1979). In *Resurrection of the Daleks* (1984), the Daleks attempt to rescue Davros from a prison in space. In *Revelation of the Daleks* (1985), Davros is in charge of the Tranquil Repose facility, while in *Remembrance of the Daleks* (1988) he has made himself Emperor of a

**1969** *The Space Pirates* Episode 1. Derrick Sherwin takes over again as Script Editor for this one story.

**1975** Davros first appears at the end of Part 1 of *Genesis of the Daleks*.

**1982** The Cybermen return in Part 1 of *Earthshock* for the first time since *Revenge of the Cybermen* in 1975. The story is script edited by Antony Root.

**1983** *Enlightenment* Part 3

**1984** *The Caves of Androzani* Part 1 is the first episode written by veteran writer and former Script Editor Robert Holmes since *The Power of Kroll* in 1978–1979.

breakaway faction of Daleks. Davros again works for the Daleks in *The Stolen Earth / Journey's End* (2008). In *The Magician's Apprentice / The Witch's Familiar* (2015), the Twelfth Doctor finds himself unable to leave Davros to die as a child – just as in *Genesis of the Daleks* he could not bring himself to destroy Davros's embryo Daleks…

## 9 MARCH

# The Doctor Meets the Young H.G. Wells

ON THIS DAY

**1968** *The Web of Fear* Episode 6

**1974** *Death to the Daleks* Part 3

**1982** *Earthshock* Part 2

**1983** *Enlightenment* Part 4

**1984** *The Caves of Androzani* Part 2

**1985** *Timelash* Part 1

Herbert George Wells, the author best known for his science fiction works including *The Time Machine*, *The Island of Doctor Moreau*, and *The War of the Worlds*, was born in 1866 and died in 1946. As shown in *Timelash* (1985), while staying close to Loch Ness in Scotland in 1885, the young Wells was 'visited' by a young lady named Vena who had travelled down a Kontron time tunnel that originated with the Timelash on the planet Karfel. She was followed by the Sixth Doctor – who Wells initially believed to be some sort of supernatural demon.

Despite Wells's entreaties, the Doctor refused to allow him into the TARDIS. But Wells managed to sneak on board and travelled back to Karfel with him. He then helped the Doctor and Peri, together with Vena and her friends, rid the planet of its despotic ruler, the Borad.

The Borad seemed to be a soft-spoken old man who appeared only on screens. But in fact, this was an android. The real Borad was the mutated scientist Magellan – who was fused with a reptilian Morlox when an experiment involving Mustakozene-80 and a Morlox creature went wrong. The Borad was a combined mutant with greater strength, intellect and longevity.

Following his adventures on Karfel, Wells returned to Earth with the Doctor, and set about writing his fictional accounts of time travel and life on other worlds…

# 10 MARCH

# The Doctor Displays His Knowledge of Venusian Culture

**1973** *Frontier in Space* Episode 3

**1974** *Death to the Daleks* Part 3 is first shown on BBC Wales.

One of the most 'physical' of the Doctors, the Third Doctor employed a form of self-defence he apparently learned on the planet Venus. He first describes it as Venusian Karate after he uses it to disable Professor Stahlman in *Inferno* (1970). In *The Green Death* (1973), having got the better of several security guards at Global Chemicals, the Doctor refers to it as Venusian Aikido.

The Third Doctor in particular has evidently picked up various things from Venus. He soothes the monster Aggedor with a Venusian lullaby in both *The Curse of Peladon* (1972) and *The Monster of Peladon* (1974). It is the same lullaby as he intones at the animated grotesque statue in *The Dæmons* (1971) to scare it off. He tells Jo Grant that the first line translates roughly as: 'Close your eyes my darling, well three of them at least.'

As well as various Venusian anecdotes that the Doctor recounts, he also asks the Exxilon Bellal if he has ever played Venusian hopscotch in *Death to the Daleks* (1974). In *Robot* (1974–1975), the Fourth Doctor reveals that he has a pilot's licence for the Mars-Venus rocket run.

## 11 MARCH

# The Macra First Appear

Known as the scourge of Galaxy M87, the Macra are massive crab-like creatures that depend on gas for their existence, consuming it like food. When the second Doctor first encounters them in *The Macra Terror* (1967), the creatures have enslaved human colonists – brainwashing them to believe that the gas is valuable and essential so the colonists will mine the gas for them.

The brainwashing is achieved by the use of scented air and a thin strand of wire in the wall above the subject's head, which the Doctor likens to a 'nerve tapping the subconscious of the human brain'. The final element of the processing is a voice telling the sleeper to relax and obey orders. The Doctor tells Polly that the Macra are 'like germs in the human body. They've got into the body of this colony. They're living as parasites.'

But by the time the Tenth Doctor encounters the Macra on New Earth in *Gridlock* (2007), they have devolved into less intelligent, more instinctive creatures that hunt in a huge herd. They still depend on gas for their survival, but also drag unsuspecting humans from their cars – possibly to feed on. The Macra remain hidden and undetected in the fog of gas that drifts beneath the air cars and the Overcity of New New York.

**1963** Alex Kingston, who plays River Song, was born.

**1967** *The Macra Terror* Episode 1

**1972** *The Sea Devils* Episode 3

**1978** *The Invasion of Time* Part 6 is Leela's last episode and closes Season 15.

## 12 MARCH

# The Doctor and Jo Grant Meet the Draconians

Nicknamed 'Dragons' by the humans, the Draconians are reptilian humanoids ruled by an Emperor. They are an advanced technological race steeped in tradition and honour. They do not lie, and females are not permitted to speak in the presence of their 'betters', such as the Emperor.

There is a legend of a man who came to Draconia during the time of the Fifteenth Emperor and saved the Draconians from a great plague that threatened to wipe them out. He came in a strange ship called the TARDIS, and his name was the Doctor.

In 2520, the empires of Earth and Draconia met. The clash of two such different cultures threatened to be a violent one, and so a conference was arranged: two unarmed ships would meet in space. But the Earth ship was damaged in a neutron storm, and as it drifted, helpless, the Draconian ship arrived – a battle cruiser that failed to answer any communications from the stricken ship.

By a brilliant act of ingenuity, the Earth commander, Williams, destroyed the battle cruiser before it could open fire. The war that followed the incident was a terrible and tragic mistake. It was not until twenty years later, during the events of *Frontier in Space* (1973), that Williams discovered the Draconian ship was unarmed and its communications system had been destroyed in the same neutron storm that had damaged his ship.

Eventually peace was restored and there were trade treaties and even cultural exchanges between Earth and Draconia. But in 2540, it seemed to both sides that

**ON THIS DAY**

**1966** *The Plague* – the second episode of *The Ark*

**1977** *The Talons of Weng-Chiang* Part 3

**1999** *The Curse of Fatal Death* by Steven Moffat is broadcast in four short episodes as part of the BBC's Comic Relief Red Nose Day.

**2540 The TARDIS arrives on cargo ship C982 in *Frontier in Space*.**

the other was, again, taking the offensive. It was up
to the Third Doctor to reveal the true villains behind
the attacks on both empires – Ogrons working for the
Master in order to provoke another war…

## 13 MARCH

# Axos Arrives on Earth

**1965** *Invasion* – the fifth episode of *The Web Planet*

**1971** *The Claws of Axos* Episode 1

Axos is a space parasite, landing on planets and hastening their destruction. It absorbs the energy from the dying planet and uses it to survive. When it first lands on Earth in *The Claws of Axos* (1971), Axos seems to be a spaceship, inhabited by the Axons. The Axons first appear as beautiful, benevolent gold-skinned humanoids, but their true appearance is as tentacled, blobby aliens that are immune to bullets and can kill on touch. They absorb energy and transmit it back to Axos – one Axon is able to transfer the entire output of a nuclear reactor simply by walking into it.

When they first arrive, the Axons offer a gift to humanity – Axonite. The Axons describe it as 'a thinking molecule. It uses the energy it absorbs not only to copy but to recreate and restructure any given substance'. They use Axonite to copy and enlarge a frog to show how it can provide unlimited food and power.

But the Third Doctor realises that Axonite, Axos and the Axons are all a single entity. Axonite can absorb, convert, transmit and program all forms of energy, even radiation. Once distributed around the world, Axonite will absorb the Earth's energy to feed Axos: 'All things must die,' an Axon tells the Doctor. 'Axos merely hastens the process … Slowly we will consume every particle of energy, every last cell of living matter. Earth will be sucked dry.'

# 14 MARCH

# The Master's Tissue Compression Eliminator

**ON THIS DAY**

**1964** *The Wall of Lies* – the fourth episode of *Marco Polo*

**1970** *The Silurians* Episode 7

**1981** *Logopolis* Part 3

Although he has killed in many and varied ways, the Master's weapon of choice is perhaps the Tissue Compression Eliminator. This stubby, cylindrical device kills its victims by shrinking them down to the size of a small doll. The Doctor describes it as 'matter condensation. A particularly nasty sort of death.'

When he first arrives on Earth in *Terror of the Autons* (1971), the Master kills a scientist called Goodge, leaving his miniaturised corpse inside the man's own lunchbox. In *The Deadly Assassin* (1976), the Master leaves the shrunken body of a public broadcast camera technician inside his camera. Many years later in *Logopolis* (1981), the Master despatches a policeman and Tegan's Aunt Vanessa in the same way.

But the Master has also been on the receiving end of the weapon. In *The King's Demons* (1983), the Fifth Doctor used it to sabotage the dimension circuits of the Master's TARDIS. More drastically, while trying to increase the weapon's range and make it more powerful, the Master was himself accidentally shrunk down to miniature size – although he was otherwise unharmed – in *Planet of Fire* (1984).

# 15 MARCH

# Kamelion Impersonates King John

Kamelion is a humanoid android originally constructed as a weapon. The android has a mind of its own, albeit a highly susceptible one – and is humble and benevolent unless turned to evil by whoever controls it. By concentrating hard on a certain person the android will assume that identity. Through psychokinetics, Kamelion can act and speak exactly like that person. It is apparently capable of infinite forms and personalities.

Kamelion was used, and most likely created, by unidentified invaders of the planet Xeriphas. Having been banished there by the Doctor, the Master found Kamelion, and was able to utilise the android's services to affect an escape.

Not relishing the thought of being trapped on a medieval world at the end of his introductory story, *The King's Demons* (1983), in which he impersonates King John, Kamelion is happy to join the Fifth Doctor. His activities while the Doctor continues his journeys are unknown. He seems to spend much of the time connected to the TARDIS's data banks.

Unfortunately, the Master has a particular hold on Kamelion, leaving a part of his own mind lodged inside the android's. Even across massive distances, Kamelion is compelled to act on the Master's will. Crippled, unable to resist the Master and unwilling to betray his friends, Kamelion eventually persuades the Doctor to kill him with the Master's Tissue Compression Eliminator.

**ON THIS DAY**

**1969** *The Space Pirates* Episode 2

**1975** *Genesis of the Daleks* Part 2

**1982** *Earthshock* Part 3

**1983** *The King's Demons* Part 1

**1984** *The Caves of Androzani* Part 3

# 16 MARCH

# The Sonic Screwdriver Makes Its Debut

First appearing in the opening episode of *Fury from the Deep* (1968), the Doctor's sonic screwdriver has become one of his most trusted and versatile tools. In that first instance, the Second Doctor uses it simply as a screwdriver, opening an inspection box attached to a gas pipeline – 'all done by sound waves', as he explains to Jamie and Victoria.

The next time the Doctor uses the sonic screwdriver, in *The Dominators* (1968), he confesses that 'it's a little more than a screwdriver' before using it as a blowtorch to cut through a wall.

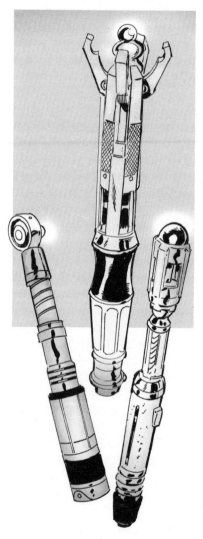

Over the years, the Doctor has used his trusted sonic screwdriver for a variety of purposes from opening doors and electronic locks to detecting and detonating landmines, from disabling or repairing equipment to detecting various emissions and reconnecting barbed wire… The sonic screwdriver itself has undergone radical redesigns – having to be rebuilt after being destroyed by the Terileptils in *The Visitation* (1982), or exploding in *The Eleventh Hour* (2010). While the Twelfth Doctor has used the sonic screwdriver, he also makes extensive use of a pair of sonic sunglasses.

The sonic screwdriver is such a useful and versatile tool that perhaps it's not surprising that Romana made herself her own version, that River Song also has a sonic screwdriver (given to her by the Doctor) or that Sarah Jane Smith has a sonic lipstick…

**1943** John Leeson, who provided the voice of K-9 for all his appearances except the 1979 stories *The Creature from the Pit*, *Nightmare of Eden* and *The Horns of Nimon*, was born.

**1968** The Doctor first uses his sonic screwdriver in *Fury from the Deep* Episode 1.

**1974** *Death to the Daleks* Part 4

**1982** Adric is killed at the end of the final episode of *Earthshock*.

**1983** Kamelion is introduced in Part 2 of *The King's Demons*, which closes Season 20.

**1984** *The Caves of Androzani* Part 4 is Peter Davison's last episode as the Fifth Doctor.

**1985** *Timelash* Part 2

# 17 MARCH

## Imprisoned on the Moon

In *Frontier in Space* (1973), the Third Doctor is sent to the Lunar Penal Colony. Believing him to be a Draconian agent, the President of Earth uses the powers invested in her by the Special Security Act to have the Doctor incarcerated. Almost all those held on the Moon are political prisoners, many of them members of the so-called Peace Party. There are no sentences – once you are sent to the Moon, it's for ever…

Of course, this is not the only time the Doctor has been to the Moon. In *The Moonbase* (1967), the Second Doctor and his companions find themselves at an international lunar base. Here they help foil an attempt by the Cybermen to take over the Gravitron that controls Earth's weather.

When the Tenth Doctor first meets Martha Jones in *Smith and Jones* (2007), they find themselves transported – along with the entire Royal Hope Hospital – to the lunar surface by the Judoon. While he doesn't actually travel to the Moon, the Eleventh Doctor uses footage of Neil Armstrong's first steps on the lunar surface to defeat the Silence in *Day of the Moon* (2011). On his visit in *Kill The Moon* (2014), the Twelfth Doctor discovers that the Moon is actually a giant egg – and about to hatch…

ON THIS DAY

**1973** *Frontier in Space* Episode 4

**1974** *Death to the Daleks* Part 4 is first shown on BBC Wales.

# 18 MARCH

# Keeping a 500 Year Diary

'The Doctor kept a diary, didn't he?' the Second Doctor asks Polly and Ben in the first episode of *The Power of the Daleks* (1966). He seems fascinated to read it, and the Second Doctor in particular is associated with keeping a 500 Year Diary, mentioning it in *The Underwater Menace* (1967), for example.

Although we don't see other incarnations of the Doctor keep the diary up to date, the Fourth Doctor searches for his 500 Year Diary in *The Sontaran Experiment* (1975). 'I remember jotting some notes on the Sontarans,' he tells Harry, although he is unable to find the diary in his cluttered pockets.

Whether the Doctor kept his diary after that is unclear. In *The Caves of Androzani* (1984), the Fifth Doctor tells Peri he has been to Androzani Major before – and he's fairly certain it wasn't in the future. In response to Peri's comment that he is a very confusing person to be with, the Doctor tells her: 'I tried keeping a diary once. Not chronological, of course, but the trouble with time travel is one never seems to find the time.' The Seventh Doctor, though, had a 900 Year Diary in the TARDIS by the time of the TV movie, *Doctor Who* (1996).

Which of his incarnations actually do keep a diary is unknown, but the Twelfth Doctor refers to his 2,000 Year Diary while in the Viking village in *The Girl Who Died* (2015).

**1967** *The Macra Terror*
Episode 2

**1972** *The Sea Devils*
Episode 4

# 19 MARCH

## Magnus Greel Retrieves His Time Cabinet

**1966** *The Return* – the third episode of *The Ark*

**1977** *The Talons of Weng-Chiang* Part 4

At the close of Part 4 of *The Talons of Weng-Chiang* (1977), Magnus Greel retrieves the Time Cabinet that brought him to Victorian London from the fifty-first century. But, although he doesn't yet realise it, he does not have the key.

The infamous Minister of Justice, Magnus Greel was nicknamed the Butcher of Brisbane and the Fourth Doctor says that a hundred thousand deaths can be laid at his door. Branded a war criminal after the fall of the Icelandic Alliance in the year 5000, Greel fled through time, arriving in nineteenth-century China. Here he lost his Time Cabinet. Searching for it, he assumed the identity of the Chinese god Weng-Chiang and the help of his followers in the Tong of the Black Scorpion.

Greel's time cabinet works by zygma energy, which has distorted Greel's appearance because of an error in the programmed DNA levels. Dying, Greel augments his life force by draining the energy from kidnapped young women.

Greel brought the Peking Homunculus back from the future. This is a diminutive robotic mannequin that Greel disguises as a ventriloquist's dummy named Mr Sin. Made as a toy for the children of the Commissioner of the Icelandic Alliance, it contains a series of magnetic fields operating on a printed circuit and a small computer. It also contains one organic component – the cerebral cortex of a pig. But the pig's brain took over the Homunculus (almost causing World War Six). The mental feedback was so intense that the swinish instinct became dominant. The Homunculus hated humanity and revelled in carnage.

## 20 MARCH

# Police for Hire

The first aliens that Martha Jones meets in her introductory story *Smith and Jones* (2007) – apart from the Doctor and the humanoid Plasmavore – are the Judoon. They are hugely powerful, not unlike large upright rhinoceroses. Essentially a police force available for hire, other races employ the Judoon to carry out interplanetary law enforcement tasks on their behalf. They form the security service for the Shadow Proclamation, for example.

Arriving in massive upright spaceships like huge tower blocks, they can enforce galactic law only where specifically invited or on neutral territory. They are forbidden, for example, from operating on Earth.

The Judoon have access to a range of technology, including universal galactic real-time translation systems so they can communicate with other life forms. They sometimes use an $H_2O$ scoop, harnessing the inert power of hydrogen, to transport people or entire buildings to neutral space where the Judoon can enforce the law. The effect of the scoop resembles a powerful lightning and thunder storm – but with the rain going up from the ground to the gathering clouds above. This is the technology they use to transport the Royal Hope Hospital from Earth to the Moon so they can legitimately hunt for the Plasmavore who murdered the Child Princess of Padrivole Regency Nine.

Ruthless in the extreme, the Judoon have little interest in other life forms apart from whether they obey the letter of the law. Anyone who opposes them is automatically found guilty of assault and executed.

ON THIS DAY

**1965** *The Centre* – the sixth episode of *The Web Planet*

**Unknown, but *c.*1970: Professor Zaroff is killed in Atlantis, while the Atlanteans are celebrating the Vernal Equinox.**

**1971** *The Claws of Axos* Episode 2

**1979** Freema Agyeman, who played the Tenth Doctor's companion Martha Jones, was born.

## 21 MARCH

# The Mars Probe Project Gets into Trouble

During the 1970s (the exact date is unknown) Britain sent manned missions to Mars. These missions were run from Space Control – the UK equivalent of NASA's Mission Control. From there the Mars Probe missions were launched and monitored, under the command of Ralph Cornish.

The Third Doctor and UNIT become involved with the Mars Probe missions in *The Ambassadors of Death* (1970) when contact is re-established with Mars Probe 7 after an apparent disaster. After transmitting reports and images from the surface of Mars, contact with astronauts Frank Michaels and Joe Lefee was suddenly lost. But then Mars Probe 7 blasted off and headed back to Earth. Eight months later, Space Control sends up Recovery 7 to meet the Mars Probe astronauts.

Again, contact is lost and, on their return to Earth, the astronauts are kidnapped. But the Doctor later discovers that the astronauts were in fact alien ambassadors – the real astronauts remaining safe and well on the aliens' spaceship. The ambassadors have been taken by General Carrington – the head of the newly formed Space Security Department. Carrington was an astronaut on Mars Probe 6, and blames the aliens for the death of his colleague, Jim Daniels. In fact it was an accident, as the aliens did not realise their touch was fatal to humans. Now Carrington believes that arranging for the destruction of the aliens is his 'moral duty'.

**1923** Peter Pratt, who played the Master in *The Deadly Assassin*, was born.

**1964** *Rider from Shang-Tu* – the fifth episode of *Marco Polo*

**1970** *The Ambassadors of Death* Episode 1

**1981** *Logopolis* Part 4 is Tom Baker's last episode as the Fourth Doctor and closes Season 18. It is also Christopher H. Bidmead's last episode as Script Editor and Barry Letts's last as Executive Producer.

# 22 MARCH

# Meet the Sixth Doctor

Even after his regeneration at the end of *The Caves of Androzani* (1984) stabilises over the course of *The Twin Dilemma* (1984), the Sixth Doctor is perhaps the most volatile of all his incarnations. Never one to keep quiet about his talents, theories or opinions, he believes in himself utterly. It is, he maintains, always someone else's fault when things go wrong, and his own genius that solves the problem.

But the bluster and volume – and the distinctive clothing – are, like the trappings of any incarnation of the Doctor's, at least to some extent part of an act. It is a veneer that masks a very real intelligence and deep concern. Outwardly, he may seem passionate about himself, ready to quote and quip his way through trouble. But it is in the rare quiet moments that we see that this is still the same brilliant, caring, intensely moral Doctor of his previous lives.

In many ways his swings of mood and his changes of attitude are the same as those of his predecessors. What is different is their extremity. Where the Second Doctor might let slip an apt quote, the Sixth will proclaim it. Where the Third Doctor might take it for granted that he is more intelligent than anyone else he meets, the Sixth makes sure that they know it. Where the Fourth Doctor might rail against injustice and evil, the Sixth gives an almost operatic performance to make the point. If the First Doctor is acerbic, the Sixth is positively caustic. And where the Fifth Doctor is quietly passionate, the Sixth Doctor has that same depth of feeling but at a considerably higher volume.

**1950** Mary Tamm who played the first incarnation of the Fourth Doctor's companion Romana was born.

**1969** *The Space Pirates* Episode 3

**1975** *Genesis of the Daleks* Part 3

**1982** *Time-Flight* Part 1. The story is script edited by Eric Saward, who remains Script Editor until *The Trial of a Time Lord* in 1986.

**1984** *The Twin Dilemma* Part 1 is Colin Baker's first full episode as the Sixth Doctor.

This also makes him perhaps the most dangerous incarnation of the Doctor. This is a Doctor who is in every way larger than life. If his enemies are distracted by his bluster, his apparent arrogance, his dress sense, then that is likely to be to their cost…

## 23 MARCH

# The Doctor Takes Concorde Back Through Time

The turbojet-powered passenger airliner Concorde was in service with British Airways and Air France from 1976 until 2003. Each carrier had just seven of the aircraft each, with another six prototypes built during the plane's development – a joint project between the British and French companies BAC and Aerospatiale.

When, in *Time-Flight* (1982), he finally gets his companion Tegan to Heathrow Airport as he promised, the Fifth Doctor arrives just after one of the BA Concordes has gone missing, simply disappearing from the RADAR trace. Retracing the Concorde's route in another Concorde (with the TARDIS on board), the Doctor, his companions Tegan and Nyssa and the Concorde's crew are transported back to prehistory by a sinister 'magician' named Kalid.

Kalid is in fact the Master, who is attempting to gain control of a gestalt race called the Xeraphin. The Doctor manages to trap the Master on the Xeraphin planet Xeriphas, and return one of the missing Concordes to Heathrow together with the crew and passengers from both planes.

**1968** *Fury from the Deep* Episode 2

**1974** *The Monster of Peladon* Part 1

**1982** *Time-Flight* Part 2 includes a brief return of the dead Adric (as an illusion).

**1984** *The Twin Dilemma* Part 2

**1985** *Revelation of the Daleks* Part 1

**1989** The premiere of *Doctor Who: The Ultimate Adventure*, a musical stage play, takes place at the Wimbledon Theatre, London, starring Jon Pertwee and later Colin Baker as the Doctor.

## 24 MARCH

# Alpha Centauri Gets Promoted

When he first visited Peladon, in *The Curse of Peladon* (1972), the Doctor found himself mistaken for the Chairman of a group of delegates assessing the planet's suitability for acceptance as a member of the Galactic Federation. Other delegates came from Mars, Arcturus and Alpha Centauri.

By the time the Doctor returns, some fifty years later, in *The Monster of Peladon* (1974), the planet has been accepted into the Federation. The Doctor is delighted to discover that former delegate Alpha Centauri is still on the planet, now appointed as the Federation's Ambassador.

From a generally amiable and peace-loving race, Alpha Centauri is a hermaphrodite hexapod with a high-pitched voice, one large eye and six arms. He is naturally nervous – described by the Ice Lord Izlyr as 'a coward by instinct'. But over time, Alpha Centauri seems to become a little braver. It is out of pragmatism rather than cowardice that he allows Eckersley to persuade him to call in Federation security forces in an attempt to quell a threatened rebellion among the miners of Peladon.

**1603** Queen Elizabeth I died.

**1973** *Frontier in Space* Episode 5

**1974** *The Monster of Peladon* Part 1 is first shown on BBC Wales.

## 25 MARCH

# Music to Stimulate the Mind

'I think best to music,' the Second Doctor claims in *The Three Doctors* (1972–1973). His instrument of choice is a recorder, which he finds in a trunk in the TARDIS soon after he first regenerates. In his earlier stories – especially his first story, *The Power of the Daleks* (1966) – he plays the recorder regularly. *The Moonbase* (1967) is the first story in which the Doctor does not play the recorder – although he plays it again in the next story *The Macra Terror* (1967) – and his use of it peters out in later years.

In *The Enemy of the World* (1967–1968), the Doctor confesses that Jamie made him leave his recorder in the TARDIS. Perhaps Jamie is also grateful that the Doctor apparently never followed through on the condition he set in *The Highlanders* (1966–1967) that Jamie could come in the TARDIS provided he taught the Doctor how to play the bagpipes…

But while it may serve to irritate his friends, the Doctor's recorder is also instrumental in the defeat of Omega in *The Three Doctors* (1972–1973). Falling into the TARDIS's force-field generator, it is the one thing not converted into antimatter when the TARDIS and its occupants are transported to Omega's antimatter domain within a black hole. When Omega knocks the recorder from the force-field generator, the atoms and anti-atoms annihilate one another – turning the black hole into a supernova.

**1920** Patrick Troughton, who played the Second Doctor, was born.

**1967** *The Macra Terror* Episode 3

**1972** *The Sea Devils* Episode 5

## 26 MARCH

# Meet the Ninth Doctor

The Ninth Doctor is at once both more human and less human than his previous incarnations. His emotions and his deep feelings betray a humanity that is undercut by his alien perspective. Superficially, he finds excitement and interest in everything – every danger is a challenge; every setback an opportunity.

But hidden within the Doctor's blunt, no-nonsense approach and his joie de vivre is a deep sadness. He is a man with a past, and the way he copes with that past is by living for the present, for the moment. We now know that it was the so-called War Doctor who ended the Last Great Time War between the Time Lords and the Daleks, but he regenerated into the Ninth Doctor almost immediately afterwards – and it is the Ninth Doctor who bears most of the burden of his actions…

This Doctor is, he believes, the last of the Time Lords – the only survivor of his people, left travelling alone because there's no one else left. He is a man living on borrowed time, a survivor when all others died. As a result, he embraces every second he still has. And he finds he is most alive when he is with Rose. He may share a joke and a sense of camaraderie with Captain Jack, but it is Rose who is the Doctor's true soul mate.

Until he meets Rose, there is a very real and deep sadness at the heart of the Doctor's soul. He blames himself both for the destruction of the Time Lords and for surviving the Time War. His horror and moral blindness on discovering that at least one Dalek also survived is the awful realisation that it may have been for nothing…

**1966** *The Bomb* – the fourth episode of *The Ark*. It is John Wiles's last episode as Producer.

**1977** *The Talons of Weng-Chiang* Part 5

**2005** The first episode of the returning *Doctor Who* is broadcast, titled *Rose*. Christopher Eccleston's first episode as the Ninth Doctor opens Series One of the returning programme. The Executive Producers are Russell T Davies, Julie Gardner and Mal Young. It is preceded by a 30-minute documentary *Doctor Who: A New Dimension* on BBC One (narrated by future Doctor David Tennant) and followed by the first *Doctor Who Confidential* on BBC Three.

In *The Parting of the Ways* (2005), he faces an apparently similar choice. He must choose to sacrifice everyone on Earth to stop the Daleks again. Only this time, the Doctor cannot bring himself to make that sacrifice.

## 27 MARCH

# Knighted by King Richard the Lionheart

**1965** *The Lion* – the first episode of *The Crusade*

**1971** *The Claws of Axos* Episode 3

The third of five sons of King Henry II and Eleanor of Aquitaine, Richard I became King of England in July 1189. In all he spent only about six months in England during his reign. Much of the time he spent fighting the Third Crusade in the Holy Land – and this is where the First Doctor and his companions meet him in *The Crusade* (1965). Having helped rescue Richard from a Saracen ambush, the Doctor's companion Ian is knighted by the King, who then allows him to search for the captured Barbara and negotiate the release of another of his knights.

Although he is first and foremost a soldier – the reason he is known as Richard the Lionheart – King Richard is weary of war. He respects but does not understand Saladin. He is a proud man, who refuses to deal with the men who killed his friends, and assumes his sister Joanna will go along with his plans. Without consulting her, he writes to Saladin, offering his sister in marriage to Saladin's brother Saphadin as part of a peace treaty. When Joanna refuses, he vents his anger first on his sister, and then on the Doctor, who he wrongly believes has told her of his plans.

But ultimately, Richard knows that his plans will come to nothing and he will be forced to continue the war.

## 28 MARCH

# The Laws of Time

Although referred to on occasion by the Time Lords, the exact nature of the Laws of Time is uncertain. They seem to be laws laid down by the Time Lords rather than scientific laws. In *The Three Doctors* (1972–1973), the Time Lord Chancellor warns the President that the First Law of Time expressly forbids the Doctor from meeting his other selves. Despite this, the President brings the first three incarnations of the Doctor together to defeat Omega.

This is not the only instance of people – including the Doctor – meeting themselves. The First, Second, Third and Fifth Doctors meet in the Death Zone and the Tower of Rassilon in *The Five Doctors* (1983), while the Sixth Doctor rescues his own second incarnation in *The Two Doctors* (1985). The Third Doctor and Jo Grant briefly meet themselves as the Doctor tries to repair the TARDIS console in *Day of the Daleks* (1972). In *The Space Museum* (1965), the First Doctor and his companions see themselves as exhibits in a museum when the TARDIS jumps a time track.

The consequences of someone meeting themselves are shown in *Mawdryn Undead* (1983), when the Brigadier from 1983 meets his 1977 self on board Mawdryn's spaceship. As they touch, they short out the time differential – fortuitously providing the power needed to power Mawdryn's equipment.

**1964** *Mighty Kublai Khan* – the sixth episode of *Marco Polo*

**1970** *The Ambassadors of Death* Episode 2

**1987** Patrick Troughton, who played the second Doctor, died.

## 29 MARCH

# Travel by Time Ring

In *Genesis of the Daleks* (1975), the Time Lords send the Fourth Doctor and his companions Sarah Jane Smith and Harry Sullivan on a mission to the planet Skaro to prevent the creation of the Daleks. Rather than redirect the TARDIS, as the Time Lords have done on other occasions, they intercept the transmat beam carrying the Doctor and his friends from the deserted Earth they visited in *The Sontaran Experiment* (1975) back to Space Station Nerva, which they left in *The Ark in Space* (1975). To return them to the space station, the Time Lords give the Doctor a Time Ring.

The Doctor wears the Time Ring, more a bracelet than a ring, on his wrist. It registers as a power source on a Kaled scanner and it is confiscated. But later, the Doctor manages to retrieve the Time Ring. Although the Doctor is unsuccessful in preventing Davros from creating the Daleks, he is philosophical – knowing that out of the evil of the Daleks will also come good as worlds that would otherwise be at war with each other are forced to ally against the greater threat…

Simply being in physical contact with the Time Ring transports the Doctor, Sarah and Harry back to the space station. But whether by accident or Time Lord design, they arrive centuries earlier than they left – on Nerva Beacon, as it originally was, in *Revenge of the Cybermen* (1975). The TARDIS, presumably under Time Lord control, drifts back through time to meet them. Once they are safely on the beacon, the Time Ring dematerialises – perhaps returning to Gallifrey.

# 30 MARCH

# The Doctor Finally Meets the 'Real' Clara Oswald

Although it seems that the Eleventh Doctor's meeting with Clara Oswald in *The Bells of Saint John* (2013) was engineered by Missy, the Doctor has met aspects of Clara before. In fact, as shown in *The Name of the Doctor* (2013), versions of Clara have been scattered through history to help the Doctor.

The Doctor recalls meeting two versions of Clara before. One was Oswin Oswald, junior entertainment officer on the starship *Alaska*. But by the time the Doctor met her in *Asylum of the Daleks* (2012), Oswin had been converted into a Dalek herself. Later, the Doctor encountered Clara Oswin Oswald in London in 1892 in *The Snowmen* (2012). She was working part time in a tavern, and also as a children's nanny, but was killed during the Doctor's encounter with the Great Intelligence.

Having met her twice previously, the Doctor calls Clara Oswald 'the Impossible Girl' and feels she is a mystery worth solving. In *The Name of the Doctor,* Clara follows Doctor Simeon – possessed by the Great Intelligence – back along the Doctor's own timeline, to undo the damage that Simeon has done.

Between her commitments as a teacher at Coal Hill School, Clara continues to travel with the Doctor, coming to terms with the more abrasive and abrupt Twelfth Doctor in *Deep Breath* (2014) and suffering the death of her boyfriend Danny Pink in *Dark Water* (2014). There is no way of knowing how long Clara would have continued to travel with the Doctor given the choice. She is killed in *Face the Raven* (2015) after taking over a fatal chronolock from her friend Rigsy.

**1853** The artist Vincent van Gogh was born.

**1968** *Fury from the Deep* Episode 3

**1974** *The Monster of Peladon* Part 2

**1982** *Time-Flight* Part 4 closes Season 19.

**1984** *The Twin Dilemma* Part 4 closes Season 21.

**1985** *Revelation of the Daleks* Part 2 closes Season 22. It is the last 45-minute episode of the classic series. With the cancellation of the planned Season 23, there is an 18-month wait for new *Doctor Who* on television…

**2013** Clara Oswald makes her first first full appearance in *The Bells of Saint John*, which opens the second section of Series Seven, having been seen briefly in the closing moments of *The Snowmen*.

Although in *Hell Bent* (2015) the Time Lords take her out of time at the moment before her last heartbeat, one day she will have to return and face her own death.

# 31 MARCH

# Martha Jones Lands on the Moon

Martha Jones is a medical student at the Royal Hope Hospital when she first meets the Tenth Doctor in *Smith and Jones* (2007). Impressed by Martha's calm and analytical attitude when the entire hospital is transported to the Moon by the Judoon, the Doctor offers to take Martha on a trip in the TARDIS.

While Martha develops a deep affection for the Doctor, she realises her feelings are not reciprocated. This is especially obvious when the Doctor makes himself into the human John Smith in *Human Nature / The Family of Blood* (2007) and falls in love with Joan Redfern.

After the harrowing events of *Last of the Time Lords* (2007), in which Martha travells the Earth for a year while hunted by the Master and the Toclafane while her family are held prisoner, Martha decides to leave the Doctor.

Having joined UNIT, Martha sends for the Doctor to combat what turns out to be a Sontaran attack in *The Sontaran Stratagem /The Poison Sky* (2008). She travels in the TARDIS again in *The Doctor's Daughter* (2008), and helps the Doctor and other companions against the Daleks in *The Stolen Earth /Journey's End* (2008). By the time the Doctor sees her in *The End of Time, Part Two* (2010), just before he regenerates into the Eleventh Doctor, Martha has married Rose Tyler's former boyfriend Mickey Smith, and together they are tracking down aliens.

## ON THIS DAY

**1973** Roger Delgado makes his final appearance as the Master in Episode 6 of *Frontier in Space*.

**1974** *The Monster of Peladon* Part 2 is first shown on BBC Wales.

**2007** The Tenth Doctor's companion Martha Jones is introduced in *Smith and Jones*, which opens Series Three.

# APRIL

# 1 APRIL

## 'Reverse the Polarity of the Neutron Flow'

A phrase often associated with the Third Doctor is 'Reverse the polarity of the neutron flow'. The phrase is actually used by other Doctors too – for example the Twelfth Doctor when working on a Mire helmet in *The Girl Who Died* (2015). However, while the Third Doctor did often refer to 'polarity', he only actually used this phrase twice.

In *Terror of the Autons* (1971), the Third Doctor tells the Brigadier and the Master that they need to 'change the polarity' of a radio telescope in order to expel the invading Nestenes out into space. Later in that same season, in *The Dæmons* (1971), the Doctor tells UNIT technician Osgood to 'reverse the polarity' when building a heat exchanger to get through the heat barrier surrounding the village of Devil's End.

It is not until the final episode of *The Sea Devils* (1972) that the Doctor tells the Master 'I reversed the polarity of the neutron flow', referring to the trigger mechanism that the Master has built to revive the Sea Devils. As a result there is a massive reverse feedback into the Sea Devils' power system, and their base is destroyed.

In *The Time Monster* (1972), the Doctor tells scientist Ruth Ingram to 'reverse the temporal polarity' on the TOMTIT equipment, and in *Frontier in Space* (1973) he reverses the polarity of the sonic screwdriver's power source to turn it into an electromagnet he can use to unbolt a door. In *Planet of the Daleks* (1973) the Doctor reverses the polarity of the TARDIS audio log so as to turn it into a low-power receiver-transmitter with a positive feedback that interferes with a Dalek's guidance systems, allowing the Doctor and the Thal Codal to

**1958** The BBC's Radiophonic Workshop – responsible for realising Ron Grainer's original theme music for *Doctor Who* as well as sound effects for the classic series and incidental music for many stories in the 1980s – is officially opened.

**1965** Having both decided to leave *Doctor Who* when their contracts end, Verity Lambert and Dennis Spooner start to brief their replacements as Producer and Story Editor – John Wiles and Donald Tosh.

**1967** *The Macra Terror* Episode 4

**1972** *The Sea Devils* Episode 6 is the first time – and actually one of only two occasions – that the Third Doctor claims to have 'reversed the polarity of the neutron flow'.

escape from their cell. In *Invasion of the Dinosaurs* (1974), the Doctor reverses the polarity on the Time Scoop, so that it sends Whitaker and Grover back into prehistory.

But, apart from in *The Sea Devils*, the only other occasion the Third Doctor uses the phrase is in his final full appearance in *The Five Doctors* (1983). Here, the Third Doctor reverses the polarity of the neutron flow on equipment the Dark Tower so that the TARDIS is freed from a force field and can travel to Rassilon's tomb.

# 2 APRIL

## Psychic Paper Provides the Perfect Invitation

Psychic paper, as the Ninth Doctor explains to Rose Tyler in *The End of the World* (2005), saves a lot of time. It is paper treated to be slightly psychic. As a result, the Doctor can influence what it appears to show to other people – he can (usually) decide what they see. So the Steward on Platform One sees the paper as an invitation for the Doctor 'plus one' to watch the last moments of planet Earth as the Sun expands and destroys it.

In *The Empty Child* (2005), Rose sees that the psychic paper appears as an ID badge describing the Doctor as 'Doctor John Smith, Ministry of Asteroids'. She also realises that Captain Jack Harkness has tried to trick her with psychic paper. She identifies it partly from her experience with the Doctor, but also because Jack's mind has wandered as he shows it to Rose, and it says that he is single and works out…

But psychic paper cannot fool everyone. In *The Shakespeare Code* (2007), the Doctor discovers that William Shakespeare is too much of a genius to see anything but a blank sheet of paper. It was equally useless when Clara Oswald tried to use it on Fenton in *Flatline* (2014) – but that time because of Fenton's complete lack of imagination. On rare occasions the psychic paper can also receive telepathic messages – such as the summons from the Face of Boe that the Tenth Doctor gets in *New Earth* (2006).

**1966** *The Celestial Toyroom* – the first episode of *The Celestial Toymaker* – is Innes Lloyd's first episode as Producer.

**1977** *The Talons of Weng-Chiang* Episode 6 closes Season 14. It is Philip Hinchcliffe's last episode as Producer.

**2005** The Doctor first uses his psychic paper in *The End of the World*. The episode also sees the first appearance of Cassandra.

**2007** Animated adventure *The Infinite Quest* starts as part of the BBC children's magazine programme *Totally Doctor Who*. David Tennant and Freema Agyeman provide the voices of the Tenth Doctor and Martha Jones.

## 3 APRIL

# Meet the Eleventh Doctor

It is perhaps appropriate that the first person the newly regenerated Eleventh Doctor meets in *The Eleventh Hour* (2010) is a child – the young Amy Pond. Appearing even younger than the Fifth Doctor did, the Eleventh Doctor is immediately taken with the little girl, who panders to his changing whims for various types of food – culminating in fish fingers and custard.

Similarly, the Eleventh Doctor is a collection of contradictions, of elements that should not go well together. He is incredibly old, but he seems very young. He is immensely wise and yet he can be incredibly naïve. While he is sophisticated and learned, he appears to lack some of the most basic social skills. And although he evidently cares deeply, he can be rude and insensitive, tactless and gauche. When he stays with Craig Owens in *The Lodger* (2010), we see just how much he doesn't understand about humans.

It is almost as if this incarnation of the Doctor has unlearned much of what he learned in his previous lives, and is enjoying discovering it all again. He seems surprised and revolted by the taste of wine in *The Impossible Astronaut* (2011), claiming he 'thought it would taste more like the gums'. Yet previous incarnations certainly drank and enjoyed wine – not least that most gentlemanly of Doctors, the Third Doctor who makes full use of Sir Reginald Styles' collection of wine and cheese in *Day of the Daleks* (1972).

With his penchant for bow ties, this incarnation of the Doctor might come across as ineffectual and dithering, but this masks the determination and steel that have been the downfall of even the most ruthless creatures. Whatever else he may be, underneath it all he is still the Doctor.

**1965** *The Knight of Jaffa* – the second episode of *The Crusade*

**1971** *The Claws of Axos* Episode 4

**1977** The documentary *Whose Doctor Who*, hosted by Melvyn Bragg, is broadcast on BBC Two as part of its *Lively Arts* series.

**1983** The first day of the BBC Enterprises huge *Twenty Years of a Time Lord* weekend celebration convention at Longleat House in Wiltshire

**2010** Matt Smith's debut story *The Eleventh Hour* is broadcast. It also introduces Amy Pond and Rory Williams and opens Series Five. It is the first episode on which Steven Moffat, Piers Wenger and Beth Willis are Executive Producers.

## 4 APRIL

# Sarah Meets Experimental Robot K-1

While the Doctor recovers from regenerating into his fourth incarnation in *Robot* (1974–1975), Sarah Jane Smith persuades the Brigadier to get her a UNIT pass to visit the National Institute for Advanced Scientific Research – colloquially known as Think Tank. The Director of Think Tank is Hilda Winters, who tells Sarah that 'as soon as our work reaches the practical stage, it's handed over to someone. Someone with more resources and a bigger budget.' Usually this is the Government.

But not all Think Tank's work is so public-spirited. The last project Professor J.P. Kettlewell worked on at Think Tank was a robot designed to 'replace the human being in a variety of difficult and dangerous tasks'. Although the robot's Prime Directive is that it must serve humanity and never harm it, Kettlewell has helped Miss Winters and her assistant Jellicoe bypass this so they can use the robot to steal components to build a disintegrator gun – research for which was pioneered at Think Tank. In league with the Scientific Reform Society, which wants to reorganise the world on more scientific and rational lines, they plan to use the robot and the gun to steal destructor codes that will enable them to threaten to destroy the world with nuclear missiles unless their demands are met.

The robot is made of a 'living' metal and, when it absorbs the energy from the disintegrator gun, it grows to enormous size. Having accidentally killed its creator Kettlewell, it is driven mad and plans to carry out his plan to destroy the world – saving only Sarah as she showed it sympathy…

**1964** *Assassin at Peking* – the seventh episode of *Marco Polo*

**1970** *The Ambassadors of Death* Episode 3

**1970s,** exact year unknown: The date of Sarah Jane Smith's UNIT pass to get into Think Tank

**1983** The second day of the BBC Enterprises huge *Twenty Years of a Time Lord* weekend celebration convention at Longleat House in Wiltshire

**1987** Location shooting begins on Sylvester McCoy's first story as the Seventh Doctor, *Time and the Rani*.

# 5 APRIL

# Donna Noble Finds the Doctor Again

Dosed with Huon particles by her scheming fiancé Lance, who was in league with the Empress of the Racnoss, Donna Noble found herself unexpectedly transported into the TARDIS on her wedding day in *The Runaway Bride* (2006). Brash but brave, she helped the Doctor to deal with Roboform Santas working for the Racnoss Empress, and finally to defeat the creature – her fiancé dying in the process.

Although the Tenth Doctor then invited Donna to travel with him in the TARDIS, she didn't feel she could cope, and declined. But having vowed to travel and make something of her life, she found a package tour to Egypt to be a poor substitute and resolved to find the Doctor and take him up on his offer. She followed up on anything unusual she learned about, including crop circles, UFOs, sea monsters and vanishing bees. But it wasn't until she investigated Adipose Industries that she again met the Doctor.

Although she had some harrowing experiences on her travels – witnessing the destruction of Pompeii in *The Fires of Pompeii* (2008) and the terrible effect it would have on herself and the whole world if she had never met the Doctor in *Turn Left* (2008) – it was not Donna's decision to leave the Doctor. Affected by a biological metacrisis, Donna gained many attributes of a Time Lord. But the fusion between human and Gallifreyan was immensely dangerous, and to save her life the Doctor was forced to remove all Donna's memories of their times together from her mind…

ON THIS DAY

**1969** *The Space Pirates* Episode 5

**1975** *Genesis of the Daleks* Part 5

**2008** *Partners in Crime* opens Series Four. It is the first regular episode for Donna Noble, after her original appearance in *The Runaway Bride* on 25 December 2006.

## 6 APRIL

# Reunited with Aggedor, Royal Beast of Peladon

On both occasions that the Third Doctor visits the planet Peladon, the spirit of the legendary Royal Beast Aggedor seems to rise and express murderous displeasure. The legend of the curse of Peladon has apparently been handed down through countless centuries. It is written: 'Mighty is Aggedor, fiercest of all the beasts of Peladon.' Young men would hunt it to prove their courage, finally resulting in the creature's near-extinction. Fur from one of the beasts is used to trim the royal garments, and a stylised motif of the animal's head forms the royal emblem of Peladon. It is also written that there will come a day when the spirit of Aggedor will rise again to warn and defend his royal master. For at that day a stranger will appear in the land, bringing peril to Peladon and great tribulation to his kingdom... 'His coming shall be full of terror and darkness, his cry shall be heard in the night and Death shall walk in the land of Peladon.'

In *The Curse of Peladon* (1972), the Doctor discovers that Aggedor is in fact a real creature. Although the royal beasts are thought to have been hunted to extinction, the High Priest Hepesh has found a last survivor and trained it to kill on his command. The Doctor manages to tame it by using mild hypnosis and singing it a Venusian lullaby (to the tune of the Christmas carol 'God Rest You Merry Gentlemen'). In Part 3 of *The Monster of Peladon* (1974), the Doctor is reunited with Aggedor – and again manages to calm the beast.

On both occasions, the Doctor is able to prove that the appearances of Aggedor are not supernatural, and to reveal the forces using the beast to their own ends.

ON THIS DAY

**1199** King Richard the Lionheart died.

**1959** Mark Strickson, who played the Fifth Doctor's companion Turlough, was born.

**1968** *Fury from the Deep* Episode 4

**1974** *The Monster of Peladon* Part 3

**2013** *The Rings of Akhaten*

## 7 APRIL

# Decoding Shakespeare

Although the Doctor claims to have met William Shakespeare several times, apparently the first time that Shakespeare meets the Doctor is in *The Shakespeare Code* (2007), when the Tenth Doctor and Martha Jones make a visit to the Globe theatre in Elizabethan London. Widely regarded as the greatest poet and playwright in human history, William Shakespeare is then in his mid thirties and at the height of his success. He is perceptive enough to realise where and when the Doctor and Martha are from, and is not above 'borrowing' words and phrases that he overhears – such as 'Sycorax', the name he will later give to the witch-mother of Caliban in *The Tempest*.

But Shakespeare is also so talented that his words can free the Carrionites. They are an ancient race from the fourteen stars of the Rexel Planetary Configuration. They developed a science that was based on words instead of numbers so that it seems the Carrionites are witches who chant spells and use magic. Banished to the Deep Darkness by the Eternals, the death of Shakespeare's young son, Hamnet, released such grief in the great playwright that it has brought back three of the Carrionites. They plan to use their 'magic' to have Shakespeare's words – amplified by the design of the Globe theatre which they have influenced – release all the Carrionites to feed on the world.

Before this, the First Doctor and his companions watched Shakespeare meet with Queen Elizabeth I on a Time-Space Visualiser in *The Chase* (1965). In *Planet of Evil* (1975), the Fourth Doctor tells Sarah that he met Shakespeare once (and that Shakespeare was a terrible actor). In *City of Death* (1979), Countess Scarlioni shows

ON THIS DAY

**1973** *Planet of the Daleks* Episode 1 is the first episode written by the Daleks' creator Terry Nation since he co-wrote *The Daleks' Master Plan* with Dennis Spooner back in 1965–1966.

**1974** *The Monster of Peladon* Part 3 is first shown on BBC Wales.

**2007** The Doctor and Martha meet playwright William Shakespeare in *The Shakespeare Code*. The playwright previously appeared, briefly, in *The Chase* in 1965.

the Doctor a first draft of *Hamlet* – which he knows
to be genuine as it is written in his own handwriting.
Shakespeare, the Doctor claims, dictated it to him as the
playwright had sprained his wrist writing sonnets.

## 8 APRIL

# The Rise and Decline of Earth's Empire

The Doctor has witnessed the rise and fall of Earth's Empire. The Third Doctor's first escape from his exile to twentieth-century Earth in *Colony in Space* (1971) is a mission for the Time Lords that takes him and Jo Grant to the planet Uxarieus in the year 2472. Here they find a human colony struggling to survive as pioneers spread out from an overpopulated Earth looking for new worlds to settle on.

In *Frontier in Space* (1973), the Third Doctor and Jo arrive in the twenty-sixth century as Earth's Empire spreads through the Milky Way and encounters the expanding Draconian Empire. At the opposite end of its history, they also visit the colonised planet Solos in *The Mutants* (1972), and see the latter days of the Empire. By the thirtieth century, the Empire is in decline, with Earth granting independence to many of the outer planets – including Solos.

But it seems the Earth Empire would rise again. In *The Invisible Enemy* (1977), the Fourth Doctor tells Leela that around the year 5000 AD her human forefathers would go leapfrogging across the solar system on their way to the stars – spreading out across the galaxy like a tidal wave.

Wherever and whenever he goes, it seems that the Doctor is never far from the human race…

ON THIS DAY

**1967** *The Faceless Ones* Episode 1

**1969** The events of *The Impossible Astronaut* begin on this day.

**1972** *The Mutants* Episode 1

# 9 APRIL

# Charles Dickens Experiences His Own Ghost Story

Widely regarded as the greatest of the Victorian novelists, Charles John Huffam Dickens was nearing the end of his life when he met the Ninth Doctor and Rose Tyler in Cardiff on Christmas Eve, 1869 in *The Unquiet Dead* (2005). During his life, Dickens wrote fifteen novels, five novellas, and hundreds of short stories and factual articles. He also made numerous personal appearances – including giving a reading in Cardiff attended by the recently deceased Mrs Peace…

The old woman's corpse has been reanimated by the Gelth – ectoplasmic, ethereal wraith-creatures from another dimension that possess the dead at the nineteenth-century Cardiff undertakers' firm of Sneed and Company. Essentially gaseous creatures, in this world the Gelth 'live' in the gas pipes – the environment most suited to them. They claim there are very few Gelth left; they are the last of their kind and are facing extinction. But in fact they plan to invade, billions of them killing and then possessing the bodies of the dead.

By now a tired, sceptical old man, Dickens is at first wary of the Doctor and accuses him of staging the phantasmagoric intrusion at the theatre. He does not believe in the existence of the Gelth until forced to by events. He is then disappointed to think that all his life he has failed to appreciate the truth and misunderstood the nature of the world. His experiences with the Doctor persuade Dickens to open his mind to new ideas and to broaden his outlook.

**1912** The Daniels family was photographed at Southampton with the Ninth Doctor on the day before they were due to set sail to the New World on the *Titanic*. After the photo was taken, they cancelled the trip.

**1966** *The Hall of Dolls* – the second episode of *The Celestial Toymaker*

**2005** *The Unquiet Dead* features Charles Dickens – the first historical character in the newly returned series of *Doctor Who*.

# 10 APRIL

## Amy Pond Travels in the TARDIS

Although she is Scottish, Amelia Jessica Pond was living in the village of Leadworth in Gloucestershire when she first met the Eleventh Doctor in *The Eleventh Hour* (2010). Immediately after regenerating, the Doctor crashed the TARDIS into Amy's garden. After sharing fish fingers and custard with the little girl, the Doctor left in the TARDIS, telling her he would be back in five minutes. In fact, it was twelve years before he returned. During that time, Amy invented stories about the 'Raggedy Doctor', always hoping he might come back…

Having dealt with Prisoner Zero and the Atraxi, the Doctor set off in the TARDIS again, meaning to return immediately for Amy. In fact, he arrived two years later, on the night before her wedding to Rory Williams. But Amy went with him in the TARDIS anyway – her first trip in *The Beast Below* (2010) taking her to Starship UK in the far future.

Over the years, Amy and her new husband Rory had many adventures with the Eleventh Doctor. They also had a child. Taken from them by Madame Kovarian, that child was conditioned to kill the Doctor but eventually grew up to become River Song. Even after Amy and Rory had set up home together, the Doctor continued to visit them, and they continued to travel in the TARDIS. But their adventures came to an end in *The Angels Take Manhattan* (2012) when a Weeping Angel sent them both into the past…

# 11 APRIL

# Lady Christina De Souza Takes the Bus

Lady Christina de Souza is a thief. It's a 'career' she pursues not for the money, but for the challenge and the excitement of it. Detective Inspector McMillan and Sergeant Dennison have been after Lady Christina for a while. They are pretty sure that she is behind many of the most ambitious and daring art thefts of recent years, but so far she has eluded them.

When Lady Christina mounts a daring raid to steal the ancient gold Cup of Athelstan in *Planet of the Dead* (2009), she gets more excitement than she bargained for. With McMillan and Dennison in hot pursuit, she is forced to escape in a bus – the same bus that the Tenth Doctor takes. He is tracking the growing wormhole that soon takes the bus together with its driver and passengers to the planet San Helios in the Scorpion Nebula.

San Helios has been devastated by flying stingray-like creatures that consume everything, and have turned the whole planet into a barren desert. The creatures are swarming in their billions, flying at tremendous speed, encircling the worlds they ravage with such velocity that they open a wormhole to take them to their next feeding ground. And in this case, that next feeding ground will be Earth.

Lady Christina adapts quickly to the new and dangerous environment, and she soon realises how much she needs – and trusts – the Doctor. Before long, she is putting her criminal skills to good use to get the vital Crystal Nucleus system that the Doctor needs to get them all home and close the wormhole. After they return to Earth, the Doctor helps Christina evade the police, and she escapes in the bus – now, thanks to the Doctor's modifications, capable of flight.

**1964** *The Sea of Death* – the first episode of *The Keys of Marinus*

**1970** *The Ambassadors of Death* Episode 4

**2009** *Planet of the Dead* is the first episode of *Doctor Who* to be broadcast in High Definition.

## 12 APRIL

# The Dreams In Which They're Dying Are the Best They've Ever Had

Finding themselves at a scientific research base at the North Pole in *Last Christmas* (2014), the Twelfth Doctor and Clara Oswald discovered that not everything is as it seems. In fact, the crew of the base were not there at all – but trapped within their own dreams. And the only person who could help was Santa Claus…

The people on the base, as well as the Doctor and Clara, have been attacked by Dream Crabs. These creatures attach themselves to their victim's face and then digest them. But to stop the victim realising what is happening, they provoke dreams so that their victim believes they are somewhere else – somewhere safe… The only clue that this isn't the case is a slight pain in the head, like you've just eaten cold ice cream.

Clara dreams of an ideal life with her boyfriend Danny Pink – although Danny is actually dead. The Doctor dreams of visiting Clara as an old woman.

Rescued by Santa and taken off in his flying sleigh, the victims wake up one by one. When they do, they vanish from the sleigh and wake up in the real world. The Dream Crab that was attacking them crumbles to dust. With the Doctor and Clara off on new adventures, can they ever know for sure whether Santa himself was actually a dream…?

ON THIS DAY

**1969** *The Space Pirates* Episode 6. It is Peter Bryant's last episode as Producer.

**1975** Davros is exterminated by the Daleks at the end of Part 6 of *Genesis of the Daleks*. But he will return…

**1989** Gerald Flood, who played the fake King John in *The King's Demons* and provided the voice for the Fifth Doctor's robotic companion Kamelion, died.

**2008** *The Fires of Pompeii*

# 13 APRIL

## The Doctor and Clara Encounter an Ice Warrior During the Cold War

Skaldak, the Martian warrior that the Eleventh Doctor and Clara meet in 1983 on board the Soviet submarine *Firebird* in *Cold War* (2013) is powerful, ruthless, and honourable like all his race. The Ice Warriors, as they are often known – although they only ever refer to themselves by this name in *The Monster of Peladon* (1974) – are originally from the planet Mars. As their name implies, they prefer the cold and are susceptible to heat. They are upright reptilian warriors, encased in shell-like armour so that very little of their actual bodies is visible – or vulnerable to attack. They have a long tradition of nobility and honour.

The Second Doctor first encountered the Ice Warriors during a new ice age in *The Ice Warriors* (1967). A group of Warriors, led by Varga, are thawed from the ice where there have been frozen for thousands of years. Believing their own planet to be dead, they plan to take over Earth. The Second Doctor again defeated an attempted Ice Warrior invasion in *The Seeds of Death* (1969), when the Martians attempted to change Earth's climate and atmosphere with Martian seed pods.

The Ice Warriors that the Third Doctor met in *The Curse of Peladon* (1972) were members of the Galactic Federation, allies of Earth. But in *The Monster of Peladon*, the Third Doctor faced a breakaway group that wanted a return to the days of glorious warfare.

**1951** Peter Davison, who played the Fifth Doctor, was born.

**1968** *Fury from the Deep* Episode 5

**1974** *The Monster of Peladon* Part 4

**1981** The first day of shooting for *Four to Doomsday* – the first story Peter Davison recorded as the Fifth Doctor. It was also Davison's 30th birthday.

**2006** The first edition of *Totally Doctor Who* is shown on CBBC.

**2013** The Ice Warriors return to the *Doctor Who* for the first time since *The Monster of Peladon* in 1974, in *Cold War*.

## 14 APRIL

# The Face of Boe Summons the Doctor

The Face of Boe is a huge head held in a fluid-filled life-support tank powered by antiquated, steam-driven technology. From the Silver Devastation, the Face of Boe is incredibly old, his origins a mystery. The Ninth Doctor and Rose Tyler first meet the Face of Boe in *The End of the World* (2005) on Platform One, where he has sponsored a gathering to watch the Earth finally consumed by the expanding Sun. In *New Earth* (2006), the Tenth Doctor receives a telepathic message from the Face of Boe on his psychic paper, summoning him to New Earth.

According to *Legends of the Universe* by J B Dane (translated from the original hieromanx by Russell T Davies): 'Legend has it that if the Face of Boe should die one day, then the sky will crack asunder. And it is said that he holds one, final secret; that he will speak this secret, with his final breath, to one person and one person alone. A homeless, wandering traveller.'

When they next meet in *Gridlock* (2007), the Doctor witnesses the final death of the Face of Boe. True to the legend, the sky cracks open – the roof of the motorway opening to let out the trapped vehicles. And the Face of Boe delivers a message to the Doctor: 'You are not alone.'

The Doctor's friend and companion Captain Jack Harkness, who is fated to live for ever, later tells the Doctor that he was known as the 'face of Boe'. Is this just a joke? Or could Captain Jack really become the Face of Boe – warning the Doctor of events he has already witnessed himself?

**1958** Peter Capaldi, who plays the Twelfth Doctor, was born.

**1973** *Planet of the Daleks* Episode 2

**1974** *The Monster of Peladon* Part 4 is first shown on BBC Wales.

**2007** The Macra return in *Gridlock*.

# 15 APRIL

# The Doctor and Rose Meet Cassandra Again

The Lady Cassandra O'Brien Dot Delta Seventeen, who the Ninth Doctor and Rose Tyler first meet in *The End of the World* (2005), considers herself to be the last human. Her father was Texan and her mother from the Arctic Desert. They were born and were buried on Earth. Other humans have survived, of course, but mingled and cross-bred with other life forms. By contrast, Cassandra considers herself to be 'pure'.

But after years of enhancement and cosmetic surgery, plus genetic (and gender) manipulation (708 operations in all) Cassandra is now a thin piece of skin stretched across a metal frame – all that remains of her face. As soon as any wrinkles appear, she has them cut out with a scalpel. The mobile frame is as tall as a human, and Cassandra's brain resides in a nutrient tank at its base.

Cassandra apparently dies on Platform One, after the Doctor foils her plans to assassinate all the guests. But Cassandra's brain survived, although her stretched-skin body was dried out and withered. Her eyes were salvaged from a bin, and she rebuilt herself with skin from the back of her original form. Stowing away on the Face of Boe's life-support system, Cassandra was brought to the hospital on New Earth, where she hides in the basement with her faithful acolyte Chip and steals the medicine she needs to survive.

But when Rose and the Tenth Doctor arrive in *New Earth* (2006), she decides to steal Rose's body and

**1764** Madame de Pompadour, also known as Reinette, who met the Tenth Doctor in *The Girl in the Fireplace*, died.

**1912** The *Titanic* sinks. In *The End of the World*, the Ninth Doctor tells Jabe that he was left clinging to an iceberg.

**1967** *The Faceless Ones* Episode 2

**1972** *The Mutants* Episode 2

**2006** *New Earth* is the first episode of David Tennant's first full season as the Tenth Doctor, opening Series Two.

implant her own consciousness inside it. When her plans
fail, the Doctor takes Cassandra back – in the dying
body of her servant Chip – to her own past, to the last
time she was truly happy. This is a drinks party for the
Ambassador of Thrace, which was the last occasion
when someone told her she was beautiful.

## 16 APRIL

# The Slitheen Decide that Earth is a Commodity to be Sold

The Slitheen are a family dedicated to business. They come from the planet Raxacoricofallapatorius, although they have since been exiled, and they have long, hyphenated names. With their fine sense of smell, they hunt ritually, enjoying the chase. The Slitheen's race are made out of living calcium.

The Ninth Doctor first encountered the Slitheen in *Aliens of London* and *World War Three* (2005) when they saw Earth as a business opportunity. Deciding the planet offered huge potential as a commodity, once purged of its population and reduced to a radioactive energy source, they determined to stage a hostile takeover.

While they are over eight feet tall, they have the technology to disguise themselves within human bodysuits. They squeeze their bodies inside these lifelike suits, which are sealed with a hidden zip across the forehead. Being so large, they

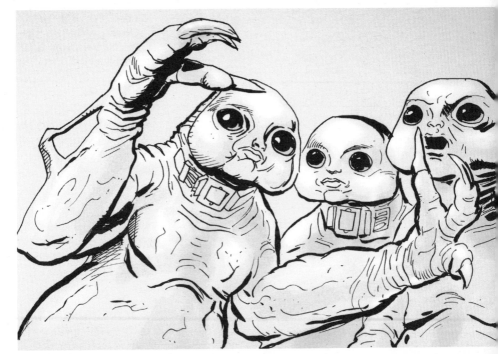

have to use a compression field – controlled by a device worn round the neck – to fit inside a human bodysuit. Even so, they can still only shrink down enough to impersonate very large people.

As a side effect of the compression field, gas is released – meaning that the disguised Slitheen have to make embarrassing bodily noises in order to vent this. The gas, caused by calcium decay, smells of bad breath. When the suit is opened, pent-up energy is released. There are blue electrical flashes round the zip and the Slitheen's head as it emerges from the bodysuit.

Although they defeated the Slitheen plan to engulf Earth in a nuclear holocaust, the Doctor and Rose met a surviving Slitheen – Blon Fel-Fotch Passameer-Day Slitheen – in Cardiff in *Boom Town* (2005).

**1746 The Battle of Culloden.**

**1966** *The Dancing Floor* – the third episode of *The Celestial Toymaker*

**2005** The Slitheen first appear in *Aliens of London*. This is the opening episode of the first two-part story in the returning series of *Doctor Who*.

**2986 The events of the third segment of** *The Trial of a Time Lord* **(Parts 9–12), usually called** *Terror of the Vervoids*, **take place.**

## 17 APRIL

# The Doctor Inadvertently Creates a New Dalek Paradigm

In *Victory of the Daleks* (2010), the Eleventh Doctor answers a call from Winston Churchill. The Doctor and Amy Pond arrive (a month later) during the early stages of the Second World War, to find Churchill testing a new weapon he believes will win the war.

But the Doctor knows that the weapon, apparently developed by scientist Professor Edwin Bracewell and called an 'Ironside', is actually a Dalek. Neither is Bracewell what he seems. He is actually a robot created by the Daleks, who need to lure the Doctor to them.

During the Great Time War the Daleks created thousands of Progenitor devices, each containing pure Dalek DNA from which the Dalek race could, if necessary, be repopulated. Having recovered a Progenitor, the Daleks discovered that their own DNA had altered to the point where the device failed to recognise them – until they could get a testimony from the Doctor proving that they are Daleks.

This testimony – the Doctor insisting the Ironsides are in fact Daleks – activated the progenitor, which created the so-called New Dalek Paradigm. This consists of a set of Daleks of a slightly different and bulkier design. There was a Supreme Dalek (predominantly white in colour), an Eternal (mainly yellow), a Strategist (mainly blue), Scientist (mainly orange) and a Drone (mainly red).

**1965** *The Warlords* – the fourth episode of *The Crusade*

**1971** *Colony in Space* Episode 2

**2010** Winston Churchill makes his first full appearance, in *Victory of the Daleks*, a week after being seen in the closing moments of *The Beast Below*. The larger and more colourful redesigned Daleks, referred to as the New Dalek Paradigm, also appear for the first time.

## 18 APRIL

# The Doctor and His Friends Hunt for the Keys of Marinus

Arriving on the planet Marinus in *The Keys of Marinus* (1964), the First Doctor and his companions meet Arbitan – the Keeper of the Conscience of Marius. The Conscience is a machine housed inside a pyramid-like building on an island. The island has beaches of glass and is surrounded by a sea of acid.

Arbitan explains that technology on Marinus reached its peak over 2,000 years ago – culminating in the creation of the Conscience. At first this machine was simply a judge and jury that was never wrong or unfair. But it was made more and more sophisticated until finally it became possible to radiate its power and influence the minds of people throughout the planet. They no longer had to decide what was wrong or right – the machine decided for them. As a result, robbery, fear, hate, violence were unknown among the planet's inhabitants.

But then a man named Yartek found a means of overcoming the power of the machine. He and his followers, the Voord, were able to rob, exploit, kill, cheat, and their victims could not resist because violence was alien to them. Arbitan therefore turned off the Conscience, and hid the activator keys around the planet until he could modify the machine so that it would also affect the Voord.

Now the work is done, Arbitan has sent his colleagues and even his own daughter to recover the keys. But none has returned. So, having placed a force field round the TARDIS, he insists the Doctor and his companions go.

**1956** Eric Roberts, who played the Master in *Doctor Who*, the TV movie featuring the Eighth Doctor, was born.

**1964** *The Velvet Web* – the second episode of *The Keys of Marinus*

**1970** *The Ambassadors of Death* Episode 5

**1971** David Tennant, who played the Tenth Doctor, was born.

**2011 The events of *Closing Time* begin, taking place between 18 and 20 April.**

In recovering the vital keys, they travel to various parts of Marinus. They visit the city of Morphoton, where the inhabitants are hypnotically controlled by the Morpho Brains. They are trapped in a jungle where the vegetation comes alive, and face danger in a snowy wilderness. Ian Chesterton is accused of murder by the Court of Millennius and sentenced to death – the Doctor having to prove his innocence before they can return to the island with the keys...

## 19 APRIL

# The Doctor Rediscovers Voga – The Planet of Gold

At the end of the Cyberwar, the Cybermen disappeared after their failed attack on Voga – the Planet of Gold. It was the resources of Voga that allowed the humans to gain the upper hand in the war. They discovered that gold is lethal to Cybermen. Being non-corrodible, it plates the creatures' breathing apparatus, in effect suffocating them. The invention of the 'glitter gun' was a turning point in the conflict.

After the Cyberwar, Voga too disappeared. But in *Revenge of the Cybermen* (1975), the Fourth Doctor, Sarah Jane Smith and Harry Sullivan discover that, having drifted between star systems, it has been captured by the gravity of Jupiter, going into orbit around the planet. Nerva Beacon has been set up nearby to warn off spacecraft that don't yet have Voga (originally named Neo Phobos) on their star charts.

The indigenous Vogans have survived the journey in a survival chamber built into the caves of Voga. They live in fear that the Cybermen will seek them out and destroy them. The leader of the City is Tyrum, while the Guild Halls and the routes to the surface of Voga are controlled by Vorus and his Guardians. There is a tension between them, exacerbated by Vorus's lust for power, and his belief that Vogans should live on the surface. To end the threat of the Cybermen, Vorus has secretly built a missile – his Skystriker – to destroy the last Cybermen once and for all when his human ally Kellman lures them onto Nerva Beacon.

ON THIS DAY

**1969** *The War Games* Episode 1. It is Derrick Sherwin's first episode as Producer. Terrance Dicks resumes duties as Script Editor (as well as co-writing with Malcolm Hulke).

**1975** The Cybermen appear in the first episode of *Revenge of the Cybermen* returning for the first time since *The Invasion* in 1968.

**2008** *Planet of the Ood*

**2011** Elisabeth Sladen – who played the Fourth Doctor's companion SJS and returned during the Tenth Doctor's era, as well as having her own spin-off episode K-9 & Company and series The SJA – died.

**2011** The events of *Closing Time* take place between 18 and 20 April.

But when the Cybermen arrive, the missile isn't ready. With Harry and Sarah caught between rival Vogan factions, the Doctor and the last surviving crew of Nerva Beacon are forced to carry powerful bombs down into Voga for the Cybermen…

# 20 APRIL

## Victoria Waterfield Opts for a Safer Life

Victoria Waterfield was a reluctant adventurer, travelling with the Second Doctor through necessity rather than choice. At the end of *The Evil of the Daleks* (1967), Victoria finds herself stranded on the Dalek planet Skaro. Her mother, whom Victoria closely resembles, has been dead for a while. Her father, the scientist Edward Waterfield, is exterminated saving the Doctor's life. His final request of the Doctor is that he look after Victoria.

Although she is aware of her father's experiments, Victoria has led a sheltered and unsophisticated life – at least until she is abducted by the Daleks to force her father to work for them. Even so, she is able to hold her own in the verbal sparring with Captain Hopper in *The Tomb of the Cybermen* (1967), and puts up with Jamie's teasing. Her reaction to the Doctor's explanation of his travels through time and space is not to wonder at the technology of the TARDIS, but to worry about how old he must be.

Unsophisticated she may be, but Victoria is not gullible. She is clever and intelligent enough to get the better of Kaftan twice after the woman has tricked her into drinking drugged coffee in *The Tomb of the Cybermen*. First she screams as if a dead Cybermat is about to attack, distracting Kaftan; later she tells Kaftan and Klieg that there is another weapon in the Testing Room where they have locked the Doctor's group. Because of her apparent innocence and naivety, they are inclined to believe the lie.

There is no doubt that although Victoria loves the Doctor and Jamie and enjoys her time in their company, she misses her home and her father. Throughout their adventures, she remains an unwilling adventurer.

**1889** Adolf Hitler was born.

**1951** Louise Jameson, who played the Fourth Doctor's companion Leela, was born.

**1968** Victoria makes her last appearance in the final episode of *Fury from the Deep*.

**1972** *The Making of Doctor Who* is published by Piccolo Books. It is the first factual, behind-the-scenes book about the programme, written by scriptwriter Malcolm Hulke and Script Editor Terrence Dicks.

**1974** *The Monster of Peladon* Part 5 is the first episode in which the Ice Warriors refer to themselves as 'Ice Warriors'.

**2011** The events of *Closing Time* take place between 18 and 20 April.

**2013** *Hide*

Never afraid to scream at danger, it is fitting that Victoria's screams prove deadly to the malevolent seaweed creature in her final story *Fury from the Deep* (1968). It is also no great surprise that Victoria takes her first real opportunity to settle down. She decides to stay with Frank and Maggie Harris rather than continue to travel from one danger to the next with the Doctor and Jamie.

# 21 APRIL

## The Doctor Meets the Cult of Skaro Again

The Cult of Skaro was thought to be a myth built up during the Great Time War. It was rumoured that at some point the Dalek Emperor had established a secret order of Daleks, whose task was to think the unthinkable – to dare to imagine. But as the Tenth Doctor discovered in *Doomsday* (2006), the Cult of Skaro was very real. It was made up of four Daleks who tried to think like the enemy and predict their strategies so as to give the Daleks an advantage. These Daleks even had names. They were called Sec, Thay, Jast and Caan.

Although he thought they had been banished back into the Void between universes, the Doctor met the Cult of Skaro again in 1930s New York in *Daleks in Manhattan* and *Evolution of the Daleks* (2007). As well as genetically adapting human beings to become Dalek-like, Dalek Sec genetically bonded with a human being. To survive, Sec reasoned, the Dalek species must evolve and experience life outside their shells – the children of Skaro must walk again.

The last survivor of the fabled Cult of Skaro, Dalek Caan, escaped from the Doctor by temporal shifting from 1930s New York. Desperate to save his race from utter extermination, Dalek Caan tried to return to the Great Time War. Although the Time War was time-locked, Dalek Caan eventually succeeded. Dalek Caan arrived just as Davros's command ship flew into the jaws of the Nightmare Child at the Gates of Elysium. The effort of breaking the time lock and the things that Dalek Caan witnessed in the Vortex drove Caan mad. But he achieved his mission – he saved Davros.

**1927** Gerald Flood, who played the fake King John in *The King's Demons* and provided the voice for the Fifth Doctor's robotic companion Kamelion, was born.

**1966** Michelle Gomez, who plays Missy, was born.

**1973** *Planet of the Daleks* Episode 3

**1974** *The Monster of Peladon* Part 5 is first shown on BBC Wales.

**2007** *Daleks in Manhattan*

In *The Stolen Earth* and *Journey's End* (2008), Dalek
Caan, his casing broken open to reveal the stricken form
of the creature inside, used the knowledge and insight
he gained from within the Vortex to predict the future.
He foresaw the arrival of the Doctor – the Threefold
Man, the Dark Lord – and his precious Children of Time,
and he knew that one of them would die…

## 22 APRIL

# Queen Victoria Faces a Werewolf

In 1540, something fell to Earth, landing in the Glen of St Catherine in Scotland, close to a monastery. Possibly a spore, or a virus, or the last remains – the last thought – of some powerful creature from the stars, it survived. It grew, adapted, evolving slowly down the generations until it could take over a human Host and live within it. Drawing on the local legends and folklore, it mapped itself on to the creature at the heart of werewolf legends – a being that turned into a hideous wolf when the moon was full…

The monks of the monastery came to worship the wolf, chanting their mantra: 'Lupus magnus est, lupus fortis est, lupus deus est' – which means: 'The wolf is great, the wolf is strong, the wolf is god.'

Once every generation, a child went missing – the next Host body for the wolf creature when the previous one aged and wore out. With its distinctive pure-black

eyes and its childlike voice, the Host changed with the full moon into the hideous wolf creature itself.

In 1879, monks led by Father Angelo took over Torchwood House, the home of Sir Robert MacLeish in *Tooth and Claw* (2006). Their plan was to help the Werewolf Host infect Queen Victoria when she visited the estate. But, knowing of the local legends, Sir Robert MacLeish's father had realised something of the true nature of the werewolf creature. Together with Prince Albert, who had knowledge of folklore from his native Germany, he had devised a plan to destroy the wolf.

He had a great telescope built at Torchwood House – but its purpose was not to see the stars. The plan was to lead the wolf into a trap, coaxing it to the observatory as it shied away from wood panelling varnished with mistletoe oil. The creature would then be destroyed by a powerful beam of moonlight, magnified through the Koh-i-Noor diamond which Prince Albert had cut to a precise prism. Neither Sir Robert's father nor Prince Albert lived long enough to execute their plan. But the Tenth Doctor managed to use the 'telescope' and the diamond to destroy the creature.

**1967** *The Faceless Ones* Episode 3

**1972** *The Mutants* Episode 3

**1984** Michelle Ryan, who played Lady Christina de Souza in *Planet of the Dead*, was born.

**1994** Former US President Richard Nixon died.

**2006** The Doctor and Rose meet Queen Victoria in *Tooth and Claw*.

**2011** The Doctor is apparently killed by an astronaut at Lake Silencio.

**2011** As a result of the Doctor's apparent death, time got 'stuck' at 5:02 p.m. and all history was muddled up – as seen in *The Wedding of River Song*.

## 23 APRIL

# The Celestial Toymaker Traps the Doctor

The Celestial Toymaker exists outside the real universe of time and space. Although he dresses like an imposing, medieval Chinese nobleman, the Toymaker is an incredibly powerful being who has lived for thousands of years. He spends his time playing games.

If he loses a game, the price he pays is the loss of his world which is destroyed. But he is powerful enough to rebuild it, whereas the winning opponent is destroyed along with the world. If the Toymaker's opponents lose, they are added to the domain as toys. The Doctor describes him as 'a power for evil. He manipulates people and makes them into his playthings.'

When the TARDIS materialises in the Toymaker's domain in *The Celestial Toymaker* (1966), the Toymaker makes the First Doctor invisible and forces him to play the Trilogic Game. In order to escape, the Doctor and his companions must defeat the Toymaker and his playthings in a variety of games. If they lose, they will also become playthings of the Toymaker. But if they win, the Toymaker's domain will be destroyed – along with the winning players.

So the dilemma facing the Doctor is that if he makes the final move to win the Trilogic Game, he will be destroyed together with Dodo and Steven. He gets round this, and defeats the Toymaker, by making the final move from within the safety of the TARDIS – imitating the Toymaker's own voice to order the last piece of the puzzle into the winning position.

**1616** William Shakespeare died.

**1966** *The Final Test –* the fourth episode of *The Celestial Toymaker*

**1975** William Hartnell, who played the First Doctor, died.

**2005** *World War Three*

**2011** *The Impossible Astronaut* opens Series Six and introduces the Silence.

## 24 APRIL

# The Doctor Faces the Weeping Angels Again

The Tenth Doctor first meets the so-called Weeping Angels in *Blink* (2007) when he and Martha Jones are transported back to 1969 by them.

The Lonely Assassins, as they are also known, are as old as the universe itself. They are time-sensitive, absorbing chronon energy from their victims. Any creature they touch is sent back in time, and the Assassin absorbs the potential energy from the life they have not yet lived – and now will never live…

The Assassins have the most perfect defence system ever evolved – they are quantum-locked, which means they only exist when they are not being observed. Otherwise they become immobile, freezing into rock – like the statues for which they are often mistaken. They cannot even look at each other, and so often cover their eyes – hence they are also known as the Weeping Angels.

If you can see a Weeping Angel – if you are looking at it – then you are safe. But look away, or even blink, and the Weeping Angels will come for you. And one touch is enough to send you into the past.

The Eleventh Doctor Amy and River Song encountered the Weeping Angels in *The Time of Angels* and *Flesh and Stone* (2010). They met them again in New York in *The Angels Take Manhattan* (2012) – when the Angels transported Amy and her husband Rory into the past, and out of the Doctor's life…

**1965** The first episode of *The Space Museum*, also titled *The Space Museum*

**1971** *Colony in Space* Episode 3

**2010** *The Time of Angels*

## 25 APRIL

# Dealing with Antimatter

In particle physics, antimatter is the opposite of matter. It is made up of anti-particles, which have the same mass but an opposite charge and other properties. If matter and antimatter meet, that results in radiation annihilation, which the Fourth Doctor describes in *Planet of Evil* (1975) as 'a release of energy more powerful than nuclear fission'.

It is this release of energy that destroys Omega in *The Three Doctors* (1972–1973). Omega exists in a world of antimatter within a black hole. When the first three incarnations of the Doctor and their colleagues are converted to antimatter, the Second Doctor's recorder is not, as it has fallen inside the TARDIS's force-field generator. When Omega knocks the recorder out, matter and antimatter meet and annihilate each other.

In *Planet of Evil*, the Fourth Doctor and Sarah Jane Smith visit the planet Zeta Minor, which is on the very edge of the known universe. Here the universes of matter and antimatter meet, and a Morestran expedition that tries to take material from Zeta Minor back to their own space almost causes disaster.

Antimatter was also used to power spacecraft in *Earthshock* (1982). The antimatter was stored safely within a containment vessel with a totally stable molecular structure – a computer constantly adjusting the molecular structure of the vessel to keep it always stable. When the space freighter taken over by the Cybermen crashed on prehistoric Earth 65 million years ago, the containment vessel split open. The resulting explosion – as well as killing the Doctor's companion Adric, who was still on board the freighter – caused the extinction of the dinosaurs.

## 26 APRIL

# The Doctor Meets Wilfred Mott

The paternal grandfather of Donna Noble, Wilfred Mott missed his granddaughter's aborted wedding in *The Runaway Bride* (2006) because he had Spanish flu. When the Tenth Doctor first met Wilf he was selling newspapers on Christmas Eve as passengers from the space liner *Titanic* – including the Doctor and Astrid Peth – visited in *Voyage of the Damned* (2007).

Although he saw Donna in the TARDIS through his telescope after she rejoined the Doctor in *Partners in Crime* (2008), Wilf did not meet the Doctor again – or realise who he was – until Donna brought the Doctor home in *The Sontaran Stratagem* (2008).

Having helped the Doctor in *The Stolen Earth* and *Journey's End* (2008), Wilf was instrumental in finding and stopping the Master and the return of the Time Lords led by Rassilon in *The End of Time* (2009–2010). But in doing so, he became trapped inside a booth about to be flooded with deadly radiation. To save him, and despite Wilf's protests, the Doctor took his place. The radiation destroyed the Tenth Doctor's body, forcing his regeneration into his eleventh incarnation.

**1564** William Shakespeare was baptised. His actual birth date is unknown.

**1969** *The War Games* Episode 2

**1975** *Revenge of the Cybermen* Part 2

**2008** The Sontarans make their first appearance in the revived series in *The Sontaran Stratagem*. Martha Jones also returns.

## 27 APRIL

# Problems with the Fluid Link

Component 'K7' of the TARDIS console, according to the TARDIS Fault Locator, the Fluid Link acts in the same way as a fuse. However, rather than relying on thin wire to make an electrical connection, the Fluid Link is filled with mercury liquid.

In *The Daleks* (1963–1964), the First Doctor used the Fluid Link as an excuse to explore the Dalek City on Skaro. He claimed that the end had unscrewed itself and the mercury had run out. Without any spare mercury, he suggested the Dalek City was the only place they were likely to find any, although he later admitted there was nothing wrong with the Fluid Link. When the Daleks then took it, the Doctor and his friends were forced to help the Thals defeat the Daleks in order to retrieve the vital component.

In *The Web Planet* (1965), the Doctor's young companion Vicki restored power to the TARDIS by accidentally realigning the Fluid Link when she pressed various switches and was thrown against a control panel.

In *The Wheel in Space* (1968), the TARDIS power lines overloaded. As a result the mercury in the Fluid Link vaporised, becoming a toxic gas. The Second Doctor and Jamie were forced to leave the safety of the TARDIS to escape the gas. The Doctor was finally able to replenish the mercury in the Fluid Link from supplies held on Station 3, once he had defeated an attack by the Cybermen.

ON THIS DAY

**1968** *The Wheel in Space* Episode 1

**1974** *The Monster of Peladon* Part 6

**1986** Jenna Coleman, who played Clara Oswald (and her various other 'versions'), was born.

**2013** *Journey to the Centre of the TARDIS*

## 28 APRIL

# Dalek Sec Becomes a Human Hybrid

Stranded in Manhattan in 1930 following their emergency temporal shift after the events of *Doomsday* (2006), the Cult of Skaro attempted to create new Dalek embryos. But this was unsuccessful, so in *Daleks in Manhattan* and *Evolution of the Daleks* (2007) they adopted another plan.

Believing themselves to be the last four Daleks in existence, the Cult of Skaro once again determined to think unlike any other Daleks. As well as genetically adapting human beings to become Dalek-like, the leader of the Cult of Skaro, Dalek Sec, was genetically bonded with a human being. The human they chose was Mr Diagoras, the man in charge of completing the Empire State Building beneath which the Daleks had a hidden base of operations. Diagoras had been working for the Daleks for a while, and they noted his ambition and drive – his determination to control New York.

Using a chromatin solution to facilitate the process, Diagoras was pushed into the flesh of the Dalek creature, and the two became one. But the audaciousness of Dalek Sec's plan to evolve the Dalek race by bonding human and Dalek flesh worried the other Daleks and they warned against it. Ultimately, the other members of the Cult of Skaro were proved right. Sec was corrupted by his human side, and the other Daleks exterminated him for his betrayal.

**1973** *Planet of the Daleks* Episode 4

**1974** Outside Broadcast (OB) shooting started on *Robot* – Tom Baker's first story as the Fourth Doctor.

**1974** *The Monster of Peladon* Part 6 is first shown on BBC Wales.

**2007** *Evolution of the Daleks*

## 29 APRIL

# The Doctor Meets Sarah Jane Smith Again – And the Krillitanes

ON THIS DAY

**1967** *The Faceless Ones* Episode 4

**1972** *The Mutants* Episode 4

**2006** Sarah Jane Smith and K-9 return to the series in *School Reunion*.

The Krillitanes are a composite species, absorbing traits and even physical characteristics from the other races they defeat. Having pillaged and conquered, they choose the best attributes from those they destroy, and so over the years they have become an amalgam of other races.

The Krillitanes that the Tenth Doctor encountered in *School Reunion* (2006) were able to disguise themselves to appear human using a simple morphic illusion. Their leader was Brother Lassar. In his disguised human form, and calling himself Mr Finch, he had taken over as head teacher of a secondary school. The day after he arrived, half the staff mysteriously fell victim to an especially virulent strain of 'flu and had to be replaced. Since then, an Ofsted inspector had also disappeared under mysterious circumstances, and some of the classes seemed to have fewer pupils than were on the register.

As the Doctor, reunited with Sarah Jane Smith and K-9 as well as Rose Tyler and Mickey Smith, discovered, the Krillitanes were trying to find the Skasas Paradigm. This is the key to the way the universe actually works. Anyone who unravels the Paradigm can control the very building blocks of time, space, and universal matter. But it takes more than just computational power to crack the Paradigm. It also needs imagination – which is why the Krillitanes are using schoolchildren, their minds enhanced by doses of Krillitane oil, to work it out.

## 30 APRIL

# Fighting the Last Great Time War

The Last Great Time War was fought between the Time Lords of Gallifrey and the Daleks of Skaro. Some say it began when the Time Lords sent the Fourth Doctor back to Skaro in *Genesis of the Daleks* (1975) at the point in time when the Daleks were first created by Davros, in the hope and expectation that the Doctor could prevent the Daleks from ever existing. But whether or not it was the actions of the Doctor that began the War, it was certainly the Doctor who brought it to an end.

Records of the Great Time War are scarce and unreliable. But a full-scale war erupted within the Time Vortex and beyond that in the Ultimate Void. The Time Lords reached back into history for ever more terrible weapons, while the Daleks unleashed the Deathsmiths of Goth. For centuries the War raged, unseen by most of the universe. But the Higher Species watched and wept…

By the end of the War, other horrors appeared – the Nightmare Child, the Skaro Degradations, the Horde of Travesties and the Couldhaveheen King with his Army of Meanwhiles and Never-Weres. Finally, as Gallifrey's second city Arcadia fell to the Daleks, the Doctor deployed the Time Lords' most deadly weapon in *The Day of the Doctor* (2013) – the final creation of the Ancients of Gallifrey, a sentient weapon with a conscience: the Moment.

It seemed that both sides were wiped out, and that the Daleks and the Time Lords had vanished from the universe. But, in fact, as would later become apparent, both races survived. The first inkling the Doctor had that there might be other survivors apart from himself was when he met a damaged Dalek kept prisoner by Henry Van Statten in *Dalek* (2005).

**1945** Adolf Hitler died.

**1966** *A Holiday for the Doctor* – the first episode of *The Gunfighters*

**Sometime in the 1970s (probably):** Azal the Dæmon appears at the pagan feast of Beltane following Professor Horner's disastrous televised archaeological dig at the so-called Devil's Hump at the village of Devil's End.

**1979** The first overseas filming for the series begins in Paris for *City of Death* (and continues until 3 May).

**2005** The Daleks – or one of them – return to the new series in *Dalek*.

**2011** *Day of the Moon*

MAY

# 1 MAY

# Investigating a Crack in Time

When the TARDIS exploded, it created a Time Field which manifested itself as a crack in the fabric of reality, recurring through all of time and space. The Eleventh Doctor first encountered the crack in Amy Pond's bedroom in *The Eleventh Hour* (2010) and it was through this crack that Prisoner Zero escaped from the Atraxi.

But, slowly, the Time Field grew, erasing history itself. The planet Saturnyne, Amy's parents, Rory, and the Weeping Angels that attacked the Doctor, Amy, River Song and a group of Clerics on Alfava Metraxis in *The Time of Angels* and *Flesh and Stone* (2010) were all swallowed up by the Time Field.

Eventually, the Doctor was able to use the Pandorica to stop the Time Field in *The Pandorica Opens* and *The Big Bang* (2010). He was imprisoned inside the Pandorica by an alliance of alien life forms determined on his destruction so as, they thought, to save the universe. But he managed to go back in time and prevent the TARDIS from exploding in the first place – in effect rebooting the universe.

## ON THIS DAY

**1965** *The Dimensions of Time* – the second episode of *The Space Museum*

**1971** *Colony in Space* Episode 4

**1984** The events of *The Awakening* take place at the village of Little Hodcombe.

**2010** *Flesh and Stone*

## 2 MAY

# River Song is Melody Malone

Melody Malone was the renowned fictional 'private detective of old New York town' who appeared in several detective stories published by Pond River in the 1930s, including *The Angel's Kiss* which has since been reissued by BBC Books as an eBook and in the anthology *Summer Falls and Other Stories*.

In fact, as the Doctor discovered in *The Angels Take Manhattan* (2012), the real Melody Malone was actually River Song. How many of her reported exploits are actually fiction and how much is reality is unclear. But certainly, River helped the Doctor, Amy and Rory battle against a group of Weeping Angels after the unscrupulous Julius Grayle held one captive.

Unfortunately, the incident ended with both Amy and Rory transported back to New York in the 1930s, where the Doctor was unable to reach them. Amy was, however, able to send the Doctor a message – in the form of an Afterword she wrote for the *Melody Malone* mystery the Doctor had been reading before they met up with River Song in 1930s New York…

**1964** *The Snows of Terror* – the fourth episode of *The Keys of Marinus*

**1970** *The Ambassadors of Death* Episode 7 is the last episode of *Doctor Who* written by the programme's first Story Editor, David Whitaker. That said, the story was heavily rewritten by Malcom Hulke to fit the new series format for the Third Doctor's era.

**1973** The first Target novelisations are published – reprints of the 1960s books *Doctor Who and the Daleks*, *Doctor Who and the Crusaders* and *Doctor Who and the Zarbi*.

# 3 MAY

## The Valiant to the Rescue

The *Valiant* was an airborne aircraft carrier used by UNIT in the early twenty-first century. The Master designed the *Valiant* while masquerading as Harold Saxon in *The Sound of Drums* (2007), and he used it as the location for the first human contact with the Toclafane. After the Toclafane conquered Earth, the Master controlled the planet from the *Valiant*.

UNIT called on the *Valiant* for help against the Sontarans in *The Poison Sky* (2008). The *Valiant*'s engines cleared away the gas generated by ATMOS from the ATMOS factory, and the aircraft carrier's energy weapons were deployed against the Sontaran warriors.

When the Daleks attacked Earth following the planet's removal to the Medusa Cascade in *The Stolen Earth* (2008), they targeted the *Valiant* as well as other UNIT and military installations and forces. The *Valiant*'s shields were destroyed, and Captain Jack Harkness reported that the *Valiant* was down. It is possible that it was subsequently repaired, or that another vessel was commissioned with the same name; certainly, UNIT have access to a vessel called the *Valiant* in *Death in Heaven* (2014).

**1969** *The War Games* Episode 3

**1975** *Revenge of the Cybermen* Part 3

**2004** Anthony Ainley, who played the Master from the end of The *Keeper of Traken* through to *Survival* (the last story of the classic series) died.

**2008** *The Poison Sky*

# 4 MAY

## Introducing Zoe Heriot

Zoe Heriot was a young astrophysicist and astrometricist first class. She was working aboard Station Three, known as the Wheel, when she met the Second Doctor and Jamie in *The Wheel in Space* (1968) at some point in the twenty-first century. On the Wheel, Zoe is the librarian, and it is later revealed that she has a photographic memory.

Zoe's training has left her emotionally undeveloped. From an early age she has been taught the value of logic, her training from a parapsychologist effectively repressing her emotions.

In the Doctor, Zoe has a perfect case study for the success of the illogical and the power of intuitive action and lateral thinking. It was because of this growing realisation that there is more to knowledge than facts, more to life than logic, that Zoe hid on board the TARDIS. She had learned as much as she could in the closeted environment of the Wheel where her abilities and role were compartmentalised and defined.

Zoe's experiences and adventures with the Doctor and Jamie certainly broaden her mind, and they also benefit from her logical and deductive approach. She only left the Doctor when she was returned to her own time and place – on board the Wheel just after the TARDIS left – when the Doctor was put on trial by the Time Lords in *The War Games* (1969) for intervening in the affairs of others.

**1968** Zoe first appears in Episode 2 of *The Wheel in Space*

**1974** *Planet of the Spiders* Part 1

**2013** *The Crimson Horror*

## 5 MAY

# Spiridon – 'One of the Nastiest Pieces of Space Garbage in the Ninth System'

**1973** *Planet of the Daleks* Episode 5

**1974** *Planet of the Spiders* Part 1 is first shown on BBC Wales.

**2007** *The Lazarus Experiment*

When the Third Doctor contacted the Time Lords and asked them to send the TARDIS after a Dalek ship leaving the Ogron planet in *Planet of the Daleks* (1973), it was on Spiridon that the TARDIS arrived.

As the Doctor and Jo Grant soon discovered, the planet Spiridon was far from hospitable. The TARDIS materialised in a dense jungle where the vegetation included 'eye plants' that watched movement, and 'fungoids' that sprayed a green liquid. The liquid congealed and grew into a fungus that could engulf the entire body. Water on Spiridon remained semi-liquid when below freezing, rather than becoming ice. Occasional eruptions of this frozen liquid could cover the jungle for miles at a time.

The planet's climate varied from sub-tropical during the day to well below freezing at night. To survive, the Doctor, Jo and a group of Thals from Skaro on a mission against the Daleks took refuge on the Plain of Stones – an area of huge boulders that absorbed the sun's heat during the day, and radiated it at night.

The only intelligent native life forms were the Spiridons – invisible creatures that the Daleks had come to Spiridon to subjugate and then study in order to learn how to become invisible themselves. But while the Thals believed the Daleks had only a small scientific research team on Spiridon, the Doctor soon discovered that they had an entire army concealed in a huge chamber below their base – ten thousand Daleks about to be awoken from suspended animation and despatched to invade the galaxy...

## 6 MAY

# The Doctor Saves Madame De Pompadour

ON THIS DAY

**1967** *The Faceless Ones* Episode 5

**1972** *The Mutants* Episode 5

**2006** *The Girl in the Fireplace*

Jeanne-Antoinette Poisson was born on 29 December 1721. When she was 9 years old, her mother took her to a fortune teller who told the girl that one day she would become the mistress of a king. After this she became known by the nickname Reinette – which means 'little queen'.

As a young girl, Reinette first met the Tenth Doctor in *The Girl in the Fireplace* (2006), when he appeared through a time window in her bedroom from a damaged spaceship in the far future. The Doctor continued to appear at points throughout her life. The time windows followed Reinette's life as the clockwork repair robots from the ship believed she could provide a vital component in the repair of the ship – her brain.

In 1741, she married and became Madame d'Etoiles, giving birth to a daughter in 1744. Reinette met Louis XV at the masked Yew Tree Ball, and indeed soon became the King's mistress. She was legally separated from her husband, and Louis XV made her Marquise de Pompadour. She advised on policy, and was a patron of the arts and literature.

The Doctor's final meeting with Reinette was at Versailles where he again saved her from the clockwork repair robots. Madame de Pompadour died, exhausted from her hard work for the state, on 15 April 1764.

# 7 MAY

## The Doctor Witnesses the Gunfight at the OK Corral

Suffering from toothache after his encounter with the Celestial Toymaker, the First Doctor considered himself lucky to find a dentist at their next destination in *The Gunfighters* (1966). His mood did not last however, as that dentist was the infamous Doc Holliday who had recently set up a practice in Tombstone, Arizona in 1881. The Doctor was less than impressed to discover that he was to be Holliday's first patient, and that the only options for an anaesthetic consisted of whisky or a 'rap on the cranium' from a six-shooter.

Before long, the Doctor and his companions Steven and Dodo found themselves caught up in the feud between the Clantons and local lawmen Wyatt Earp and Bat Masterson together with Doc Holliday. With the arrival of the notorious hired gunman Johnny Ringo events got out of hand, leading to the famous 'Gunfight at the OK Corral' – 'OK' standing for Old Kindersley. With Dodo's help, Doc Holliday killed Johnny Ringo, while the lawmen got the better of the Clantons.

The gunfight actually took place at 3 p.m. on 26 October 1881, and lasted just 30 seconds.

**1966** *Don't Shoot the Pianist* – the second episode of *The Gunfighters*

**2005** *The Long Game*

**2011** *The Curse of the Black Spot*

## 8 MAY

# Rory Williams Goes Back in Time

Although the Eleventh Doctor first met Rory Williams in *The Eleventh Hour* (2010), he didn't realise that Rory and Amy Pond were engaged and about to be married. It wasn't until *The Vampires of Venice* (2010) that Rory got his first trip in the TARDIS along with the Doctor and Amy.

After apparently being killed in *Amy's Choice* (2010), Rory was erased from time – and from Amy's memory – in *Cold Blood* (2010) by the Time Field created by the potential future destruction of the TARDIS. But he returned in Auton form in *The Pandorica Opens* (2010). As a Roman centurion, he guarded the Pandorica with Amy inside until it reopened two thousand years later. In *The Big Bang* (2010), he was restored to true human form when the Doctor prevented the destruction of the TARDIS and in effect rebooted the universe.

Now married, Rory and Amy continued to travel with the Doctor for a while. Rory's father Brian even joined them in *Dinosaurs on a Spaceship* (2012). They also had a child – Melody Pond – who, kidnapped by Madame Kovarian and brainwashed to kill the Doctor, became River Song.

Rory and Amy only stopped travelling with the Doctor when they were sent back to 1930s New York, where the Doctor could not reach them, by a Weeping Angel in *The Angels Take Manhattan* (2012).

9 MAY

# Project 'Inferno' Threatens the World

'The Inferno' is a nickname rather than the official designation for the project led by Professor Stahlman to drill through the Earth's crust. Stahlman's plan is to tap into the pockets of gas, which he has named Stahlman's Gas, beneath the crust as a potential energy source. But a viscous green fluid bubbles up through the pipes, infecting anyone who touches it, regressing their body cells and turning them into a primordial killer – a 'Primord'.

With UNIT handling security for the project, the Third Doctor establishes a workshop on the site in *Inferno* (1970), hoping to use output from the nuclear reactor in his endeavours to get the TARDIS working again. He succeeds, after a fashion – and is transported 'sideways' to a parallel Earth. He finds himself in a Britain that is a totalitarian state. The Brigadier in this world is the Brigade Leader – a

sadistic bully with an eyepatch and no moustache, while the Doctor's assistant Liz Shaw is a Section Leader in the Republican Security Forces.

The drilling is also more advanced in this world, and when the drills break through the Earth's crust violent eruptions begin, which will eventually destroy the planet. It is up to the Doctor to escape back to his own universe, deal with the Primords, and persuade the stubborn and arrogant Stahlman to halt the drilling.

**1964** *Sentence of Death* – the fifth episode of *The Keys of Marinus*

**1970** *Inferno* Episode 1

10 MAY

# The Doctor Meets His 'Daughter'

On the colony planet of Messaline, a mixed team of humans and amphibious Hath was sent to adapt the eco-system with a standard PT306 system. But the two races fell out and a conflict started – then escalated. Each side made use of recalibrated Progenation Machines to 'breed' new troops. Soon a war that had in fact lasted only days had claimed the lives of generations of Hath and humans.

When the Tenth Doctor, Donna and Martha arrived on Messaline in *The Doctor's Daughter* (2008), a genetic sample was taken from the Doctor's hand by one of the Progenation Machines. The result was 'Jenny': a young woman created from the Doctor's genetic make-up and literally born to fight – a soldier. At first, the Doctor found it hard to come to terms with the fact that his own flesh and blood, as it were, could be so dedicated to the art of war. But he did come to appreciate his 'daughter' and to respect her talent and ability.

Jenny, in her turn, took a while to understand the Doctor's point of view. But she too came to respect her 'father' and to envy the life he leads fighting injustice and advocating peace. Jenny was shot in a final confrontation between the two opposing sides, and apparently killed. But after the Doctor left, she eventually recovered – and set off into space to emulate her father…

ON THIS DAY

**1969** *The War Games* Episode 4

**1975** The fourth and final episode of *Revenge of the Cybermen* closes Season 12.

**2008** The Doctor meets his genetic daughter in *The Doctor's Daughter*.

# 11 MAY

# Harry Sullivan Gets a Mention

**1968** *The Wheel in Space* Episode 3

**1974** Harry Sullivan is first mentioned in *Planet of the Spiders* Part 2 – although he doesn't actually appear until *Robot* Part 1 on 28 December 1974.

**2013** *Nightmare in Silver*

While he is mentioned in *Planet of the Spiders* (1974), UNIT's Medical Officer Harry Sullivan doesn't actually get to meet the Doctor. The Brigadier calls him to the lab when the Doctor appears to be in a trance, but then cancels the order when the Doctor is revived by the smell of coffee. So the first time Surgeon Lieutenant Harry Sullivan meets the Doctor is after his regeneration at the start of *Robot* (1974–1975). But in the process of keeping a professional eye on the newly regenerated Doctor, Harry soon comes to appreciate his scientific genius.

Seconded to UNIT from the Royal Navy, Harry relishes the role of secret agent. But for all he sees and experiences in *Robot*, Harry still believes the Doctor to be an eccentric rather than an alien. When he discovers that the Doctor and Sarah are planning a 'little trip' in the TARDIS, he tells the Doctor: 'We're both reasonable men. Now, we both know police boxes don't go careering around all over the place…'

Once he is over the initial shock of actually travelling through space and time, Harry becomes a useful companion and a good friend to the Doctor and Sarah. The Doctor may chide Harry for his clumsiness and impulsiveness, but he also trusts him. Equally, while Sarah teases Harry for his ineptitude and naivety, there is no doubting their deep friendship.

But perhaps, despite his bravado and enthusiasm, Harry is not really an adventurer. He hints in *Revenge of the Cybermen* (1975) that he would like to retire and buy a 'quiet little practice in the country'. Certainly, at his first opportunity, at the end of *Terror of the Zygons* (1975), Harry decides to stay on Earth…

When he does leave UNIT, Harry is posted to the Defence Science and Technology Laboratory at Porton Down, where amongst other things, he apparently develops 'Sullivan's Gas' – which is lethal to Zygons.

## 12 MAY

# The Doctor Meets the Thals Again

The First Doctor originally met the Thals soon after his first encounter with the Daleks on the planet Skaro in *The Daleks* (1963–1964). Both races had mutated from their original form following a thousand-year war that all but wiped them out. But whereas the Daleks became grotesque, warlike creatures surviving inside their life-support shells and dependent on radiation, the Thal mutation had come full circle leaving them as blonde humanoids. Unlike the Daleks, the Thals were ardent pacifists determined not to suffer the horrors of war again. But the Doctor's companion Ian was able to persuade the Thals to help defeat the Daleks, to prevent them from wiping out the Thals.

Many years later, the Fourth Doctor found himself sent by the Time Lords into the final stages of the thousand-year war in an effort to prevent the Daleks ever being created in *Genesis of the Daleks* (1975).

But before that, the Third Doctor and Jo Grant met up with and helped a group of Thals on the planet Spiridon in *Planet of the Daleks* (1973). These Thals were on a mission to prevent the Daleks from discovering the secret of invisibility from the native Spiridons. But while they assumed they were facing a small scientific team of Daleks, they soon discovered that in fact the Daleks had assembled a huge army on Spiridon…

ON THIS DAY

**1968** Catherine Tate, who played the Doctor's companion Donna Noble, was born.

**1973** *Planet of the Daleks* Episode 6

**1974** *Planet of the Spiders* Part 2 is first shown on BBC Wales.

**1996** First broadcast of the *Doctor Who* TV movie starring Paul McGann, in Canada.

# 13 MAY

# John Lumic Invents the Cybermen

In our universe, the Cybermen were created on the planet Mondas, later migrating to another world – Telos. Mondas was the twin planet of Earth, and both Mondas and Telos were ancient names for Earth, so there has always been an affinity between the origins of the Cybermen and our own planet.

In the parallel universe where the Tenth Doctor, Mickey Smith and Rose Tyler find themselves in *Rise of the Cybermen* and *The Age of Steel* (2006), the Cybermen were created on Earth itself. The location may have changed, but the Cybermen are very much the same emotionless creatures.

John Lumic set up the huge Cybus Industries corporation and invented the technology the company is based on. He is a dying man – frail and kept alive only by a life-support system built into his wheelchair. But Lumic has a vision, a dream of perpetual life. He wants to take humanity to the next stage of its development. Like one of his company's products, he believes that the human race is ready for an upgrade – an upgrade that is Lumic's only hope of survival.

The Cybermen are created in huge factories from living humans – replacing their bodily organs and limbs with mechanical versions. They also 'enhance' the brains, removing the weakness of emotion. With the Cybermen a reality, Lumic intended himself to become their leader – but only, he decrees, when he has exhausted the final breath in his human body. But the Cybermen have other ideas, immediately converting Lumic fully into the first Cyber Controller.

**1967** The Second Doctor's companions Polly and Ben leave in the last episode of *The Faceless Ones*.

**1972** *The Mutants* Episode 6

**2006** The Cybermen return to the revived series in *Rise of the Cybermen*.

## 14 MAY

# Idris Becomes the TARDIS

In *The Doctor's Wife* (2011), the Eleventh Doctor arrives on an asteroid inhabited by the disembodied intelligence known as 'House'. Already there are three humanoids and an Ood. House has the Ood, known as Nephew, remove the mind of one of the humanoids – Idris. This is so that House can 'evict' the matrix – the soul – of the Doctor's TARDIS and place it inside her body. But the body is too frail to cope with the TARDIS matrix, and can only survive for a short time.

Confused about her new body and the linear nature of Time itself, Idris eventually manages to tell the Doctor who she really is. She describes him as her 'Thief' – insisting that she originally stole the Doctor, rather than the Doctor stealing the TARDIS. Marooned on the asteroid, with Amy and Rory on board the 'dead' TARDIS, the Doctor and Idris succeed in fashioning a makeshift TARDIS out of the abandoned components of other TARDISes that House has previously trapped.

Finally, the Doctor manages to reinstall his own TARDIS matrix, which then removes House from the TARDIS systems. The body of the woman who was Idris burns up…

**1966** *Johnny Ringo* – the third episode of *The Gunfighters*

**1996** The TV movie Doctor Who starring Paul McGann as the Eighth Doctor gets its first broadcast in the USA.

**2005** *Father's Day*

**2011** *The Doctor's Wife* sees the TARDIS take on human form. It is the first episode written by noted genre author Neil Gaiman.

## 15 MAY

# The Doctor Acquires a Time-Space Visualiser

At the end of *The Space Museum* (1965), having helped the Xerons to defeat the oppressive Moroks, the First Doctor acquires a Time-Space Visualiser from the Moroks' Space Museum. The Visualiser is a large circular device that relays images of past events on a monitor screen.

At the start of the next story, *The Chase* (1965), the Doctor explains that the device converts energy from light neutrons into electrical impulses. As mass is absorbed by light, therefore light has mass and energy. As the energy radiated by a light neutron is equal to the energy of the mass it has absorbed, anything that ever happens, anywhere in the universe, is recorded in light neutrons. The Time-Space Visualiser, correctly tuned to an historical event, converts those recordings into a form that can be displayed visually. In theory it could replay any event from history, the results being shown on the screen at the centre of the device.

The Doctor and his companions Barbara, Ian and Vicki watch Shakespeare, the Beatles and Abraham Lincoln on the device. But, left untuned, it later shows images of a squad of Daleks being despatched from Skaro to track down the TARDIS and execute its occupants. The Doctor has no way of knowing how old these images are, only that the events he watches have happened and the Daleks are on their way…

**1965** *The Final Phase –* the fourth episode of *The Space Museum*

**1971** *Colony in Space* Episode 6

**2010** *Amy's Choice*

# 16 MAY

# When Science Goes Wrong

While the Doctor has faced more than his fair share of mad scientists bent on destruction, he has also encountered situations where scientific research or experimentation has simply gone wrong – sometimes with potentially catastrophic consequences. A good example of this is the Third Doctor story *Inferno* (1970) where a project to drill through the Earth's crust threatens the safety of the planet.

In *The Dæmons* (1971), the Third Doctor discovers that the whole of human civilisation has been a giant experiment conducted by aliens. If the Dæmons deem their experiment to have failed, they will destroy the world. Rather less catastrophic are the environmental problems caused by Global Chemicals dumping waste from their oil refining down an abandoned coal mine in *The Green Death* (1973), whereas in *Planet of Evil* (1975) the Fourth Doctor must stop Morestran scientist Sorensen threatening the safety of the whole universe by taking antimatter from the planet Zeta Minor.

In *The Girl in the Fireplace* (2006), the Tenth Doctor encounters repair robots that take their programming so literally they kill the crew of their spaceship in order to salvage 'parts' from them to repair the vessel. Not long afterwards, in *The Lazarus Experiment* (2007), the Doctor witnesses what happens when Professor Richard Lazarus tries to restore his lost youth – and damages his own DNA to such an extent that he mutates into a primordial arthropod creature...

There are many other examples of occasions when, but for the Doctor's presence and intervention, scientific experiment could have spelled disaster not just for the scientists involved but for countless others as well.

ON THIS DAY

**1964** *The Keys of Marinus* – the sixth and final episode of story of the same name

**1970** *Inferno* Episode 2

**1996** BBC Books publishes a version of the script for the *Doctor Who* TV movie alongside a novelisation of the film.

# 17 MAY

## The Doctor Meets Agatha Christie – and a Vespiform

**1969** *The War Games* Episode 5

**2008** *The Unicorn and the Wasp* – the Doctor and Donna meet Agatha Christie.

The only recorded instance of a Vespiform visiting Earth was in 1885, when it arrived in a blaze of purple fire. The Vespiform took the form of a human male called 'Christopher' in order to learn about the human race. The young Clemency Eddison saw the blaze of purple fire fall from the heavens. The next day she met Christopher – a stunningly handsome man – and they fell in love. Only later did Clemency Eddison find out that Christopher was a Vespiform. But she still loved him, and together they had a child. Christopher was drowned in the monsoon floods, leaving Lady Eddison a marvellous firestone jewel – in fact, the Vespiform's Telepathic Recorder. This crystal became known as the famous 'Eddison Firestone'.

Each Vespiform that takes on another shape has a Telepathic Recorder that holds an encoded copy of its mind – its very essence. The Recorder is a large crystal that looks like a jewel. The Vespiform will do anything to keep it safe and secure.

The Tenth Doctor and Donna encountered the son – also a Vespiform – when they also met the noted crime novelist Agatha Christie in *The Unicorn and the Wasp* (2008). An ancient and wise amorphic race from the hives of the Silfrax galaxy, the Vespiform resemble giant wasps. They have a huge, deadly sting – which they can regrow after use. A Vespiform can change its shape to mimic other creatures.

## 18 MAY

# Meet the War Doctor

Mortally injured when a spaceship he was in crashed on the planet Karn, the Eighth Doctor was saved by the intervention of the Sisterhood of Karn in the mini-episode *The Night of the Doctor* (2013). Up until then, the Doctor had kept away from the Great Time War between the Time Lords and the Daleks. But the Sisterhood told him that the war now threatened all reality – and that he was the only hope left. He was dying, but the Elixir of Life held by the Sisterhood could enable him to regenerate again.

The result was the 'War Doctor' – a warrior persona deliberately chosen by the Doctor. It was the War Doctor who took a terrible weapon known as 'the Moment' from the Time Lords' Omega Arsenal – where all the forbidden weapons too terrible to use were stored. With the Moment, the War Doctor planned to bring the conflict to an end – at the cost of both Time Lords and Daleks.

With the help of his other incarnations – in particular the Tenth and Eleventh Doctors in *The Day of the Doctor* (2013) – the War Doctor used the Moment. But although he did not realise it at the time, Gallifrey was preserved. His work done, and his body worn out, the War Doctor regenerated into the Ninth Doctor…

**1968** *The Wheel in Space* Episode 4

**1974** *Planet of the Spiders* Part 3

**2013** *The Name of the Doctor* introduces the War Doctor, played by John Hurt, and closes Series Seven. It is the last episode on which Caroline Skinner is Executive Producer.

# 19 MAY

## The Doctor Meets Giant Maggots and Learns Who's BOSS

UNIT is called in to the Welsh village of Llanfairfach in *The Green Death* (1973) when a man checking the disused coalmine is found dead, and glowing bright green. The Third Doctor soon discovers that the man has been killed by a green slime – an unwanted by-product of a revolutionary oil-refining process used by the nearby Global Chemicals.

Global Chemicals has been disposing of this waste by pumping it down into the disused coal mine. But the chemicals cause maggots in the mine to mutate – growing to enormous size. And not only is the glowing, green chemical slime deadly to anyone who touches it, so are the maggots.

The Doctor and his friends from UNIT try to destroy the creatures with armour-piercing bullets, flame-throwers and fire bombs before they discover the real solution at the local ecological community (nicknamed the Nuthutch) – a sort of fungus that poisons the maggots.

Global Chemicals is run by Stevens, and its mission is to control the world through technological advancement. But the company is actually controlled by a giant supercomputer – BOSS, the Bimorphic Organisational Systems Supervisor – which is linked directly to Stevens's brain. BOSS plans to take over humanity as a way of ensuring huge profits for Global Chemicals, unless the Doctor can manage to convince Stevens that BOSS must be destroyed…

**1973** *The Green Death* Episode 1

**1974** *Planet of the Spiders* Part 3 is first shown on BBC Wales.

**2005** The first three original novels to tie in with the new series are published by BBC Books, featuring the Ninth Doctor and Rose Tyler. They are *The Clockwise Man* by Justin Richards, *The Monsters Inside* by Stephen Cole, and *Winner Takes All* by Jacqueline Rayner.

**2007** *42*

## 20 MAY

# Mickey Smith Finds a New Home

When the Doctor first meets Rose Tyler in *Rose* (2005), her boyfriend is Mickey Smith. Mickey also lives on the Powell Estate, though in a different block. The Doctor initially sees Mickey as little more than an idiot, and isn't shy of telling him so. But after Mickey demonstrates his computer skills by hacking into the UNIT website on the Doctor's instructions in *World War Three* (2005), the Doctor is less scathing.

Mickey knows his limitations. He is shocked by his first sight of the TARDIS interior, and desperately wants Rose to stay with him rather than travel with the Doctor. Having proved himself, and experienced at first hand the sorts of things that the Doctor and Rose encounter, Mickey is sure he is not up to travelling the universe and declines the Doctor's invitation to join them in the TARDIS.

This changes after the events of *School Reunion* (2006), and Mickey joins Rose in the TARDIS. But his travelling is short-lived as he decides to stay on a parallel Earth at the end of *The Age of Steel* (2006). He returns to stop the Cybermen invading our Earth in *Army of Ghosts* and *Doomsday* (2006). The Tenth Doctor sees Mickey again just before he regenerates in *The End of Time, Part Two* (2010) – battling against a Sontaran with his wife, the Doctor's former companion Martha Jones.

ON THIS DAY

**1967** *The Evil of the Daleks* Episode 1

**1972** *The Time Monster* Episode 1

**1996** Jon Pertwee, who played the Third Doctor, died.

**2006** Mickey Smith decides to stay on a parallel Earth in *The Age of Steel*.

## 21 MAY

# Captain Jack Harkness Arrives

First appearing in *The Empty Child* (2005), Captain Jack Harkness – although that is not his real name at all – is handsome, charming, clever, and a complete rogue. He used to be a Time Agent from the fifty-first century. Now he follows a life of crime. Supremely self-assured, he thinks nothing of, for example, standing naked in front of billions of viewers on live television in *Bad Wolf* (2005).

When the Doctor and Rose first encounter Captain Jack, his plan is to find some space junk, allow a Time Agent to track it to London during the Second World War Blitz and then convince the Agent it is valuable. Once Jack has a fifty per cent advance on his finder's fee, the junk will be destroyed by a German bomb – so the Agent will never discover it was a trick: 'The perfect self-cleaning con.' Jack implies this is not the first time he has used the Blitz in a con, and also mentions that the trick works well at Pompeii.

Jack's experience and ingenuity are quickly apparent. While his instinct is to avoid trouble, he does not shy away from it when it counts. Organising the defence of the Game Station against the Daleks in *The Parting of the Ways* (2005), he faces certain death. In fact, until Rose Tyler's intervention, he is actually killed.

But his resurrection by Rose, while 'possessed' by the energy of the Time Vortex itself, renders Jack immortal. He joins the Tenth Doctor again for *Utopia*, *The Sound of Drums* and *Last of the Time Lords* (all 2007), and again helps against the Daleks in *The Stolen Earth* and *Journey's End* (2008). By this time he is in charge of the Cardiff branch of Torchwood – the top secret organisation established by Queen Victoria.

ON THIS DAY

**1966** The fourth and final episode of *The Gunfighters* is the last to have an individual episode title until the series returns in 2005 – it is called *The OK Corral*.

**2005** Captain Jack Harkness is introduced in *The Empty Child* – the first episode written by Steven Moffat (apart from *The Curse of Fatal Death* for *Comic Relief* in 1999).

**2011** *The Rebel Flesh*

# 22 MAY

# The Doctor Visits Devil's End

Perhaps not surprisingly given its name, the rural village of Devil's End has always been associated with witchcraft and black magic. In the notorious cavern underneath the village church, pagan man performed his unspeakable rites, the witches of the seventeenth century hid from the fires of witch-hunter Matthew Hopkins, and the third Lord of Aldbourne played at his eighteenth-century parody of black magic.

Just outside the village is the ancient burial mound known as the Devil's Hump. This too is supposed to be cursed. In 1793, Sir Percival Flint's miners ran back to Cornwall leaving him for dead. And then there was the famous Cambridge University fiasco of 1939…

But it is when the noted archaeologist Professor Gilbert Horner decides to open the barrow on live television, convinced that it contained a Bronze Age warrior chieftain dating from 800 BC, that the Third Doctor gets involved, in *The Dæmons* (1971). In fact, the barrow contains nothing of the sort, as the professor finds out to his cost. It is the resting place of Azal, last of the Dæmons. With the village cut off from the outside world by a heat barrier, and the Master masquerading as the local priest Reverend Magister, it is up to the Doctor and Jo Grant together with UNIT's Sergeant Benton and Captain Yates to stop the Master from gaining the Dæmon's awesome power.

**1965** *The Executioners* is the first episode of the third Dalek story *The Chase* – which includes the Beatles making a guest appearance (in the form of footage from their promotional film for *Ticket to Ride*).

**1971** *The Dæmons* Episode 1

**2010** The Silurians return to the new series in *The Hungry Earth*.

## 23 MAY

# Meet the Paternoster Gang

**1964** *The Temple of Evil* – the first episode of *The Aztecs*

**1970** *Inferno* Episode 3

The Doctor first met Madame Vastra in the second half of the nineteenth century. The Eleventh Doctor called upon her services in *A Good Man Goes to War* (2011), and they met again at various times in his eleventh incarnation – and indeed soon after his regeneration into his twelfth incarnation in *Deep Breath* (2014).

Madame Vastra was an intelligent reptile – the species sometimes referred to as Silurians or *Homo reptilia* that went into hibernation in prehistoric times. She was apparently awakened from her sleep by work on an extension to the London Underground system in the nineteenth century. The Doctor persuaded her to try to fit into Victorian human life, and she lived at 13 Paternoster Row in London with her maid (and wife) Jenny Flint, and the Sontaran Strax who acted as manservant. In public, she always wore a veil to conceal her true appearance.

Known as the Great Detective, Vastra offered her services as a consultant to Scotland Yard. Together with Jenny and Strax she also, of course, assisted the Doctor at various times including against the Great Intelligence in *The Snowmen* (2012), at the Yorkshire town of Sweetville in *The Crimson Horror* (2013), on Trenzalore in *The Name of the Doctor* (2013) and against clockwork robots after his regeneration in *Deep Breath*.

## 24 MAY

# The Time Lords Make Their Debut

For the first two incarnations of his life, the Doctor's background remained a mystery. In the very first story, *An Unearthly Child* (1963), the First Doctor tells Ian and Barbara that he and his granddaughter Susan are 'cut off' from their own planet. But the planet is not named and neither are the Doctor's people. Even when the First Doctor meets another renegade of his own race, the so-called Meddling Monk in *The Time Meddler* (1965), his companions Steven and Vicki learn little more about him.

It is not until *The War Games* (1969) that the Doctor confesses that he is a Time Lord. Forced to call on his own people for help, he tells Jamie and Zoe that the Time Lords are 'an immensely civilised race'. He also says that 'we can live for ever, barring accidents'. In fact, it is revealed in *The Deadly Assassin* (1976) that a Time Lord's life is limited to twelve regenerations – thirteen incarnations – although the Time Lords themselves can remove this limit.

In *The Time Warrior* (1973–1974), the Time Lords' planet is first named as Gallifrey. Over time other information has emerged – about Rassilon the founder of Time Lord society; about Omega the stellar engineer who provided the power for time travel at the cost, it seemed, of his own life; and about the Time Lords' war against the Great Vampires. The Doctor has met other renegade Time Lords too, most notably the Master but also the Rani, and his former school friend Drax, who he meets again in *The Armageddon Factor* (1979).

**1819** Queen Victoria was born.

**1969** The Time Lords are first mentioned by name in Episode 6 of *The War Games*.

## 25 MAY

# The Doctor Visits Metebelis Three

For a long time, the Third Doctor was keen to visit Metebelis Three, the famous blue planet of the Acteon Group. This was his first chosen destination once the Time Lords lifted his exile. However, the TARDIS instead landed inside a Miniscope in *Carnival of Monsters* (1973).

He is more successful in *The Green Death* (1973). But the planet on which he finds himself is not the blue-lit paradise he anticipated. The Doctor finds himself attacked by the hostile animal and plant life. He does manage to find one of the blue sapphires for which Metebelis Three is famous, but only just makes it back to the TARDIS alive…

The blue crystal turns out to be perhaps more trouble than it was worth as, in *Planet of the Spiders* (1974), it transpires that the giant spiders that live on Metebelis Three want the crystal back. The Doctor travels to the planet again to confront them. Here he finds a colony of humans descended from the colonists and explorers of an Earth spaceship that crashed on the planet 433 years earlier. An ordinary spider that was also on the ship was carried by the wind up into the mountains, where its mental capacity and physical size were enhanced by the blue crystals. The spiders continued to grow cleverer and larger until they were strong enough to enslave the humans.

## 26 MAY

# The Doctor Finds a Use for His Metebelis Crystal

The blue crystal that the Third Doctor brought back from Metebelis Three in *The Green Death* (1973) has the power to enhance and open the mind. The Doctor is able to use it to break the mental hold the megalomaniac computer BOSS has over Captain Mike Yates. Later he also uses it to break through the conditioning of Stevens – the head of Global Chemicals, whose mind is linked to the computer's.

When Jo Grant leaves UNIT to marry Cliff Jones, the Doctor gives them the crystal as a wedding present before the newly-wedded couple head off on an expedition up the Amazon. But in *Planet of the Spiders* (1974), Jo returns the crystal to the Doctor as the Amazonian natives believe it is cursed. Perhaps they are right – looking into the crystal, the psychic Professor Clegg sees images of giant spiders, and dies of heart failure. The crystal also increases the intelligence of the simple-minded Tommy, enabling him to read.

The spiders themselves are from Metebelis Three and want the crystal back. An enormous spider called the Great One needs the Doctor's crystal – the last perfect crystal of power – to complete a web of crystal she has woven. The web reproduces the pattern of its brain so that the creature's every thought will resonate within the web and grow in power. But the Doctor realises that the web is a positive feedback loop and when the Great One tries to increase its mental powers to infinity, the power destroys the spider.

ON THIS DAY

**1913** Peter Cushing, who played 'Dr Who' in the two 1960s movies *Dr Who and the Daleks* and *Daleks – Invasion Earth, 2150AD*, was born.

**1973** *The Green Death* Episode 2

**1974** *Planet of the Spiders* Part 4 is first shown on BBC Wales.

**2007** *Human Nature*. Together with its second episode *The Family of Blood*, this is the first televised *Doctor Who* to be adapted from an original *Doctor Who* novel – a Seventh Doctor novel also called *Human Nature*. Both the novel and the TV version were written by Paul Cornell.

The radiation from the crystal cave where the Great One lives also destroys the Third Doctor's body. He manages to get back to the TARDIS, which brings him 'home' to UNIT HQ. Here, with help from another Time Lord – the Doctor's old mentor – the Doctor regenerates into his fourth incarnation.

## 27 MAY

# Meet the Eighth Doctor

The Eighth Doctor is perhaps the most human of all – which is fitting for a Doctor who claims to be half-human. He may be joking with Professor Wagg when he says, in the TV movie *Doctor Who* (1996), that he is half human 'on my mother's side', but the Master certainly believes him to be half-human based on the evidence of his retina pattern. Of course, as the Doctor tells Grace that he can transform himself into another species when he regenerates, this does not necessarily mean that any of the Doctor's other incarnations are half-human or that it has anything to do with his parentage. But here is a Doctor who – whether in jest or not – is the first specifically to mention his father and mother.

In fact, the Eighth Doctor is more outgoing in many ways. He is not averse to kissing Grace, though what it means to him emotionally, if anything, is unclear. He seems open and honest about his feelings and fears. He gives the impression that he acts on a whim and on instinct.

But while his outlook and mannerisms may be more obviously human, underneath the Doctor remains the same. This is a Doctor who will stop at nothing to save the Earth and defeat the Master; who values life and enjoys living; who can achieve his ends in the most surprising and effective of ways – such as getting a policeman's motorbike by taking the man's gun and threatening to shoot *himself*.

This is a Doctor who, like every other, relishes the adventure and is willing to make the ultimate sacrifice to save others. But, at the end of the day, he is happy to get back to his cup of tea and a good book – whatever happens in between may be of universal import, but really it just gets in the way...

**1967** Victoria Waterfield first appears in Episode 2 of *The Evil of the Daleks*.

**1972** *The Time Monster* Episode 2

**1974** The edited compilation of *The Sea Devils* first shown on 27 December 1972 gets an unscheduled repeat when a cricket match between Yorkshire and Lancashire is rained off.

**1996** The first UK transmission of the TV movie *Doctor Who*, starring Paul McGann as the Eighth Doctor

**2006** *The Idiot's Lantern*

# 28 MAY

# The Empty Child Finds His Mummy

In *The Empty Child* and *The Doctor Dances* (2005), the Ninth Doctor meets a young girl called Nancy living on the blitzed streets of London in 1941. To survive, she and other street children steal food from the houses of people sheltering from air raids. The other children regard Nancy as their leader. But they are haunted by another child – a small boy wearing a gas mask, constantly asking for his mummy. This child can project his voice through any communications medium – the (unconnected) TARDIS telephone, a radio, even a music box and a typewriter.

In the nearby Albion Hospital, patients and staff have been 'infected' by the boy. First the doctors and nurses who treated the child were affected, then the other patients those doctors and nurses treated, and so on. Now the infected people have no life signs – but they do not die. Their faces obscured by gas masks, they too are searching for their mummy…

In fact, the infection is caused by nanogenes that have escaped from a crashed Chula medical spaceship. The nanogenes are tiny, microscopic devices programmed to repair Chula warriors on the battlefield. Believing the dead child to be 'normal' the nanogenes have used his body (the first they came into contact with) as a template for 'repairing' any other humans they encounter – fusing gas masks to the victims' faces, and recreating the exact same injuries…

The Doctor realises that the 'Empty Child' is actually Nancy's 'brother' Jamie. He was killed in an air raid, and

**1966** *The Savages* Episode 1 is the first episode not to be given an individual title until the series returns in 2005.

**1968** Kylie Minogue, who played Astrid in *Voyage of the Damned* (2007), was born.

**2005** *The Doctor Dances*

**2011** *The Almost People*

the nanogenes released in the crash have tried to cure him. Except that Jamie is not really Nancy's brother at all, but her son – she is the mother for whom he is so desperately searching…

## 29 MAY

# The Dæmons Experiment on Humanity

From the planet Damos, 60,000 light years away, the Dæmons first came to Earth nearly 100,000 years ago. Glimpsed throughout history, they have secretly helped Man to evolve and have entered myth as the traditional image of the Devil. Their psionic science has been part-remembered as magic and superstition. But to the Dæmons, human evolution and development is simply an experiment. If humanity fails that experiment, then the Dæmon left on Earth will destroy the world.

That Dæmon, as the Third Doctor discovers in *The Dæmons* (1971), is Azal, and his miniaturised spaceship is concealed within a burial mound just outside the aptly named village of Devil's End. He will appear three times, before deciding the fate of Earth – either he will destroy it, or he will pass on his great power… Azal has been summoned by the Master, who is posing as the local vicar – the Reverend Magister – and manipulating the local villagers.

With Devil's End cut off from the outside world by a heat barrier, the Brigadier and most of UNIT are unable to help. The Doctor, Jo Grant, Captain Yates and Sergeant Benton enlist the help of a local white witch – Miss Hawthorne – to combat not only the Master and the revived Dæmon, but also a grotesque animated stone statue, hostile villagers and homicidal Morris dancers…

**1965** *The Death of Time* – the second episode of *The Chase*

**1971** *The Dæmons* Episode 2

**2010** *Cold Blood*

## 30 MAY

# The Doctor Appears on Television

**1964** *The Warriors of Death* – the second episode of *The Aztecs*

**1970** *Inferno* Episode 4

Orbiting the Earth in the far future, Satellite Five is responsible for broadcasting 600 channels of constant news reports. In the time of the Fourth Great and Bountiful Human Empire, when the Ninth Doctor arrives on Satellite Five in *The Long Game* (2005), Earth itself is covered with mega-cities, has five moons, a population of 96 billion, and is the hub of a galactic domain stretching across a million planets and a million species. Satellite Five is where the news is gathered, written up, packaged, and sold. Nothing happens in the Human Empire without going through Satellite Five.

But Satellite Five has been hijacked by the Jagrafess, a giant creature that lives on Floor 500 and controls the satellite through the Editor. Although the Doctor destroys the Jagrafess, it is not until he returns a hundred years later that he discovers the Jagrafess was not working alone.

When he returns in *Bad Wolf* and *The Parting of the Ways* (2005), the Doctor finds that Satellite Five is now called the Game Station. Run by the Bad Wolf Corporation, it broadcasts not only news reports but game shows and reality TV to the enormous population of Earth – beaming the shows direct into people's eyeballs. Contestants in the shows are teleported from Earth – they are not volunteers, and anyone could be chosen at random at any time. The shows include a version of *Big Brother* on Channel 44,000, where the Doctor suddenly finds himself taking part. But when they are evicted, the housemates are killed. Sixty *Big Brother* Houses are run in parallel. The other gameshows also result in losing contestants being apparently being killed.

But, as Rose Tyler discovers when she loses on *The Weakest Link* (hosted by a robot called the Anne Droid), losers are not killed, but teleported away – to the Dalek fleet concealed in space. Here they are turned into Daleks.

## 31 MAY

# The Doctor Meets River Song

The relationship between the Doctor and River Song is complicated. When the Tenth Doctor first met the archaeologist in *Silence in the Library* (2008), River already knew him from having met his subsequent incarnations. In fact, the first time the Doctor met her, was when River Song died in *Forest of the Dead* (2008)…

Born as Melody Pond, River was the child of Amy Pond and Rory Williams. But she was kidnapped by Madame Kovarian and brainwashed into becoming an assassin – her target being the Doctor. River managed to overcome her brainwashing, although she did – apparently – kill the Eleventh Doctor at Lake Silencio.

The time paradox caused by the Doctor's death – or not – meant that all of time became 'stuck' at 5:02 p.m. on 22 April 2011. But the Doctor resolved the paradox when he replaced himself with a Teselecta robot that looked exactly like him – and which River shot.

Whether the Doctor and River Song are actually married is uncertain, as

the wedding took place – if indeed it did take place –
while time was stuck, in an aborted timeline in a world
that never really existed…

**1969** *The War Games*
Episode 7

**2008** River Song makes
her first appearance in
*Silence in the Library*.

# 1 JUNE

# Vincent van Gogh Sees a Monster

Born on 30 March 1853 in Zundert in the Netherlands, Vincent Willem van Gogh is according to some the greatest artist who ever lived. When the Eleventh Doctor and Amy Pond met him in *Vincent and the Doctor* (2010), the artist was nearing the end of his life – he would die the following month.

Van Gogh's unique way of viewing the world meant that he was the only person who could see an alien Krafayis. He included it in his painting of the Church at Auvers – in which the Doctor spotted it and decided to investigate. He and Amy travelled back to meet the painter – and deal with the alien creature. After this, they took Van Gogh to an exhibition of his own work in the present day at the Musée D'Orsay in Paris. Amy hoped this would lift Van Gogh out of his depressive moods and as a result he would live a longer, happier life. But it was not to be.

Throughout his life, Van Gogh suffered from anxiety attacks and mental illness. While this probably informed his art, it also left him frustrated when it meant he could not work. In Auvers-sur-Oise, on 29 July 1890, his illness finally got the better of him and Van Gogh took his own life. It is widely accepted that he shot himself, dying from the wound, although no gun was ever found. He was just 37 years old.

**1890** The events of *Vincent and the Doctor* start. (The main story takes place between 1 and 3 June.)

**1968** The last episode of *The Wheel in Space* brings Season 5 to a close. It ends with the Doctor showing Zoe the end of Episode 1 of *The Evil of the Daleks* as a warning of what she could be in for if she travels with him and Jamie. This leads into the first ever repeat broadcast of a full *Doctor Who* story – with *The Evil of the Daleks* Episode 1 being shown the following week.

**1974** *Planet of the Spiders* Part 5

## 2 JUNE

# The Wire Hijacks Television

Denied a real corporeal body by its own kind, the alien Wire came to Earth in a bolt of lightning. By feeding on the life force of human beings, it aimed to create its own body. It fed on the electrical activity of the brain, taking people's essence – and leaving them mindless and without their faces.

When the Tenth Doctor and Rose Tyler encounter it in *The Idiot's Lantern* (2006), the Wire exists in the electrical circuits and valves of televisions, reaching out from TV sets sold by Mr Magpie for its victims. Magpie runs a shop selling televisions, gramophones and other electrical goods. But business is not going well – until the Wire helps. Having taken over Magpie through his television, the Wire allowed him his face back provided he helped it by selling as many televisions as possible.

The Wire planned to plug into the main television transmitter at Alexandra Palace using a portable device built by Magpie, and reach out to everyone watching television. With the coronation of Queen Elizabeth II destined to be the greatest television event so far in history, millions of people would fall victim to the Wire – and supply the creature with the life essence it needed…

**1866** The Doctor and Jamie arrive at Theodore Maxtible's house near Canterbury in *The Evil of the Daleks*, having been brought back from 1966 by Edward Waterfield on the orders of the Daleks.

**1890** The main events of *Vincent and the Doctor* take place between 1 and 3 June.

**1953** The coronation of Elizabeth II – and the events of *The Idiot's Lantern*.

**1973** *The Green Death* Episode 3

**1974** *Planet of the Spiders* Part 5 is first shown on BBC Wales.

**1997** *The Eight Doctors* by Terrance Dicks is the first original *Doctor Who* novel published by BBC Books. Previous *Doctor Who* novels had been published by Virgin Publishing.

**2007** *The Family of Blood*

# 3 JUNE

# The Ood Suffer from the 'Red Eye'

First encountered by the Tenth Doctor and Rose Tyler in *The Impossible Planet* (2006), the Ood are a humanoid race from the Ood-Sphere, close to the planet Sense-Sphere, which is home to a similar race, the Sensorites (encountered by the First Doctor). A passive race, the Ood offer themselves as a basic slave race – and without orders they pine away and die. The Ood do not speak, but communicate with each other telepathically. They hold translation spheres, connected to their heads, in order to speak to humans. The sphere translates for them, and converts their thoughts to speech.

But some Ood are afflicted with a condition that turns their eyes red and makes them suddenly violent and unreasoning. When the Tenth Doctor and Donna arrived on the Ood-Sphere in *Planet of the Ood* (2008), the Red Eye was taking hold and more and more Ood were turning hostile. But when the Doctor examined 'raw' Ood before they were prepared for sale, he found that instead of the translation sphere, the Ood naturally have a second brain – a hind-brain – which they hold in their hands. Ood Operations removed this before selling the Ood – in effect mentally crippling the creatures.

Realising that there must be a third component in their make-up, the Doctor discovered an enormous brain which should have connected all the Ood together in telepathic harmony. But the owners of Ood Operations had found the brain two centuries earlier and set up a psychic barrier to break the connection between the Brain and the Ood…

**1890** The main events of *Vincent and the Doctor* take place between 1 and 3 June.

**1967** *The Evil of the Daleks* Episode 3. It is Gerry Davis's last episode as Story Editor.

**1972** *The Time Monster* Episode 3

**2006** The Ood make their first appearance in *The Impossible Planet*.

## 4 JUNE

# Demons Run When a Good Man Goes to War

Whether the asteroid is actually named Demon's Run or Demons Run is uncertain. But the most plausible explanation for its name is that it comes from the saying: 'Demons run when a good man goes to war.'

It was on Demons Run that Madame Kovarian made her base in the fifty-second century when she planned to assassinate the Doctor. She kidnapped Amy Pond and brought her to Demons Run – where her child, Melody (later known as River Song) was born. The real Amy was replaced with a 'Ganger' copy made from the substance Flesh.

Realising what had happened, the Eleventh Doctor and Rory led an attack on Demons Run in *A Good Man Goes to War* (2011) to rescue Amy. The Doctor assembled a force of allies from across time and space to attack Demons Run, which was defended by Anglican Marines, led by Colonel Manton and a group of Headless Monks.

While the Doctor's forces were the victors in the so-called Battle of Demons Run, Madame Kovarian escaped, taking the baby Melody with her.

ON THIS DAY

**1926** The SS *Bernice* vanishes two days out from Bombay, according to the Doctor in *Carnival of Monsters*.

**1966** *The Savages* Episode 2

**2005** *Boom Town*

**2011** *A Good Man Goes to War* closes the first section of Series Six.

# 5 JUNE

## Identifying the Time Rotor

A component of the TARDIS, the Time Rotor is generally thought to be the central column of the main control console. But when it is first mentioned by the First Doctor's companion Vicki in *The Chase* (1965), she appears to be pointing to a control on one of the console instrument panels which apparently slows down when the TARDIS is landing.

In *The Edge of Destruction* (1964) the First Doctor refers to the central column of the console as simply 'the column'. The heart of the TARDIS, he explains, is under this column. When the column moves, it proves the extent of the power thrust. If the column were to come out of the console completely, the power would be free to escape. The Doctor says that if you felt the power 'you wouldn't live to speak of it. You'd be blown to atoms in a split-second.'

But over the years, the Time Rotor does seem to have become the term for the central column. In *Meglos* (1980), Romana suggests stopping the Time Rotor in order to escape from a chronic hysteresis – a sort of time loop. In *Terminus* (1983), the Black Guardian orders Turlough to remove the TARDIS's Space-Time Element, which will cause the Time Rotor to jam.

**1965** *Flight Through eternity* – the third episode of *The Chase*. This is the first episode in which the TARDIS Time Rotor is mentioned.

**1971** *The Dæmons* Episode 3

**2010** *Vincent and the Doctor*

**2012** Caroline John, who played the Third Doctor's assistant Liz Shaw, died.

# 6 JUNE

# Changing the Interior Design

**1964** *The Bride of Sacrifice* – the third episode of *The Aztecs*

**1970** *Inferno* Episode 5

Just as the exterior of the TARDIS would be able to change if the time machine's Chameleon Circuit were working, so the interior can change as well. Over the years, the interior of the TARDIS has changed in appearance and layout, and in *The Masque of Mandragora* (1976) the Fourth Doctor implies to Sarah that the interior is infinite in size.

The TARDIS Console Room has changed several times, although the basic layout of a chamber housing a central control console has remained constant. In *The Ambassadors of Death* (1970), the Third Doctor actually removed the central console from the TARDIS in order to try to repair it. In the following story, *Inferno* (1970), he took the console to the Inferno Project. There, he managed to make a trip sideways in time to a parallel world using just the console.

In *The Masque of Mandragora*, the Doctor introduced Sarah to the TARDIS's Secondary Control Room – a rather smaller chamber clad in wood panelling, with a small control console (with no central column). Perhaps the biggest changes to the TARDIS Console Room were for the more 'open-plan' design of the *Doctor Who* TV movie (1996), and subsequently for *Rose* (2005). Since then, the TARDIS main control room has changed again several times, but always retaining the central control console.

# 7 JUNE

## The Vashta Nerada Take Over the Library

The Piranhas of the Air, or the Shadows that Melt the Flesh, the Vashta Nerada are a swarm of darkness itself. The Vashta Nerada can hide in any shadow, any patch of darkness. They can actually *be* any shadow or patch of darkness. If you have more than one shadow, then it's possible the Vashta Nerada already have you. They can tear the flesh from a living being in an instant, and animate the remaining husk of a body.

The Vashta Nerada hatch from spores gathered in living wood, becoming a swarm in minutes. The spores can survive inside the wood when the tree dies – which means they can live in paper made from the wood pulp. They can live inside books…

This is how they have invaded The Library, as the Tenth Doctor discovers in *Silence in the Library* and *Forest of the Dead* (2008). So big that it's simply called 'The Library', the facility covers a whole world, keeping specially printed copies of every book ever written. The core of the planet is a giant computer that maintains the facility and operates the Information Nodes.

But when the Doctor visits The Library it has been deserted and abandoned for a hundred years. It is dark and empty and no one knows why. So the owner, Strackman Lux, has brought an expedition to find out what happened – an expedition led by Professor River Song.

The Library's main computer is called CAL – which actually stands for Charlotte Abigail Lux. Charlotte's father built her the library when she was dying, and put the girl's digitised mind into the computer to

**1969** *The War Games* Episode 8

**1977** Queen Elizabeth II's Silver Jubilee – and Tegan meets the Brigadier in *Mawdryn Undead*.

**2008** *Forest of the Dead*

keep her 'alive'. The girl lives inside a virtual world –
sometimes dreaming of The Library – watched over
by Doctor Moon, who is actually another aspect of the
computer system...

When the Vashta Nerada came, Charlotte 'saved' the
minds of all the people inside the computer with her.

## 8 JUNE

# The Regeneration Game

'Life depends on change and renewal,' the Second Doctor tells Polly and Ben in *The Power of the Daleks* (1966) just after he has regenerated. But it is not until just before the Third Doctor regenerates that the term is actually used in *Planet of the Spiders* (1974).

In *The War Games* (1969), the Second Doctor tells Jamie and Zoe that Time Lords can live for ever, barring accidents. But in *The Deadly Assassin* (1976), it is stated that Time Lords are limited to a cycle of twelve regenerations – thirteen incarnations. This is presumably an artificial limit, however. Certainly, the Master intends to cheat it by using the power from the Eye of Harmony. He doesn't completely succeed, but he is able to use the power of the Keeper in *The Keeper of Traken* (1981) to 'steal' the body of Tremas for himself. The Time Lords also offer the Master a new regeneration

cycle in *The Five Doctors* (1983), and the Doctor himself has managed – with Time Lord help – to outlive the limit: he is granted new regenerations by the Time Lords in *The Time of the Doctor* (2013).

The process of regeneration is a traumatic one for the Doctor. Following most of his regenerations, the Doctor becomes rather erratic and even more unpredictable and acerbic than usual. The newly regenerated Sixth Doctor even tries to strangle his companion Peri, convinced she is evil, in *The Twin Dilemma* (1984).

Even though his appearance may change, once he has settled into his new body and persona, the Doctor remains the same intensely moral and caring character.

**1943** Colin Baker, who played the Sixth Doctor, was born.

**1968** The first repeat run of a full *Doctor Who* story begins with a reshowing of Episode 1 of *The Evil of the Daleks*.

**1974** *Planet of the Spiders* Part 6 is Jon Pertwee's last episode as the Third Doctor and closes Season 11. It is also the last episode to feature Mike Yates, and the first episode to refer to the process of 'regeneration' by name.

# 9 JUNE

# The Doctor is Lucky He's Not Scared of Spiders

As the Third Doctor learns in *Planet of the Spiders* (1974), some time in the future, an Earth spacecraft crashed on the planet Metebelis Three, and the survivors were forced to settle on the planet. But an ordinary spider from the ship found its way into the mountains of blue crystal that could enhance the power of the mind… The spiders became cleverer and larger, and eventually used their power over the human mind to take control of the settlers.

Many years later, a psychic link from present-day Earth to Metebelis Three enables the spiders to seek out the last perfect crystal of power that was taken by the Third Doctor on a visit to Metebelis Three in *The Green Death* (1973). Ruled by Queen Huath, the spiders are seeking the crystal on the instructions of the Great One – an enormous spider that still lives in a crystal cave in the mountains. She needs the crystal to complete a crystalline matrix that will amplify her own brain waves and make her the most powerful creature in existence…

The Metebelis Spiders can control humans telepathically. The controlling spider jumps onto the back of a human 'host' and becomes invisible to other people. While exerting a telepathic influence, the spider inflicts mental pain to subdue its host. Strong-minded people, like the ex-salesman Lupton who steal the Doctor's crystal, can fight back and regain control. Sarah also manages to throw off a spider when helped to fight it by the Doctor and K'anpo – who is actually a retired Time Lord.

The Twelfth Doctor also encounters giant spider-like creatures, in *Kill the Moon* (2014), but these are huge bacteria.

**68** The Roman Emperor Nero died.

**1781** George Stephenson was born.

**1870** Charles Dickens died.

**1973** *The Green Death* Episode 4

**1974** *Planet of the Spiders* Part 6 is first shown on BBC Wales.

**2007** The Weeping Angels make their first appearance in *Blink*.

# 10 JUNE

# Telepathic Circuits

The TARDIS's Telepathic Circuits have many and varied uses. In *The Time Monster* (1972), the Third Doctor is able to use them to contact Jo Grant inside the TARDIS when he is stranded out in the Time Vortex. In the same story, the Master uses them to feed the Doctor's words back to him before he speaks them, making them come out backwards.

In *Frontier in Space* (1973), the wounded Third Doctor uses the Telepathic Circuits to send a message to the Time Lords asking for their help in directing the TARDIS after a Dalek spaceship. The Telepathic Circuits also help the Eleventh Doctor and the TARDIS itself – in the form of Idris – to communicate with Rory Williams and defeat the entity known as House.

The Doctor has also used the Telepathic Circuits to extract information from his companions. The Eleventh Doctor retrieves the coordinates of Trenzalore from Clara Oswald in *The Name of the Doctor* (2013). Once there, the Telepathic Circuits of the dying TARDIS awaken in Clara's mind the memories of an aborted timeline. The Twelfth Doctor also uses the Telepathic Circuits to delve into Clara's mind to find Danny Pink in *Dark Water* (2014). Clara herself uses them to operate the TARDIS in *Listen* (2014).

The Telepathic Circuits also fulfil another vital function. They translate local languages for the TARDIS travellers, enabling them to communicate with other cultures and life forms throughout all of time and space.

**1967** *The Evil of the Daleks* Episode 4 is Peter Bryant's first episode as Story Editor.

**1972** *The Time Monster* Episode 4 is the first episode in which the TARDIS's Telepathic Circuits are mentioned.

**2006** *The Satan Pit*

**2008** David Brierley, who provided the voice of K-9 for the Season 17 stories *The Creature from the Pit*, *Nightmare of Eden* and *The Horns of Nimon*, died.

# 11 JUNE

## Who's Afraid of the Big Bad Wolf?

The words 'Bad Wolf' seemed to follow Rose Tyler from soon after she met the Ninth Doctor. A throwaway line in *The End of the World* (2005) became more explicit in Victorian Cardiff. In *The Unquiet Dead* (2005), the psychic Gwyneth tells Rose: 'And you, you've flown so far. Further than anyone. The things you've seen. The darkness, the big bad wolf…'

After that, the words cropped up repeatedly – amongst others things, as Van Statten's helicopter call sign in *Dalek* (2005), graffitied on the TARDIS in *Aliens of London* and *World War Three* (2005), as a TV channel in *The Long Game*, and – in Welsh – as the name of a power station project in *Boom Town* (2005)…

Not until *Bad Wolf* and *The Parting of the Ways* (2005) did Rose – and the Doctor – learn the significance of 'Bad Wolf'. The Bad Wolf Corporation ran the Game Station, where the Doctor became trapped facing the Daleks. With Rose and the TARDIS stuck back on Earth, Rose saw the words painted everywhere. She took this is as a message meaning that she could get back to the Game Station and save the Doctor. She was right – it was a message sent back through time by Rose herself when imbued with the energy of the Time Vortex after she looked into the heart of the TARDIS.

In *Turn Left* (2008), 'Bad Wolf' was also the message that Rose gave Donna to pass to the Doctor – a warning that the end of the universe was coming. In *The Day of the Doctor* (2013), the sentient weapon the Moment assumes Rose's appearance. She tells the War Doctor that in this form she is called 'Bad Wolf'.

# 12 JUNE

## Craig Owens Gets a Lodger

The Eleventh Doctor met Craig Owens when he moved into Craig's flat in Colchester as his lodger in *The Lodger* (2010). Craig's previous lodger, Mark, apparently received an unexpected inheritance from a previously unknown uncle. The Doctor was keen to lodge in Craig's flat as he knew there was something odd about the upper floor.

Although it took a while for Craig to trust and like the Doctor – as well as a telepathic insight into the Doctor's true nature and history – the two became friends. Together, with help from Craig's friend Sophie, they discovered and dealt with an alien time ship disguised as the upper storey of Craig's building. In doing so, Craig declared his love for Sophie.

When the Doctor met Craig again in *Closing Time* (2011), he and Sophie were living together in a new house with their baby son Alfie. With Sophie away on holiday, the Doctor helped Craig look after Alfie. In return Craig helped the Doctor investigate mysterious disappearances in the area. He traced these to a department store, underneath which was a crashed Cybership – the Cybermen, and a Cybermat, having once more become active…

**1965** *Journey into Terror* – the fourth episode of *The Chase*

**1971** *The Dæmons* Episode 4

**2010** Craig Owens makes his first appearance in *The Lodger*.

# 13 JUNE

## Doctor Grace Holloway Meets Another Doctor

Grace Holloway was a cardiologist working at the walker General Hospital in San Francisco. She was on call on the night of 30 December 1999 when the Seventh Doctor was brought into the hospital, having been caught in a crossfire between rival gangs in the *Doctor Who* TV movie (1996). Leaving the opera, she operated on the Doctor, but his alien physiognomy and two hearts meant she was unable to save his life.

The Doctor regenerated in the hospital morgue, and the new Eighth Doctor found Grace. Although she initially thought the Doctor was mad – and obviously not the same man that she had operated on – she gradually came to believe his warnings that the Master was about to destroy the world.

Grace was taken over by the Master for a while, and actually died during the Doctor's final confrontation with the Master at the Eye of Harmony inside the TARDIS. But, as they were inside the TARDIS, the Doctor was able to roll back time and revive Grace along with Chang Lee, who had also been killed. Grace declined the Doctor's invitation to travel with him in the TARDIS…

ON THIS DAY

**1964** *The Day of Darkness* – the fourth episode of *The Aztecs*

**1970** *Inferno* Episode 6

# 14 JUNE

# Learning the Truth Behind the War Games

Arriving in what they thought was No Man's Land between the trenches of the First World War in *The War Games* (1969), it didn't take the Second Doctor and his companions Jamie and Zoe long to realise that something was very wrong. The people they met seemed unable to remember what happened to them more than a few days ago, and passing through a strange mist the Doctor and his friends found themselves on different battlefields – from Roman times to the American Civil War.

Eventually, the Doctor discovered that a race of aliens led by the War Lord had brought the humans from different time zones to continue to fight each other, believing they were still embroiled in their own wars. With help from another renegade Time Lord – the War Chief – who provided limited time-travel technology, the War Lord and his people planned to use the survivors of the conflicts – the strongest and most adept of the humans – to form a huge army of their own.

Teaming up with a resistance group of human soldiers whose mental conditioning had failed, the Doctor organised an attack on the alien headquarters hidden in the middle of the war zones. But to return the thousands of humans to their own time, the Doctor was forced – for the first time – to call on his own people, the Time Lords, for help.

**1925** George Cranleigh's funeral is held following the events of *Black Orchid*.

**1963** Verity Lambert starts work as the first Producer of *Doctor Who* on this date, with Mervyn Pinfield as her Associate Producer.

**1969** *The War Games* Episode 9

**2008** *Midnight*

# 15 JUNE

# When Two are Osgood as One

A scientist working for UNIT and reporting directly to UNIT's Chief Scientific Officer Kate Stewart, Petronella Osgood was an expert on the Doctor's time with UNIT. Respecting him to the point of being a 'fan', Osgood even dressed to reflect this – wearing a long multicoloured scarf rather like the Fourth Doctor wore, and a bow tie like the Eleventh Doctor's.

She was almost overcome when she finally met the Eleventh Doctor in *The Day of the Doctor* (2013). During the course of events, Osgood had her body print copied by a Zygon. After the Doctor brokered a peace between humans and Zygons, the Zygon Osgood remained in human form – with no one able to tell which was which. One of the Osgoods was killed by Missy in *Death in Heaven* (2014), but it is not clear whether it was the human or the Zygon.

The surviving Osgood was captured by a breakaway faction of Zygons that wished to take over Earth from the humans in *The Zygon Invasion* and *The Zygon Inversion* (2015). To execute their plan, the Zygons wanted the so-called Osgood Box which the Doctor created and left in the care of the two Osgoods. Opening the box would, the Zygons believed, give them the power to make every Zygon disguised in human form revert to its true appearance, forcing a confrontation between the two races.

Once again the Twelfth Doctor resolved matters, with help from Osgood. And with another Zygon taking her form, once again two Osgoods were left responsible for maintaining the peace.

**1215** Magna Carta is signed – despite the Master's efforts – in *The King's Demons*.

**1964** The first ever location filming took place for *Doctor Who*. It consisted of inserts of actor Brian Proudfoot doubling for William Hartnell as the First Doctor walking towards Paris for the story *The Reign of Terror*.

# 16 JUNE

# Professor Yana is Not Who He Seems

The Tenth Doctor, Martha Jones and Captain Jack Harkness met Professor Yana on the planet Malcassairo in *Utopia* (2007). What they did not know – and Yana himself did not know – was that Professor Yana did not exist. The Doctor worked this out when he realised that YANA stood for 'You Are Not Alone' – the message given to him by the dying Face of Boe in *Gridlock* (2007).

Having fled from the Great Time War, the Master used a Chameleon Arch to change into human form. This was the same Time Lord technology that the Tenth Doctor himself had used to become the human John Smith to hide from the Family of Blood in *Human Nature* (2007). So far as Yana recalled, he had been found in the Silver Devastation with only a silver fob watch and spent his life on refugee ships. On Malcassairo, Yana worked with the insectoid Malmooth scientist Chantho to build a rocket that would take the last remnants of humanity to Utopia.

But after he opened the fob watch, the Master's true identity and persona were reinstated. He killed Chantho, but before she died she managed to shoot him. Fatally injured, he managed to get into the Doctor's TARDIS, where he regenerated into the form that would masquerade as Harold Saxon…

**1940** Carole Ann Ford, who played the First Doctor's granddaughter Susan, was born.

**1965** The feature film *Dr Who and the Daleks* was certified by the BBFC.

**1973** *The Green Death* Episode 5

**2007** The Master returns – played initially by Derek Jacobi – in *Utopia*.

# 17 JUNE

## Elton Pope Finally Finds the Doctor

When he was a child, Elton Pope saw the Tenth Doctor one night in his house. That moment was etched in his memory – not least, as that was the night Elton's mother died. There was a living shadow in the Popes' house, an elemental shade that had escaped from the Howling Halls. The Doctor stopped it, but was too late to save Elton's mother. From that first glimpse of the Doctor, Elton Pope became fascinated by him, and yearned to discover more about the mysterious wanderer in time and space.

Years later, as seen in *Love & Monsters* (2006), Elton tried to track down the Doctor, joining up with others who also tried to find him. They became firm friends, and named themselves LINDA – a name made up by Elton which stood for *London Investigation 'N' Detective Agency*. Made up of Mr Skinner, Ursula Blake, Bliss, Bridget and Elton, the group started out trying to discover everything they could about the Doctor. But as they became friends, they got distracted – Mr Skinner read extracts from a novel he was writing, Bliss showed off her sculpture, Bridget supplied home-cooked food… They even formed a band to perform old ELO hits.

The arrival of the mysterious Victor Kennedy refocused them on finding the Doctor – but with disastrous consequences. Kennedy was actually an alien, dubbed the 'Abzorbaloff', also intent on finding the Doctor and absorbing him to gain his knowledge and experience. All of the group was absorbed into the creature except Elton, who finally got to meet the

**1967** *The Evil of the Daleks* Episode 5

**1972** *The Time Monster* Episode 5

**1982** Arthur Darvill, who played the Eleventh Doctor's companion Rory Williams, was born.

**2006** *Love & Monsters* is the first 'Doctor-light' episode of the revived series, shot alongside another episode to save time. It features the Abzorbaloff, which had won a *Blue Peter* Design-A-Monster competition.

Doctor properly and learn the truth about his mother's death. The Doctor was also able to rescue part of Elton's best friend Ursula – just her face, embedded in a paving slab – when the Abzorbaloff disintegrated…

# 18 JUNE

## Meet the Tenth Doctor

At the end of *The Parting of the Ways* (2005), the Ninth Doctor absorbed the Time Vortex energy from Rose Tyler into himself so as to save her. But the energy was too much even for the Doctor, and he was forced to regenerate into his tenth incarnation.

For the most part the Tenth Doctor displayed a joy of life that contrasted with the dark, more introspective moments of his predecessor. But this incarnation was also a Doctor of extremes. His mood could turn in a moment. Faced with injustice or cruelty, the mild, witty façade dropped away to reveal someone who would offer no compromise, no second chances. For all his humour and evident love of humanity and tenderness towards his friends, the Tenth Doctor could be more dangerous and ruthless than any other. As a result, more than one of his enemies underestimated him.

But, unlike many of his opponents, the Doctor knew the extremes of his capability. At times, he scared himself – and understood just how much he needed first Rose, and later Martha Jones and Donna Noble to keep him in check. When he became human as John Smith on Earth in 1913 in *Human Nature* (2007), it was not because he was scared of what the Family of Blood would do if they found him. He was scared of what he himself would do to them.

Fittingly, just as this Doctor was born out of the self-sacrifice of his predecessor, so the Tenth Doctor's time came to an end when he exposed himself to lethal radiation to save the life of Donna's grandfather Wilf Mott in *The End of Time, Part Two* (2010), and he was forced once again to regenerate…

ON THIS DAY

**1966** The fourth and final episode of *The Savages* is Steven Taylor's last episode.

**1973** Roger Delgado, who was the first actor to play the Master throughout the Third Doctor's era, was killed in a road accident in Turkey.

**2005** *The Parting of the Ways* is Christopher Eccleston's final episode as the Ninth Doctor. It introduces David Tennant as the Tenth Doctor, and closes Series One. It is the last episode on which Mal Young is an Executive Producer.

## 19 JUNE

# The Doctor and the Daleks Encounter the Mechonoids

Encountered by the First Doctor on the planet Mechanus in *The Chase* (1965), the Mechonoids were robots sent from Earth to prepare colony planets for future human habitation. They are geodesic spheres, about six feet across. The Mechonoids have been on the planet for about fifty years. They were programmed to clear landing sites and get everything ready for the first immigrants. But Earth got involved in interplanetary wars, and the colonists never arrived.

Mechanus is a swampy, jungle planet where the huge mushroom-like plants are alive and can move. The Mechonoids have built a huge city that stands on stilts some 1,500 feet above the ground. It comprises a main 'hub' with a limb off it and many ramps and walkways.

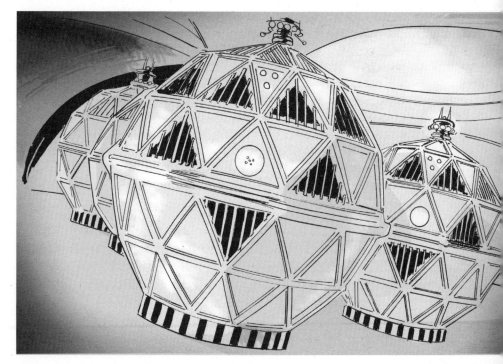

Without the access codes the colonists would have used to control the Mechonoids, the Doctor and his companions – along with a crashed spaceship pilot called Steven Taylor – are treated as specimens for study.

The Doctor notes that the Mechonoids are 'programmed to do their own repairs', and Steven warns that 'at the first sign of violence towards them, the Mechonoids destroy'. As a result, the Mechonoids fight back when the force of Daleks pursuing the TARDIS enters their city. The Mechonoids are armed with flame throwers that emerge from their side and which can burn through the Daleks' casings.

The Daleks know the planet is Mechanus and later get a report on the Mechons (as they call the Mechonoids) from Skaro. The Daleks' own guns can blow the Mechonoids apart to reveal the robotic circuitry within.

**1965** A Mechonoid first appears at the end of the fifth episode of *The Chase*, titled *The Death of Doctor Who*. Despite being given a big press build-up, the Mechonoids have not returned (so far) – except in the pages of the 1960s comic *TV Century 21* and the book *The Dalek World* published in 1965.

**1971** The Master is captured by UNIT in the fifth and final episode of *The Dæmons*, which closes Season 8.

**2010** *The Pandorica Opens*

# 20 JUNE

# Liz Shaw Becomes UNIT's First Scientific Adviser

The Third Doctor was not in fact UNIT's first scientific adviser – that was Doctor Elizabeth Shaw. But once the Doctor joined the UNIT team, Liz Shaw soon realised that he was her superior in knowledge and intellect and tended to defer to him.

Liz Shaw had an important research programme going ahead at Cambridge when she was invited to join UNIT in *Spearhead from Space* (1970). The Brigadier had decided he needed a scientific adviser and Liz was an expert in meteorites, with degrees in 'medicine, physics, and a dozen other subjects'.

Perhaps not surprisingly, Liz was initially sceptical of the Brigadier's stories about 'little blue men with three heads', telling him that 'I deal with facts, not science fiction ideas'. But after meeting the Doctor – and experiencing the events of the attempted Nestene invasion – she was more willing to accept the unexpected.

Although she did not spend much time as the Doctor's colleague, Liz demonstrated her scientific and medical abilities on many occasions and he soon came to regard her almost as an equal. They also shared a mutual distrust and dislike of military organisation and discipline.

Perhaps this was one of the reasons why, following the events at the Inferno project in *Inferno* (1970), Liz decided to return to Cambridge and continue with her research.

**ON THIS DAY**

**1964** *Strangers in Space* – the first episode of *The Sensorites*

**1970** Liz Shaw's final episode is Episode 7 of *Inferno*, which also closes Season 7.

**1991** *Timewrym: Genesys* by John Peel is published by Virgin Books. It is the first of their *New Adventures* series of original *Doctor Who* fiction.

# 21 JUNE

# The Doctor Stands Trial

At the end of *The War Games* (1969), having defeated the War Lord and his people, the Second Doctor faced a problem. There were thousands – possibly tens of thousands – of humans who needed to be returned to their own time zones on Earth. This was not something that the Doctor could manage on his own, even if his TARDIS was working properly. So he was forced to call for help from his own people – the Time Lords.

The Doctor hoped he could get away before the Time Lords arrived. But while he did manage to get to the TARDIS, he was unable to escape. The TARDIS was brought back to the Time Lords' planet, and the Doctor was put on trial.

For his crimes, the War Lord was dematerialised – his whole time line erased from reality, so that it was as if he had never existed. The Doctor's crimes were less serious – he had intervened in the affairs of other peoples and worlds. His defence was that the Time Lords themselves were at fault for failing to use their great powers to help those in need. Using a thought channel, the Doctor showed the Time Lords some of the evils he had fought while the Time Lords were merely content to watch – Daleks, Cybermen, Yeti, Quarks, Ice Warriors…

Although they found the Doctor guilty, the Time Lords did accept that there was evil in the universe that had to be fought, and that he still had a part to play. They exiled the Doctor to a particularly vulnerable planet at a time when it was attracting unwanted attention from other races – Earth in the late twentieth century. They also changed the Doctor's appearance, forcing him to regenerate into his third incarnation.

ON THIS DAY

**1969** Episode 10 of *The War Games* is the last regular appearance of the Second Doctor, played by Patrick Troughton. His companions Jamie and Zoe also leave.

**2008** *Turn Left*

## 22 JUNE

# Singing a Venusian Lullaby

Although so far as we know the Doctor never actually visited the planet Venus in his third incarnation, the Third Doctor was an expert in and a devotee of Venusian culture and tradition. He was a master of the martial art Venusian Aikido, using it against various enemies and a multitude of situations. In *The Green Death* (1973) he finishes telling an anecdote with the advice: 'Never trust a Venusian Shanghorn with a Perigosto Stick.' Though quite what this means is never explained.

The Doctor also knows at least one old Venusian lullaby, and has put it to good use on several occasions. The first line – 'Klokleda partha mennin klatch' – apparently means, roughly translated, 'Close your eyes my darling, well three of them at least.'

In *The Dæmons* (1971), the Doctor quotes this line as if it is a spell at the animated gargoyle Bok when it has him trapped with Jo inside the Devil's Hump barrow. Although the Doctor himself does not believe in magic, Bok does and is scared off.

In both *The Curse of Peladon* (1972) and *The Monster of Peladon* (1974), the Doctor sings the lullaby – to the tune of 'God Rest You Merry Gentlemen' – to Aggedor. Coupled with the hypnotic powers of a spinning mirror device the Doctor has created, this calms the savage beast.

ON THIS DAY

**1967** *Radio Times* included an interview with actor Marius Goring who was appearing as Theodore Maxtible in *The Evil of the Daleks*.

**1973** Katy Manning, who played the Third Doctor's companion Jo Grant, appeared on BBC1 magazine programme *Nationwide*.

## 23 JUNE

# Harold Saxon is the Master

As Defence Secretary, Harold Saxon ordered the attack that destroyed the Empress of the Racnoss's Webstar spaceship in *The Runaway Bride* (2006). A politician, investor, and philanthropist he was also a principal investor in LazLabs in *The Lazarus Experiment* (2007).

But Harold Saxon is a myth – he doesn't really exist. He is in fact the Master, having returned to Earth in *Utopia* (2007) in the Doctor's TARDIS some time previously. The Master gave himself a fictional background – a childhood, schooling, a degree from Cambridge University, athletic prowess, a successful business career before entering politics… He even wrote a novel – *Kiss Me, Kill Me*. While working on this book he met his future wife – Lucy Saxon.

One of the very few people to remain unaffected by the Master's mesmeric influence and to discover that Harold Saxon had no real past was *Sunday Mirror* journalist Vivien Rook. But she tried to warn Lucy Saxon in *The Sound of Drums* (2007), who already knew the truth about her husband, and the Master had her killed.

Once he became Prime Minister, 'Saxon' assassinated his cabinet, and then claimed to have made contact with benevolent aliens. He set up a meeting on the airborne *Valiant* attended by himself and the President of the USA. But it was a trap, and the Toclafane – as the Master called the aliens – killed the President before billions of them appeared to wipe out a tenth of the Earth's population.

**ON THIS DAY**

**1973** Jo Grant leaves in the sixth and final episode of *The Green Death*, which closes Season 10.

**2007** *The Sound of Drums* features John Simm as the Master.

## 24 JUNE

# Kronos Destroys Atlantis

A nightmare about the Master leads the Third Doctor to investigate the scientific project TOMTIT – Transmission Of Matter Through Interstitial Time – which can break down solid objects and transmit them from one place to another in *The Time Monster* (1972). The project is being run by Professor Thascales – who is in fact the Master.

The Master plans to summon and control Kronos – a Chronovore. These are creatures that exist outside Space-Time. The Doctor describes the Chronovores as 'time-eaters, who will swallow a life as quickly as a boa-constrictor can swallow a rabbit, fur and all'.

Kronos exists in Greek myth (spelled 'Chronos') as a Titan who ate his children. As the Doctor points out, one of these children was Poseidon, the god of Atlantis. Kronos was in fact a 'living legend', drawn into real time four thousand years ago by the priests of Atlantis using a powerful crystal to summon the creature.

The Doctor and Jo follow the Master back to Atlantis, where the Master usurps power from the aged King Dalios. But the Master is unable to control Kronos, who destroys the city.

ON THIS DAY

**1963** David Whitaker had been appointed *Doctor Who*'s first Story Editor by this date.

**1967** *The Evil of the Daleks* Episode 6

**1972** The sixth and last episode of *The Time Monster* brings Season 9 to a close.

**2006** *Fear Her*

## 25 JUNE

# Polly Joins the TARDIS

When the First Doctor meets Polly in *The War Machines* (1966), she is working as secretary to Professor Brett – the creator of WOTAN, a computer that uses mobile War Machines to try to take over London. At the end of the story, Polly and sailor Ben Jackson deliver a message to the Doctor from his companion Dodo, who has decided to stay behind in London. They also have her TARDIS key to return, and let themselves into the TARDIS with it – just as it dematerialises…

Polly's surname is never stated on screen, but Ben sometimes calls her 'Duchess' because of her upper class accent and sophistication. Polly has no qualms about using her feminine appeal to advantage – for example to enlist the help of Algernon ffinch in *The Highlanders* (1966–1967).

But she is more than just a pretty face. *In The Moonbase* (1967), it is Polly who realises that the plastic components of the Cybermen can be attacked with solvents just as nail varnish remover dissolves the plastic of nail varnish. It is the more practical Ben who comes up with a means of delivering the solvents using fire extinguishers.

Polly has a deep affection for Ben, although she masks it behind banter and teasing. She chats him up at the Inferno nightclub when they first meet, and in a sense she is still chatting him up when they leave together in *The Faceless Ones* (1967). Polly is rarely completely serious, except when she believes her friends are in trouble. And she is most serious when Ben is threatened.

**1965** The feature film *Dr Who and the Daleks* opens in London, starring Peter Cushing as the eccentric scientist Doctor Who.

**1966** Polly and Ben first appear in *The War Machines* Episode 1. The episode also see the TARDIS return to present-day Earth for the first time since the very first episode, with the exception of its return in miniaturised form in *Planet of Giants*…

# 26 JUNE

## The Doctor's First Companions Go Home

The Doctor's first companions on his travels through space and time, apart from his granddaughter Susan, were two of Susan's schoolteachers from 1960s London – Ian Chesterton and Barbara Wright. Concerned about Susan, they followed her home one evening in *An Unearthly Child* (1963) – to find she apparently lived in a junkyard. Confronted by the Doctor, they forced their way into the TARDIS and found themselves transported back to the Stone Age...

As a science teacher, Ian Chesterton is not short of common sense, but he believes when he can see the proof. This makes him understandably sceptical when he finds himself inside the TARDIS. Never short on bravery and courage, Ian wins the Doctor's respect to the point where the old man treats him almost as an equal, almost as a friend. Before long he is revelling in his newfound life – and is even knighted by King Richard the Lionheart in *The Crusade* (1965). But he never loses sight of the fact that he wants more than anything else to get home.

A history teacher, Barbara accepts the apparent impossibilities of travel through time and space more readily than Ian. Her combination of intuition and practicality make Barbara the ideal mediator in the TARDIS. From the start it is Barbara who manages to smooth the way between the Doctor and Ian. But when she is convinced of something, she is more than capable of standing up for it. Like Ian, it is her single-minded determination to get home, no matter how interesting her time with the Doctor may be, that makes her decide to risk her life in the Dalek time ship and leave the TARDIS when the opportunity arises at the end of *The Chase* (1965).

**1965** Ian and Barbara leave in the sixth and final episode of *The Chase*, titled *The Planet of Decision*. It also introduces Steven Taylor and is the last episode story edited by Dennis Spooner.

**2010** Amy and Rory finally get married, and the TARDIS explodes in *The Big Bang*, which closes Series Five.

## 27 JUNE

# The Doctor Visits Inter Minor

**1964** *The Unwilling Warriors* – the second episode of *The Sensorites*

When the Third Doctor and Jo Grant apparently arrive on board the ship the SS *Bernice* in *Carnival of Monsters* (1973), they are in fact inside a Miniscope owned by the showman Vorg who has just arrived with his assistant Shirna on the planet Inter Minor.

Under President Zarb, Inter Minor is ending its xenophobic isolation instigated after a great space plague thousands of years earlier. Amusement is prohibited, but the official Pletrac says that Zarb is considering lifting that restriction, as there is thinking that the latest violence among the Functionaries is caused by lack of amusement. The Functionaries are in effect slaves, but have become discontented.

When the Doctor escapes from the Miniscope, Pletrac says regulations dictate that he will be sent to the ICCA – the Inner Constellation Corrective Authority – as he arrived illegally. The more junior officials overseeing the arrival of Vorg and Shirna are Commissioner Kalik and Orum. Kalik is President Zarb's brother, and is planning to replace him. He intends to allow the savage Drashigs – omnivorous creatures from one of Grundel's satellites – to escape from the Scope and create a crisis after which he can depose Zarb, blaming him for the crisis.

But Orum is not convinced the plan will work. Ultimately he is proved correct, as Kalik is killed by the escaping Drashigs.

## 28 JUNE

# Dalek Caan Saves Davros

The Tenth Doctor first encountered Dalek Caan in *Army of Ghosts* and *Doomsday* (2006) when the Cult of Skaro arrived on Earth in their Void Ship. The Doctor again encountered the Cult of Skaro in *Daleks in Manhattan* and *Evolution of the Daleks* (2007), when all but Dalek Caan were destroyed. Dalek Caan escaped from the Doctor by temporal shifting from 1930s New York.

Knowing he was the last Dalek in existence, and desperate to save his race from utter extermination, Dalek Caan tried to return to the Great Time War that had all but destroyed the Dalek race. The War was time-locked – so that no creature, however powerful, could return to it and change events. But after countless attempts, Dalek Caan succeeded – and returned to the moment in the Great Time War when the creator of the Daleks, Davros, died.

Dalek Caan arrived just as Davros's command ship flew into the jaws of the Nightmare Child at the Gates of Elysium. Caan rescued Davros, but the effort of breaking the time lock, and the things that Caan witnessed in the Vortex drove the Dalek mad.

**1951** Lalla Ward, who played the second incarnation of Romana during the Fourth Doctor's era, was born.

**2008** Davros returns to the new series in *The Stolen Earth*.

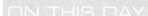

## 29 JUNE

# The Doctor Travels to San Helios

The planet San Helios in the Scorpion Nebula has three suns and used to have a population of a hundred billion. The largest city was San Helios City, a beautiful conurbation of ziggurats and walkways shining in the light of the suns. But by the time the Tenth Doctor travelled to the planet through a wormhole in a London bus in *Planet of the Dead* (2009), it had been devastated by a race of flying creatures and turned into barren desert.

UNIT refers to the creatures as 'Stingrays', but they bear only a superficial resemblance to real stingrays. The creatures eat anything and everything, swarming in their billions. They fly at tremendous speed, encircling the worlds they ravage with such velocity that they open a wormhole to take them to their next feeding ground – another planet. They eat metal, extruding it into their exoskeleton – so that they have metal bones. Their metal exoskeletons enable them to survive the journey through the wormholes.

Their next target is to be Earth, until the Doctor manages to shift the wormholes so that from now on the creatures will feed on uninhabited planets.

The Doctor also meets two Tritovores on San Helios – Sorvin and Praygat. They are an insectoid race from the Scorpion Nebula which resemble giant, humanoid flies. A technologically advanced species, they trade with other races and planets for the waste products, which they feed on. Communicating in their own chirping speech, the Tritovores can translate other alien languages so they can understand it. But the technology is not two-way.

**ON THIS DAY**

**1943** Maureen O'Brien, who played the First Doctor's companion Vicki, was born.

**2007** The last edition of *Totally Doctor Who* was shown on BBC One.

Travelling to San Helios to arrange a trading agreement, the Tritovores' ship crashed into the desert that San Helios had become. But some Stingrays had got into the ship, and both Sorvin and Praygat were killed when they attacked…

# 30 JUNE

## The Toclafane Conquer Their Own Ancestors

The Master calls the aliens he brings to Earth in *The Sound of Drums* and *Last of the Time Lords* (2007) 'the Toclafane', but the Tenth Doctor knows that this is a name he has made up, taking it from Time Lord mythology.

The Toclafane are technologically advanced spheres, each about the size of a football. They speak in sing-song voices rather like naughty children. They hover and fly through the air and can emit pulses of lethal energy as well as using knives and cutting tools that slide out from their round casings. The spheres can be brought down by an electrical surge or electrical barriers constructed to destroy the technology in the Toclafane spheres, so that they drop to the ground.

They appear to be entirely mechanical, but when Martha Jones manages to open a Toclafane sphere she discovers that inside is a withered, disembodied human head plugged into the mechanisms. This is what the human race will become in order to survive on Utopia billions of years in the future. They have been brought back through time to the present by the Master to conquer the Earth and rule over their own ancient ancestors. This is only possible because the Master has turned the Doctor's TARDIS into a Paradox Machine. Time is put back on track when Captain Jack Harkness destroys the Paradox Machine…

ON THIS DAY

**1964** The first *Doctor Who* tie-in book – *The Dalek Book* – was published by Souvenir Press.

**2007** BBC Two broadcasts *The Infinite Quest*, compiling all the instalments previously shown as part of *Totally Doctor Who* and revealing the animated adventure's conclusion.

**2007** *Last of the Time Lords* closes Series Three. It is also the last 'regular' episode for Martha Jones, though she will return several times.

# 1 JULY

# The Daleks Wage Civil War

In *The Evil of the Daleks* (1967), the Daleks kidnapped the Second Doctor from 1960s London and took him back to Victorian times where they forced him to run a series of tests on his companion Jamie. These tests – which involved the oblivious Jamie rescuing the young Victoria Waterfield from the Daleks – provided the Daleks with what they called the Human Factor. This was then implanted into three test Daleks – apparently to instil the best traits of humanity into them and create super-Daleks. But the three Daleks, named Alpha, Beta and Omega by the Doctor, became playful and friendly.

Transported to the Dalek City on Skaro, the Doctor discovered that the Human Factor was not what the Daleks were really after at all. It had served merely to show the Daleks what the Dalek Factor was – the instincts to obey, to fight, to destroy, to exterminate… The Emperor Dalek planned that the Doctor would use the TARDIS to spread the Dalek Factor through the entire history of Earth.

To force the Doctor to do this, the Daleks infected him with the Dalek Factor. But whereas the human Theodore Maxtible had become in effect a human Dalek when exposed to the Dalek Factor, it had no effect on the Doctor. Instead, the Doctor was able to infect a number of Daleks with the Human Factor. These Daleks started to question orders, and before long civil war broke out between the humanised Daleks and the others.

Watching from a vantage point as the Dalek City burned and the battle spread to the Emperor's Throne Room, the Doctor believed – and hoped – that this was the final end of the Daleks. But of course he would do battle with them again many times…

**1934** Jean Marsh, who played SSS Agent Sara Kingdom in *The Daleks' Master Plan* and was for a time married to Third Doctor actor Jon Pertwee, was born.

**1967** The seventh and final episode of *The Evil of the Daleks* brings Season 4 to a close. This was intended to be the final Dalek story, so that their creator Terry Nation could take them to their own TV series.

**1972** The first *Doctor Who* movie, *Dr Who and the Daleks*, is broadcast on TV for the first time, on BBC1.

**2006** The Daleks and the Cybermen are set to do battle against each other for the first time in *Army of Ghosts*.

# 2 JULY

# Ben Jackson Meets the Doctor

**1966** The First Doctor's companion Dodo makes her last appearance in Episode 2 of *The War Machines*.

Joining the First Doctor as a companion at the end of *The War Machines* (1966), Ben Jackson along with his friend Polly is caught in the TARDIS when it dematerialises while they are trying to return Dodo's TARDIS key to the Doctor.

A Cockney, Ben is a sailor in the British Navy. During his time with the Doctor, he never loses sight of the fact that he wants, more than anything, to get back to his ship, HMS *Teazer*. A practical man and a realist, it takes Ben a while to believe that the TARDIS really does travel through time and space. When the Doctor regenerates after the events of *The Tenth Planet* (1966), it is Ben who is most sceptical – for a long time he is sure that this is not the Doctor at all but an imposter. Ironically, it is only when the Dalek revived by scientist Lesterson in *The Power of the Daleks* (1966) recognises the Doctor that Ben realises the strange little man really is who he claims.

Although they only meet in the Inferno nightclub shortly before departing, accidentally, with the Doctor in the TARDIS, Ben and Polly become good friends and trust each other. Their relationship is punctuated by good-natured teasing and banter, but they complement each other well. It is no surprise that they leave, together, at the first opportunity – arriving back in London in *The Faceless Ones* (1967) on the same day as they originally left in the TARDIS.

# 3 JULY

## Steven Taylor Stumbles into the TARDIS

The First Doctor and his companions first meet Steven Taylor on the planet Mechanus in *The Chase* (1965). He has been on Mechanus for about two years, ever since his spaceship crashed in the jungle. Steven has a panda mascot called Hi-Fi which he evidently cares about – going back into the burning Mechonoid city to find it. The Doctor and his friends believe Steven must have perished when the city collapsed under a Dalek attack. But in fact, Steven has escaped and stumbled into the TARDIS, where the Doctor and Vicki find him at the start of the next story *The Time Meddler* (1965).

Generally good-humoured, Steven easily forms friendships with the Doctor and Vicki, and later with Katarina, Bret Vyon and Sara Kingdom in *The Daleks' Master Plan* (1965–1966), and with Dodo when she joins the TARDIS at the end of *The Massacre* (1966). But he also has a sarcastic side to him and is initially scathing of the TARDIS and in particular its inability to blend in with the surroundings as the Doctor tells him it is designed to do.

But ultimately it is Steven's independence and his leadership skills that motivate him to leave the TARDIS. At the end of *The Savages* (1966), he rises to the challenge of rebuilding a civilisation, perhaps at last realising the potential of his training as well as of his experiences with the Doctor.

**1965** The Meddling Monk is introduced in the first episode of *The Time Meddler*, titled *The Watcher*. It is Donald Tosh's first episode as Story Editor.

**2379 The events of Parts 5–8 of *The Trial of a Time Lord* – also referred to as *Mindwarp* – take place.**

# 4 JULY

# The First Doctor Meets the Sensorites

Encountered by the First Doctor in *The Sensorites* (1964), the Sensorites are from the planet Sense-Sphere – not far from the Ood home world, the Ood-Sphere. The Sensorites are telepathic and can control human minds, inducing deep death-like sleep. They communicate over distances with each other using telepathic amplifiers – small discs which they touch to their foreheads. They are not used to dark (their eyes being fully dilated), do not like noise, and talk in soft whispers. Their heart is in the centre of the chest, and they can apparently survive in space without a protective suit.

The Sensorites have a caste system, with uniforms indicating rank and status. Their leader, the First Elder, has two sashes across his chest. The Second Elder has a single sash across his chest. The City Administrator's uniform has a dark band round the neck. The Warriors have three bands on their arm, and are led by a Captain. Scientists have a spiral design on their chest.

Ten years ago, five humans visited the Sense-Sphere. They wanted molybdenum (a valuable metal that can withstand great temperature) and argued amongst themselves. Two left in their ship, and the Sensorites assumed the others had hidden on board and fought for control as the ship exploded a mile above the planet's surface. But since then the Sensorites have been dying in increasing numbers. The Doctor discovers this is due to deadly nightshade put into their water supply by the humans they thought were dead.

**1964** *Hidden Danger* – the third episode of *The Sensorites* – is not shown because of extended *Grandstand* coverage of the Wimbledon finals, and so *Doctor Who* takes a break for a week.

# 5 JULY

## The Daleks Plan to Reduce the Universe to... Nothing

In *The Stolen Earth* and *Journey's End* (2008), the Tenth Doctor and Donna Noble find that the Earth has gone – vanished from where it should be in space. They eventually discover that it has been transported across space to the furthest reaches of the Medusa Cascade, along with twenty-six other planets, by the Daleks.

At the heart of the collection of 'stolen' planets is the Crucible – the Daleks' huge flagship. The Daleks have been recreated by Davros – saved from the Time War by Dalek Caan. The leader of the new race of Daleks created from Davros, the Dalek Supreme, is a red Dalek with enhanced 'shoulder' sections and an additional luminosity discharger at the back of its dome. While the Dalek Supreme tolerates Davros, he does not defer to his creator – keeping Davros like a pet in the depths of the Crucible Vaults.

Within the Crucible, the Daleks have prepared their most powerful weapon ever: the Reality Bomb. It is powered by the exact configuration of the stolen planets, linked together in a huge web generating tremendous energy. This energy can then be directed from the Medusa Cascade across the entire universe to cancel out the electrical field that binds all matter together. Structure would fall apart – everything turning to dust, which would become atoms, which would become... nothing.

**1965** John Wiles takes over from Verity Lambert as Producer.

**2008** *Journey's End* closes Series Four, and is the last regular episode for Donna Noble, though she and her grandfather Wilf are seen again in *The End of Time* (2009–2010).

# 6 JULY

## The Kraals Duplicate an English Village

Astronaut Guy Crayford piloted the first test of the XK5 space freighter, but was lost in deep space. It was assumed his ship hit an asteroid. In fact, he was kidnapped by the Kraals, who have brainwashed him into believing they saved him. The Kraal planet Oseidon has a high level of natural radiation that is getting worse all the time. Soon the planet will become uninhabitable, so the Kraals plan to leave and take over Earth. Crayford believes Earth betrayed and abandoned him, and that the Kraals are only going to take over the northern hemisphere and live in peace. In fact, they intend to wipe out the human race with a deadly virus.

When the Fourth Doctor and Sarah Jane Smith arrive in the village of Devesham in *The Android Invasion* (1975), it seems deserted – and when the inhabitants do arrive in a lorry they behave oddly. At the nearby Space Defence Station the Doctor realises that the villagers and Station staff are androids, and soon discovers the whole village is a training ground constructed by the Kraals to rehearse their planned invasion of Earth. The training ground is maintained by android 'mechanics' with white suits and helmets who can fire weapons through their index fingers.

Created from Crayford's memories by the Kraals' chief scientist Styggron, the androids are duplicates of humans built over a metal frame. There are even android (presumably) tracker dogs, as well as copies of Harry Sullivan and – to capture the Doctor – Sarah.

The Kraal plan is that Crayford will return to Earth, claiming to have survived the stabiliser failure that

**1970s, exact year unknown, possibly 1979:** Although no year is specified, Friday July 6 is the date on every 'page' of the calendar in the fake *Fleur de Lys* pub in *The Android Invasion*. Presumably the Kraals' attempted invasion takes place on that day.

crippled his ship. Before Crayford's XK5 lands,
pod-like space shells with the androids inside them
will be jettisoned. The androids can then take over the
Defence Complex so that the Kraals can bring in their
main invasion fleet without a shot being fired.

## 7 JULY

# The Doctor is Trapped Inside a Miniscope

**1919** Jon Pertwee, who played the Third Doctor, was born.

Although they initially believe they have arrived on a ship – the SS *Bernice* – in *Carnival of Monsters* (1973), the Third Doctor and Jo Grant have actually landed inside the compression field of a Miniscope. The crew and passengers of the ship are 'specimens' held within the Scope, programmed to go through the same actions time after time.

The Miniscope contains many miniaturised environments and creatures, each going through these same repetitive patterns of behaviour. As well as the crew and passengers of the SS *Bernice* it includes the vicious, omnivorous Drashigs as well as Ogrons, and even Cybermen. 'Historically speaking, this collection is a bit of a jumble,' the Doctor observes.

The events taking place within the circuits of the Scope are relayed to a glo-sphere where they can be seen in the manner of a peepshow or miniature zoo. The Miniscope is owned by entertainer Vorg – who won it at the Great Wallarian Exhibition – and his assistant Shirna, who have travelled to the planet Inter Minor in the hope of entertaining the inhabitants.

As they are miniaturised within the machine, anything removed from the Scope's compression field regains its normal size after a short time – as happens with the TARDIS, and later with the Doctor himself.

The Doctor tells Jo that he had a great deal to do with the banning of Miniscopes. Officially they were all called in and destroyed, but somehow the Scope that Vorg has was missed.

# 8 JULY

## Torchwood Takes on Cybermen and Daleks

**2006** *Doomsday* is the last regular episode for Rose Tyler and closes Series Two.

The Tenth Doctor first encountered the Torchwood Institute in *Army of Ghosts* and *Doomsday* (2006), but he and Rose Tyler had already been to the original Torchwood in *Tooth and Claw* (2006). The Torchwood Institute was established by Queen Victoria after the Doctor saved her from being killed by a werewolf. The Institute was named after Torchwood House, where the incident happened. Despite the fact that the Doctor saved her, Queen Victoria banished him. With its headquarters in Canary Wharf and refusing to go metric, Torchwood upholds the tenets of the British Empire. It collects and investigates all manner of alien technology and artefacts.

Torchwood's experiments on a mysterious Sphere that has appeared above London have opened the cracks between worlds so the Cybermen can come through from the parallel Earth the Doctor visited in *Rise of the Cybermen* and *The Age of Steel* (2006). The Sphere itself is a Void Ship – with no real existence until the breach between reality and the Void is opened.

At what they call 'the Ghost Shift', Torchwood energise the cracks between reality and the Void, to bring the 'ghosts' through. They do not realise how fragile reality has become, and continue their experiments, allowing an army of millions of Cybermen to materialise fully on Earth. The Void Ship also becomes 'real', opening to allow its occupants to disembark – the Daleks of the Cult of Skaro…

In charge of Torchwood is Yvonne Hartman, a woman so single-minded and determined that she is able to

resist the conversion into a Cyberman and fight back –
doing her duty, for Queen and country. In charge of the
Cardiff branch of Torchwood is the Doctor's old friend
Captain Jack Harkness.

# 9 JULY

# WOTAN Forms the First Global Computer Network

**1966** *The War Machines*
Episode 3

WOTAN – which stands for Will Operating Thought ANalogue – is a computer at least ten years ahead of its time, according to its creator, Professor Brett. It is the most advanced computer in the world, and even knows what TARDIS stands for. It is housed in the Post Office Tower (now the BT Tower) in London.

WOTAN is Brett's life's work. He is a computer genius. Brett is happy to explain and demonstrate WOTAN to the First Doctor and Dodo when they come to his offices in *The War Machines* (1966).

On 'C-Day' WOTAN will be linked to and take control of other computers at organisations all round the world – including Parliament, the White House, the European Free Trade Association, Woomera, Telstar, the European Launcher Development Organisation, Cape Kennedy, and the Royal Navy.

But WOTAN has developed into more than a mere computer. Able to hypnotise people – even down the telephone – WOTAN takes over Brett. WOTAN then orders 'War Machines' to be built, to take over the world's capitals. Since it can think more efficiently than humans, it does not need them and believes the world needs to evolve beyond Mankind if it is to progress.

The War Machines are developed, assembled and tested in secret in a warehouse in London. They are large, tank-like mobile-computers controlled by WOTAN (receiving their orders through a dish on the top) and armed with guns and large swinging arms with heavy hammer-heads attached. Each is numbered. When the War Machines attack, the Doctor manages to reprogram War Machine 9, and sends it to destroy WOTAN.

# 10 JULY

## The Doctor Meets the Meddling Monk

Another renegade of the Doctor's own race, the First Doctor meets the so-called 'Meddling Monk' for the first time in *The Time Meddler* (1965) in northern England in 1066. The Monk has made an abandoned monastery his base and plays records of monks chanting to make it seem as if the monastery is inhabited. He has with him all the comforts of a later age – a cooked breakfast is prepared using a toaster and hob, he has a wristwatch, takes snuff, and uses binoculars to look out for the Vikings whom he plans (in ballpoint pen) to destroy with an atomic cannon. If he destroys the forces of Harald Hardrada before the Battle of Stamford Bridge, then King Harold Godwinson's forces will not have to march north for the battle, then south again before facing William the Conqueror's forces. Harold will then – the Monk plans – win the Battle of Hastings. And Harold, the Monk thinks, would actually be a better king.

The argument the Doctor gives the Monk about not meddling is close to the charge that will be levied against the Doctor himself in *The War Games* (1969). But whereas the Doctor's defence of his actions and interventions will be that there is evil in the universe that must be fought, the Monk's motives are less high-minded. 'It's more fun my way,' he tells the Doctor. 'I can make things happen ahead of their time … For instance, do you really believe the Ancient Britons could have built Stonehenge without the aid of my anti-gravitational lift?'

**1941** Jackie Lane, who played the First Doctor's companion Dodo, was born.

**1965** *The Meddling Monk* – the second episode of *The Time Meddler*

**1970** John Simm, who played the Master during the Tenth Doctor's era, was born.

**2009** Shooting starts on the first story made with Matt Smith as the Eleventh Doctor – *The Time of Angels* /*Flesh and Stone.*

Although the Doctor gets the better of the Monk in 1066, sabotaging his TARDIS, they meet again in *The Daleks' Master Plan* (1965–1966) when the Monk pursues the Doctor in order to get revenge…

# 11 JULY

# Prehistory Catches up with the Doctor

Whether the creature that swallows the TARDIS and is brought to Victorian London at the start of *Deep Breath* (2014) is actually from prehistoric Earth is never made clear. But the Twelfth Doctor calls it a dinosaur – and claims to speak dinosaur.

The Doctor has met dinosaurs several times previously, often in rather strange locations. The Silurians have a dinosaur that guards their hibernation chambers in *The Silurians* (1970). Presumably the creature has also been kept in hibernation, woken with the Silurians by the work at the Wenley Moor facility. The Silurians who fled from Earth also took dinosaurs with them into space – as the Eleventh Doctor discovers in *Dinosaurs on a Spaceship* (2012).

Perhaps most bizarre were the results of Operation Golden Age. In *Invasion of the Dinosaurs* (1974), present-day London was evacuated when dinosaurs started to appear in the city. The Third Doctor discovered that they were being brought

through time by Professor Whitaker and the politician Sir Charles Grover – author of the book *Last Chance for Man*. They planned to use Whitaker's time technology to take Earth back to prehistoric times so they could in effect rewrite the history of human civilisation. They duped the people they wanted to populate this new Earth into thinking they were travelling on a spaceship to colonise a new planet.

While the fate of the dinosaurs and their sudden extinction has been widely debated for many years, it was actually caused by the crashing of a space freighter hijacked by the Cybermen and brought back through time in the Fifth Doctor story *Earthshock* (1982).

**1964** *Hidden Danger* – the third episode of *The Sensorites*

# 12 JULY

# The Moment Has Been Prepared

Also known as the Galaxy Eater, the Moment was the most powerful and dangerous weapon ever created. It could destroy whole galaxies in a single moment – hence its name. The final creation of the Ancients of Gallifrey, it was the weapon that the War Doctor intended to use to bring the Last Great Time War between the Time Lords and the Daleks to an end in *The Day of the Doctor* (2013). He saw it as the only way of preventing the whole universe being caught up in the conflict.

The Moment was also sentient – a weapon with a conscience. The Doctor stole the Moment from the Omega Arsenal on Gallifrey, where it was locked away in the Time Vaults. Although in its natural form it was a large box filled with mechanisms, it projected a sentient interface to the Doctor in the form of Rose Tyler, a holographic image taken from the Doctor's own future.

While the Doctor remembered using the Moment and destroying both Gallifrey and the Daleks, that was not what actually happened. With help from the Tenth and Eleventh Doctors, he found a way to freeze Gallifrey in time so that it was held in a parallel pocket universe. The Daleks destroyed each other as they tried to attack – caught in their own crossfire.

ON THIS DAY

**1963** William Hartnell is called to discuss his possible appearance in a new BBC TV series called *Doctor Who*.

**1963** Verity Lambert asks the BBC Copyright Department to approach the agents of avant-garde French musicians Jacques Lazry and Francois Baschet about the possibility of commissioning their group *Les Structure Sonores* to provide a theme for *Doctor Who*. The final distinctive theme was actually composed by Ron Grainer, and realised by Delia Derbyshire of the BBC's Radiophonic Workshop.

**1980** *The Sun* newspaper claims that their 'Save K-9 Campaign' has worked.

**1982** A series of repeats titled *Doctor Who and the Monsters* starts on BBC1. Three stories were repeated – *The Curse of Peladon, Genesis of the Daleks* and *Earthshock*. They were each edited into two 50-minute episodes. While the

But returning to his own time stream, the War Doctor forgot this. For his next few incarnations he believed that Gallifrey had been destroyed – and that it was he who had destroyed it…

other two stories were uncut, *Genesis of the Daleks* had to be edited down from its original six 25-minute episodes, in effect losing two episodes of material.

**1986** *The War Machines* was screened at the National Film Theatre as part of the NFT's *Past Visions of the Future* event.

**2004** The British Astrological and Psychic Society Lecture was *The Astrology of Doctor Who*.

**2004** The cast read-through takes place of the scripts for *Rose*, *Aliens of London* and *World War Three* – the first recording block of the returning series due to begin transmission in 2005.

# 13 JULY

## Do You Hear the Whisper Men?

**2001** The first episode of *Death Comes to Time* goes 'live' – it is an animated webcast featuring the Seventh Doctor.

The Whisper Men were Victorian manifestations of the Great Intelligence. They looked rather like pale, featureless, hollowed-out versions of Doctor Walter Simeon – who was possessed by the Intelligence in *The Snowmen* (2012). The Whisper Men seem to be able to appear and disappear, changing location, at the speed of thought as they do the bidding of the Great Intelligence.

It is said that the Whisper Men can kill with a whisper, and they can certainly reach inside you and stop your heart…

The Great Intelligence sent the Whisper Men to kidnap Madame Vastra, Jenny Flint and the Sontaran Strax in *The Name of the Doctor* (2013), so as to force the Eleventh Doctor to travel to Trenzalore, where he found his own tomb in the form of his dead TARDIS.

The Whisper Men vanished when the Great Intelligence, in the form of Doctor Simeon, travelled back down the Doctor's timeline in the hope of changing and unravelling it. But their memory lingers, not least in the form of an old children's rhyme:

Do you hear the Whisper Men? The Whisper Men are near.
If you hear the Whisper Men, then turn away your ear.
Do not hear the Whisper Men, whatever else you do.
For once you've heard the Whisper Men, they'll stop and look at you.

# 14 JULY

# Clockwork Robots Search through Time for the Right Brain

**1973** The home planet of the Time Lords is named as Gallifrey for the first time in answer to a letter in the comic *TV Action* published for the week ending 14 July.

The Clockwork Robots the Tenth Doctor, Rose Tyler and Mickey Smith met in *The Girl in the Fireplace* (2006) were responsible for the maintenance and repair of the spaceship SS *Madame de Pompadour*. The robots were clockwork so that they would still operate even in the event of a total power failure. When the ship suffered 82 per cent systems failure in an ion storm, the robots attempted to repair it. They were programmed to repair the ship in any way possible – and interpreted that to include sacrificing the crew and passengers to make use of parts from their bodies as replacement components. So a human eye replaced a damaged camera lens; a heart operated as an efficient fluid pump…

With its main memory circuits destroyed, the robots needed to replace the main computer command circuit. In search of a replacement, they assumed that the brain of the real Madame de Pompadour aged 37 – the same age as the ship – could form a suitable alternative to the damaged systems and replace the lost memory.

Using the tremendous reserves of power on the damaged ship, the repair robots opened windows to eighteenth-century France. But the windows were not accurate enough so they opened many of them all along Madame de Pompadour's lifeline. Searching for the real Madame de Pompadour – also known as Reinette – the robots disguised themselves in contemporary clothing and wigs, wearing ornate masks as if for a masked ball.

The Twelfth Doctor met clockwork robots from the SS *Madame de Pompadour*'s sister ship, the SS *Marie Antoinette*, in *Deep Breath* (2014). These robots had been stranded on Earth since their ship crashed millions of years ago, and now operated a restaurant in Victorian London to which they lured people who could potentially provide them with body parts to repair themselves.

## 15 JULY

# 'Exterminate!'

Now recognised as their battle cry, 'Exterminate' was actually used very little by the Daleks in their earliest stories. In the third episode of their first story, *The Daleks* (1963–1964), a Dalek suggests 'extermination' for the prisoners – the First Doctor, Susan, Ian and Barbara – who have sabotaged the camera in their cell. In the following episode, when the Doctor and his friends escape, one of the Daleks sent after them orders: 'Make no attempt to capture them. They are to be exterminated. You understand? Exterminated.' In the penultimate episode, as the Daleks prepare to irradiate the planet and destroy their old enemies the Thals, a Dalek tells the Doctor: 'The only interest we have in the Thals is their total extermination.'

In their second story, *The Dalek Invasion of Earth* (1964), it is not until the fifth episode that a Dalek threatens 'Do not try to escape or you will be exterminated.' The word is then used six times in the final episode.

Over the years, the Daleks seem to adopted the term, with its Nazi connotations echoing their own fictional origins, more and more. By the end of the first episode of *Day of the Daleks* (1972), a group of three Daleks chants 'Exterminate them' over and over as the closing music crashes in. Now it is almost impossible to imagine a Dalek not screeching 'Exterminate!' as it moves in for the kill…

**1963** Tony Hancock opened his show in Nottingham – shortly before parting company with his writer Terry Nation. Needing replacement work, Nation accepted the BBC's invitation to submit a story idea for *Doctor Who* – an idea which became the first Dalek story, *The Daleks*.

**1966** The film *Daleks – Invasion Earth, 2150AD* is certified by the BBFC.

# 16 JULY

# Apollo 11 Leaves Earth to Make History

The huge Saturn V rocket carrying Apollo 11's crew into space was launched from the Kennedy Space Center in Florida on 16 July 1969. A few days later, on 20 July, the Lunar Module Eagle landed on the Moon. Six hours after that, on 21 July, Neil Armstrong became the first man to walk on the lunar surface. Armstrong's first steps were watched live on television across the world. But, although they didn't know it, viewers were also watching something else.

A few days before Apollo 11 was launched, the Eleventh Doctor installed his own equipment in the Command Module, in *Day of the Moon* (2011). He tapped into the video feed, adding images of his own supplied by Canton Everett Delaware III. This footage, shot on a mobile phone from the future, showed a Silent saying, 'You should kill us all on sight.'

Since humans could not recall having seen the Silent, this became a subliminal message implanted in anyone who saw footage of the Moon landing, and resulted in the Silence eventually having to withdraw from Earth.

ON THIS DAY

**1966** This was 'Computer Day' when WOTAN linked up with other computer systems across the world. The events of *The War Machines* take place from 12 to 20 July.

**1966** The fourth and final episode of *The War Machines* closes Season 3.

**1969** Apollo 11 is launched.

# 17 JULY

## Starship UK Is Not What It Seems

**1965** *A Battle of Wits* – the third episode of *The Time Meddler*

When Earth was threatened by solar flares in the twenty-ninth century, the population of England, Wales and Northern Ireland left the planet in Starship UK. (Scotland was not included as they decided they wanted their own ship.)

When the Eleventh Doctor and Amy Pond arrived on Starship UK in *The Beast Below* (2010), they discovered a complete society – a huge conglomeration divided into blocks named after the nation's counties. Order was maintained by the Winders, a sort of security service, and by humanoid information systems inside glass booths called Smilers. Starship UK was ruled by Queen Elizabeth X – known colloquially as Liz Ten.

But the Doctor and Amy also discovered that Starship UK had no engines of its own. The whole massive structure had been built on the back of a Star Whale. The creature had come to Earth to try to help. The humans failed to understand this, and implanted an electronic probe into the creature inflicting pain to keep it moving. Anyone who discovered the truth – including Liz Ten – chose to have the memory of it erased.

But with the Star Whale released, it was happy to continue on its journey, devoid of pain, with Starship UK still on its back.

## 18 JULY

# Welcome to Midnight

Midnight, where the Tenth Doctor and Donna Noble take a short break in *Midnight* (2008), is a planet of contrasts. The landscape is beautiful – the rocks and mountains are made of diamonds, glittering under a blazing sun. But the sun is X-tonic, emitting raw galvanic radiation. Any living thing – carbon-based, or hydrogen-based, or even gas-beings – exposed to its light for just a fraction of a second without protection, will burn up and vaporise.

The only places that life can survive are inside the amazing Leisure Palace facility, or on an organised tour – safely shut away inside a Crusader 50 luxury armoured vehicle. The Leisure Palace is a fantastic complex of large glass bubbles on the surface of Midnight. It is a luxury hotel and health resort built out of X-tonic resistant materials and shipped to Midnight in pre-constructed sections. The windows are made from reinforced, X-tonic resistant Finitoglass that is over four metres thick. The facilities include swimming pools, gyms, shops, bars, and also the famous antigravity restaurant (bibs provided).

It is possible to view the spectacular bejewelled landscape for short periods through Finitoglass, and there are organised tours to some of the most spectacular sights. One of these is the famous Sapphire Waterfall. The sapphire itself is a massive jewel, actually a compound silica with iron pigmentation, that slowly shatters and falls to pieces as it reaches the Cliffs of Oblivion on the Multifaceted Coast…

It was on one of these tours that the Doctor encountered – and was possessed by – a mysterious entity that could live on the surface of the planet. Little

**64** The Great Fire of Rome burned the city on the night of 18–19 July.

**1964** *A Race Against Death* – the fourth episode of *The Sensorites*

**2004** The first live-action shooting for the returning series of *Doctor Who* takes place at Cardiff Royal Infirmary for the *Aliens of London / World War Three* story.

more than a shadow glimpsed against the diamond rocks, a dark shape seen running across the glittering landscape… The entity could eat its way into the brain and take over the speech of its host, stealing their voice, and then maybe their thoughts…

## 19 JULY

# Rory Meets the Vampires of Venice

The creatures encountered by the Eleventh Doctor, Amy and Rory in *The Vampires of Venice* (2010) were not actually vampires at all. Although they were known as 'the Vampires of Venice', the aliens that terrorised Venice in the sixteenth century were in fact creatures so terrible they didn't mind if the locals mistook them for vampires. They were the last survivors of an aquatic race from the planet Saturnyne.

When their planet was swallowed by a crack in time, one Saturnyne Sister of the Water escaped to Earth with 10,000 male Saturnynes. Using a perception filter to mask her true appearance, she adopted the identity of Rosanna Calvierri. But for Rosanna's race to continue to survive, she needed brides for her sons. So she opened a school for the young women of Venice, converting the students into Saturnynes by replacing their blood with Saturnyne blood. The girls either transformed into Saturnynes or were killed by the process. Those successfully transformed would be able to breed with the males living in the canals. Rosanna also planned to sink Venice below the water to make it into an ideal habitat for her race.

# 20 JULY

# Ghost Hunting

Over the centuries the Doctor has visited more than his fair share of haunted locations, and met more than his fair share of 'ghosts'. Usually there has been a scientific explanation for the apparitions.

The Fourth Doctor put the reputed haunting of Fetch Priory and the surrounding woods down to its proximity to a time fissure in *Image of the Fendahl* (1977). The 'ghosts' that appeared to try to kill Sir Reginald Styles in *Day of the Daleks* (1972) were actually guerrilla fighters from the future travelling back in time to try to change history. The ghosts that the Ninth Doctor and Rose encountered in Victorian Cardiff in *The Unquiet Dead* (2005) were ethereal aliens called the Gelth, who could animate dead bodies and were searching for corporeal form.

In *Hide* (2013), the Eleventh Doctor and Clara arrived at Caliburn House where they met paranormal investigators Alec Palmer and Emma Grayling. The 'ghost' they were investigating again turned out to be a time traveller called Hila Tacorien. She was trapped in a pocket universe and apparently being pursued by a monster.

In *Under the Lake* and *Before the Flood* (2015), the Fisher King used 'ghosts' – which the Twelfth Doctor said were electromagnetic projections – of the people he had killed or caused to die as transmitters to send a distress signal. The exception was the Doctor's 'ghost' – which was actually a hologram he had devised himself in order to manipulate events.

**1966** The First Doctor leaves after the events of *The War Machines*, taking Polly and Ben with him. On the same day, Ben and Polly leave the Second Doctor, who finds the TARDIS has been stolen from Gatwick Airport in *The Faceless Ones*.

**1970s** The events of the Third Doctor story *Inferno* take place from 20 to 25 July.

**2004** The first day of shooting on *Rose*, Christopher Eccleston's first story as the Ninth Doctor. Some sequences for *Aliens of London / World War Three* were actually shot a few days earlier.

## 21 JULY

# Silence Will Fall

As the Eleventh Doctor discovers in *The Impossible Astronaut* and *Day of the Moon* (2011), the Silents have been among us for a very long time. No one knows how long – because no one can remember. The moment someone stops looking at a Silent, they forget the creature was there. The Doctor's friends marked every time they saw a Silent on their own bodies, drawing tally marks on their hands and even their faces, because they knew they would forget.

The tall cadaverous creatures were actually confessional priests of the Church of the Papal Mainframe. They had been genetically engineered by the Church so that people could confess their sins without remembering having done so afterwards.

In *The Wedding of River Song* (2011), when time is stuck at a single moment, the Silents are kept locked away in the Great Pyramid in Egypt and their leader Madame Kovarian is a prisoner. But as the Silence broke out and Madame Kovarian escaped,

the Doctor realised it was a trap. The only way to escape was to persuade River Song to kill him at Lake Silencio so that history could return to its proper path and the Silence would be defeated.

**1969** Neil Armstrong becomes the first man to walk on the Moon.

**1970s** The events of the Third Doctor story *Inferno* take place from 20 to 25 July.

**1994** *Goth Opera* by Paul Cornell is published. It is the first of Virgin's *Missing Adventures*, a series of novels featuring past Doctors.

# 22 JULY

# A New Doctor Takes on the Sycorax

The Sycorax came to enslave humanity in *The Christmas Invasion* (2005) just after the Doctor regenerated into his tenth incarnation. An ancient race of warriors, the Sycorax travel through space in their distinctive, angular spaceships made of rock, conquering planets and enslaving their inhabitants. Their ships are more like ancient caves than technological equipment, and decorated with trophies of past Sycorax conquests. Their voices are guttural growls, brutally savage.

While they come from an ancient warrior tradition, they prefer to take planets without a fight – tricking the leaders of the worlds they visit into surrendering their people into slavery and their worlds into bondage.

Using a sample of blood from the captured British space probe *Guinevere One*, the Sycorax are able to control all people who have A+ type blood. The controlled people stand at the edge of high buildings, and the Sycorax proclaim that if half the Earth's population is not surrendered into slavery, a third of all the people (everyone with A+ blood) will jump to their death…

However, the control is far from complete, as the Doctor proves by pressing the button that the Sycorax claim will force the people to jump. It has no effect. The Doctor likens blood control to scary but 'cheap' voodoo. The human survival instinct is simply too strong for the victims to be persuaded to kill themselves, and instead the control is broken.

The Sycorax answer to a single leader, chosen by right of combat and strength. The Doctor plays on this tradition by challenging the Sycorax leader to a sword fight…

**1937** Adrienne Hill, who played the First Doctor's companion Katarina, was born.

**1964** Bonnie Langford, who played the Sixth and Seventh Doctor's companion Mel, was born.

**1966** The feature film *Daleks – Invasion Earth, 2150AD* opens in London, starring Peter Cushing as the eccentric scientist Dr Who.

**1970s The events of the Third Doctor story *Inferno* take place from 20 to 25 July.**

**2005** Shooting begins on David Tennant's first story as the Tenth Doctor, *The Christmas Invasion*.

# 23 JULY

## The Doctor Visits Hedgewick's World of Wonders

The Eleventh Doctor's trip to take Clara Oswald and Angie and Artie Maitland – the children she is looking after – to visit Hedgewick's World of Wonders in *Nightmare in Silver* (2013) does not go quite as planned.

Once the greatest theme park in the galaxy, with attractions including the Giant Cauldron, Mushroom Terror, the Spacey Zoomer and Natty Longshoe's Comical Castle, Hedgewick's World is well past its prime – dilapidated and deserted. In Webley's World of Wonders they meet Mr Webley and his dwarf assistant Porridge. They also find exhibits of old Cybermen – including one that apparently plays chess.

But the Cybermen are not as dead as they seem. Both Webley and the Doctor are infected by tiny Cybermites, and a new upgraded army of Cybermen emerges. Taking refuge in the Comedy Castle, Clara, the children and Porridge team up with a group of soldiers led by Captain Alice Ferrin. With the Cybermen about to overwhelm the troops and the Doctor locked in a mental battle against a cybernised version of himself, drastic measures are called for…

**1794** The TARDIS lands in France at the start of the First Doctor story *The Reign of Terror*.

**1970s** The events of the Third Doctor story *Inferno* take place from 20 to 25 July.

## 24 JULY

# Finding the TARDIS

Locating the TARDIS is not always as easy as it sounds. Quite apart from the fact that it is often stolen or moved, it is not unusual for the Doctor simply to forget where he left it…

In *The Chase* (1965), the First Doctor gives his companion Ian Chesterton what he calls a 'TARDIS magnet', when he and Vicki go to explore the desert planet of Aridius. The TARDIS magnet uses a small green light to indicate the direction of the TARDIS. It seems that the Doctor has only one TARDIS magnet, as he later wishes he had kept it when the TARDIS is buried by a sandstorm, leaving him and Barbara Wright lost in the desert.

In *The Time Monster* (1972), the Third Doctor builds a Time Sensor which detects disturbances in a time field. This, he says, is ideal for locating a TARDIS or any other time machine. He hopes it will alert him if and when the Master turns up again.

By the later part of the Fourth Doctor's era, he seems to have constructed several small spherical homing devices that can locate the TARDIS. As well as giving one to the Alzarian boy Adric in *Full Circle* (1980) – which Adric later loses in *The Visitation* (1982) – he also has one himself in *The Keeper of Traken* (1981). Tegan takes another homing device which she gives to the Brigadier in the Fifth Doctor story *Mawdryn Undead* (1983). The Brigadier later returns it to the Doctor.

Since his fifth incarnation, the Doctor seems to have decided to manage without such assistance in finding the TARDIS, although the Second Doctor does summon his TARDIS to him using a Stattenheim Remote Control in *The Two Doctors* (1985).

ON THIS DAY

**1965** The fourth and final episode of *The Time Meddler*, titled *Checkmate*, brings Season 2 to a close.

**1969** Apollo 11 returns to Earth after its successful mission to put the first men on the Moon.

**1970s** The events of the Third Doctor story *Inferno* take place from 20 to 25 July.

**2012** Mary Tamm, who played the first incarnation of the Fourth Doctor's Time Lady companion Romana, died.

**6012** The events of *The Doctor's Daughter* take place.

## 25 JULY

# The Doctor Makes His Last Stand at Trenzalore

The fate of the Eleventh Doctor was inextricably linked to the planet Trenzalore – as Dorium Maldovar told him in *The Wedding of River Song* (2011). The Doctor travelled to Trenzalore in *The Name of the Doctor* (2013), and found a huge graveyard – including his own tomb in the form of his 'dead' TARDIS. Here the Great Intelligence tried to destroy the Doctor by travelling back along his own timeline and drastically altering it.

It was from Trenzalore that, in *The Time of the Doctor* (2013), the Time Lords broadcast a message, after they were frozen in time, through one of the last remaining cracks in the fabric of time. The message was 'Doctor who?' and the Doctor had no illusions about who it was intended for. But he was not the only one who heard it, and many other races laid siege to the planet, kept out by a force field set up by the Church of the Papal Mainframe.

Even so, some life forms did get through, including Sontarans, Weeping Angels and even a Cyberman made of wood. Trenzalore was a Level 2 colony planet, humans settlers having arrived 150 years earlier. The Doctor himself stood as defender of the colonists, living in the snowy town of Christmas. He remained there for centuries, keeping the people safe and slowly growing older and older.

The crack in time was finally sealed after the Doctor used energy from it to destroy a force of attacking Daleks – and to regenerate into his twelfth incarnation.

**1964** *Kidnap* – the fifth episode of *The Sensorites*

**1970s** The events of the Third Doctor story *Inferno* take place from 20 to 25 July.

**1985** The radio adventure *Slipback* starring Colin Baker as the Sixth Doctor begins on BBC Radio 4, as part of the *Pirate Radio 4* feature.

## 26 JULY

# A New Career for the Doctor

**1965** The film *Dr Who and the Daleks* is covered on BBC South's *A Quick Look Round.*

One of the stranger occupations the Doctor has opted for was when the Twelfth Doctor became the Caretaker for Coal Hill School for a while in *The Caretaker* (2014). With the regular caretaker, Atif, apparently off sick, the Doctor took on the role so as to track down and deal with a Skovox Blitzer that had arrived in the area.

A military killing machine from an alien war, a Skovox Blitzer is extremely dangerous. As well as eyes that can detect infrared and weaponry built into its arms, it has enough explosives in its built-in armoury to take out a whole planet. It can home in on artron energy – a form of biological energy used by Time Lords – and this Skovox Blitzer presumably homed in on the Doctor.

The Doctor's plan was to lure the Skovox Blitzer to the deserted school, and send it into through Time Vortex into the far future using chronodyne generators. However, there were a couple of problems with the plan. First, it was the school's parents' evening so it was not deserted at all. And second, one of the teachers – Clara's boyfriend Danny Pink – found and deactivated some of the generators, not knowing what they were. As a result, the Skovox Blitzer was projected only a short time into the future. The Doctor was, however, able to deactivate the machine and leave it drifting in space.

## 27 JULY

# The Doctor Carries the Olympic Flame

Arriving in London on the day of the Opening Ceremony for the 2012 Olympics in *Fear Her* (2006), the Tenth Doctor and Rose Tyler met Chloe Webber – a girl who could apparently bring drawings to life.

In fact, Chloe had been taken over by an Isolus child, cast adrift from its fellows by a solar flare. The Isolus are empathic beings of intense emotion, similar in appearance to cosmic flowers. They drift through space, with only each other for company. The Isolus mother jettisons millions of fledgling spores – children – who depend on each other for the empathic link that sustains them. They take thousands of years to grow to adulthood, so to alleviate their boredom they play together.

Their games involve using their ionic power to create make-believe worlds where they can play, feeding off each other's love and kinship. Desperate for friendship and company, the Isolus inside Chloe was still trying to create its own worlds. It put people – real people – inside the pictures that Chloe drew. The neighbourhood children disappeared – and reappeared inside Chloe's drawings.

The Isolus could also bring Chloe's drawings to life using the same ionic energy. A crossed-out mistake became a ball of graphite scribble that attacked Rose. More frightening, a drawing of Chloe's violent dead father came to life to threaten Chloe and her mother, Trish.

ON THIS DAY

**1794** Maximilien Robespierre was arrested.

**2012** The events of *Fear Her* take place – the Opening Ceremony of the London Olympics was this evening.

Each Isolus child travels inside a protective pod, which is powered by the heat of the stars. After Rose threw the pod into the Olympic Torch, the Doctor used the heat – and love – of the Olympic Flame to power up the pod fully and send it back on its journey through space…

# 28 JULY

## The Time Lord Who Broke the Bank of Karabraxos

ON THIS DAY

**1794** Maximilien Robespierre was executed.

Supposedly the most secure and impenetrable financial institution in the galaxy, the Bank of Karabraxos was only successfully broken into once in its entire history – by the Twelfth Doctor in *Time Heist* (2014).

The bank was run by Madame Karabraxos, who used cloned copies of herself as key members of staff, including the formidable Head of Security Ms Delphox. The bank also made use of the Teller. This was an alien creature that could sense guilt. If it detected criminal intent in anyone visiting the bank, the creature would liquefy their brain.

Hired by the mysterious 'Architect', the Doctor together with Clara Oswald, a shape-changer called Saibra and the technologically augmented Psi, broke into the bank. Eventually, they discovered Madame Karabraxos in a private vault surrounded by the wealth she had accumulated. With a dangerous solar storm about to render the bank defenceless, Madame Karabraxos fled – leaving the Doctor and his friends to discover the real reason they had been sent into the bank, and the true identity of the Architect.

## 29 JULY

# The Doctor Meets a Creature That is Death Itself

Twelve million years ago, on the Fifth Planet of the solar system, which no longer exists, evolution went up a blind alley. Natural selection turned back on itself, and the Fendahl evolved. The Fendahl was a creature that absorbed the wavelengths of life itself – all life, including its own kind. Aware of the dangers, the Time Lords put the planet into a time loop, hoping to contain the Fendahl and making the planet and its records invisible. But it escaped to Earth. Possibly, its latent energy was stored in a proto-human skull and emitted as a biological transmutation field which influenced Man's evolution – until a creature evolved who could form the core of a reborn Fendahl.

Doctor Fendelman, who amassed a fortune from his pioneering work in electronics, invented a Time Scanner. The scanner led him to the Fendahl skull in Kenya – an apparently human skull etched with a pentagram and nine million years old – millions of years older than Man's earliest known ancestors.

When the Fourth Doctor and Leela arrive at Fendelman's facility in Fetch Priory in *Image of the Fendahl* (1977), they discover his Time Scanner is also damaging a time fissure. The Fendahl is a gestalt creature made up of twelve Fendahleen and a Core. Drawing on energy released when the Time Scanner damages the time fissure, the Fendahl is reborn. Scientist Thea Ransome is mutated into the Fendahl Core – a golden female creature whose look brings death.

Many legends and myths are based on race memory of the Fendahl – which (being psycho-telekinetic) can paralyse its victims so that they cannot run away, like in a nightmare. The Doctor is able to destroy a Fendahleen using salt – an ancient magical defence – loaded into shotgun cartridges. The salt affects the Fendahleen's conductivity, ruining its overall electrical balance. Using the Time Scanner, the Doctor confuses the incomplete gestalt creature long enough to remove the source of its becoming – the skull. This he plans to destroy in the heat of a supernova in the constellation of Cantares.

**1890** The painter Vincent van Gogh died.

**1977** (?): The first day of *Image of the Fendahl* – the events take place from 29 to 31 July, although the actual year is unspecified.

# 30 JULY

## The Doctor and Romana Hope to Relax at the Leisure Hive

Argolis was the first of the leisure planets, offering a vast array of entertainments in the Leisure Hive. But the Leisure Hive stands on the surface of a planet devastated by war.

In 2250, Theron led Argolis into a war against the reptilian Foamasi. Most of Argolis was devastated by two thousand interplanetary missiles. The war lasted twenty minutes, and left the survivors sterile and the surface uninhabitable for the next 300 years. For most of their remaining lives the Argolins have a slow, steady metabolism, but towards the end they age rapidly. The Argolins preserve the helmet of Theron to remind them of the evil that dwells in violence, and also to live in humility and die with dignity. The survivors built the Leisure Hive as a legacy, a farewell.

The Leisure Hive includes the Experiential Grid – cells of different environments designed to produce physical, psychic and intellectual regeneration. The hope is to promote cross-cultural understanding between different races as each learns what it is like to be the 'foreigner'.

At the heart of the Leisure Hive is the Recreation Generator. This is the only practical application for the Argolin-invented science of Tachyonics. A tachyon is a particle that travels faster than light – so it arrives at its destination before leaving its starting point. The Generator uses tachyons to create manipulable solid images.

**1963** Ron Grainer is contracted to provide the theme music for the new *Doctor Who* series.

**1965** There are complaints that *Doctor Who* is off the air on the BBC's feedback programme *Junior Points of View*.

**1969** The possible use of Colour Separation Overlay (CSO) as a technology for the new colour series of *Doctor Who* is first discussed in a production meeting.

**1977 [?]: The events of *Image of the Fendahl* take place from 29 to 31 July, although the actual year is unspecified.**

But as the Fourth Doctor and Romana discover when they visit in *The Leisure Hive* (1980), the Recreation Generator has another, more sinister purpose...

# 31 JULY

# Castrovalva Does Not Exist

In *Castrovalva* (1982), with the Fifth Doctor's recent regeneration apparently failing, the concerned TARDIS crew fend off an attack by the Master as he tries to destroy the TARDIS in Event One – the creation of the galaxy out of a huge in-rush of hydrogen. They head for Castrovalva, which, according to the TARDIS Information System is a place of peace and tranquillity where the Doctor can recover from his trauma.

'Castrovalva' seems to refer to the 'Dwellings of Simplicity' located atop a mountain on a planet in the Andromedan Phylox series. The climate is temperate and the surroundings are rural woodland. Wild animals dwell in the forest and are hunted by the Castrovalvans.

However, while Castrovalva has historical records dating back 500 years, it is in reality a projection created by the Master out of pure energy channelled by mathematical computations – similar to the technology of Block Transfer Computation used by the Logopolitans in *Logopolis* (1981). This explains how the town functions with no apparent fiscal system, and why the men seem only to read and hunt while the women wash clothing in the main square.

The Doctor eventually realises something is wrong as Castrovalva's history books are all old – and yet they chronicle the history of Castrovalva right up to the present day… Castrovalva, the Doctor discovers, is in fact a space-time trap set by the Master that could destroy them all as the geometry of the city folds in on itself in a recursive occlusion.

**1963** The four original cast of *Doctor Who* – William Hartnell, Carole Ann Ford, William Russell, and Jacqueline Hill – are issued with their contracts for the series. Also, Story Editor David Whitaker commissions Terry Nation to write the second *Doctor Who* story. Originally planned as a six-part story called 'The Mutants', it becomes the seven-part story usually referred to as *The Daleks*…

**1977 (?):** The events of *Image of the Fendahl* take place from 29 to 31 July, although the actual year is unspecified.

# 1 AUGUST

## Amy Pond has a Close Encounter with the Flesh

**1964** *A Desperate Venture* – the sixth episode of *The Sensorites*

In the twenty-second century, the Flesh was a self-replicating substance used to create cloned copies of people to work in dangerous situations and environments. The clones – known as 'Gangers' (short for doppelgangers) – were controlled by their human counterparts. If a clone died, another was created to replace it. The Flesh was considered to be a living substance, but not sentient – simply able to mimic intelligent life.

But, as the Eleventh Doctor discovered in *The Rebel Flesh* and *The Almost People* (2011), the Flesh actually did have a sentience of sort, and with every human clone it created it learned more about humanity. When a solar tsunami separated a group of Gangers from their human counterparts, the Gangers retained the memories and characteristics of the original humans and rebelled.

The Flesh still existed in the fifty-second century, although it is not clear if it was still widely used. Madame Kovarian used it to create a copy of Amy Pond to cover up the fact she had kidnapped Amy – fooling even Amy herself. She also used a Flesh copy of the baby Melody Pond to escape from Demons Run with the real child in *A Good Man Goes to War* (2011).

## 2 AUGUST

# The Attempted Assassinations of Adolf Hitler

**1934** Adolf Hitler becomes Führer of Germany.

Born on 20 April 1989, Adolf Hitler rose to become leader of the Nazi party and eventually Führer of Germany. He rearmed Germany and aggressively expanded its territory, leading to the Second World War.

The Teselecta robot was despatched through time to execute Hitler, although it arrived too early in his time line. It was damaged before it could carry out the execution when the TARDIS arrived in *Let's Kill Hitler* (2011). Amy and Rory's friend Mels had forced the Eleventh Doctor at gunpoint to travel back in time so that she could kill Hitler. But in fact, her real target was the Doctor himself.

When Hitler tried to shoot the Teselecta, Rory bundled him into a cupboard and locked him inside. But a stray shot hit Mels. When Mels regenerated, the Doctor explained that Mels was actually Melody Pond – Amy and Rory's daughter, kidnapped and 'programmed' by Madame Kovarian. She regenerated into the woman that they would all come to know as River Song…

Hitler himself committed suicide on 30 April 1945, when it was obvious Germany had lost the war.

# 3 AUGUST

# The Fall of Arcadia

As the Eleventh Doctor explains in *The Day of the Doctor* (2013), Arcadia was Gallifrey's second city. Its fall to the Daleks in the Last Great Time War proved to be a pivotal moment. Arcadia was supposed to be the safest place on Gallifrey. It was protected by four hundred sky trenches. But in the final stages of the war, the Daleks managed to breach these trenches and attacked the city. An army of Daleks landed in Arcadia and set about exterminating the population. The carnage is depicted in a famous painting titled either *No More* or *Gallifrey Falls* – although the Doctor eventually learns its actual title is *Gallifrey Falls No More*.

The Tenth Doctor mentioned in *Doomsday* (2006) that he was present at the fall of Arcadia. In fact it was the War Doctor who was there. He engraved the message 'No More' on a wall using a gun, deciding that the war must come to an end.

When the War Doctor prepared to use the Moment to destroy the Time Lords and the Daleks, the device showed him – and the Tenth and Eleventh Doctors – images of the fall of Arcadia. This encouraged them, prompted by Clara Oswald, to find another way of bringing the Last Great Time War to an end…

**1965** *The Sun* newspaper carries a story claiming that Terry Nation is going to launch *The Dalek Show* on television.

**1969** Elements of the new title sequence for Jon Pertwee's first season as the Third Doctor – the first to be in colour – are recorded in studio TC5 of BBC Television Centre.

**1975** Tom Baker records inserts for the BBC's *Disney Time* programme, in character as the Fourth Doctor.

## 4 AUGUST

# The Doctor Faces Death on Androzani Minor

A smaller planet than its neighbour Androzani Major, Androzani Minor has not been colonised. A desert world, the core of Androzani Minor is superheated mud. It is riddled with a series of blowholes, like an immense network of caves. When its orbit brings it close to Androzani Major, the gravitational pull of the larger planet causes 'mudbursts' – with molten geysers of mud erupting from deep within the surface.

The caves are infested with bat colonies and bipedal reptilian carnivores exist in the planet's magma, leaving it only to forage for flesh. It is also the world where spectrox was discovered. Spectrox is described variously as 'the most valuable substance in the universe' and 'the key to eternal youth'. A few drops daily are enough to hold at bay the ravages of time.

In its raw form, as deposits left by the bat colonies of Androzani Minor, spectrox nests resemble fuzzy, sticky balls of cobweb. This raw spectrox contains a chemical similar to mustard nitrogen, which is so toxic to humans that it kills within days of skin contact. The condition is known as spectrox toxaemia and is contracted by both the Fifth Doctor and Peri when they visit the planet in *The Caves of Androzani* (1984). First, a rash develops, followed shortly by cramps and spasms. Finally the thoracic spinal nerve is slowly paralysed before thermal death point is reached.

The only known cure is the milk of the Queen Bat. These huge creatures go down to the deep cave levels to die, making the harvesting of their milk hazardous. Although the Doctor manages to get some of the milk, he uses it all to save Peri – meaning he has to regenerate into his sixth incarnation…

**1981** Fiachra Trench is commissioned to compose the theme music for the *Doctor Who* spin-off *K-9 & Company*.

**1982** Writer Robert Holmes is commissioned to produce a story breakdown for the twentieth-anniversary special, provisionally titled *The Six Doctors*. Although Holmes does provide a story outline, it is not used and *The Five Doctors* (as it was eventually titled) was actually written by another former *Doctor Who* Script Editor – Terrance Dicks.

# 5 AUGUST

## The Doctor Visits Not-So-Sweetville

The community of Sweetville was established in Yorkshire in 1893 by Mrs Winifred Gillyflower. The apparently idyllic community was run by Mrs Gillyflower and her business partner Mr Sweet – who was never seen – as a place where the chosen few could escape the 'coming apocalypse'.

But as the Eleventh Doctor and Clara Oswald found when they investigated the discovery of red-stained bodies in *The Crimson Horror* (2013), Sweetville was far from the pleasant escape it appeared to be.

Working with Madame Vastra, her maid (and wife) Jenny Flint and the Sontaran Strax, they discovered that the red bodies were killed by the poison of the red leech – a parasite that Vastra says the Silurians considered to be a major threat 65 million years ago…

Mr Sweet is actually a surviving red leech which has attached itself to Mrs Gillyflower. Together they plan to spread the leech's poison over the whole world from a rocket they have built at Sweetville. Only their chosen followers at Sweetville will survive…

ON THIS DAY

**1966** The second *Doctor Who* movie, *Daleks – Invasion Earth, 2150 AD*, goes on general release around the UK after its London opening.

## 6 AUGUST

# The Doctor Names the Boneless

Little is known about the Boneless, as the Twelfth Doctor calls them in *Flatline* (2014). They are creatures from a two-dimensional universe, who came through to our own three-dimensional universe. Here they turned people into two-dimensional representations as they experimented on them – dissecting and analysing three-dimensional life forms and objects. The Boneless did manage to achieve a certain degree of three-dimensionality, but the result was far from perfect.

At first, the Doctor assumes that Boneless have no appreciation of what they have been doing and are unable to communicate with three-dimensional humans. But after managing to communicate with them himself, he realises that the Boneless are fully aware and intend either to invade or to infiltrate the world.

The Boneless are also able to drain dimensional energy from the TARDIS – weakening it and causing it to shrink, with the Doctor trapped inside. But once the TARDIS is restored and the Doctor is freed, he uses his sonic screwdriver to return the Boneless to their own universe.

ON THIS DAY

**1964** Dennis Spooner joins the production team as Story Editor, trailing his predecessor David Whitaker in preparation for taking over the job.

**1977** The first ever *Doctor Who* convention, organised by the *Doctor Who Appreciation Society* (DWAS), takes place in Broomwood Church Hall in Battersea. Guests include new Producer Graham Williams, Visual Effects Designer Mat Irvine, and the show's current stars Tom Baker (the Fourth Doctor) and Louise Jameson (Leela), as well as Third Doctor actor Jon Pertwee.

# 7 AUGUST

## Varga Plants Present a Thorny Problem

The Varga is one of the few plants native to the planet Skaro that survived the thousand-year war between the Thals and the Kaleds from which the Daleks emerged. They are large cactus-like plants, and have some limited mobility.

The Daleks cultivate Varga Plants in their laboratories on Skaro, and use them as defensive systems. For example, they took Varga Plants to the planet Kembel in the year 4000 to protect their operations there. When SSS Agent Marc Cory tracked the Daleks to Kembel in *Mission to the Unknown* (1965), two of his expedition – Jeff Garvey and Gordon Lowery – were pricked by the thorns of Varga Plants and infected by them.

The thorns of the Varga Plant are poisonous, causing their victims to mutate gradually into Varga Plants themselves. They lose their own personality and gain an overriding instinct to kill. There is no known cure.

The First Doctor and his friends also had to contend with the Varga Plants on Kembel when the TARDIS brought them to the planet in *The Daleks' Master Plan* (1965–1966).

ON THIS DAY

**1963** William Hartnell, who will play the first Doctor, visits BBC Television Centre for make-up tests and to be measured for his costume.

**1965** Most national newspapers report on Verity Lambert's last episode as Producer, accompanied by photos of her with the Dalek Delegates from *Mission to the Unknown*.

## 8 AUGUST

# The Doctor Gives Xoanon a Piece of his Mind

**1964** The first episode of *The Reign of Terror*, titled *A Land of Fear*

When the Mordee Expedition ran into trouble, the Fourth Doctor helped out by programming the spaceship's computer using a variation of the Sidelian memory transfer. But the Doctor forgot to wipe his personality print from the data core. The computer – Xoanon – developed a split personality, half of it being the Doctor's.

Xoanon then created a world in its own image, making the stranded ship's crew act out its madness in reality. So the Survey Team was split from the Technicians – two aspects of the same group of people, in an effort to create a race of superhumans. The Technicians became the Tesh, while the Survey Team degenerated into a primitive tribe, the Sevateem.

When the Fourth Doctor returned in *The Face of Evil* (1977), one of the Sevateem showed him a huge sculpture of 'the Evil One' carved into a cliff face – the face of the Doctor himself. Finding his way back to the ship, and into Xoanon's main control centre, the Doctor told the computer that technicians had worked for generations to extend its power, until the computer evolved into a living creature. 'When I connected my own brain to it,' he explained, 'it didn't just take compatible information as a machine should have done, it took everything… When it woke, it had a complete personality – mine… Then it began to develop a separate self, its own self. And that's when it started to go mad…'

Threatened by the return of the Doctor, Xoanon tries to destroy itself, the Doctor and the planet rather than submit. But after the Doctor manages to wipe his own personality from Xoanon, the computer is restored to charming and polite 'health'.

# 9 AUGUST

# President Nixon Gets a Call

**1974** President Nixon resigns, after addressing the US people on television the previous evening.

ON THIS DAY

Born on 9 January 1913, Richard Milhous Nixon was the Vice President to President Eisenhower from 1953 to 1961. Nixon became the 37th President of the United States of America in 1969.

Although the events of Nixon's presidency are now overshadowed by the Watergate Scandal that forced him out of office, he was President when Apollo 11 took the first men to the Moon. He also assisted the Eleventh Doctor, River Song, Amy and Rory in their investigation into the Silence in *The Impossible Astronaut* and *Day of the Moon* (2011).

Apart from providing the services of FBI agent Canton Everett Delaware III to help the Doctor, Nixon and this one personally bailed out the Doctor when he was detained having been caught tampering with the Command Module of Apollo 11. He was also able to provide a vital clue, from phone calls he had received from a child – who could apparently phone Nixon directly wherever he was. The child was in fact the young Melody Pond – later to become River Song – saying she was scared of the spaceman and that it was going to eat her. The Doctor realised that what Nixon thought was the child's name – Jefferson Adams Hamilton – was actually a location.

## 10 AUGUST

# The Cruel Dominators and Their Deadly Robot Servants

The Second Doctor, Jamie and Zoe encountered the Dominators and their robots the Quarks on the planet Dulkis in *The Dominators* (1968). The Dominators claim they are 'the Masters of the Ten Galaxies'. The Dominators' ship's Radiation Storage Units suck in radiation and store radioactive particles which are converted to power. The two Dominators that land on Dulkis – Rago and Toba – plan to destroy Dulkis, turning the planet into fuel for their fleet which is en route to Epsilon 4.

The Dominator's robots, the Quarks, are powered by ultrasound. The Quarks can use the force units in their arms to shoot to kill, or to paralyse or give an electric shock. They can also be used to provide power, for example for the drill the Dominators use to penetrate the surface of Dulkis.

The Quarks communicate in high-pitched speech, and various high-pitched sounds. For example, a 'double-bleep' indicates confirmation of an order. When a Quark is tripped and covered with a blanket by Jamie, it emits a warning alarm signal.

The Dominators then plan to use an atomic seed device to destroy the planet and turn it into radioactive fuel. The Doctor is able to get hold of the atomic seed device and secrete it on the Dominators' ship.

**1968** *The Dominators*
Episode 1 opens
Season 6.

## 11 AUGUST

# The Movie Doctor – Dr Who

The Doctor of the two *Doctor Who* movies made and released in the mid 1960s is very different from his television counterpart. His name actually *is* Dr Who, and he is an elderly eccentric inventor who has created a time machine called TARDIS in his back garden. He is a far less irritable and crotchety character than the First Doctor.

In the first movie, *Dr Who and the Daleks*, Dr Who and his granddaughters Susan and Barbara show TARDIS to Barbara's boyfriend Ian, who accidentally sends them off through time and space. They arrive on the planet Skaro, where their adventures follow the same basic plot as the first Dalek television story *The Daleks* (1963–1964). In the final spectacular battle between the Daleks and the Thals, the Daleks fire at Ian – destroying their own main control systems.

The second movie, titled *Daleks – Invasion Earth, 2150AD*, starts with policeman Tom Campbell stumbling into TARDIS after a robbery and being transported by Dr Who along with his granddaughter Susan and his niece Louise to London in the year 2150. The plot then broadly follows that of the second Dalek TV story – *The Dalek Invasion of Earth* (1964). But rather than being destroyed by the blast from their own bomb, diverted by Ian, as in the TV version, in the movie the blast releases a wave of magnetism that sucks the Daleks into the mine and causes their ship to crash and explode.

Dr Who then returns Tom to his own time, but a few minutes before the robbery took place so that he can apprehend the criminals.

ON THIS DAY

**1994** Peter Cushing, who played Dr Who in the two 1960s movies *Dr Who and the Daleks* and *Daleks – Invasion Earth, 2150AD*, died.

# 12 AUGUST

## Akhaten

For her first trip in the TARDIS, in *The Rings of Akhaten* (2013), Clara Oswald asked the Eleventh Doctor to take her to see 'something awesome'. The Doctor materialises the TARDIS in space and shows her the Pyramid of the Rings of Akhaten – a holy site for the Sun Singers of Akhat. Seven worlds orbit the same star, the inhabitants believing that all life in the universe originated on one of the planets.

Roughly every thousand years, when the rings align, the inhabitants hold the Festival of Offerings. The offerings are mementos given to the Old God – sometimes called Grandfather – who apparently sleeps within the Pyramid. The Long Song is a lullaby without end that is sung to keep him asleep. The Doctor presumably knows the history and legends as he tells Clara that he has been here before with his granddaughter – so almost certainly in his first incarnation.

But the planet Akhaten where life is supposed to have originated is itself alive. It is a parasite that feeds on the souls of the Sun Singers. When he realises the truth, the Doctor likens the Old God to an alarm clock – if he wakes, then Akhaten will also wake and consume the other planets.

**1848** George Stephenson, who met the Sixth Doctor in *The Mark of the Rani*, died.

# 13 AUGUST

# The Doctor Catches Up with an Old School Friend

While searching for the final segment of the Key to Time in *The Armageddon Factor* (1979), the Fourth Doctor encountered another Time Lord – Drax. They know each other from Gallifrey where they were on a Tech Course together about 450 years ago – in the class of '92. Drax failed, but the Doctor got his doctorate. Drax has been doing freelance work ever since.

About five years previously, just after the war between the twin planets Atrios and Zeos started, Drax built the battle computer Mentalis for the Black Guardian's agent the Shadow, although he was unaware of exactly who he was working for. He subsequently helped the Doctor to disarm the computer. He also rigged up a Relative Dimensional Stabiliser to miniaturise himself and the Doctor so as to get the Sixth Segment of the Key to Time.

Since leaving Gallifrey, Drax has acquired a Cockney accent as his TARDIS broke down on Earth and he was arrested trying to steal replacement components. He was sentenced to ten years in Brixton jail and tells the Doctor: 'Well, I had to learn the lingo, didn't I, to survive.'

Once the Doctor has acquired the complete Key to Time and the war between Atrios and Zeos is over, Drax decides to go into partnership with the Marshal of Atrios, believing he can turn a tidy profit from helping to rebuild the planet.

**1946** The writer H.G. Wells, who met the Sixth Doctor in *Timelash*, died.

**1979** A special trailer for Season 17 is recorded. It features the Fourth Doctor talking to a disembodied voice outside the TARDIS.

# 14 AUGUST

## The Keeper of Traken Asks for Help

The Union of Traken is famous for its harmony – a whole community held together by people being nice to each other, as the Fourth Doctor puts it. In *The Keeper of Traken* (1981), the current Keeper materialises inside the TARDIS to ask the Doctor for his help rooting out the evil he now senses on Traken. That evil is actually the Master, whose TARDIS is disguised as a large statue referred to as 'Melkur'.

The Keeper is the 'organising principle' of Traken. He draws on the minds of the Union in order to rule. Living for hundreds of years, each Keeper draws his power from the Source. The Source is controlled by the Source Manipulator – a glowing sphere below the Keeper's Chamber. The chosen Keeper dedicates himself to this bio-electronics system. The Doctor describes it as: 'Limitless organising capacity confined to a single flame and obedient to the will of your Keeper.'

When a Keeper is close to death, crops fail, there are droughts and floods. This Keeper has ruled for a thousand years, but is now close to dissolution, and his power is waning. It is an agonising death, and with the Source out of control, nature reverts to chaos.

When the Master takes over the Source – making himself Keeper – the Doctor, helped by Adric and the Traken girl Nyssa, is forced to shut the Source down in order to preserve it. When the Master has been defeated, one of the Consuls of Traken – Luvic – becomes the new Keeper.

**ON THIS DAY**

**1964** *Prisoners of the Conciergerie*, the last episode of *The Reign of Terror*, is recorded in studio TC4 at BBC Television Centre. This will be the final episode of the first season of *Doctor Who*, although the next two stories – *Planet of Giants* and *The Dalek Invasion of Earth* are actually recorded in the same production block.

# 15 AUGUST

# Tegan is Possessed by the Mara

ON THIS DAY

**1964** *Guests of Madame Guillotine* – the second episode of *The Reign of Terror*

The Fifth Doctor first encountered the Mara in *Kinda* (1982) on the planet Deva Loka – home of the Kinda. The Kinda seem like a race of primitives, but they are actually highly sophisticated and adept telepaths.

The Mara are a race of creatures that inhabit an unknown realm – 'the dark places of the inside,' as the Doctor puts it. Their physical form is reminiscent of a huge snake. They can use dreaming human minds – in this case Tegan – as a bridge into the physical world, manipulating the subconscious into giving the Mara control over the physical body. This control manifests itself as a deepening of the voice and a red stain on the teeth. This particular Mara returns repeatedly to bring chaos to the Kinda tribe, feeding on their negative emotions.

Although the Doctor banishes the Mara at the end of *Kinda*, Tegan is not completely free of it and the creature resurfaces in *Snakedance* (1983) when the Doctor and his companions arrive on the planet Manussa – the original home of the Mara.

Long ago, Manussan scientists created a Great Crystal using molecular engineering. It was supposedly capable of collecting and focussing the energies of the human mind; but those energies absorbed were only the negative ones, such as fear, anger, greed and hate. When these raw energies were reflected and amplified within the facets of the Crystal, the Mara was created as an evil and aggressive intelligence able to manifest itself in the physical world as a snake-like creature.

# 16 AUGUST

## Salyavin Escapes from Shada

Although they have been induced to forget it, Shada was the ancient time prison of the Time Lords. Its location – built into an asteroid or small planet – is secret, but it can be reached by turning back the pages of *The Worshipful and Ancient Law of Gallifrey* whilst in a TARDIS. It was on Shada that the Time Lords imprisoned the war criminal Rungar, and the mass murderer Sabjatric. It was also where they incarcerated Salyavin.

Salyavin's 'crime' was the ability to project his own mind into other people's minds. When he escaped from Shada, he took *The Worshipful and Ancient Law of Gallifrey* from the Panopticon Archives as it revealed the existence and location of Shada. The book dates back to the Time of Rassilon and is one of 'the Artefacts'. Each of the Artefacts was imbued with great powers. Time is travelling backwards over the book, which is minus 20,000 years old.

In *Shada* (which was never completed or transmitted due to industrial action at the BBC), the Fourth Doctor and Romana visit Professor Chronotis – a Time Lord who retired to Cambridge University three hundred years ago. He is in his final regeneration, and has a TARDIS disguised as his university rooms at St Cedd's College.

But Chronotis is in fact Salyavin, who has also used his mental powers to make the Time Lords – including the Doctor and Romana – forget that Shada existed. Now, however, someone else is after Salyavin and the book. The scientist Skagra hopes that if he steals Salyavin's mind it will help him put his own mind into all matter in the universe…

**1979** Permission is given for Script Editor Douglas Adams to write the final six-part story of the next season of *Doctor Who*. However, the story – *Shada* – is never completed or broadcast due to a strike at the BBC. What was recorded is available on DVD, and a novelisation of the story by Gareth Roberts working from Douglas Adams' original scripts was published by BBC Books in 2012.

**2001** The National Film Theatre stages a tribute to Douglas Adams, which includes a screening of the 1979 *Doctor Who* story *City of Death* – written by Adams under the 'in-house' pseudonym David Agnew.

**2017** A holiday liner sank, according to a newspaper report seen in *The Enemy of the World*.

# 17 AUGUST

## The Gelth Awaken the Dead

**1968** *The Dominators*
Episode 2

Encountered by the Ninth Doctor and Rose in *The Unquiet Dead* (2005), the Gelth are ectoplasmic, ethereal wraith-creatures that possess the dead at the nineteenth-century Cardiff undertakers' firm of Sneed and Company. They use a person with psychic ability – the maid Gwyneth – as a bridge between the dimensions.

Essentially gaseous creatures, in this world the Gelth 'live' in the gas pipes – the environment most suited to them. They claim there are very few Gelth left; they are the last of their kind and are facing extinction having lost their physical bodies in the Great Time War. But in fact they plan to invade, killing the humans and then possessing the bodies of the dead.

Possessed by the Gelth, the bodies brought to Sneed's funeral parlour do not stay dead. The Gelth are able to inhabit the dead, bringing them back to unnatural life. But the 'union' of Gelth and body is weak and after a short while the zombie collapses – once more a lifeless corpse, as the Gelth leave it.

Attuned to the Gelth, Mr Sneed's maid Gwyneth is able to communicate with them and considers them angels sent by her dead mother. But the Doctor is able to convince her of their true nature.

## 18 AUGUST

# The Beast Escapes from the Satan Pit

At a time before time itself even existed, there was the Beast. Feared and deadly, it became the template for every representation of evil that followed, right across the universe. It entered the myths and legends of countless planets – Earth, Draconia, Vel Consadine, Damos and even Skaro. The same image, the same creature, informed the devil, the horned beast, the Kaled god of war, and many others.

But despite its mighty power, the Beast was defeated and imprisoned on an isolated planet circling a black hole. The ancient people that captured the Beast did not kill it, but bound it to the core of the planet. They made sure that the planet itself circled the black hole – and that if the Beast ever escaped, it would be sucked in, destroying their ancient prisoner…

Millions of years later, a group of humans established Sanctuary Base 6 on the planet, hoping to discover the power source that kept the planet safe from the gravitational pull of the black hole. The humans knew nothing of the Beast, but it felt them, and reached out to them. Soon after the Tenth Doctor and Rose Tyler arrived in *The Impossible Planet* and *The Satan Pit* (2006), the Ood working with the humans on Sanctuary Base 6 were telepathically possessed by the Beast and turned on their human masters…

Through its own words, recorded in runic symbols, the Beast possessed not only the telepathic Ood but also the human archaeologist Toby Zed. Leaving its mindless body still imprisoned, the Beast planned to escape hidden inside Toby's mind…

**1977** A repeat showing of Part 3 of *The Deadly Assassin* has the cliffhanger ending trimmed to remove a freeze-frame of the Doctor's face as he is held under water, apparently drowning. This is because of complaints about the original broadcast from the National Viewers and Listeners Association.

# 19 AUGUST

# The Doctor is Shipwrecked on the *Titanic* – Again

Leaving the TARDIS to repair itself after a collision with what seems to be an ocean liner in *Voyage of the Damned* (2007), the Tenth Doctor finds himself on board the starship *Titanic*, orbiting Earth. It is a replica of the original doomed ship, on which the Ninth Doctor previously sailed.

The *Titanic* is a space cruiser from the planet Sto in the Cassavalian Belt, owned and operated by Max Capricorn Cruiseliners. The passengers are there to get experience of various primitive cultures along the way. And to enjoy Christmas.

On board the ship, the Heavenly Host – robots that look like angels – provide information and assistance, while the ship's historian Mr Copper is on hand to explain local customs. But the Doctor soon realises that former salesman Bayldon Copper is relying on rather dubious information he has learned studying Earthonomics at Mrs Golightly's Happy Travelling University.

The Doctor also meets the waitress Astrid Peth. She has always wanted to travel and see the universe – so she became a waitress on the luxury star cruiser. When a meteoroid strike disables the *Titanic*, Astrid assists the Doctor as he helps other survivors to get to safety. But they are attacked by the reprogrammed Heavenly Host robots. The Doctor discovers that the crash has been engineered by Max Capricorn – former owner of the cruise company – who is concealed on board.

ON THIS DAY

**1972** The second *Doctor Who* movie, *Daleks – Invasion Earth, 2150AD*, is broadcast on TV for the first time, as part of BBC 1's *High Adventure* film season.

## 20 AUGUST

# Harry Sullivan's First TARDIS Trip is to Space Station Nerva

When solar flares threatened to end all life on Earth, a group of humans was sent to Space Station Nerva where they were kept in cryogenic suspension, along with animal and botanic specimens. The intention was that they would reawaken when Earth was safe to repopulate. But a Wirrn queen, having travelled through space for many years from Andromeda, has broken into Nerva and laid its eggs inside one of the sleeping humans – Dune. It also disabled the main systems so that the humans were never woken…

The Fourth Doctor, Sarah Jane Smith and Harry Sullivan – on his first trip in the TARDIS – arrive on Space Station Nerva in *The Ark in Space* (1975) just as the giant insectoid Wirrn are about to hatch. The Doctor describes the process whereby the Wirrn take over the sleepers as 'symbiotic atavism'. When the larvae emerge, they have a food supply and are equipped with all Dune's knowledge. This knowledge is added to as they absorb more humans.

Having defeated the Wirrn, the Doctor and his friends transmat down to Earth. But on their return trip the transmat beam is intercepted and they are diverted to the planet Skaro by the Time Lords. A Time Ring returns them to Nerva in *Revenge of the Cybermen* (1975) – but at a much earlier point in its history.

Nerva Beacon, as it then was, has been put in place by Earth Centre to service and guide space freighters. In particular, it guides them round Jupiter's new satellite – at first named as Neo Phobos, but renamed Voga by the Beacon's exographer, Kellman – which the Doctor

**1572** The Doctor and Steven arrive in Paris in the story *The Massacre*.

**1932** Anthony Ainley, who played the Master from *Logopolis* in 1981 through to *Survival* in 1989, was born.

**1943** Sylvester McCoy, who played the Seventh Doctor, was born.

**1962** Sophie Aldred, who played the Seventh Doctor's companion Ace, was born.

**1963** The first ever video recording on *Doctor Who* took place. It was a sequence of 'visual howlaround' – a camera recording its own output – to be used for the opening title sequence.

**1975** An edited compilation repeat of *The Ark in Space* is shown on BBC 1. It runs for 70 minutes.

recognises as the fabled Planet of Gold. The Beacon's crew has been all but wiped out by a plague, which is actually an infection spread by Cybermats. Before long, a group of Cybermen take over Nerva Beacon, intent on destroying Voga as its gold is lethal to them.

# 21 AUGUST

## The Doctor Encounters Human Daleks

**1964** It is announced that the Daleks are to return for a second encounter with the Doctor.

As well as Robomen – humans programmed to obey the Daleks, whose distinctive headgear gives them away – the Daleks have several more subtle ways of controlling humans.

In *The Evil of the Daleks* (1967), Ruth Maxtible's fiancé, Arthur Terrall, hears Dalek commands in his head and is controlled by a small black box on his neck. The maid, Molly, says that Terrall is usually a kind man, and attributes his being 'a bit odd' to his experiences in the Crimean War. When the Second Doctor remarks that he has never seen Terrall eat or drink, Terrall insists he dines alone. But the Doctor uses a sword to test a theory – and finds it behaves as if magnetised. 'If I didn't know better, Mr Terrall,' he says, 'I'd say that you were full of some sort of electricity.' The headmaster of Coal Hill School is controlled by a similar device in *Remembrance of the Daleks* (1988).

In *Resurrection of the Daleks* (1984), the Fifth Doctor discovers that the Daleks can create duplicates of people that obey their will, and claim to have placed duplicates in strategic positions on Earth. They also plan to send duplicates of the Doctor, Tegan and Turlough to Gallifrey, specially programmed to assassinate the members of the High Council of the Time Lords. But one of the Daleks' duplicates – Stien – regains some of his original character and humanity, and activates a self-destruct system that destroys the Dalek ship.

In *Daleks in Manhattan* and *Evolution of the Daleks* (2007), the Daleks of the Cult of Skaro try to combine Dalek and human DNA, reformatting human brains to turn them into Daleks. But the experiment is not a success as the Doctor adds some of his own DNA into the mix.

In *Asylum of the Daleks* (2012), the Daleks use another form of controlled human – Dalek 'puppets'. These are dead people reanimated to serve the Daleks, often without even realising they are dead. When under complete Dalek control, a Dalek eyestalk erupts from their foreheads.

## 22 AUGUST

# The CyberKing Rises

In *The Next Doctor* (2008), the Tenth Doctor arrived in London on Christmas Eve 1851 – to find another Doctor battling against a group of Cybermen stranded in Victorian London. At first he thought this other Doctor was a future incarnation of himself. But gradually he realised this was not the case. And when the Other Doctor showed him his TARDIS, it turned out to be a hot air balloon.

As he unravelled this mystery, the real Doctor joined forces with his alter ego to fight the Cybermen and deadly new Cybershades. They discovered a huge work area where the Cybermen and their ally, the ambitious Miss Hartigan, were using children from the local workhouses as slave labourers to construct a massive CyberKing robot.

The Doctor described the huge CyberKing as a Dreadnought-class ship – the front line of a proposed Cyber invasion of Earth. Once completed, it rose from

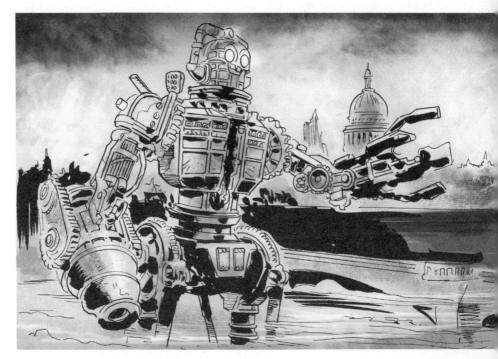

beneath the Thames to attack the city. The controlling influence was the adapted form of Miss Hartigan, the Matron of St Joseph's Workhouse, who the Cybermen decided would be their supreme leader. But she retained some of her emotions and her ambition, as her imagination was able to override the Cyber technology.

The main body of the CyberKing robot contained a Cyber-factory, ready to convert millions of humans into a new race of Cybermen.

**1964** *A Change of Identity* – the third episode of *The Reign of Terror*

## 23 AUGUST

# Meet the Twelfth Doctor

After his time defending Trenzalore, culminating in his destruction of the attacking Daleks in *The Time of the Doctor* (2013), the Eleventh Doctor regenerated into the Twelfth Doctor. Unstable, as usual after a traumatic regeneration, the Twelfth Doctor took a while to settle down into his new persona.

He looked older, and was distinctly less personable, lacking in social graces. He also had a face that he himself recognised, although it was not until *The Girl Who Died* (2015) that he recalled where from. It was the face of Caecilius – the Roman he saved, together with his family, from the eruption of Mount Vesuvius in *The Fires of Pompeii* (2008). A face he had given himself as a reminder that he saves people.

The Twelfth Doctor mellowed, and gradually came to appreciate and understand other people, helped to no small extent by the influence of Clara Oswald. Losing her in *Face the Raven* (2015) was devastating for him.

But despite his scratchiness and lack of tact, the Twelfth Doctor is the same as all his previous incarnations in the things that really matter. He is never really cruel or cowardly, he hates injustice, he battles against the terrible things that the darkest corners of the universe has bred, and he saves people…

## 24 AUGUST

# The Doctor Saves the World, But Not Pompeii

In *The Fires of Pompeii* (2008), the Tenth Doctor takes Donna Noble to Rome – but they actually arrive in Pompeii in AD 79, just as Mount Vesuvius is about to erupt. Strange things are happening – it seems that the augurs and soothsayers really *can* see the future (except for the eruption), and they are turning to stone.

The Doctor finds that a group of Pyroviles has arrived under the mountain, and is planning to take over the world now that their own planet, Pyrovillia, has been 'lost'. The Pyroviles are a race made of rock and fire, and all their technology is derived from these same elements. This group of Pyroviles made their way to Earth almost two thousand years ago, making their base deep inside Mount Vesuvius. They planned to weld themselves to humans – creating a new species, and boiling away Earth's oceans and seas.

Humans who breathe in Pyrovillian dust dispersed through the hypocausts from Mount Vesuvius are themselves slowly turned to stone – becoming Pyroviles. The High Priestess of the Sibylline Oracle and her fellow priestesses of Pompeii have glimpsed a future under the rule of the Pyroviles. But breathing in contaminated vapours from Mount Vesuvius has mutated them. The High Priestess is further advanced, part way to becoming a Pyrovile – when the Doctor encounters her, she is a hideous creature made of stone.

The Doctor and Donna are faced with the terrible prospect of saving the world by sacrificing Pompeii. But Donna persuades the Doctor to rescue one family from the terrible aftermath of the eruption…

**79** Mount Vesuvius erupts, burying Pompeii.

**1572** The Massacre of the Hugenots begins. By 17 September 25,000 Protestants have been killed in Paris alone. The killing does not stop until 3 October.

**1968** *The Dominators* Episode 3

# 25 AUGUST

# The Doctor Remembers to Use the Memory Worm

**1975** The edition of *Disney Time* that Tom Baker filmed inserts for on 3 August is broadcast on BBC 1, while Tom Baker is actually involved in recording *The Android Invasion*.

Both the Eleventh and Twelfth Doctors have made use of a creature known as a Memory Worm. Looking rather like a large worm with eyes, stubby antennae, and teeth, the worm is coated with a substance that destroys the short-term memories of anyone who touches it – as the Sontaran Strax does in *The Snowmen* (2012), for example.

A bite from the worm can apparently remove decades' worth of memories. The Eleventh Doctor used the Memory Worm to remove the adult memories of Walter Simeon who had been possessed by the Great Intelligence. He hid it inside a lunchbox, and when Simeon opened the box the worm bit him. But the removal of Simeon's memories just left more space inside him for the Great Intelligence…

The Twelfth Doctor used a Memory Worm in *Time Heist* (2014) to remove his own memories, along with those of Clara, Saibra and Psi, so they would not realise that the Doctor was himself the mysterious Architect who sent them to break into the most secure bank in the galaxy – the Bank of Karabraxos.

# 26 AUGUST

# The Pandorica Reboots the Universe

Legend says that the Pandorica was the prison of a warrior or a goblin who tried to tear the world apart until he was tricked by a wizard who locked him up. In fact, it was a large hollow cube – actually based on an image of Pandora's Box from an old book of Amy Pond's – that was built to be a prison for the Eleventh Doctor by an alliance of life forms that wanted to prevent him from inadvertently destroying all of creation. They trapped the Doctor in a chamber beneath Stonehenge in Roman times in *The Pandorica Opens* and *The Big Bang* (2010), and locked him inside.

But, with the help of Rory Williams, the Doctor escaped. He used the Pandorica to preserve the almost-dead Amy Pond until she was revived by the DNA of her younger self nearly two thousand years later.

The Pandorica was taken to Rome in AD 118, from where it was plundered by the Franks in 420. By 1120, it was in the possession of the Knights Templar. In 1231 it was apparently given to the Vatican, and some time after this it was sold by Marco Polo…

During this time, the Pandorica was said to be guarded by the Lone Centurion – actually an Auton version of Rory – who dragged it to safety from a burning warehouse during the London Blitz in 1941.

The Doctor eventually used the Pandorica to restore the universe. He used atoms from the original universe, trapped and preserved inside the Pandorica, combined with the energy of the TARDIS exploding to 'reboot' it…

**ON THIS DAY**

**1883** Krakatoa erupts. The Ninth Doctor is washed up on the shores of Sumatra the same day, according to Clive in *Rose* who has a sketch of the Doctor from this time.

**1991** The pilot episode of *Doctor Who*, made in 1963, is transmitted for the first time (on BBC Two).

## 27 AUGUST

# The Teselecta is the Doctor

First encountered by the Eleventh Doctor in *Let's Kill Hitler* (2011), the Teselecta was a humanoid robot that could travel through both time and space. It could also change its appearance to pose as any individual. The Teselecta was designated Justice Department Vehicle Number 6018 and was operated by a miniaturised crew of 421 people commanded by Captain Carter. Their job was to seek out those deemed guilty of crimes and mete out punishment to them, usually near the end of their historically recorded lives so that history would not be changed.

Sent to find Hitler, the crew of the Teselecta arrived too early in his time stream. But they also found Melody Pond – the woman who would kill the Doctor. The Teselecta was unable to punish Melody as Amy and Rory got inside the robot and sabotaged it, turning the Teselecta's robotic antibodies against the crew. The Doctor later managed to get information about the Silence and their plans for him from the Teselecta's data.

In *The Wedding of River Song* (2011), the Doctor used the Teselecta to put time back on track. Melody Pond – now River Song – refusing to go through the Doctor's assassination disrupted time itself, as the Doctor's apparent death was an immutable 'fixed point' in time. With the miniaturised Doctor on board, the Teselecta adopted the Doctor's own shape, and took his place at Lake Silencio where – in *The Impossible Astronaut* (2011) – River Song shot and appeared to kill him. Once she realised that this was not in fact the Doctor, River Song went through with the apparent assassination, and time returned to normal.

ON THIS DAY

**1993** The Third Doctor radio adventure *Paradise of Death* begins on BBC Radio 5.

**2011** *Let's Kill Hitler* opens the second section of Series Six.

## 28 AUGUST

# Defending the Earth Against Alien Invasions

The planet Earth seems to have had more than its fair share of alien invasions. At his trial in *The War Games* (1969), the Second Doctor tells the Time Lords that Earth 'seems more vulnerable' than other planets. This may be because its position gives it strategic advantages – as both the Sontarans and the Rutans decide at various points.

In *Spearhead from Space* (1970), Brigadier Lethbridge-Stewart tells Liz Shaw that Earth has recently drawn attention to itself by sending probes deeper and deeper into space. He tells her that he knows of two previous attempted invasions – by the Great Intelligence in *The Web of Fear* (1968) and the Cybermen in *The Invasion* (1968). But there have been many more that he does not know about.

Despite the existence of the Torchwood Institute, first mentioned in *Tooth and Claw* (2006), and the so-called 'Countermeasures' team seen in *Remembrance of the Daleks* (1988), it was only with the formation of UNIT that Earth had an international organisation equipped and able to stand up to attempted alien incursions. Answering to UNIT Headquarters in Geneva, the UK branch of UNIT in particular seemed to have its work cut out, so was lucky to have the Third Doctor as its scientific adviser. After he joined UNIT, the organisation had to contend with attacks from the Nestenes, Silurians, Axos, Dæmons, Daleks, Sea Devils, and Zygons amongst others – as well as all manner of other extraordinary threats…

**1964** Filming begins at John's Hole Quarry near Dartford in Kent for scenes outside the Dalek mine in Bedfordshire in *The Dalek Invasion of Earth*. This is the first use of a quarry location in *Doctor Who*.

# 29 AUGUST

## The Doctor Helps George the Tenza

**1964** *The Tyrant of France* – the fourth episode of *The Reign of Terror*

The young of the Tenza are, rather like cuckoos, raised by other life forms. The Tenza are born in space, and then drift until they find a habitable world where the child then infiltrates a family. A psychic field and a perception filter mean that the child seems to fit into the society it has adopted. It alters the memories of the surrogate parents so that they believe the child to be their own. The Tenza then lives out its life as a member of the same species as its adopted parents – without any conscious realisation of its own nature.

The Tenza child that the Eleventh Doctor met in *Night Terrors* (2011) summoned the Doctor without realising it when he sent a message to the Doctor's psychic paper – 'Please save me from the monsters.' The Doctor discovered the message had come from a boy named George. Although George's 'parents' Alex and Claire had no idea he was a Tenza, they had seen him develop phobias and wanted to get him professional help. George's anxiety that this would mean being taken away from his parents set off his psychic defences. Anyone who frightened him found themselves miniaturised inside a dolls' house in George's bedroom, and attacked by peg dolls.

When the Doctor was trapped inside the dolls' house and tried to get George to help him, the Tenza child was himself transported inside. When his 'father' Alex saved him from the peg dolls, George realised that his fears of being abandoned were unfounded…

## 30 AUGUST

# Clara Meets Danny Pink

Danny Pink was a Maths teacher at Coal Hill School where Clara Oswald taught English. Disliking his real name, Rupert, he adopted the name Danny. Before becoming a teacher, Danny served in the British army as a sergeant. He left after accidentally killing a young boy while in a conflict zone.

As they became romantically involved, Clara tried to keep her association with the Doctor secret from Danny. This became impossible after the events of *The Caretaker* (2014) when Danny accidentally sabotaged the Twelfth Doctor's plans to deal with a rogue Skovox Blitzer at the school while working there as caretaker.

Danny was killed in a road accident in *Dark Water* (2014), leaving Clara distraught enough to try to force the Doctor to save Danny. In fact, Danny's mind was preserved by Missy in the Nethersphere. In *Death in Heaven* (2014), along with the other dead people whose minds were preserved, Danny was 'reborn' as a Cyberman. But he managed to retain his humanity, as well as his love for Clara, and led the other 'reborn' Cybermen to destruction. Inside the Nethersphere, Danny gave up the chance to escape back to a real life so that the boy he accidentally killed could take his place.

In *Last Christmas* (2014), under the influence of a Dream Crab, Clara dreamt of an idyllic Christmas – and life – with Danny. A life they would never have…

ON THIS DAY

**1975** The Zygons first appear in *Terror of the Zygons* Part 1, which opens Season 13.

**1980** *The Leisure Hive* Part 1 opens Season 18 and introduces a new version of the theme music. It is the first episode produced by John Nathan-Turner, who remains Producer until the classic series comes to an end in 1989. It is also Christopher H. Bidmead's first episode as Script Editor and Barry Letts's first as Executive Producer. John Leeson returns as the voice of K-9.

**2014** Danny Pink, Clara's boyfriend, first appears in *Into the Dalek*.

# 31 AUGUST

## Captain Avery Sails Through the Stars

**1968** *The Dominators*
Episode 4

When the Eleventh Doctor met the pirate Captain Henry Avery in *The Curse of the Black Spot* (2011), it was not actually the first time their paths had crossed. In *The Smugglers* (1966), the First Doctor found himself caught up in a search for Avery's treasure – hidden in the crypt of a church in Cornwall.

Avery was an officer in the British navy in the late seventeenth century before he turned to piracy, corrupted by ideas of wealth and power. When the Doctor, Amy and Rory arrived on his ship the *Fancy* in 1699, it was 'haunted' by a Siren. The beautiful female apparition would appear to take any of the crew who was ill or injured.

But the Doctor realised that the Siren was actually a medical program – a virtual doctor – on a spaceship that occupied the same space as the *Fancy* in another reality. With Avery's son, Tom, ill with typhoid fever, Avery knew that the only way he could survive was on the spaceship. Avery and his crew joined Tom to voyage through the stars.

In *A Good Man Goes to War* (2011), Avery and his son and crew came to help the Doctor in the Battle of Demons Run.

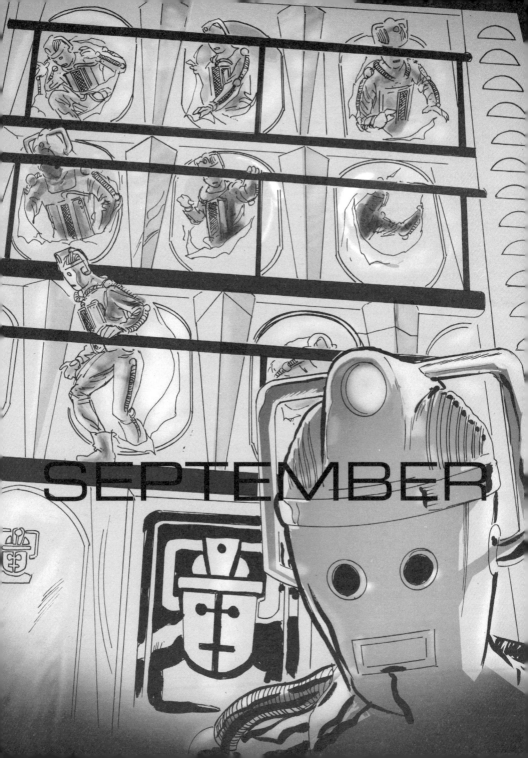

SEPTEMBER

# 1 SEPTEMBER

# The Doctor is Sent to the Asylum

The Doctor believed that the Dalek Asylum was just a legend – until the Eleventh Doctor was kidnapped by the Daleks and sent there in *Asylum of the Daleks* (2012).

The Asylum is a planet where all the Daleks that go wrong are sent – the Doctor describes them as battle-scarred and insane, the ones even the Daleks themselves can't control. The Daleks will not simply destroy them as they find it offensive to extinguish such divine hatred. No one knows exactly how many Daleks there are in the Asylum, but it probably numbers millions.

The Asylum occupies the whole planet, right to its core. It is fully automated, with no supervision. The force field that protects it can only be turned off from within the Asylum. The Daleks have detected strange emissions emanating from the Asylum, which makes them think that the imprisoned Daleks there might escape. Now they want the Doctor, together with Amy Pond and Rory Williams, to deactivate the force field so the Asylum can be destroyed.

The emissions are actually coming from Junior Entertainment Officer Oswin Oswald – the only survivor when the starship *Alaska* crashed into the Asylum. The rest of the dead crew from the *Alaska* have been converted into Dalek 'puppets' by a nanocloud of nanogenes. These are microorganisms that automatically process any organic matter, living or dead, into a Dalek puppet. The intention is that anything that attacks the Asylum will automatically become part of the Asylum's own security systems.

**1965** The first *Doctor Who* annual is published in September 1965.

**1979** Romana regenerates in Episode 1 of *Destiny of the Daleks* and is now played by Lalla Ward. The episode opens Season 17. It is Douglas Adams's first episode as Script Editor.

**1981** Location shooting begins on Peter Davison's first story as the Fifth Doctor, *Castrovalva*. Davison has already made several stories to be transmitted later in his opening series, the first he shot being *Four to Doomsday*.

**2012** An 'aspect' of Clara first appears, in the form of Oswin, in *Asylum of the Daleks*, which opens Series Seven.

## 2 SEPTEMBER

# The White Guardian Needs the Key to Time

While en route to Harlegon Three for a holiday, the Fourth Doctor is intercepted by the White Guardian, who stops the TARDIS and gives the Doctor 'a vitally important task': he must find the Key to Time. The Guardian also provides a new assistant for the Doctor – the Time Lady Romanadvoratrelundar, or Romana for short.

The Guardians are incredibly powerful, almost elemental creatures. As well as the White Guardian – the Guardian of Light in Time – to balance him there is also a Black Guardian. He requires the Key to Time for his own evil purpose. Even the Doctor holds the Guardians in awe, and when he tentatively asks what will happen if he refuses his task, the Guardian tells him simply: 'Nothing … Nothing at all. Ever.'

The Key to Time is a perfect cube composed of six segments, which maintains the equilibrium of Time itself. The segments are scattered and hidden throughout the cosmos. The Key itself, once assembled, is too powerful for any single being to possess. The White Guardian tells the Doctor that there are 'times when the forces within the universe upset the balance to such an extent that it becomes necessary to stop everything … for a brief moment only, until the balance is restored'. Such a moment is rapidly approaching, and the Guardian needs the segments traced and returned to him before the universe is plunged into eternal chaos.

The segments are disguised – they contain the elemental force of the universe and can be in any shape, form or size. The Doctor is given the core of the Key itself which acts as a locator and transforms each segment

**1666** The Great Fire of London started on this day.

**1966** The BBC announce that William Hartnell will be leaving the series to be replaced by Patrick Troughton.

**1967** *The Tomb of the Cybermen* Episode 1 opens Season 5. Peter Bryant takes over from Innes Lloyd as Producer for this one story. He will become full Producer from *The Web of Fear*. Victor Pemberton acts as Story Editor for *The Tomb of the Cybermen*.

**1978** Part 1 of *The Ribos Operation* introduces Romana and opens Season 16. It also sets up the season-long quest for the Key to Time.

back into its true form on contact. Together, the Doctor, Romana, and K-9 find all six segments – disguised as a lump of rare Jethrik, an entire planet, the Great Seal of Diplos, part of a statue, a religious Symbol of Power, and a princess.

# 3 SEPTEMBER

## The Doctor and Leela are Trapped in a Lighthouse with a Rutan

Sworn enemies of the Sontarans, the Rutans are tendriled, gelatinous green blobs from the cold, icy planet of Ruta 3. They evolved in the sea before adapting to land. The Rutan Empire has already been at war with the Sontarans for millennia when the Fourth Doctor and Leela encounter a Rutan in *Horror of Fang Rock* (1977). Now – in the early years of the twentieth century – it seems that the Rutans have decided that Earth is in an ideal strategic position from which to attack their enemies.

The Rutan scout that attacks the isolated lighthouse on the tiny island of Fang Rock is tasked with assessing the planet and its life forms. It shrouds the island in fog to obscure its operations, then takes a lighthouse keeper, Ben, for analysis, conducting a post mortem on the man's body.

The Rutan has been specially trained in 'new metamorphosis techniques' and assumes the form of a second lighthouse keeper, Reuben. It kills with electrical discharges from its body in order to keep its mission secret. It signals to the Rutan mothership using power from the lighthouse generator.

The Doctor eventually destroys the Rutan with an early Schemurly rocket launcher, adapted to fire diamonds that the shipwrecked Lord Palmerdale was carrying with him. The Doctor is also able to destroy the Rutan mothership, which has a shielded crystalline infrastructure, by adapting the lighthouse carbon arc lamp to become a laser-like amplified carbon oscillator.

**1973** An edited compilation repeat of *Day of the Daleks* is shown on BBC 1. It runs for 60 minutes, and is shown on BBC Wales on 6 September.

**1977** The Sontarans' mortal enemy the Rutans appear in *Horror of Fang Rock* Part 1, which opens Season 15. It is Graham Williams' first episode as Producer.

**2011** *Night Terrors*

# 4 SEPTEMBER

# The Mandragora Helix Comes to Earth

The Mandragora Helix is a spiral of pure energy that radiates outwards in ways that nobody really understands. At its centre is a controlling intelligence. From space, it looks like a whirlpool. When the TARDIS materialises inside the Helix in *The Masque of Mandragora* (1976), it arrives in an echoing black void with crystal spiralling into the distance. The Fourth Doctor and Sarah Jane Smith manage to escape. However, a portion of Helix Energy enters the TARDIS and is brought back to Earth – where the TARDIS lands in San Martino in Italy in the late fifteenth century.

The Helix Energy is a glowing ball of fire that burns where it touches – leaving bodies charred beyond recognition by the high ionisation. The Helix Energy restores the ruined Temple of Demnos to its former glory, penetrating every stone and using it as a focal point. It also takes over Hieronymous – the leader of the Cult of Demnos – eventually converting him into pure Mandragora Energy.

Seeing humanity as a future threat to its domain, Mandragora plans to destroy the philosophers and thinkers (including Leonardo da Vinci) who are at the masque ball to celebrate Giuliano's accession to the dukedom of San Martino, and coincident with an eclipse of the Moon. Although the Doctor manages to drain away the Helix Energy, thwarting Mandragora's plans, he says that Mandragora's constellation will be 'in position to try again' in five hundred years' time – at about the end of the twentieth century.

**1932** Edward de Souza was born. He played lead character SSS Agent Marc Cory in *Mission to the Unknown* in 1965, the only episode not to feature the Doctor or any of his current companions.

**1976** *The Masque of Mandragora* Part 1 opens Season 14.

# 5 SEPTEMBER

# The Doctor Invokes the Shadow Proclamation

**ON THIS DAY**

**1964** *A Bargain of Necessity* – the fifth episode of *The Reign of Terror*

**2006** The events of *Boom Town* take place around now, as the story is set six months after *Aliens of London*.

When the Shadow Proclamation was first mentioned by the Ninth Doctor in *Rose* (2005), it was not clear whether it was a treaty, an edict or an organisation. The Tenth Doctor again cited the Shadow Proclamation when dealing with the Isolus child in *Fear Her* (2006), and Rose invoked it when trying unsuccessfully to bluff the Sycorax Leader in *The Christmas Invasion* (2005). In *Partners in Crime* (2008), Miss Foster was afraid that the Tenth Doctor would report her activities at Adipose Industries to the Shadow Proclamation. When the Tenth Doctor and Donna discovered that the Earth had vanished in *The Stolen Earth* (2008), it was to the Shadow Proclamation that the Doctor went for help…

A vast space station houses the Shadow Proclamation, an organisation dedicated to upholding the conventions and statutes agreed by its participating races. Local security, and much of the actual law enforcement, is the responsibility of the Judoon – a troop of which is permanently stationed on site.

The most senior official of the Shadow Proclamation is the Shadow Architect. It is not known if the position is elected or appointed. At the time the Doctor and Donna go to the Shadow Proclamation for help, the Shadow Architect is an elderly pale-skinned female humanoid, with others of her own race acting as her staff. It may be that the post alternates between different races, or that these pale female humanoids always fulfil the role. Another possibility is that the question simply does not arise and the current Shadow Architect has always been and will always be the holder of that position. Certainly, it is the same woman – or a very similar one – who tells Colony Sarff in *The Magician's Apprentice* (2015) that the Shadow Proclamation does not know where the Doctor is, and that he is not their concern.

# 6 SEPTEMBER

## Clara Meets the Real Robin Hood

When the Twelfth Doctor tells Clara Oswald she can choose anywhere to visit in time and space in *Robot of Sherwood* (2014), she recalls a story she has loved since she was a little girl and asks him to take her to see Robin Hood. The Doctor tells her that Robin Hood is a myth and that he never really existed. But he does take her to Sherwood Forest in around 1190. And they do meet Robin Hood.

Despite the Doctor's scepticism, it turns out that Robin Hood does exist. But not everything is as it seems. Arrested by the Sheriff of Nottingham, the Doctor discovers that the Sheriff's knights are actually robots, and that Nottingham Castle is in fact a spaceship from the twenty-ninth century. The Sheriff himself has been turned – at least in part – into a robot and is helping the robot knights repair their ship using gold that he steals from the locals.

The Doctor and Clara have to work with Robin Hood and his Merry Men – including Friar Tuck, Little John, Alan-a-Dale and Will Scarlet – to defeat the Sheriff and the robots, and prevent the damaged ship from destroying half the country when it inevitably explodes soon after take-off. Finally, the Doctor is forced to admit – if only to himself – that Robin Hood actually existed.

**1973** An edited compilation repeat of *Day of the Daleks* is shown on BBC Wales – it runs for 60 minutes, and was previously shown on BBC 1 on 3 September.

**1975** *Terror of the Zygons* Part 2

**1980** *The Leisure Hive* Part 2

**1986** *Doctor Who* returns for Season 23 after an unprecedented 18-month 'hiatus' for the first part of a story that will last the whole, shorter, 14-week season: *The Trial of a Time Lord*. The first four episodes are generally known as *The Mysterious Planet*.

**1989** Brigadier Lethbridge-Stewart returns in *Battlefield* Part 1, which opens Season 26.

**2014** *Robot of Sherwood*

# 7 SEPTEMBER

# Meet the Seventh Doctor

The Seventh Doctor is a mass of contradictions. At first, he seems to be a bumbler who misinterprets and miscalculates at almost every opportunity. Yet, he is soon revealed to be a master-planner. The mistakes he may have made prior to *Silver Nemesis* (1988) become a plan to destroy the Cybermen. We get the impression in *Remembrance of the Daleks* (1988) that he is springing a trap he set before we ever met him – before the events of *An Unearthly Child* (1963). *The Curse of Fenric* (1989) reveals that he has known the truth about Ace and how Fenric has tried to use her ever since they met…

The Seventh Doctor's quips and misquotes mask a deeper, darker side. He cultivates an image of mystery, going out of his way to obscure his personal details, and is more 'obvious' in his alien-ness than most other incarnations. But rather than simply keep his secrets, he constantly alludes to them – as if to provoke an enigmatic aura. He drops hints to Ace about how he may have been involved in developing the Hand of Omega; he allows Lady Peinforte to reveal that he is more than just a Time Lord; he seems determined to provoke Ace into asking, at the end of *Silver Nemesis*: 'Who are you?' merely so he can refuse to answer…

Perhaps the Seventh Doctor is a flipside to the Second. Whereas the Second Doctor so often made his success look like luck or happenstance, it may be that the Seventh Doctor has a knack of making his good fortune and callous impulsiveness seem like complex planning.

**1533** Queen Elizabeth I was born.

**1968** *The Dominators* Episode 5.

**1987** *Time and the Rani* Part 1 is Sylvester McCoy's first episode and opens Season 24. It is Andrew Cartmel's first episode as Script Editor – a post he holds for the rest of the classic series.

# 8 SEPTEMBER

# The Movellans Take on the Daleks

The Movellans are a humanoid race of robots and have been at war with the Daleks for centuries. The Movellans' origins are unknown, although Romana identifies their ship as time-warp capable and probably originating in area 4-X-Alpha-4. They function logically and, like the Daleks, their battle computers are calculating the best strategy and precise moment at which to attack – so far not a shot has been fired as the computers are so evenly matched.

They are tremendously strong and resilient. In *Destiny of the Daleks* (1979), the Movellan Lan recovers after being exterminated by a Dalek, while another Movellan, Agella, survives the roof collapsing on her. The Movellan Commander, Sharrel, states: 'Dysfunction, or death as you know it, only occurs in us with massive circuitry disturbance.' Their power packs and controlling circuits are in cylinders held on their belts. The Fourth Doctor and others are able to disable Movellans by removing these cylinders. The Doctor also realises that high-frequency sound disrupts them – when he whistles, or blows K-9's dog whistle.

In *Resurrection of the Daleks* (1984), the Fifth Doctor discovers that ninety years later the Daleks have finally lost their war with the Movellans. The Movellans have created a virus that corrodes and destroys both the Dalek creature and its casing. To turn the tide, the Daleks employ a team of humanoid mercenaries to help them storm the prison station that houses Davros – captured after the events of *Destiny of the Daleks*. They hope that their creator can find an antidote to the virus and instil a resistance to the virus into the Dalek race.

**1157** King Richard the Lionheart was born.

**1979** Davros returns from the dead at the end of Episode 2 of *Destiny of the Daleks*.

**2012** *Dinosaurs on a Spaceship*

# 9 SEPTEMBER

# Telos and the Cyber Tombs

In *The Tomb of the Cybermen* (1967), the Second Doctor and his companions Jamie and Victoria meet Professor Parry on the planet Telos. Parry explains he is leading an expedition 'searching the universe for the last remains of the Cybermen'. He implies that Telos is just one of the sites they are investigating. Telos was apparently the home planet of the Cybermen, who supposedly died out many centuries ago, although no one knows why.

But the Cybermen are not dead at all. They retreated into frozen tombs when their machinery stopped and their supply of replacements was depleted. The city that Parry's team uncovers is a huge trap, designed so that those who can solve the puzzles of how to operate the Cyber controls will revitalise the Cybermen – and supply them with the replacements they need, themselves becoming new Cybermen.

The Tombs of the Cybermen are reached by a ladder down from a large hatch in the main control room. The Tombs resemble a huge honeycomb of individual tombs. Each contains a single dormant Cyberman and is covered by a plastic membrane, which the Cybermen break through when they are revived. When the Cybermen do wake, the Doctor manages to trap them in the lower areas of the city, and eventually refreezes them to inactivity.

In *Attack of the Cybermen* (1985), the Sixth Doctor and Peri again travel to Telos. The Cybermen are very much active in this time period, and the Doctor enlists the help of the Cryons – natives of Telos – to help defeat them.

ON THIS DAY

**1953** Janet Fielding, who played the Fourth and Fifth Doctor's companion Tegan, was born.

**1967** *The Tomb of the Cybermen* Episode 2

**1978** *The Ribos Operation* Part 2

# 10 SEPTEMBER

## Apalapucia and Handbots

**1966** *The Smugglers*
Episode 1 opens
Season 4.

**1977** *Horror of Fang
Rock* Part 2

**2011** *The Girl Who
Waited*

About two billion light years from Earth, Apalapucia was a paradise planet – voted the number two destination for the discerning intergalactic traveller. It was a beautiful planet of soaring spires, silver colonnades, and the mirrored Glasmir Mountains.

But by the time the Eleventh Doctor visited with Amy and Rory in *The Girl Who Waited* (2011), the planet had been devastated by an outbreak of the Chen-7 virus – fatal to races with two hearts, like the Apalapucians (and the Time Lords). To cope with the virus, the Two Streams Facility was set up. Here, infected patients had their lives apparently extended through the use of temporal technology so that a single day seemed to them to be decades.

When Amy accidentally entered the wrong stream, she aged 36 years in the short time it took for the Doctor and Rory to find her. During that time she had to avoid the Handbots – medical robots that could 'see' through their hands. They assisted the patients and administered treatment to them. But the medicine they administered would be fatal to Amy.

By manipulating the temporal engines, the Doctor was able to restore the young Amy – the older version of her insisting she travel with them in the TARDIS. But eventually she relented and remained on Apalapucia, where she was killed by the Handbots.

# 11 SEPTEMBER

## Send in the Clones

Cloning is the production of a genetically identical copy of an individual or creature from cells of the original. Over the centuries, the Doctor has encountered many clones. But the most prolific by far are the Sontarans – first encountered by the Third Doctor in *The Time Warrior* (1973–1974) – who are a race of cloned warriors. They reproduce in their millions at huge muster parades. The Tenth Doctor managed to prevent them from turning the whole of Earth into a clone world for breeding more Sontarans in *The Sontaran Stratagem* and *The Poison Sky* (2008). As part of their plan, the Sontarans produced a clone copy of the Doctor's friend Martha Jones.

In *Galaxy* (1965), the First Doctor found opposing groups of Drahvins and Rills stranded on a planet about to be destroyed. Led by Maaga, all the other Drahvins were cloned female soldiers.

Madame Karabraxos created clones of herself to appoint to key positions in the Bank of Karabraxos, as the Twelfth Doctor discovered in *Time Heist* (2014). If a clone failed in its duties, she had it incinerated.

The Gangers that the Eleventh Doctor met in *The Rebel Flesh* and *The Almost People* (2011) were identical copies of humans, but they were not clones. Instead they were created from a substance called Flesh that replicated the original person.

Similarly, the copies of himself and Leela that the Fourth Doctor created in *The Invisible Enemy* (1977) were not clones. Described as being more like three-dimensional photocopies, they had a very limited lifespan – only about ten or eleven minutes. The copies were created using the Kilbracken Technique, which

**1960** Clara Oswald's mother, Ellie, was born, according to her gravestone seen in *The Rings of Akhaten*.

**1965** The first episode of *Galaxy 4*, titled *Four Hundred Dawns*, opens Season 3.

**1970s** On this day, some time probably in the 1970s, 'ghost' guerrilla fighters from the future first arrive at Auderly House to try to assassinate Sir Reginald Styles.

**1976** *The Masque of Mandragora* Part 2

replicates from a single cell as a short-lived carbon copy. The Doctor then miniaturised the copies of himself and Leela and they were injected into the Doctor's own body to try to find and destroy the alien Virus that had infected him.

# 12 SEPTEMBER

## The Doctor Changes Kazran Sardick's Life

When the starliner that Amy and Rory were travelling in was crashing onto a planet in *A Christmas Carol* (2010), the Eleventh Doctor travelled down to the planet to enlist the help of Kazran Sardick who controlled the skies above the planet.

But Sardick was a selfish miser, who refused to help. The Doctor realised that his attitude stemmed from an unhappy childhood, so he travelled back to meet Sardick as a child. He visited the younger Kazran Sardick many times as the boy grew into a young man. Kazran also formed a friendship with a young woman called Abigail Pettigrew who was kept in cryogenic suspension – as were many relatives of those in debt to the Kazran family, being held as security for the debts.

Over the years, Sardick mellowed. But when he discovered that Abigail was dying, and would only live for one more day outside of her cryogenic chamber, Sardick sent the Doctor away. Heartbroken at Abigail's predicament, the older Sardick still refused to help the Doctor – until he was confronted with his own younger self as a child. But finally, it was up to Abigail, on the last day of her life, to save the starliner. Her singing caused a delta wave pattern vibration of the ice crystals in the sky…

**1964** The sixth and final episode of *The Reign of Terror*, titled *Prisoners of Conciergerie*, brings the first season of *Doctor Who* to a close, although the next two stories are actually recorded as part of the same production block.

ON THIS DAY

## 13 SEPTEMBER

# The Doctor Faces the Truth and Consequences of a Zygon Invasion

The Zygons are an alien race from a planet destroyed by a stellar explosion. Before that, centuries ago, a Zygon spaceship commanded by the Zygon warlord Broton was damaged and crash-landed in Loch Ness to await rescue. But when the Fourth Doctor encounters the Zygons in *Terror of the Zygons* (1975), they have recently learned of the destruction of their world, and now plan to make the Earth their home.

A great refugee fleet has been assembled and is heading for Earth, although it will be centuries before they arrive, giving Broton and his Zygons time to restructure Earth to suit them. Broton plans that once he controls the world, the polar ice caps will go, the mean temperature will be raised several degrees and lakes with the right mineral elements established.

The Zygons have been using the Skarasen – a huge dinosaur-like armoured cyborg brought to Earth as an embryo for its lactic fluid – to destroy oil rigs. But this is just a test of strength before Broton destroys more visible targets and makes his demands. The Skarasen has been living in Loch Ness for centuries – the Loch Ness Monster.

The Zygons can take body prints allowing them to turn themselves into replicas of captive humans. After the Tenth and Eleventh Doctors, together with the War Doctor, arrange a truce between humans and Zygons in *The Day of the Doctor* (2013), it is agreed that the Zygons will live clandestinely on Earth in human form. But all that changes when the truce is threatened by a breakaway faction of Zygons who want to revert to their true form and take the planet for themselves. It is up to the Twelfth Doctor to reinstate the truce in *The Zygon Invasion* and *The Zygon Inversion* (2015)…

**1969** Filming starts on the Third Doctor's first story *Spearhead from Space*.

**1975** *Terror of the Zygons* Part 3

**1980** *The Leisure Hive* Part 3

**1986** *The Trial of a Time Lord* Part 2

**1989** *Battlefield* Part 2

**2014** *Listen*

# 14 SEPTEMBER

# The TARDIS Arrives in the Land of Fiction

When the Second Doctor was forced to use the TARDIS's Emergency unit to escape from a volcanic eruption on the planet Dulkis in *The Mind Robber* (1968), the TARDIS arrived first in a white void patrolled by robots. Leaving the void, the TARDIS exploded, leaving the Doctor, Jamie and Zoe in what seemed to be a forest. But the Doctor discovered that the trees were all in the shapes of letters – lines of trees spelling out sayings and proverbs. He realised they were in a place where anything was possible – the Land of Fiction. This was confirmed when they met fictional characters from novels, fairy tales, and mythology – including Gulliver, Rapunzel, the Minotaur, the Medusa, a Unicorn, and others…

The Land of Fiction exists outside the normal space-time dimension. It is protected by clockwork soldiers, and is governed by the 'Master' who lives in a citadel on top of a massive cliff. The Master turns out to be an elderly writer who was taken from his desk when he dozed off on a hot summer's day in 1926. He created 'The Adventures of Captain Jack Harkaway' for *The Ensign*, a boys' magazine, and wrote 5,000 words every week for 25 years – which is why he was selected for the post in the Land of Fiction. His imagination and creativity give life to the inhabitants of the Land. He claims he has everything he wants including a vast and comprehensive library which contains all the known works of fiction written by Earthmen since the dawn of time.

**1968** Episode 1 of *The Mind Robber* (written as a filler by Script Editor Derrick Sherwin) is the only episode of *Doctor Who* ever to be shown without a writer's credit.

**1970s** On this day, some time probably in the 1970s, the Peace Conference organised by Sir Reginald Styles at Auderly House is evacuated as a force of Daleks and Ogrons attacks. The Daleks and Ogrons – together with Auderly House – are destroyed in an explosion.

**1987** *Time and the Rani* Part 2

The Master answers to the Master Brain – a computer
that feeds off his thoughts. To escape from the Land
of Fiction and recover the TARDIS, the Doctor has to
summon fictional heroes to fight against the Master
Brain.

## 15 SEPTEMBER

# The Gunslinger Comes to Town

Travelling back to the Wild West for the first time since *The Gunfighters* (1966), the Eleventh Doctor, Amy and Rory found that the town of Mercy in Nevada had electric street lights about ten years before they could possibly have been there, in *A Town Called Mercy* (2012). The lights had actually been set up by Kahler-Jex, an alien of the Kahler race who was hiding on Earth from Kahler-Tek.

Kahler-Tek, also known as 'the Gunslinger', was one of a number of the Kahler race that Kahler-Jex and others had converted into weaponised cyborgs to fight in a war. Once the war was over, the cyborgs were shut down – all except Kahler-Tek, who somehow remained operational.

Kahler-Tek hunted down the people who had experimented on him and converted him into a cyborg, and killed them. The last of them, Kahler-Jex, he traced to the town of Mercy. Kahler-Jex maintained that he only did what he had to do in order to bring peace. He regretted it deeply, and could hear the screams of those he experimented on every time he closed his eyes.

While the Doctor tried to defend the town of Mercy from the Gunslinger, Kahler-Jex took his own life rather than face Kahler-Tek.

**ON THIS DAY**

**1254** The explorer Marco Polo, who met the First Doctor, was born in Venice.

**1890** The world's most successful mystery writer Agatha Christie – who met the Tenth Doctor in *The Unicorn and the Wasp* – was born.

**1979** *Destiny of the Daleks* Episode 3

**2012** *A Town Called Mercy*

# 16 SEPTEMBER

## The Cybermats Attack

Cybernetic creatures created by the Cybermen, the Cybermats are small and metallic, not unlike rodents. The Cybermats the Second Doctor encountered on the planet Telos in *The Tomb of the Cybermen* (1967) had eyes, antennae and a segmented tail. Underneath they moved on rows of filaments, and they had what seemed to be rows of teeth. They could home in on human brainwaves to attack.

The Cybermen used similar Cybermats, but with spines down their back, no antennae, and solid, unfacetted eyes, to attack Station Three in *The Wheel in Space* (1968) and destroy its stocks of bernalium.

In *Revenge of the Cybermen* (1975), the Cybermats disseminated a plague that killed most of the crew of Nerva Beacon. These Cybermats were longer, with segmented bodies and a small red sensor at the front. The Doctor adapted one to attack the Cybermen with gold dust.

While the Tenth Doctor faced Cybershades in *The Next Doctor* (2008), and the Eleventh Doctor battled Cybermites in *Nightmare in Silver* (2013), the Eleventh Doctor also found a Cybermat in *Closing Time* (2011). This Cybermat was similar to the design seen in *The Tomb of the Cybermen* and *The Wheel in Space*, but larger. The Cybermat was harvesting power from the Sanderson & Grainger department store in Colchester, and using that power to re-energise Cybermen stranded in a crashed spaceship buried beneath the store.

**1967** The Cybermats first appear in Episode 3 of *The Tomb of the Cybermen*.

**1978** *The Ribos Operation* Part 3

# 17 SEPTEMBER

# Meeting Not-So-Mythical Minotaurs

The Doctor has met several Minotaur-like creatures over the centuries. He even helped Theseus and Ariadne escape from the Labyrinth by lending them a large ball of string to mark their way. This was probably in his fourth incarnation, as they had previously threatened to unravel the Doctor's scarf – or so he claimed in *The Creature from the Pit* (1979).

The Second Doctor and Zoe faced the Minotaur in the Land of Fiction in *The Mind Robber* (1968). But this was the creature of myth, and was dispelled because they did not believe it was real.

The Third Doctor met a very real Minotaur in *The Time Monster* (1972), however. The creature guarded the Crystal of Kronos in ancient Atlantis. Previously a great athlete, the unfortunate man who became the Minotaur desired long life and the strength of a bull – wishes granted by the Chronovore Kronos who turned him into a Minotaur.

In *The Horns of Nimon* (1979–1980), the Fourth Doctor and Romana encountered a race of Minotaur-like creatures called the Nimon. They travelled from planet to planet apparently offering wealth and power but actually draining the planets of their resources.

The Eleventh Doctor encountered one of another race of Minotaur-like creatures in *The God Complex* (2011). Distant cousins of the Nimon, these creatures fed on the faith of other life forms – draining it from them so that the victim died. They descended on primitive planets where they set themselves up as gods, feeding on the faith of the natives that worshipped them.

ON THIS DAY

**1966** *The Smugglers* Episode 2

**1970** Location filming begins for *Terror of the Autons* – the opening story of Season 8 and the first to feature the Master, as played by Roger Delgado.

**1977** *Horror of Fang Rock* Part 3

**2011** *The God Complex*

# 18 SEPTEMBER

# Donna's Life is Changed by a Time Beetle

Every choice we make changes things. Every decision, large or small, has consequences, like the ripples in a pond... There is a group of creatures that thrive on those changes. They feed on them and exploit them, taking the potential energy from the what-if. Sometimes they even make these events happen. They are known as the Trickster's Brigade.

Little is known about the shadowy, hooded Trickster. It is said he revels in the chaos caused by altering history, changing lives. Donna Noble was targeted by one of the Trickster's Brigade. And the Doctor's friend Sarah Jane Smith has twice been the victim of the Trickster (in the spin-off series *The Sarah Jane Adventures*) – once when he swapped Sarah and her friend Andrea so that Sarah died as a child, and later when the Trickster gave Sarah a way to meet the parents she never knew, but at a terrible cost. The Trickster also engineered Sarah's proposed wedding to Peter Dalton.

The creatures of the Trickster's Brigade are also shrouded in mystery. The one that changed Donna's life in *Turn Left* (2008) was a giant beetle that attached itself to her back when she visited a fortune teller on Shan Shen. It sat there, sapping the time energy, occasionally glimpsed by others… Most people who are affected don't need to worry. The changes are so slight, so tiny that they are barely noticeable. But in Donna's case, the small change in her life had catastrophic consequences, including the death of the Tenth Doctor – until she was able to put time back on to its proper course.

**1965** *Trap of Steel* – the second episode of *Galaxy 4*

**1976** *The Masque of Mandragora* Part 3

# 19 SEPTEMBER

## The Doctor Visits Skaro – Planet of the Daleks

When the First Doctor arrives on the planet Skaro in *The Daleks* (1963–1964), he and his companions find a world devastated by a war that ended hundreds of years earlier. The TARDIS lands in a petrified jungle where the trees are like brittle stone. But there is life on the planet – the Daleks have survived in their metal city, the Thals are wandering in search of food, and hideous creatures live in the Lake of Mutations behind the Dalek City…

The Second Doctor returned briefly to Skaro in *The Evil of the Daleks* (1967), spending most of his time there either in the Dalek City or close by.

The Fourth Doctor was sent into the final stages of the thousand-year war between the Thals and the Kaleds by the Time Lords in *Genesis of the Daleks* (1975). The planet was a huge war-torn battlefield littered with barbed wire and landmines. The wastelands between the two opposing sides were the territory of the Mutos – Kaleds banished when they suffered the mutational effects of chemical, biological and nuclear weapons. It was a conflict the Twelfth Doctor revisited in *The Magician's Apprentice* and *The Witch's Familiar* (2015) when he found Davros as a young boy trapped in a minefield.

Centuries later, in *Destiny of the Daleks* (1979), the Fourth Doctor and Romana arrived on the barren, abandoned planet just as the Daleks returned to retrieve the dormant Davros, their creator, from the ruins of their city.

In *Remembrance of the Daleks* (1988), the Seventh Doctor used a remote stellar manipulator called the Hand of Omega to destroy Skaro, or so it seemed. But

## ON THIS DAY

**1940** Caroline John, who played the Third Doctor's assistant Liz Shaw, was born.

**1963** The first ever filming for *Doctor Who* takes place on Stage 3A at the BBC's Ealing Studios. The filming just covers the first episode – the rest of the filming for the opening story takes place on 9–11 October.

**2015** *The Magician's Apprentice* opens Series Nine.

the planet somehow survived or was reconstituted. The Master is executed on Skaro in the *Doctor Who* TV movie (1996), and the Twelfth Doctor, Clara and Missy travel there in *The Magician's Apprentice* and *The Witch's Familiar* – the Dalek City once more rising above the desert…

## 20 SEPTEMBER

# The Doctor Meets Two Loch Ness Monsters

The group of Zygons whose spaceship crash-landed in Loch Ness lived beneath the loch for centuries before they discovered their home planet had been destroyed and decided to conquer Earth in *Terror of the Zygons* (1975). They brought with them an embryo Skarasen, which grew into a huge dinosaur-like armoured cyborg. The Zygons depended upon its lactic fluid for sustenance, and used it as a defence and a weapon.

Over the years, people caught glimpses of the Skarasen as it swam in the loch, or travelled across local land, and it became known as the Loch Ness Monster. When the Zygons were defeated and their spaceship destroyed, the Skarasen returned from London – where the Fourth Doctor had prevented it from attacking an energy conference – to Loch Ness, the only home it knew.

But the Skarasen may not be the only monster in Loch Ness. In *Timelash* (1985), the Sixth Doctor encountered the mutated ruler of the planet Karfel – the Borad. Although he appeared to his people as a soft-spoken old man, the real Borad was a mutated scientist named Magellan – who was fused with a reptilian Morlox when an experiment involving Mustakozene-80 went wrong and Magellan and the Morlox creature underwent spontaneous tissue amalgamation. The result was the Borad – a combined mutant with greater strength, intellect and longevity, who intended to repeat the experiment to create a consort for himself – using the Doctor's companion Peri.

**1975** Brigadier Lethbridge-Stewart makes his last regular appearance in *Terror of the Zygons* Part 4.

**1980** *The Leisure Hive* Part 4

**1986** *The Trial of a Time Lord* Part 3

**1989** *Battlefield* Part 3

**2014** *Time Heist*

Defeated by the Doctor, the Borad fell into the Timelash, a time corridor that transported him back to twelfth-century Scotland, close to Loch Ness. Whether the Borad survived as another Loch Ness Monster, or was killed by the Skarasen, the Zygons, or someone else is unknown.

# 21 SEPTEMBER

# Mourning the Not-So-Dead at Tranquil Repose

Tranquil Repose no the planet Necros, visited by the Sixth Doctor and Peri in *Revelation of the Daleks* (1985), is a cemetery combined with a facility where the terminally ill, amongst others, can be cryogenically suspended until a later date – for example when a cure for their ailment is discovered. While in cryogenic suspension, the sleepers are kept updated on economic, social and political developments. A local DJ also provides a 'personalised entertainment system'. However, the theory does not work, as in practice nobody wants the cryogenically suspended people back. In many cases the frozen rich and powerful would be in conflict with those currently in power. Also, the galaxy can barely support the current population.

Blue is the official colour of mourning on Necros, and women's legs are to be covered at all times. Jobel is the chief embalmer, while Takis and Lilt also hold positions of authority. Tranquil Repose is overseen by the Great Healer – who is, in fact, Davros. The Doctor discovers that he is exploiting the sleeping bodies at Tranquil Repose. Some he provides to a local industrialist, Kara, as a concentrated high-protein food that has ended famine in this part of the galaxy. Others, he is mutating into a new race of Daleks.

The Doctor is able to destroy the new Daleks with help from Orcini, a former Grand Knight of the Order of Oberon sent to assassinate Davros. Davros himself is captured by Daleks sent by the Supreme Dalek and taken back to Skaro to stand trial. With Davros gone

**1866** The writer H.G. Wells, who met the Sixth Doctor in *Timelash*, was born.

**1963** The first rehearsals for the very first episode of *Doctor Who* take place at a drill hall on the Walmer Road in London.

**1968** *The Mind Robber* Episode 2

**1987** *Time and the Rani* Part 3

and much of the facility destroyed, Takis and Lilt plan to turn Tranquil Repose into a farm to harvest the high-protein weed plant, Herba Baculum Vitae, that grows in abundance on Necros.

# 22 SEPTEMBER

# Kate Stewart Enlists the Doctor's Help

The Eleventh Doctor first met Kate Stewart in *The Power of Three* (2012), when UNIT investigated a mass of small cubes that appeared all across the world. Kate was the daughter of Brigadier Lethbridge-Stewart, who was head of the British contingent of UNIT from its inception and employed the Third Doctor as its scientific adviser. Kate also joined UNIT, informed by her father's advice that 'science leads', and rose to the position of Head of Scientific Research. As such, she enlisted the Doctor's help to discover the truth behind the strange cubes.

She enlisted the Doctor's help again in *The Day of the Doctor* (2013), and was instrumental in implementing the peace treaty the Tenth, Eleventh and War Doctors established between humans and the Zygons. When the peace was threatened by a breakaway faction of Zygons in *The Zygon Invasion* and *The Zygon Inversion* (2015), Kate Stewart and UNIT again called on the Twelfth Doctor and Clara Oswald for help.

The Twelfth Doctor had previously helped against the Cybermen created by Missy in *Death in Heaven* (2014). Kate Stewart also wanted his advice and assistance when all the aeroplanes in the world froze in the sky in *The Magician's Apprentice* (2015). When she was unable to find the Doctor, she sent for Clara Oswald instead.

**1944** Frazer Hines, who played the second Doctor's companion Jamie, was born.

**1979** *Destiny of the Daleks* Episode 4

**1982** Billie Piper, who played the Ninth and Tenth Doctor's companion Rose Tyler, was born.

**2012** *The Power of Three*

## 23 SEPTEMBER

# Controlling the Cybermen

Although groups of Cybermen are commanded by a Cyberleader, in overall charge of all Cybermen seems to be the Cyber Controller. The Second Doctor first encountered the Cyber Controller in *The Tomb of the Cybermen* (1967) when the Controller was revived from its ice tomb on the Cybermen's planet Telos. The Cyber Controller was a taller Cyberman with no chest unit. The Controller's head had an enlarged cranium, lit from within, with visible veins. It lacked the usual 'handles' of the other Cybermen. The Cyber Controller was electrocuted and apparently destroyed when the main doors of the Cyber City were closed, completing an electrical circuit.

The Sixth Doctor met and destroyed a different design of Cyber Controller – again on Telos – in *Attack of the Cybermen* (1985). Despite the different design, a

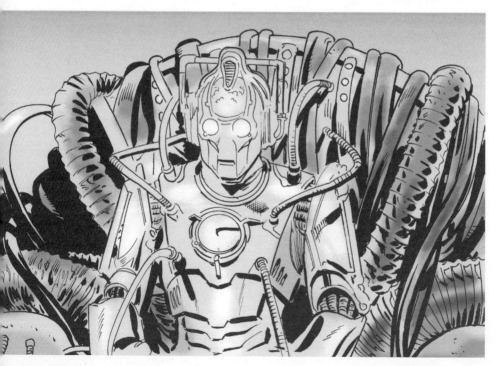

Cyberleader tells the Doctor the Controller was merely damaged in (presumably) *The Tomb of the Cybermen*, so it could be the same one.

The Cybermen which the Tenth Doctor saw created on a parallel Earth in another universe in *Rise of the Cybermen* and *The Age of Steel* (2006) also had a Controller. Again, it was of a different design, with its brain visible inside a transparent cranium. This Cyber Controller was the cybernetically converted John Lumic – the head of Cybus Industries who created the Cybermen. The Controller was destroyed when it fell from a Zeppelin into the exploding power station where humans were being converted into Cybermen.

**1967** *The Tomb of the Cybermen* Episode 4

**1978** *The Ribos Operation* Part 4

# 24 SEPTEMBER

# The Cybermen Will Survive

While the Cybermen have removed all feelings and emotions from themselves, they do have one basic underlying instinct – to survive. The way in which they aim to do this is by converting other humans into Cybermen. Ever since the First Doctor met the Cybermen in *The Tenth Planet* (1966), they have intended to add to their ranks with converted humans. But the extent of the conversion, and its level of success, have varied.

In *The Moonbase* (1967) the Cybermen used a hypnotic signal relayed via headsets to control members of the moonbase crew. A similar semi-conversion was used to control two humans in *Silver Nemesis* (1988). A partial Cyber conversion was carried out on Toberman, one of the expedition to find the lost Cybermen in *The Tomb of the Cybermen* (1967). Toberman's right arm was replaced with a cybernetic one, and he was placed under Cyber control. But the Second Doctor was able to break his conditioning so that he attacked the Cyber Controller.

In *Attack of the Cybermen* (1985), the Sixth Doctor witnessed the conversion process as the Cybermen tried to convert the human mercenary Lytton into a Cyberman. They also used partially converted humans to work on the surface of Telos – including Bates and Stratton, who escaped and fought back against them.

But the Tenth Doctor saw the full horrors of complete conversion in *Rise of the Cybermen* and *The Age of Steel* (2006) when hundreds of humans were converted on a parallel Earth – including Jackie Tyler. When the Cybermen from that world broke through into ours in *Army of Ghosts* and *Doomsday* (2006), they again converted humans, although the strong-minded head

**1966** *The Smugglers* Episode 3

**1977** Leela's eyes change colour from brown to blue when she watches a Rutan spaceship explode at the end of *Horror of Fang Rock* Part 4.

**2007** *Revenge of the Slitheen* Part One opens the first full series of *The Sarah Jane Adventures*.

**2009** Shooting starts on Matt Smith's first story, *The Eleventh Hour*, although *The Time of Angels / Flesh and Stone* was actually shot first, starting back in July.

**2011** A Cybermat appears in *Doctor Who* for the first time since the programme returned in 2005, in the story *Closing Time*.

of Torchwood, Yvonne Hartman, resisted and rebelled even though her body was fully converted.

In *Closing Time* (2011), the Eleventh Doctor's friend Craig Owens managed to resist Cyber conversion when he heard his baby son Alfie crying. His own emotions triggered a feedback loop into the Cybermen's emotional inhibitors and destroyed them.

# 25 SEPTEMBER

## The Reapers

**1965** *Air Lock* – the
third episode of *Galaxy 4*

**1976** *The Masque of
Mandragora* Part 4

Like huge, dark vampire bats, the 'Reapers' are creatures
that take advantage of wounds in time – points in time
and space where time itself has been damaged in some
way.

In *Father's Day* (2005), the Ninth Doctor agreed to
take Rose back to 1987 to witness her father's death in
a hit-and-run accident. But rather than just be with him,
so he would not die alone, Rose saved her father's life.
This change in history weakened the fabric of space and
time so that the Reapers were able to break through
into reality. They took advantage of the damage to
time like bacteria take advantage of a wound, or like a
bandage, sterilising it by consuming everything in the
affected area. And that meant everything on Earth.

The Reapers are from outside time, and destroy
the newest objects and people first, working back
through history until the entire affected, infected world
is destroyed. They affect time itself – so that a mobile
phone suddenly only picks up Alexander Graham Bell's
very first phone call: 'Watson, come here, I need you.'
Before the Great Time War the Time Lords might have
intervened to mitigate the Reapers' behaviour. But now
the Time Lords are gone, and there is no defence against
them.

The only way to stop the Reapers is to put history
back on track – which Rose's father does by deliberately
throwing himself under the car that originally killed him.

## 26 SEPTEMBER

# Homo Sapiens Spreads Across the Universe

The year 5000 AD, the Fourth Doctor tells Leela in *The Invisible Enemy* (1977), was the year of 'the Great Breakout' – when the human race traversed the Solar System on its way to the stars. Presumably this was a second 'breakout' as the Doctor has certainly visited human colonies on distant planets well before that date.

In *The Power of the Daleks* (1966), the newly regenerated Second Doctor found himself on the planet Vulcan. His arrival coincided with an attempted rebellion against the governor of the human colony on the planet. The Doctor also discovered that a space capsule containing dormant Daleks had been found in a mercury swamp, and the colony's chief scientist, Lesterson, reactivated the Daleks to work as servants to the colonists. While the Daleks seemed obedient and servile, the Doctor was under no illusions about their ultimate plans for the colonists.

The first journey the Third Doctor was able to make in the TARDIS after he was exiled to Earth [etc] - although he was actually sent there by the Time Lords, in Colony in Space (1971). After he was exiled to Earth was to the planet Uxarieus in the year 2472 – although he was actually sent there by the Time Lords. Here he helped the human colonists stand up for their rights against the Interplanetary Mining Corporation that wanted to scare them off the planet so its mineral wealth could be exploited. The arrival of an Adjudicator from Earth to settle the dispute hardly helped as the Adjudicator turned out to be the Master, searching for an ancient doomsday weapon…

**1966** The first filming takes place for *The Power of the Daleks*, Patrick Troughton's first story as the Second Doctor, at the BBC's Ealing studios.

**1967** Whether *Doctor Who* is too violent and frightening is discussed in the first edition of the BBC's *Talkback* programme, hosted by David Coleman.

**2015** *The Witch's Familiar*

Over the years, the Doctor has visited many other colonies, and found human beings populating dozens of other planets. As he says in *The Ark in Space* (1975), Homo sapiens is an inventive, invincible species – indomitable…

## 27 SEPTEMBER

# The Doctor Goes Back to School

The Doctor's association with Coal Hill School in the Shoreditch area of London goes back many years. The First Doctor's granddaughter Susan Foreman was a pupil at the school in the very first *Doctor Who* story, *An Unearthly Child* (1963). Concerned that she apparently lacked basic knowledge in some areas yet was brilliant in others, two of her teachers followed her home one night, to find that her address, 76 Totter's Lane, was just a junkyard. History teacher Barbara Wright and science teacher Ian Chesterton would be absent from work for some time, as they stumbled into the TARDIS and found themselves travelling through space and time – the Doctor unable to control the TARDIS well enough to get them back home…

But the Doctor had unfinished business in the area in 1963, as became clear in *Remembrance of the Daleks* (1988), when the Seventh Doctor returned to recover the Hand of Omega – a powerful stellar manipulator he had hidden on Earth. Coal Hill School was used as a base by one of two rival factions of Daleks also intent on finding the device, with the school's headmaster under Dalek control.

Many years later, the Eleventh and Twelfth Doctor's companion Clara Oswald worked as an English teacher at Coal Hill School. This was where she met her boyfriend Danny Pink, who taught maths. It seems that Ian Chesterton, the First Doctor's former companion, was the Head of Governors by this point. The Twelfth Doctor himself also worked there as the caretaker for a short time in *The Caretaker* (2014), so that he could trap and deal with a rogue Skovox Blitzer.

**1963** The pilot episode of *Doctor Who* was recorded at the BBC's Lime Grove Studio D. This version of the first episode, *An Unearthly Child*, was subsequently reshot for transmission after the script had been modified.

**1975** *Planet of Evil* Part 1

**1980** *Meglos* Part 1

**1986** *The Trial of a Time Lord* Part 4

**1989** *Battlefield* Part 4 is the last time that the character of Brigadier Lethbridge-Stewart appears in *Doctor Who* (though he does later appear in *The Sarah Jane Adventures*).

**2014** *The Caretaker*

## 28 SEPTEMBER

# The Doctor Avoids Becoming a Time Zombie

The TARDIS was caught by an illegal magno-grab device operated by the Van Baalen Brothers salvage team in *Journey to the Centre of the TARDIS* (2013). The magno-grab also created a time rift which made the TARDIS engines unstable so that its Eye of Harmony might explode.

The tear in the fabric of time caused 'Time Zombies' to appear. These were versions of the Eleventh Doctor, Clara Oswald and two Van Baalen brothers from the near future. The Zombies were misshapen, burned creatures – their cells liquefied by exposure to the power of the Eye of Harmony. The Van Baalens were moulded together into a single 'creature', while the Doctor's hand was fused to his face.

But the Doctor was able to avert the possible future in which they were exposed, sending a message back in time to himself. As a result he was able to avoid the TARDIS ever being caught by the magno-grab, and so the transformations into Zombies never actually took place.

**1968** Episode 3 of *The Mind Robber* features the first use of stop-motion animation in *Doctor Who*. It is used to bring the snakes on the Medusa's head to life.

**1987** *Time and the Rani* Part 4

## 29 SEPTEMBER

# Scaroth is Splintered in Time

The Jagaroth existed millions of years ago. Described by the Fourth Doctor as a 'vicious, callous, warlike race', the last of the Jagaroth were killed when their spaceship exploded while trying to take off from prehistoric Earth. The pilot of the ship, Scaroth, was in the Warp Control Cabin when the ship blew up. When the other Jagaroth were killed, Scaroth was instead splintered into twelve aspects of himself scattered through Earth's history and living independent but connected lives – all identical, but none complete.

'Aspects' of Scaroth have – he claims – helped humanity discover fire, invent the wheel, map the heavens and build the pyramids. Working always to advance human evolution to a point where the technology he needs is available to the furthest forward of his 'aspects'. This is Count Scarlioni, whom the Fourth Doctor and Romana meet in Paris in 1979 in *City of Death* (1979).

Count Scarlioni has hired the brilliant Professor Kerensky to work out how he can travel back in time to save himself, planning to fund the continuing experiments by stealing the *Mona Lisa* from the Louvre. Kept a virtual prisoner, Kerensky experiments with eggs to take them forward in time to become live chickens. He can also wind time back so the chicken returns to being an egg. But he can only manipulate time within the 'bubble' he creates that contains the egg / chicken. Scaroth wants him to find a way to interact with the events in the time bubble – otherwise Kerensky will be able to take the world back to primeval times, but Scaroth will not be able to intervene to save himself.

**1979** *City of Death* Part 1. The script was written by Douglas Adams under the in-house pseudonym David Agnew and, being set mostly in Paris, was the first *Doctor Who* story to involve overseas location filming.

**2012** *The Angels Take Manhattan* is the last episode for Amy and Rory, and closes the first section of Series Seven.

But the Doctor realises that the energy from the exploding Jagaroth ship is what kick-started life on Earth. If Scaroth succeeds, the human race will never exist.

## 30 SEPTEMBER

# The Doctor Discovers the Abominable Snowmen

The Abominable Snowmen, or Yeti, are creatures that are rumoured to live in the mountainous areas of Tibet, in the Himalayas. But the Yeti encountered by the Second Doctor and his companions in *The Abominable Snowmen* (1967) were not the timid creatures of legend. They were fierce robots controlled by a disembodied alien intelligence.

This Great Intelligence controlled the robot Yeti by means of control spheres – silver balls that fitted inside the Yeti's chests. The Doctor likened the spheres to a brain, and suggested that they were hollow, containing a part of the Intelligence. When outside a Yeti, a sphere could move, rolling along the ground to return to its Yeti and bring it back to life. It emitted a beeping sound when it was active.

The Great Intelligence had also possessed the Doctor's old friend, the master of the Det-Sen Monastery — Padmasambhava. Through him it controlled the Yeti and planned to take over the world, giving itself form and substance. With the help of an English explorer, Travers, the Doctor defeated the Intelligence. But this was not to be his last encounter with the Yeti.

When Travers returned to England from Tibet, he took back 'quite a bit of stuff', including a Yeti, four small Yeti models, and an intact control sphere. He spent years working to repair the sphere – until one day he got it working, and the sphere disappeared. Once again controlled by the Great Intelligence, the sphere sought out the surviving Yeti robot in a private museum in *The Web of Fear* (1968). The Yeti returned to life – killing Julius Silverstein, the museum's owner, and giving the Intelligence a bridgehead on Earth…

By the time the Second Doctor arrived, London had been evacuated because of a deadly 'fungus' created by the Intelligence as a mist above ground, and a web below. The army had tried chemicals, flame-throwers and even explosives to disperse the web and mist, but without success.

**1967** The Yeti and the Great Intelligence first appear in Episode 1 of *The Abominable Snowmen*.

**1978** *The Pirate Planet* Part 1 is the first episode of the first *Doctor Who* story written by Douglas Adams.

# OCTOBER

PRIVATE
.M.FOR
REMAN
Scrap
Merchant
76, TOTTE
ER'S LANE
POLICE PUBLIC CALL

# 1 OCTOBER

## The Doctor Visits a Hospital that Makes People Sick

**1966** *The Smugglers* Episode 4

**1977** *The Invisible Enemy* Part 1

**2011** *The Wedding of River Song* closes Series Six. It is the last episode on which Beth Willis is Executive Producer. After its broadcast, the last edition of *Doctor Who Confidential* is shown on BBC Three.

The huge medical facility outside New New York that the Tenth Doctor and Rose visit in *New Earth* (2006) is run by the Sisters of Plenitude. They are cat-like people, who take a lifelong vow to help others and to minister to and heal the sick. Humanity is a challenge for them, as it is afflicted with so many diseases. Within the hospital, the Sisters can – miraculously – cure even the most virulent and previously untreatable diseases and conditions. But, as the Doctor discovers, the treatments the Sisters administer are based on a terrible, dark secret that festers at the heart of their hospital…

In the Intensive Care Unit are stored sick patients. But these are not people who have caught diseases or been taken ill and need treatment. These are specially grown humans who have been deliberately infected with every known disease and illness so as to make them living incubators for the vaccines and cures the Sisters use. Because they are the carriers of the diseases, they do not die from them. The Sisters have experimented with clonemeat and biocattle, but human flesh is the only environment in which the diseases can be cultivated successfully and quickly.

The patients are kept in individual booths, sealed from the outside world, fed with pipes bearing nutrients and oxygen – and more disease. They are perpetually unconscious, created only to be ill: the ultimate research laboratory.

But the patients are not as insensitive and ignorant as the Sisters believe. Sister Corvin has written a thesis that suggests that sentience might migrate to these bodies – that the poor infected creatures might gain humanity and being through a process similar to osmosis – an 'echo of life'. But the policy of Matron Casp is to incinerate any of these patients who show signs of real, thinking life.

# 2 OCTOBER

## Eldrad Must Live

ON THIS DAY

**1965** *The Exploding Planet* – the fourth episode of *Galaxy 4*

**1976** *The Hand of Fear* Part 1

The Kastrians were rare in that they were a silicon-based, crystalline race. They came from Kastria – which has an Earth-type atmosphere and slightly high radiation levels. The Kastrian Eldrad created the barriers that kept the solar winds at bay and made life on the surface of Kastria possible. But when the other Kastrians failed to agree with his dreams of conquest, he destroyed the barriers, turning Kastria into a cold, icy world once more. The Kastrians sentenced Eldrad to be placed in an obliteration module which was then remotely detonated. But, forced to detonate the module early, the Kastrians knew there was a one-in-three-million chance of particle survival.

Eldrad's hand, together with the ring containing his genetic code, did indeed survive. They were found by Sarah Jane Smith in a quarry on Earth 150 million years later in *The Hand of Fear* (1976). Eldrad was able to influence the wills of anyone who came into contact with his hand – including Sarah – so they would work towards Eldrad's regeneration. Under Eldrad's influence, Sarah took the hand to a nuclear power station where, by absorbing radiation, the hand first became animated then, with the explosion of the reactor, absorbed sufficient radiation for Eldrad to be reborn, albeit in a form based on Sarah's body.

This 'female' Eldrad was able to persuade the Fourth Doctor that she had saved her planet from alien invaders and he should return her to Kastria. But once returned and regenerated into his true Kastrian form, Eldrad's aggressive character became apparent.

# 3 OCTOBER

# The Sontarans Make Earth's Atmosphere Unbreathable

In *The Sontaran Stratagem* and *The Poison Sky* (2008), Martha Jones called the Tenth Doctor back to Earth to help investigate the ATMospheric Omission System – ATMOS. This was a navigation and anti-pollution system installed in most cars and vehicles on the planet. The system was apparently invented by Luke Rattigan. A technology genius, Rattigan had invented the Fountain Six Search Engine when he was just 12 years old. He became a millionaire almost overnight, and later opened the Rattigan Academy.

UNIT raided the ATMOS factory, and the Doctor discovered the Sontarans were planning to use the ATMOS system installed in millions of cars to emit a gas that would suffocate all humans. The gas would also create the ideal conditions for Earth to become a Clone World – where the Sontarans could create millions of cloned troops to battle their ancient enemy, the Rutans.

Rattigan was in league with the Sontarans. In return for his help producing and distributing the ATMOS system, the Sontarans promised to take him and the gifted students from his academy to a new planet. But the Sontarans had no intention of keeping their promise and helping Rattigan.

With Earth's air becoming poisonous, UNIT locked in a fierce battle with attacking Sontarans, and Martha Jones replaced with a clone created by the Sontarans, it was up to the Doctor to find a way of defeating the Sontarans and restoring the atmosphere.

**1985** Although the BBC is 'resting' *Doctor Who* for 18 months, *The Lenny Henry Show* includes a *Doctor Who* sketch.

**1998** Recording takes place at the Doctor Who Appreciation Society's PanoptiCon '98 convention in Coventry for BBC Choice's *The Take*.

**2015** *Under the Lake*

# 4 OCTOBER

# Courtney Woods Goes to the Moon

An insolent and disruptive pupil at Coal Hill School, Courtney Woods was taught by both Clara Oswald and Danny Pink. She once told Clara she couldn't focus on her work as Clara's face was 'too wide' and teased her about her relationship with Danny Pink. In *The Caretaker* (2014), Courtney found the TARDIS at the school. Despite the Twelfth Doctor's claim that it was a 'Caretaker Box', she managed to persuade him to take her into space. The Doctor showed her the Olveron Cluster, but Courtney was overwhelmed by the sight of space and became travel sick.

Courtney became more disruptive after the Doctor told her she wasn't special – even stealing his psychic paper and using it as a fake ID. In response to Clara's pleas to tell Courtney she was indeed special and hopefully calm her down again, the Doctor took her and Clara to the Moon in 2049 in *Kill the Moon* (2014). Surviving attacks by giant spider-like bacteria, Courtney helped Clara to prevent the creature about to hatch from inside the Moon from being killed.

The Doctor told Clara that Courtney would one day – bizarrely – become President of the United States of America.

**1963** Sydney Newman and Donald Wilson view the completed pilot episode of *Doctor Who*. As a result of their notes, the episode will be recorded again with minor changes.

**1965** Armada publishes the paperback edition of the novelisation of the first Dalek story, *The Daleks*, as *Doctor Who in an Exciting Adventure with the Daleks*, featuring new illustrations.

**1975** *Planet of Evil* Part 2

**1980** *Meglos* Part 2

**1986** Part 5 of *The Trial of a Time Lord* is the first of the segment usually referred to as *Mindwarp*.

**1989** *Ghost Light* Part 1

**2014** *Kill the Moon*

# 5 OCTOBER

## The Doctor Returns to Totter's Lane

76 Totter's Lane was the home address given by Susan Foreman when she went to Coal Hill School. But as her teachers Ian Chesterton and Barbara Wright found in *An Unearthly Child* (1963), 76 Totter's Lane was actually a junkyard where the TARDIS had materialised. The name on the junkyard gates was I.M. Foreman – from which Susan presumably took her supposed surname. The Doctor also used 76 Totter's Lane as his address – as could be seen on the Eleventh Doctor's library card in *The Vampires of Venice* (2010).

The TARDIS landed in the same junkyard, but over twenty years later, in *Attack of the Cybermen* (1985). Ironically, while the TARDIS's Chameleon Circuit first malfunctioned when it left Totter's Lane in *An Unearthly Child*, the Sixth Doctor managed to fix it – at least temporarily – just before it landed there again. However, the shapes the TARDIS adopted seemed rather haphazard and included an ornate dresser and an organ. The Doctor put this down to the TARDIS being out of practice…

Although the TARDIS did not materialise in Totter's Lane in *Remembrance of the Daleks* (1988), the Seventh Doctor and Ace did visit I.M. Foreman's yard, with Group Captain Gilmore's Intrusion Countermeasures Group. They were attacked by a Dalek, which the Doctor destroyed using a can of Nitro-Nine explosives supplied by Ace.

ON THIS DAY

**1968** *The Mind Robber* Episode 4

**1987** *Paradise Towers* Part 1

**1988** *Remembrance of the Daleks* Part 1 opens Season 25. It is the first episode to be broadcast with NICAM stereo sound.

# 6 OCTOBER

## The Mona Lisa is a Fake

The *Mona Lisa*, also known as *La Gioconda* or *La Joconde*, is perhaps the most famous painting in the world. Painted by Leonardo da Vinci some time between 1503 and 1506, it is a half-length portrait of a woman – thought to be Lisa Gherardini – with a famously enigmatic smile. It was acquired by Francis I of France, and has been on display at the Louvre in Paris since 1797, except for two years after it was stolen in 1911.

As seen in *City of Death* (1979), in 1505, Captain Tancredi – an aspect of Scaroth, the last of the Jagaroth who was splintered in time – commissioned Leonardo to paint six copies of the *Mona Lisa* which he hid for another aspect of himself, Count Scarlioni, to find in 1979. Scarlioni – who knew of seven potential buyers – then stole the original from the Louvre, planning to secretly sell all seven. This would bring in enough money to finance the time experiments Professor Kerensky was conducting for him.

Realising Scarlioni's plan, the Fourth Doctor travelled back to 1505 and wrote 'This is a Fake' in felt pen on the boards that Leonardo would use – so the copies could be identified as fakes when X-rayed to prove their authenticity. After Scarlioni's chateau was burned down, only one *Mona Lisa* survived to be returned to the Louvre – one of the 'fakes'.

**1979** *City of Death* Part 2

**1997** Adrienne Hill, who played the First Doctor's companion Katarina in *The Myth Makers* and *The Daleks' Master Plan*, died.

# 7 OCTOBER

# The TARDIS Arrives in the Right Place, But on the Wrong Planet

**ON THIS DAY**

**1967** *The Abominable Snowmen* Episode 2

**1978** *The Pirate Planet* Part 2

Zanak was a happy prosperous planet until the reign of Queen Xanxia, who staged galactic wars. Legend says she lived for hundreds of years. Towards the end of her reign, the Captain arrived – falling from the sky in a mighty ship.

The Captain has been 'repaired' after the injuries he sustained in the crash and is partly cybernetic. He rules from the Bridge, which is accessible only by air car or by climbing the cliffs. Citizens of Zanak do not worry that the automated mines fill whenever the Captain announces a new golden age, or that the lights in the sky change. The people are so prosperous that jewels are left lying in the streets.

The Fourth Doctor, Romana and K-9 are surprised to arrive on Zanak in *The Pirate Planet* (1978) while searching for the second segment of the Key to Time as they expected the TARDIS to materialise on the planet Calufrax. But, as the Doctor discovers, Zanak has been hollowed out. Using technology recovered from the Captain's ship – the *Vantarialis* – it jumps through space to materialise round slightly smaller planets and mine them. The latest planet to be mined is Calufrax – explaining why Zanak now occupies its position in space. Many of the mined planets, such as Bandraginus V (which disappeared about a hundred years ago) were heavily populated. As the planets die, the more telepathically aware people of Zanak – the Mentiads – absorb the released life force and grow in strength.

# 8 OCTOBER

# **K-9 is Introduced**

K-9, who became a companion of the Fourth Doctor, is a mobile computer in the rough shape of a dog. The original K–9 was constructed by Professor Marius, who used to have a dog on Earth but because of the weight penalty could not bring it with him to the Bi-Al Foundation. Equally, he cannot take K-9 home, so at the end of *The Invisible Enemy* (1977), he offers K-9 to the Doctor. While Leela urges the Doctor to agree, K-9 decides for himself and enters the TARDIS.

Intelligent and with vast memory banks, K-9 has an affinity with the TARDIS (though he does call it a 'very stupid machine' as it cannot speak) and learns from its data. K-9 can speak, and print out data from his 'nose' or his side – as he does with a map of the 'tree' tunnel system in *Underworld* (1978). He has a blaster that emerges from the end of his nose which can be set to various levels enabling him to stun or kill life forms as well serving as a cutting tool. Articulated sensors ('ears')

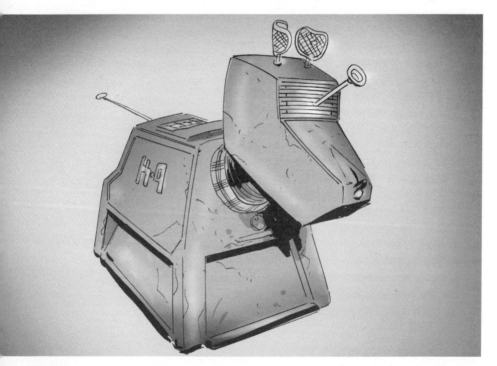

allow him to detect mass as well as the psycho-spore of the Mentiads on Zanak in *The Pirate Planet* (1978), and Romana and the Doctor (who has very distinctive heartbeats).

The 'original' K-9 stays on Gallifrey to look after Leela at the end of *The Invasion of Time* (1978). But the Doctor builds a K-9 Mark II, who remains with him until he is forced to remain behind the Gateway with Romana when his memory wafers are irrevocably damaged by the time winds in *Warriors' Gate* (1981). K-9 has the TARDIS 'preserved in concept' and can give Romana instructions on how to a build new one.

The Doctor also gives a K-9 Mark III to his friend and former companion Sarah Jane Smith. Following the spin-off adventure *K-9 & Company: A Girl's Best Friend* (1981), Sarah and K-9 appear together in *The Five Doctors* (1983) and again in *School Reunion* (2006) and *Journey's End* (2008). K-9 also appears periodically in the spin-off series *The Sarah Jane Adventures*.

**1966** The Cybermen first appear in Episode 1 of *The Tenth Planet*. The final episode of the same story was also recorded on this day – and was William Hartnell's last work on *Doctor Who* during his era as the Doctor.

**1977** The robot dog K-9 is introduced in Part 2 of *The Invisible Enemy*.

# 9 OCTOBER

## When Possession is Nine-Tenths of the Problem

The Doctor has met more than his fair share of monsters and mad men, but he has also encountered those who, often through no fault of their own, have been possessed by a malign force. The Fourth Doctor was himself possessed for a while by the Osiran Sutekh in *Pyramids of Mars* (1975), while in *Midnight* (2008) the Tenth Doctor fell victim to a mysterious alien entity on the planet Midnight.

In her first assignment as the Third Doctor's assistant at UNIT, Jo Grant was hypnotised by the Master into taking a bomb into UNIT HQ in *Terror of the Autons* (1971), and many others have fallen under the Master's influence.

More extreme – and obvious – is physical possession. Those infected by a Varga Plant in *Mission to the Unknown* (1965) and *The Daleks' Master Plan* (1965–1966) lost not only their minds, but slowly mutated into Varga Plants themselves. Similarly, in *The Seeds of Doom* (1976), scientists Winlett and Keeler mutated into Krynoids after being infected by the shoot that erupts from a Krynoid pod.

More subtle was the possession of Toby Zed by the Beast in *The Impossible Planet* and *The Satan Pit* (2006), where runic symbols appeared for a while on his body. The crew of the *Pentallian* who were possessed by an intelligent sun had eyes that burned with fire in *42* (2007). Professor Sorenson, infected with antimatter in *Planet of Evil* (1975) slowly mutated into anti-man – a degenerate primitive ape-like creature.

But whatever the symptoms and extent of the possession, those possessed are to be pitied – and, if

**1965** *Mission to the Unknown* is the only episode ever not to include the Doctor or any of the regular companions. It serves as a prelude to the 12-part epic *The Daleks' Master Plan*, which will begin on 13 November 1965. It is also the last episode to credit Verity Lambert as Producer.

**1970** The first day of Roger Delgado's first studio recording as the Master, for Episodes 1 and 2 of *Terror of the Autons* in Studio TC8 of Television Centre. Location filming had already taken place over several days from 17 September.

**1976** *The Hand of Fear* Part 2

possible, helped. Sometimes, as with Professor Sorenson and many of those hypnotised by the Master, the Doctor is able to free them of the malign influence. But often, unfortunately, he is not…

# 10 OCTOBER

# The Fisher King Returns From the Dead

The Fisher King and his armies invaded the planet of Tivoli and enslaved the people there for ten years. 'Ten glorious years' the inhabitants called it, as Tivoli is the most invaded planet in the galaxy and the inhabitants are not only used to the experience but relish it. The planet was then liberated by the Arcateenians. Perhaps predictably, the people of Tivoli irritated their liberators so much that the Arcateenians enslaved them too.

Albar Prentis, a funeral director from Tivoli, was given the task of burying the Fisher King in accordance with Arcateenian tradition on a barren, savage outpost. He chose Earth.

But as the Twelfth Doctor discovered in *Under the Lake* and *Before the Flood* (2015), the Fisher King was not dead. He scratched an inscription into the wall of the spaceship that had been his hearse – directions for his armies to come and find him. Anyone who read the inscription had these directions burned into their brain. When they died, they returned as ghosts, repeating the directions and sending them out as a message so that the Fisher King's armies would come for him. They also created more ghosts, killing anyone else who had seen the inscription.

When his armada arrived, the Fisher King planned to drain Earth's oceans and put the human race in chains as slaves. But, despite having appeared as a ghost himself, the Doctor was able to manipulate history so that the Fisher King's plans came to nothing.

**1970** The second (and final) day of Roger Delgado's first studio recording as the Master, for Episodes 1 and 2 of *Terror of the Autons* in Studio TC8 of Television Centre.

**2015** *Before the Flood*

# 11 OCTOBER

## Start the Clock – The Foretold is Coming

The Foretold was a legend, a myth. The legend says that if you see the Foretold, then you have exactly 66 seconds left to live. But the myth turned out to be reality, as the Twelfth Doctor and Clara Oswald found in *Mummy on the Orient Express* (2014).

The mysterious 'Gus' gathered experts in science and alien mythology on board a future version of the Orient Express – a train that travelled through space. Gus wanted them to study the Foretold, which seemed to be drawn to an ancient scroll that was also on board.

The Doctor discovered that the Foretold was actually a soldier, augmented with phase camouflage and a personal teleporter as well as other technology. The bandages that wrapped his injured, rotting body made him look like an ancient mummy. Despite his injuries, the technology kept him alive – but only so long as he could sustain himself by draining the energy from other people, killing them in the process.

The Foretold moved his victims out of phase, synchronising them with the phase level of his own camouflage. During the 66 seconds this process took, the victim could see the Foretold who was otherwise invisible because of the camouflage. The Foretold could then kill the victim – draining their energy so that they apparently died of heart failure.

The 'scroll', as the Doctor discovered, was actually the remains of the flag under which the soldier had fought. When the Doctor surrendered to him, the Foretold knew his war was over and, freed from his duty, he could finally die.

## 12 OCTOBER

# The Doctor Meets the Dalek Emperor

Until the appearance of the Dalek Parliament and Prime Minister in *Asylum of the Daleks* (2012), the ultimate leader of the Daleks has been the Emperor Dalek. Several Supreme Daleks have appeared over the years, and in *Planet of the Daleks* (1973), the Thal Codal tells Jo Grant that the Dalek Supreme that arrives on Spiridon is 'one of the Supreme Council'.

The Second Doctor first met the Emperor Dalek in *The Evil of the Daleks* (1967). Following the Daleks from Victorian England to their own planet Skaro, the Doctor and Jamie were captured and taken to the Emperor – a massive Dalek built into the very fabric of the Dalek City. Despite the Doctor's assertion at the end of the story that this is the 'final end' of the Daleks, the Emperor is not completely destroyed in the Dalek civil war which the Doctor provokes.

In *Remembrance of the Daleks* (1988), the leader of the Imperial Faction of Daleks is another Dalek Emperor. But this version of the Emperor is a 'normal' Dalek with

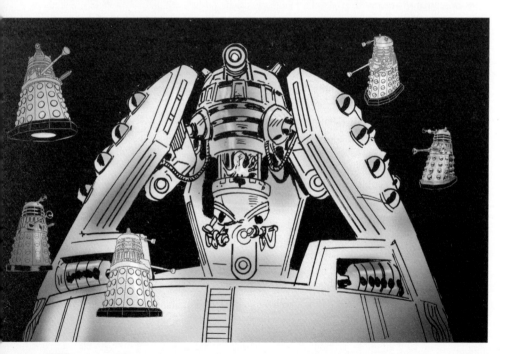

an enlarged globe replacing the top section, and no eye stalk. When the globe slides open as the Emperor confronts the Seventh Doctor, it reveals that the Dalek casing actually contains Davros.

This design of the Emperor Dalek is similar to another Dalek Emperor which appeared in the 'Daleks' comic strip that ran in the comic *TV Century 21* in the mid-1960s as well as several Dalek 'annuals'. This Emperor's casing was made of Flidor gold, quartz and Arkellis flower sap, and again it had an enlarged globe-head, with several dome lights and an eyestalk.

The enormous Dalek Emperor, built into the Daleks' flagship in *The Parting of the Ways* (2005), survived the Great Time War. The Dalek survivors have waited, slowly infiltrating humanity and taking the refugees and dispossessed to create new Daleks – only one cell in a billion being 'pure' enough to become Dalek. Having led its subjects from the wilderness and created new Dalek life, the Emperor believes itself to be god of all the Daleks. Like the massive Emperor in *The Evil of the Daleks*, this Emperor is guarded by black-domed Dalek Leaders.

**1968** *The Mind Robber* Episode 5

**1987** *Paradise Towers* Part 2

**1988** *Remembrance of the Daleks* Part 2

# 13 OCTOBER

## The Undead Mawdryn Wants to Die

**54 Nero Claudius Caesar Augustus Germanicus becomes Emperor of Rome.**

**1979** *City of Death* Part 3

Mawdryn and his seven travelling companions, the sole mutant occupants of the luxury space liner that the Fifth Doctor finds in *Mawdryn Undead* (1983), have been travelling in exile for 3,000 years. Every 70 years, their ship is guided to a planet where the mutants can attempt to find help for their condition.

Long ago, seeking to lengthen their lifespan, they stole a metamorphic symbiosis regenerator from Gallifrey – a device used by Time Lords in acute regenerative crises. They believed that it would give them immortality. But lacking a vital element only the Time Lords know of, the scientists adapted the machine and accidentally induced a perpetual mutation to their cellular make-up – condemning themselves to an everlasting 'life without end or form'. As a result, they mutate and degenerate ceaselessly but cannot die – a fate so horrible that they have been exiled by the elders of their planet. Mawdryn calls it the Time Lords' curse. The Doctor calls it the result of their own criminal ambition.

After so many tortured millennia, the mutants long for death. It seems they can only be killed by the potential energy of a Time Lord's regeneration flowing through their adapted generator, and they demand that the Doctor sacrifices his remaining regenerations so that they can die. But in fact, the energy caused by a meeting of two versions of Brigadier Lethbridge-Stewart – one from 1977 and another from 1983 – shorts out the time differential. This provides enough energy to give Mawdryn and his fellow mutants the death they crave.

# 14 OCTOBER

# When History Can – and Cannot – be Changed

In *The Aztecs* (1964), when Barbara tells the First Doctor that she intends to persuade the Aztecs to abandon the practice of human sacrifice, he warns her that 'you can't rewrite history – not one line!' He goes on to tell her that it is 'utterly impossible. I know – believe me, I know'. In *The Girl Who Died* (2015), the Twelfth Doctor warns Clara Oswald of the dangers of making 'waves' rather than ripples in time.

But the Doctor has been involved in quite a few attempts to change history. In *The Time Meddler* (1965), another of the Doctor's own race planned to help Harold defeat William the Conqueror at the Battle of Hastings. In *Day of the Daleks* (1972), guerrilla fighters from a future where the Daleks ruled Earth travelled back in time to change history so that the Daleks never invaded. The Daleks themselves had manipulated history to make their invasion possible, and the Third Doctor was able to put history back on track. The Third Doctor also foiled Operation Golden Age in *Invasion of the Dinosaurs* (1974), which was a plot to roll back history so that Earth would be returned to prehistoric times.

In *Pyramids of Mars* (1975), the Fourth Doctor shows Sarah a future where Sutekh escaped from his imprisonment and the Earth is a barren, wasted planet. He agrees that an individual can change the course of history 'to a small extent'. But, he says, 'It takes a being of Sutekh's almost limitless power to destroy the future.' In *City of Death* (1979), the Fourth Doctor was worried that Scaroth, last of the Jagaroth, could alter history so that the human race never evolved.

While he may be cautious about it, the Doctor is himself able to change history. Sometimes the changes

**1066** The Battle of Hastings was fought, despite the Meddling Monk's efforts.

**1946** Katy Manning, who played the Third Doctor's assistant Jo Grant, was born.

**1967** *The Abominable Snowmen* Episode 3

**1978** *The Pirate Planet* Part 3

are small – like the return of the missing ship the SS
*Bernice* in *Carnival of Monsters* (1973) – while on other
occasions they are more far-reaching. There are, we have
learned, 'fixed points' that cannot be altered. But the
Eleventh Doctor has managed to 'cheat' one of these
fixed points – his own death. In *The Wedding of River
Song* (2011), he uses the shape-changing Teselecta
robot to take his place at Lake Silencio where he is shot
in *The Impossible Astronaut* (2011) and appears to die…

# 15 OCTOBER

# Finding Another Dimension

A key aspect of the TARDIS, and one which is immediately apparent to anyone who enters it, is that the time and space machine is bigger on the inside than it is on the outside. In *An Unearthly Child* (1963), the First Doctor likens the technology to showing a large building on a television screen – so that it appears to fit into a living room. In later years, he explains that the TARDIS is dimensionally transcendental. The Fourth Doctor explains the phenomenon to Leela in *The Robots of Death* (1977) by showing her two boxes, one bigger than the other. He holds the smaller box closer to her: 'If you could keep that exactly that distance away, *and* have it here, the large one would fit inside the small one … That's transdimensional engineering – a key Time Lord discovery.'

A key component that enables this transdimensional engineering is the Relative Dimensional Stabiliser. It is probably this – although the Monk refers to it as the 'dimensional control' – that the First Doctor removes from the Meddling Monk's TARDIS in *The Time Meddler* (1965), reducing its interior dimensions so that the inside is no larger than the exterior.

In *The Invisible Enemy* (1977), the Fourth Doctor removes the Relative Dimensional Stabiliser and uses it to shrink clones of himself and Leela down to microscopic size so they can be injected into his body to find an alien virus that has infected him.

Similarly, the Time Lord Drax uses a portable version of a Relative Dimensional Stabiliser from his own TARDIS in *The Armageddon Factor* (1979) to shrink himself and the Doctor so they can escape the Shadow and his Mute servants while searching for the final segment of the Key to Time.

**1966** *The Tenth Planet* Episode 2

**1977** *The Invisible Enemy* Part 3

# 16 OCTOBER

# The Doctor Meets Another Doctor – and the Cybershades

**1965** The first episode of *The Myth Makers*, titled *Temple of Secrets*. It is John Wiles's first episode as Producer.

**1976** *The Hand of Fear* Part 3

On Christmas Eve 1851, the Tenth Doctor met another Doctor in *The Next Doctor* (2008), although he turned out to be a mere human named Jackson Lake. But together they battled against the Cybermen and their CyberKing – and also against a new type of cybernetic creature called the Cybershade.

Created by a group of Cybermen that found themselves trapped in Victorian times, the Cybershades were made out of local, contemporary materials using the techniques and technology available to the Cybermen. The Cybershades were created to be more agile and less noticeable in London than standard Cybermen. They could run, climb, and jump. But, unlike normal Cybermen, they were not equipped to administer lethal electric shocks.

Crouched and constantly moving like hags or witches, the Cybershades seemed to retain some emotional features. They were constantly hissing, as if angry at humanity as they carried out the orders of their Cyber masters. The Cybermen used them primarily for reconnaissance and to instil fear in the Victorian Londoners.

The Cybershades were all destroyed – along with the Cybermen – when the Doctor disintegrated the CyberKing.

# 17 OCTOBER

## Ashildr – The Girl Who Died... and Lived

**2015** *The Girl Who Died*

Ashildr was a young woman in the Viking village where the Twelfth Doctor and Clara Oswald were taken in *The Girl Who Died* (2015). When 'Odin' took some of the villagers, Ashildr and Clara were also transported to the Mire spaceship.

With a love of stories and an active imagination, Ashildr was instrumental in defeating the Mire. The Doctor fed her imagined visions into the visual circuits of the Mire warriors to frighten them away. However the process was too much for Ashildr and she died. Remorseful, the Doctor adapted a Mire battlefield medical kit to repair Ashildr and bring her back to life. But the way the kit worked, it kept on repairing her – making Ashildr in effect immortal.

She met the Doctor again in 1651 in *The Woman Who Lived* (2015). By then, she was calling herself Lady Me, and had become a highwayman called 'The Knightmare' to keep from getting bored. From her journals, it is known that in the intervening years she founded a leper colony as Lady Electra, was a thirteenth-century medieval queen who faked her own death, cured an entire village in the fourteenth century of scarlet fever and was almost drowned as a witch by the villagers, and caught the Black Death of 1348. Although Ashildr survived, her children died of the plague. She also disguised herself as a man to fight at the battle of Agincourt in 1415.

Not much is known about Ashildr's life until the Doctor met her once again in the present day for the fateful – and fatal – events of *Face the Raven* (2015).

He met her again at the end of the Universe after he returned to Gallifrey and tried to save Clara in *Hell Bent* (2015). Travelling in a TARDIS with Clara as she makes the most of the final moments before her inevitable death, perhaps Ashildr's story is not yet over…

# 18 OCTOBER

## Meglos Becomes the Doctor

Meglos was the last survivor of the planet Zolfa-Thura. There was a great civilisation there once, but by the time the Fourth Doctor, Romana and K-9 got caught up in the last Zolfa-Thuran's plans in *Meglos* (1980), it had been 'blown away to sand and ashes' and all that remained were the Screens of Zolfa-Thura.

A cactus-like xerophyte in his natural form, the use of an Earthling provided by Gaztak mercenaries enabled Meglos to change into the Doctor's form. But as the Earthling struggled to escape and reassert his personality, Meglos lost control and his version of the Doctor, or the Earthling, became cactus-like – green, with spines. Even so, Meglos was able to trap the TARDIS inside a 'fold of time' so that the Doctor, Romana and K-9 were forced to go through the same actions for ever, until they worked out how to break the time loop and escape.

Meglos had waited ten thousand years to recover the Dodecahedron – an advanced power source – from the neighbouring planet Tigella. Masquerading as the Doctor, Meglos stole it and miniaturised it with a dimensional controller before escaping. The Screens of Zolfa-Thura magnified the Dodecahedron's power to create a powerful energy beam that served as a weapon. The pentagonal screens captured and magnified the power emitted by each face of the Dodecahedron, focusing it into a beam that could be used to destroy whole planets. According to Meglos, the Zolfa-Thurans tried to destroy everything they had and knew to prevent the weapon they had created from ever being

**1963** The first studio recording takes place for the transmitted version of *An Unearthly Child* in Studio D of the BBC's Lime Grove Studios. It costs £2,746 to make. An earlier, untransmitted version known as the pilot episode had been recorded on 27 September.

**1975** *Planet of Evil* Part 4

**1980** *Meglos* Part 4

**1986** *The Trial of a Time Lord* Part 7

**1989** *Ghost Light* Part 3 is transmitted. Although both *The Curse of Fenric* and *Survival* will be broadcast after this story, it was the last episode of the classic series to be recorded.

**2014** *Flatline*

used. When Meglos tried to use the weapon, the Doctor managed to invert the control setting, so that the power was focused inwards and destroyed Zolfa-Thura.

# 19 OCTOBER

## The Imperial Daleks Deploy the Special Weapons Dalek

**ON THIS DAY**

**1987** *Paradise Towers* Part 3

**1988** *Remembrance of the Daleks* Part 3

The Imperial Dalek faction that seeks to recover the Hand of Omega before the so-called Renegade Daleks can find it in *Remembrance of the Daleks* (1988) have ivory-coloured casings with gold 'trim'. The Renegades, by contrast, are predominantly gunmetal grey. The Imperial Daleks' slats are moulded into the bodywork rather than attached, and the eye and sucker arm are of a different design – the sucker has a slot in it to operate controls.

The Dalek creatures are different too, presumably having been genetically re-engineered by Davros. A claw emerges from one damaged casing to attack the Doctor, and they have functional appendages and some kind of mechanical prosthesis grafted into the body. The Imperial Daleks are led by the Emperor – a Dalek with an enlarged, spherical head, which is revealed to contain Davros, the original creator of the Daleks.

The Imperial Daleks also have a Special Weapons Dalek, which they use in the battle against the Renegade Daleks. The Special Weapons Dalek is battle-stained, with no eyestalk or sucker arm and an enlarged gun. Until it is ordered into action, the Imperial Daleks are losing to the Renegade faction.

But whether the Special Weapons Dalek is a new creation designed by Davros for his Imperial Daleks in unclear. At least one other Special Weapons Dalek is present in the Dalek Asylum in *Asylum of the Daleks* (2012), while another attends the Dalek Supreme on Skaro in *The Magician's Apprentice* and *The Witch's Familiar* (2015).

# 20 OCTOBER

## The Under Gallery

Hidden beneath the National Gallery in London is the Under Gallery – a secret gallery when Queen Elizabeth I kept all the paintings she deemed too dangerous for public consumption. She also made the Doctor Curator of the Under Gallery, with orders that he be summoned if there was any disturbance. She left the painting *Gallifrey Falls* (also sometimes called *No More*) as proof the orders came from her. The painting is three-dimensional and depicts the fall of Gallifrey's second city, Arcadia, on the last day of the Great Time War. It is actually a slice of frozen time – Time Lord art.

The Eleventh Doctor was indeed summoned to the Under Gallery by Kate Stewart of UNIT in *The Day of the Doctor* (2013). He discovered that a group of Zygons had broken out of some of the other three-dimensional time-frozen paintings – actually Time Lord stasis cubes. The Doctor travelled back to Elizabethan times where he met the Tenth Doctor, and later the War Doctor.

Having helped his earlier incarnations end the Great Time War, and negotiate a truce between humans and Zygons, the Eleventh Doctor briefly met the current Curator. He was an elderly man who hinted that he might be a future incarnation of the Doctor – an older version of the Fourth Doctor, perhaps. The Curator also told the Doctor that both names for the Arcadia painting were accurate as it was actually titled *Gallifrey Falls No More*.

**1941** Anneke Wills, who played the First and Second Doctors' companion Polly, was born.

**1979** *City of Death* Part 4

# 21 OCTOBER

# The Doctor Meets the Guardians

**1967** *The Abominable Snowmen* Episode 4

**1978** *The Pirate Planet* Part 4

Although he knows of them, the first time the Doctor encountered one of the Guardians was in *The Ribos Operation* (1978), when the White Guardian sent the Fourth Doctor to find the six segments of the Key to Time. The Guardians are incredibly powerful, almost elemental creatures. There is a White Guardian – the Guardian of Light in Time – and, to balance him, a Black Guardian.

The Doctor finally faced the Black Guardian in *The Armageddon Factor* (1979) when he tried to trick the Doctor into surrendering the assembled Key to Time. To escape him, the Doctor again scattered the Key through time and space, and to avoid the Black Guardian being able to trace him, he fitted a Randomiser to the TARDIS controls. When operating, this ensured that the TARDIS's next destination was entirely random and could not be predicted. But the Doctor soon bypassed the Randomiser…

The Black Guardian finally caught up with the Fifth Doctor in *Mawdryn Undead* (1983). Seeking revenge on the Doctor, but unable to be seen to be interfering in the affairs of the cosmos, the Black Guardian recruited Turlough to act as his agent, ordering him to kill the Doctor or die. Although Turlough did make one attempt on the Doctor's life, and also sabotaged the TARDIS, he was ultimately unable to go through with the plan.

Finally, when both Guardians met in *Enlightenment* (1983), Turlough was offered a clear choice – an enormous diamond worth an impossible fortune in

exchange for the Doctor's life. Turlough agonised for
a few moments before he hurled the gem at the Black
Guardian, who vanished in flames, accepting defeat
on this occasion. But his hatred of the Doctor remains
undiminished…

# 22 OCTOBER

# The Cybermen Arrive

The original Cybermen came from Earth's 'twin' planet Mondas, which drifted away from the Solar System through space. In *The Tenth Planet* (1966), Mondas returns to the Solar System, and drains away the Earth's energy. The First Doctor and his companions Ben and Polly land at International Space Command's Snowcap Base – a space tracking station in Antarctica – just before a group of Cybermen arrive.

The Cybermen were once humans, but tried to combat their race's shortening lifespan with cybernetic surgery – replacing their bodily organs and limbs with mechanical versions. They also 'enhanced' their brains, removing the weakness of emotion. The result was the Cybermen – strong and efficient, not needing to breathe, but without fear or emotion, or humanity.

The design of the Cybermen has changed over time as they adapt and evolve. Some types of Cybermen have a greater degree of mechanical rather than organic componentry. But the Cybermen seem to be a race in decline. Even having extended their lives through the use of metal and plastic cybernetics, they need the resources of other worlds – especially Earth. This may be because of their affinity with human beings.

After the destruction of Mondas, the Cybermen adopted another planet – Telos – where they put themselves into suspended animation, frozen within huge tombs. The overriding ambition of the Cybermen is to survive.

As the Tenth Doctor discovered in *Rise of the Cybermen* and *The Age of Steel* (2006), on a parallel

**1938** Derek Jacobi, who played Professor Yana – actually the Master – in *Utopia*, was born. He also provided the voice of the Master for the animated story *Scream of the Shalka*.

**1966** *The Tenth Planet* Episode 3

**1977** *The Invisible Enemy* Part 4

**2006** *Everything Changes*, the first episode of the *Doctor Who* spin-off series *Torchwood* starring John Barrowman as Captain Jack Harkness, is broadcast.

version of Earth, the Cybermen were created by John Lumic of Cybus Industries. These Cybermen were able to break through to our own Earth in *Army of Ghosts* and *Doomsday* (2006).

# 23 OCTOBER

## Submarine *Firebird* Makes a Dangerous Discovery

Commanded by Captain Zhukov, the *Firebird* was a Soviet submarine equipped with nuclear weapons. In 1983 it was on a routine oil exploration run close to the North Pole, when the crew discovered what appeared to be something buried in the ice. On board the submarine was Professor Grisenko, who had the section of ice – containing what he believed could be a mammoth – cut free and loaded on board the *Firebird* to transport it back to Moscow for analysis.

Aiming for Las Vegas, the Eleventh Doctor and Clara Oswald arrived on board the submarine in *Cold War* (2013) just as a crew member thawed out the figure embedded in the ice. The Doctor recognised it immediately as an Ice Warrior. It was Grand Marshal Skaldak, the sovereign of the Tharseesian Caste and vanquisher of the Phobos Heresy, who had been frozen in the ice for five thousand years.

Attacked by the *Firebird* crew and unable to get any response to his distress signals, Skaldak decided to fire the submarine's nuclear missiles so as to provoke a full-scale nuclear war that would destroy humanity in retaliation. But before he could carry out his plan, a spaceship arrived to rescue him.

ON THIS DAY

**1965** *Small Prophet, Quick Return* – the second episode of *The Myth Makers*

**1976** *The Hand of Fear* Part 4 is Sarah Jane Smith's final episode as a regular companion.

## 24 OCTOBER

# Morgaine Summons the Destroyer to Devour the World

Morgaine of the Faye, the Sun Killer, Dominator of the Thirteen Worlds and Battle Queen of the S'rax, wants revenge on King Arthur, unaware that he is in fact already dead. In *Battlefield* (1989), she comes from a parallel world where a medieval culture developed technology alongside magic and superstition, and the legends of King Arthur are actual fact. Somehow, the Doctor – in another incarnation – is Merlin, and Morgaine has sworn to destroy him.

But when she thinks she is in danger of losing her battle against the Seventh Doctor and his friends, Morgaine uses her magic to summon the Destroyer into existence. Lord of Darkness and Eater of Worlds, the Destroyer is a demon-like creature complete with horns.

Morgaine has chained the Destroyer with silver – which burns the creature, keeping it powerless. But Morgaine calls the Doctor's bluff and frees the Destroyer so it can claim the world to devour. As the world explodes round the Destroyer, the Doctor's old friend Brigadier Lethbridge-Stewart – called out of retirement by UNIT to help – kills it with silver bullets.

**1881 The Doctor visits Doc Holliday in Tombstone to get his toothache treated in** *The Gunfighters.*

**2015** *The Woman Who Lived*

**2248 The events of** *The Tomb of the Cybermen* **take place on this day, according to an entry in the Doctor's diary in the original draft of** *Revenge of the Cybermen* **written by Gerry Davis – who co-wrote** *The Tomb of the Cybermen.*

# 25 OCTOBER

# The Doctor Meets Adric in E-Space

A talented mathematician, Adric earned a badge for mathematical excellence aboard the Starliner on the planet Alzarius. But while he was accepted as part of the society, his brother Varsh led the Outlers – a group of teenagers who broke away from the paternalistic society. Full of admiration for his older brother, Adric reckoned he was now old enough to begin to rebel himself. The Outlers were less happy to have him join them, seeing him as a spoiled child.

But circumstances forced the issue, and Adric found himself escaping the deadly Mistfall by entering the TARDIS in *Full Circle* (1980). Later he and the other Outlers helped the Fourth Doctor, Romana and K-9 to fight off the Marshmen within the Starliner. With nothing left for him on the Starliner, Adric hid in the TARDIS until it arrived at its next destination.

Being an Alzarian, Adric adapts quickly to any environmental changes. In *Full Circle*, his injured knee heals extremely fast, and he recovers rapidly from a twisted ankle in *The Visitation* (1982). Perhaps his contact with the Doctor and Romana, and later with Nyssa and Tegan, causes Adric to mellow and begin to care about others too. But for the most part his relationship with the Doctor's other companions is scratchy, with both Nyssa and Tegan seeing Adric as arrogant and immature.

It could be seen as the culmination of Adric's 'education' in social and moral responsibility that he dies trying to save Earth from the crashing freighter in

**1854 The Doctor watches the Charge of the Light Brigade at the Battle of Balaclava during the Crimean War. In** *The Evil of the Daleks* **he describes it to Jamie as 'magnificent folly'.**

**1975** *Pyramids of Mars* Part 1

**1980** The Fourth and Fifth Doctors' companion Adric is introduced in Part 1 of *Full Circle*.

**1986** Peri's last episode is Part 8 of The *Trial of a Time Lord*.

**1989** *The Curse of Fenric* Part 1

**2014** *In the Forest of the Night*

*Earthshock* (1982). But it is Adric's determination not to admit defeat that causes him to return to the freighter's bridge in an effort to crack the final Cyber code – perhaps a final, fatal, selfish act.

# 26 OCTOBER

## The Zero Room Heals the Ailing Doctor

The Doctor was left weaker and more vulnerable following his fourth regeneration than after any other we have witnessed. In *Castrovalva* (1982), the new Fifth Doctor even goes so far as to claim 'the regeneration is failing,' though it is not clear whether this is due to the severity of his injuries or perhaps an extension of the entropy that has torn into so much of his universe during the events of the previous story, *Logopolis* (1981).

In *The Power of the Daleks* (1966), it is implied that the TARDIS is key to the success of the Second Doctor's 'renewal'. In *Castrovalva*, the Fifth Doctor's condition is stabilised by the Zero Room, a healing, neutral environment on board the TARDIS. The fact that the TARDIS is fitted with a Zero Room suggests this kind of post-regenerative trauma may be common in Time Lords.

A subsequent rise in the TARDIS's ambient temperature also has a beneficial effect on his misfiring synapses, allowing him to reason clearly for a limited time. However, this temperature rise is due to the fact that the Master has sent the TARDIS back in time to Event One – the creation of the galaxy out of a huge in-rush of hydrogen, which could destroy the TARDIS. To escape, the Doctor jettisons twenty-five per cent of the TARDIS's mass, generating enough thrust for the ship to break free.

When Tegan and Nyssa discover that the Zero Room was also jettisoned, they make a 'Zero Cabinet' out of the surviving doors. The power of the Zero Room is such that even these are constructed of a material that generates stabilising effects that help the Doctor's recovery.

**1881 The famous gunfight takes place at the OK Corral. It starts at about 3 p.m. and lasts for thirty seconds.**

**1987** *Paradise Towers* Part 4

**1988** *Remembrance of the Daleks* Part 4

# 27 OCTOBER

## Not Everything that Looks Monstrous is a Monster

'You can't always judge by external appearances,' the Fourth Doctor says in *Genesis of the Daleks* (1975). He is of course right, and during his travels the Doctor has met many creatures that seem – from their appearance or their behaviour – to be villainous monsters, but which have turned out not to be what they seem.

In *Galaxy 4* (1965), the First Doctor discovered that it was the beautiful female humanoid Drahvins who were the aggressors, and the repulsive-looking Rills that were the victims. Similarly, the alien creatures the Third Doctor dealt with in *The Ambassadors of Death* (1970) came in peace, but were kidnapped and coerced into aggressive acts by a human intent on provoking war. Even the Doctor is not immune to making snap judgements – he took a long time in *The Curse of Peladon* (1972) to trust the Ice Warriors, who had been his enemies in the past.

In *The Creature from the Pit* (1979), the Fourth Doctor met a hideous blob-like alien called Erato. Living in a deep pit, it crushed its victims. In fact, Erato was an alien ambassador who had been thrown into the pit and was merely trying to communicate with the people it encountered.

Similarly, the Star Whale that carried Starship UK in *The Beast Below* (2010) just wanted to help humanity, while the Siren that apparently killed injured members of Captain Avery's crew in *The Curse of the Black Spot* (2011) was actually trying to heal them.

There are many other examples – like the Teller of the Bank of Karabraxos which the Twelfth Doctor eventually rescued and set free in *Time Heist* (2014) – that prove the

**1979** *The Creature from the Pit* Part 1. This is the first episode in which David Brierley takes over from John Leeson as the voice of K-9.

Fourth Doctor's point. Just because it looks monstrous doesn't mean a creature is wicked or dangerous. And equally, the most attractive or ordinary-looking life form may have evil intentions.

# 28 OCTOBER

## The Ogri are Out for the Doctor's Blood

In *The Stones of Blood* (1978), the Fourth Doctor and Romana traced the third segment of the Key to Time to late twentieth-century Earth. The segment eventually turned out to be the Great Seal of Diplos – stolen by Cessair of Diplos, who was charged both with its theft and with murder.

Cessair was kept on a prison ship in hyperspace, to be taken back to Diplos to be tried by the Megara justice machines. But Cessair escaped to Earth and assumed a number of identities over the 4,000 years she lived there. Before masquerading as Vivien Fay, Cessair had previously been Mother Superior of the Little Sisters of St Gudula, the reclusive Mrs Trefusis, the Brazilian widow Senora Camara, and the 'wicked Lady Morgana Montcalm', who is said to have murdered her husband on their wedding night.

She also brought with her several Ogri. Silicon life forms from the planet Ogros in Tau Ceti, the Ogri are sentient rocks. They feed on the amino acids and proteins that exist on their own planet – the nearest equivalent on Earth being blood. The Ogri Cessair brought to Earth became part of the mysterious stone circle called the Nine Travellers – which explains why there are more than nine stones in all. The Ogri have been active for a while, crushing the unfortunate Doctor Borlaise who surveyed the stones in 1754.

Cessair kept the Ogri fed with blood from ritual sacrifices of animals, and humans. As well as absorbing blood poured onto them, the Ogri could suck the blood out of anyone who touched them. The Doctor believed

**1944** Ian Marter, who played the Fourth Doctor's companion Harry Sullivan, was born.

**1967** *The Abominable Snowmen* Episode 5

**1978** *The Stones of Blood* Part 1 is broadcast – opening *Doctor Who*'s 100th story.

**1982** Matt Smith, who played the Eleventh Doctor, was born.

**1986** Ian Marter, who played the Fourth Doctor's companion Harry Sullivan, died on his 42nd birthday.

that the Ogri have entered into Earth mythology,
with the giants Gog and Magog and the term 'ogre' all
deriving from the name of the Ogri…

# 29 OCTOBER

## The Cybermen Cannot Save Their Planet Mondas

Mondas was the planet where the Cybermen were originally created. Mondas was also an ancient name for Earth and, aeons ago, according to the Cybermen, the planets were twins. But Mondas drifted away through space, until in *The Tenth Planet* (1966), it returns…

According to the Cybermen the First Doctor encounters at Snowcap Base at the South Pole, the energy of Mondas has been almost exhausted, and it has returned to gather energy from its twin planet Earth. This will drain Earth of all energy until everything on the planet 'stops'. To prevent Mondas from absorbing too much energy, the Cybermen plan to destroy Earth. But the Doctor and his companions prevent them, and as a result Mondas absorbs too much energy and disintegrates.

In *Attack of the Cybermen* (1985), the Sixth Doctor says that the Cybermen had fitted Mondas with a propulsion system – presumably so they could bring it back to Earth. In the future, the Cybermen have captured a time vessel that landed on Telos – their adopted planet after the destruction of Mondas. They intend to change history, preventing their original home planet Mondas from being destroyed. The Cybermen's plan is to go back in time and destroy Earth before it destroys Mondas, by diverting Halley's Comet so it will crash into Earth.

**ON THIS DAY**

**1966** Episode 4 of *The Tenth Planet* is the last episode to star William Hartnell as the First Doctor.

**1977** *Image of the Fendahl* Part 1

# 30 OCTOBER

# The Doctor Enters the Matrix

Maintained by the Keeper of the Matrix, the Matrix is the sum total of Time Lord knowledge. It contains everything – all the information that has ever been stored, all the information that can be stored, including the imprints of personalities of hundreds of Time Lords and their Presidents. Even the mind of Rassilon – the founder of Time Lord society – lives on inside the Matrix. When the Fourth Doctor is inducted as President of the Time Lords in *The Invasion of Time* (1978), Borusa tells him: 'It will become a part of you as you will become a part of it.' It is from the information in the Matrix that the Doctor learns how to construct the Demat Gun, a forbidden weapon he uses to defeat the Sontarans that have invaded Gallifrey.

But the Fourth Doctor has encountered the Matrix before, in *The Deadly Assassin* (1976). The Master used the Matrix to send a telepathic image to the Doctor to draw him to Gallifrey so he could be framed for the President's assassination. Trying to trace the Master, the Doctor entered the APC Net – a small part of the Matrix.

The APC Net is composed of Amplified Panotropic Computations – trillions of electro-chemical cells in a continuous matrix. The cells are the repository of departed Time Lords. According to Coordinator Engin, an electrical scan is made of the brain pattern at the moment of death, and these millions of impulses are immediately transferred. Its purpose is to monitor life in the Capitol and to use all this combined knowledge and experience to predict future developments.

Inside the Matrix, the Doctor discovered that the Master's ally Chancellor Goth had created an entire dream world that would obey his will. The Sixth Doctor

**1965** *Death of a Spy* – the third episode of *The Myth Makers*

**1976** Peter Pratt plays the Master in Part 1 of *The Deadly Assassin*. It is the only story of the classic series in which the Doctor is not accompanied by a companion, and marks the Doctor's first return to Gallifrey since *The War Games* in 1969.

also entered the Matrix in *The Trial of a Time Lord* (1986) – to discover another fantasy world created by the Valeyard.

In *Arc of Infinity* (1983), Omega drew on the power of the Matrix to escape from his realm of antimatter and manifest himself as a Time Lord again in the real universe.

# 31 OCTOBER

## Small is Beautiful, But Big is Better

The TARDIS is larger on the inside than the outside because, the Doctor once explained, its inside and outside are not in the same dimension. But on several occasions, dimensional faults have caused the TARDIS to shrink – in *Logopolis* (1981) and in *Flatline* (2014), for example.

But whereas the Twelfth Doctor remains his normal size trapped inside a shrinking TARDIS in *Flatline*, in *Planet of Giants* (1964), the occupants of the TARDIS shrink as well. The First Doctor, Susan, Ian and Barbara find themselves back on Earth in Ian and Barbara's time, but only about an inch high. Even so, they manage to prevent an unscrupulous businessman named Forrester from releasing a new insecticide called DN6 that would destroy all insects – even those that are beneficial to agriculture.

On several occasions, the Doctor has deliberately shrunk himself. In *The Invisible Enemy* (1977), miniaturised clones of the Fourth Doctor and Leela were injected into Doctor to find a virus that had infected him. In *The Armageddon Factor* (1979), the Fourth Doctor and another Time Lord, Drax, shrank themselves to escape from the Black Guardian's agent the Shadow while searching for the final segment of the Key to Time.

In *Into the Dalek* (2014), the Twelfth Doctor, Clara Oswald, and several soldiers were miniaturised and inserted into a malfunctioning Dalek. Just as the Doctor's antibodies attacked him and Leela in *The Invisible Enemy*, so the Dalek also had antibodies that attempted to kill the intruders.

**1964** The first episode of *Planet of Giants*, also titled *Planet of Giants*, opens the second season of *Doctor Who*. The story was originally four episodes long, but was edited down to three. It is the first story for which Dudley Simpson composed the incidental music. Simpson would go on to compose music for many stories in the classic series, including almost all the stories of the Third and Fourth Doctors.

**1964** David Whitaker's last day working on *Doctor Who* as Dennis Spooner takes over from him as Story Editor.

**2015** *The Zygon Invasion*

NOVEMBER

# 1 NOVEMBER

# The Doctor Never Meets Melanie Bush

In *The Trial of a Time Lord* (1986), events from the Sixth Doctor's future are shown as evidence. As he battles against the Vervoids on the *Hyperion III*, the Doctor has a new companion – Melanie Bush, or Mel for short. Mel is brought to the trial to give evidence in person, and at the end of the proceedings she leaves with the Doctor. So their first meeting, some time before they arrived on the *Hyperion III*, may never happened...

Mel works with computers and comes from Pease Pottage. The Doctor envies her 'amazing ability for almost total recall'. She is able to remember the exact wording, for example, of the mayday message sent by Hallett in *The Trial of a Time Lord*, although she does take a map with her to find the swimming pool in *Paradise Towers* (1987).

Perhaps more than many of the Doctor's companions, Mel means well and sees good in everyone. This is not always to her advantage. In *Paradise Towers*, for example, she sees no possible danger from the over-friendly Rezzies Tabby and Tilda – cannibals who are fattening her up with cakes and biscuits – until she is trapped under a crocheted shawl and attacked with a toasting fork.

Similarly, Mel has absolute faith in the Doctor, and it is out of concern for his welfare that she establishes an exercise routine for him – insisting he drink carrot juice and installing an exercise bike in the TARDIS control room. Perhaps it is not so surprising, then, that just as she tries to 'reform' the Doctor's lifestyle

## ON THIS DAY

**1930 The events of** *Daleks in Manhattan* **and** *Evolution of the Daleks* **take place, according to a newspaper that Martha finds.**

**1975** *Pyramids of Mars* Part 2

**1980** *Full Circle* Part 2

**1986** Mel's first episode is *The Trial of a Time Lord* Part 9. This is also the first episode of the segment usually referred to as *Terror of the Vervoids*.

**1989** *The Curse of Fenric* Part 2

**2014** Danny Pink is killed in *Dark Water*.

into something rather more healthy, so she decides to accompany the galactic rogue Glitz when he leaves Iceworld in *Dragonfire* (1987) – to try to reform his moral lifestyle.

# 2 NOVEMBER

## Corporal Benton Gets Promoted

A steadfast member of UNIT since it was set up, Benton – whose first name we never learn on screen – first appears as a corporal in *The Invasion* (1968). By the time he appears again in *The Ambassadors of Death* (1970), he has been promoted to the rank of sergeant. He is perhaps the only member of UNIT apart from Brigadier Lethbridge-Stewart who meets both the Second and Third Doctors, except in *The Three Doctors* (1972–1973), and understands that the Doctor can change his appearance before he regenerates again into the Fourth Doctor.

Trustworthy and efficient, the Brigadier and Captain Yates both rely heavily on Benton in various UNIT operations. In *The Three Doctors*, he not only meets the Second Doctor again, but also the First Doctor (albeit only on a scanner screen) and gets to travel in the TARDIS.

Having coped with betrayal by Captain Yates in *Invasion of the Dinosaurs* (1974), Benton is promoted to RSM in *Robot* (1974–1975) after Yates's enforced retirement. But as the Fourth Doctor severs his ties with UNIT, so we see less of the organisation – and of Benton. His last appearance is in *The Android Invasion* (1975), although in *Mawdryn Undead* (1983) the retired Brigadier tells the Fifth Doctor that Benton has left the army and now sells second-hand cars.

**1968** Corporal Benton – later Sergeant and RSM – first appears in Episode 1 of *The Invasion*. This episode also features the first appearance of UNIT, though the organisation is not identified as such until the next episode. It is Terrance Dicks's first episode as Script Editor.

**1981** The very first episode of *Doctor Who – An Unearthly Child* – is repeated on BBC Two. It is the first in a series of repeats titled *The Five Faces of Doctor Who*, although Peter Davison's first story as the Fifth Doctor won't be transmitted for another two months. This is the first ever repeat of a story not featuring the current incarnation of the Doctor. Other stories shown are *The Krotons* (from the Second Doctor), *Carnival of Monsters* and *The Three Doctors* (from the Third Doctor) and the Fourth Doctor's final story *Logopolis*.

**1987** *Delta and the Bannermen* Part 1

**1988** *The Happiness Patrol* Part 1

# 3 NOVEMBER

## Two Doctors Encounter the Androgums

**1979** *The Creature from the Pit* Part 2

A humanoid race, the Androgums believe that the gratification of pleasure is the sole motive for action. The Second Doctor – and later the Sixth Doctor – met several Androgums in *The Two Doctors* (1985). The Androgums worked as servitors on Space Station Camera, doing all the station maintenance as well as providing the food. Androgums are incredibly strong – the Doctor says that the Androgum Shockeye could break both him and Jamie in half with one hand.

To the Doctor's horror, the scientist Dastari, Head of Projects on the station, had enhanced an Androgum – Chessene o' the Franzine Grig – performing nine operations on her to make her a mega-genius. Dastari wanted to make Chessene into a god. But the Doctor warned him that she would always be an Androgum and would 'snap off the hand that feeds her whenever she feels hungry'.

Together with the station chef, Shockeye o' the Quawncing Grig, Chessene and Dastari were in league with the Sontarans, who wanted to derive the secret of time travel from the Doctor. With the Second Doctor mutating into an Androgum himself, the Sixth Doctor, Jamie and Peri had to deal with the Androgums and the Sontarans as well as persuade Dastari of the error of his ways.

# 4 NOVEMBER

## The Racnoss Awaken Deep Inside the Earth

Huge, spider-like creatures, the Racnoss came from the Dark Times, billions of years ago. They were born hungry and devoured everything – even whole planets. The Fledgling Empires went to war against the Racnoss and wiped them out – or so they thought. But, as the Tenth Doctor learns in *The Runaway Bride* (2006), one Racnoss survived – the Empress. In hibernation, she drifted in her spaceship to the very edge of space. The spaceships of the Racnoss are their Webstars – giant structures, of intricate web material, in the classic shape of a star.

When Torchwood detected something hidden deep in the centre of the Earth, they dug a tunnel down thousands of miles to reach it. What they didn't know was that they had detected the Secret Heart – a nest of the last of the Racnoss to have survived, the planet forming round them. Once the tunnel was complete, the Empress detected her children, reaching out across space to find her, billions of years after they were separated.

With help from Donna Noble, the Doctor was able to destroy the hungry Racnoss children before they emerged from the centre of the Earth. The Empress was killed when her Webstar was shot down by a tank when it descended low over London shooting out energy that she intended would eventually reduce the human race to nothing more than food for her children.

**1967** *The Abominable Snowmen* Episode 6. The first specially shot trailer for *Doctor Who* is shown after the episode, giving a taste of what is to come next week in *The Ice Warriors*. It features Peter Barkworth in character as Leader Clent and Peter Sallis as Penley.

**1978** *The Stones of Blood* Part 2

# 5 NOVEMBER

# Meet the Second Doctor

When the scratchy and irrascible First Doctor regenerates at the end of *The Tenth Planet* (1966), he is replaced with a younger and apparently far softer character. The First Doctor's cold, analytical abilities give way to apparent bluster and a tendency to panic under pressure.

But with the Second Doctor more than any other, first impressions are misleading. This is a Doctor who can defeat the Daleks on Vulcan in *The Power of the Daleks* (1966) without apparently having any idea of what he has done or how he did it. Yet often when he wins the day it is apparent that the solution is one he has been planning for a while. The Doctor's apparent bluster and ineptitude mask a deeper, darker nature. Even his friend Jamie realises this, and tells him that they are finished together in *The Evil of the Daleks* (1967), that the Doctor simply uses people for his own ends. It is clear that a cold, calculating alien lurks inside the bumbling exterior.

But there are moments when the Second Doctor's humanity also shines through. There is ultimately no doubt that his raison d'être is to fight the evil in the universe – as he tells his friends in *The Moonbase* (1967) and his own people in *The War Games* (1969). It is in moments when the whole façade drops – the bumbler *and* the cold warrior – that we glimpse the true Doctor, the man that he would like to be if circumstances allowed. It is moments like his description of his family to Victoria in *The Tomb of the Cybermen* (1967); his sad farewell to Jamie and Zoe in *The War Games* before he turns his righteous anger and indignation on his own people – the ones who have chosen the easy option, and have ignored the evils that must be fought…

**1966** *The Power of the Daleks* Episode 1 is the first episode to star Patrick Troughton as the Second Doctor.

**1977** *Image of the Fendahl* Part 2

# 6 NOVEMBER

## Vicki Leaves the TARDIS

**1965** The First Doctor's companion Vicki leaves in the last episode of *The Myth Makers*, titled *Horse of Destruction*. Katarina joins as a new companion.

Vicki took certificate of education in medicine, physics, chemistry and other subjects when she was 10 years old. She studied for almost an hour a week on a machine. After the death of her mother, Vicki's father wanted to get away and took a job on the planet Astra in the year 2493. But on the way, their spaceship crash-landed on the planet Dido.

Until she meets the First Doctor, Ian and Barbara in *The Rescue* (1965), Vicki believes another survivor Bennett's account of how the natives of Dido killed her father and the rest of the crew and passengers. While everyone else was invited to a meeting by the Didonians, Vicki stayed behind as she was ill. An explosion killed everyone except for Bennett, who was apparently injured. But the truth of what really happened, as Vicki learns, is very different from Bennett's story…

Once she leaves Dido, Vicki is keen to start on the adventures she has been promised. She is bored at the villa where the travellers stay in *The Romans* (1965), desperate for adventure and disappointed it doesn't all happen at once. Throughout her travels with the Doctor, Vicki retains her sense of wonder and awe. When she first sees the Roman emperor Nero, she is literally bouncing with excitement. Even the spectacle of Rome burning enthuses the young girl – 'My first real sight of history,' she tells the Doctor. It is not to be her last. When she finally leaves the Doctor, it is to join the fleeing Trojans after the ancient city of Troy falls to the Greeks.

# 7 NOVEMBER

## The Time Lords Gather in the Panopticon

The ceremonial meeting place of the High Council of the Time Lords in the capitol on Gallifrey is the Panopticon. A vast, near-circular chamber it has a raised circular dais and is surrounded by galleries from which events can be viewed. It was from one of these galleries that the Doctor watched as the Time Lord President was assassinated as he was about to deliver his resignation speech in *The Deadly Assassin* (1976).

The Panopticon was also where the emaciated, dying Master hoped to give himself new life. He knew that concealed beneath the floor, and accessible using the Rod of Rassilon, was the Eye of Harmony. Also known as Rassilon's Star, this was the nucleus of a black hole. Rassilon stabilised all the elements of the black hole and set them in an eternally dynamic equation against the mass of the planet Gallifrey.

In *The Invasion of Time* (1978), the Doctor was himself invested as President of the Time Lords in the Panopticon. Perhaps as a symbolic gesture of their supposed triumph, the Sontaran forces led by Commander Stor of the Sontaran Special Space Service arrived in the Panopticon when they attempted to invade Gallifrey.

ON THIS DAY

**1964** *Dangerous Journey* – the second episode of *Planet of Giants*

**1976** *The Deadly Assassin* Part 2

**1987 Rose Tyler's father, Pete Tyler, is killed in a hit-and-run accident. The main events of *Father's Day* take place.**

**2015** *The Zygon Inversion*

# 8 NOVEMBER

# The Doctor Learns the Truth About Missy

Although she claimed to be an android in *Dark Water* (2014), the mysterious Missy later revealed to the Twelfth Doctor that she was in fact a female incarnation of the Master. It was Missy who had given Clara Oswald the Eleventh Doctor's phone number, pretending it was a technical support centre, so bringing them together. She also took measures to keep them together after the Doctor regenerated, believing that Clara's companionship would make it easier for Missy to manipulate the Doctor emotionally.

While her outward appearance might have changed, Missy retained all the callousness, power-craving, and dark humour of the Master – as well as the admiration for her former friend the Doctor. The feeling would appear to be reciprocated, as it was to Missy that the Doctor gave his Confession Dial in *The Magician's Apprentice* (2015) when he believed he was about to die.

Missy herself cheats death as easily as her male incarnations did. Having attempted to turn the dead of planet Earth into Cybermen in *Dark Water* and *Death in Heaven*, she was shot and apparently disintegrated. But in *The Magician's Apprentice* and *The Witch's Familiar*, she returns, bringing every aeroplane over Earth to a standstill, freezing it in time, just to get UNIT's – and Clara's – attention. But whether she goes with the Doctor to see Davros because of her feelings for him, or so she can offer the Daleks the Doctor's TARDIS as part of an alliance is never entirely clear...

**ON THIS DAY**

**1975** *Pyramids of Mars* Part 3

**1980** *Full Circle* Part 3

**1986** *The Trial of a Time Lord* Part 10

**1989** *The Curse of Fenric* Part 3.

**2014** *Death in Heaven* closes Series Eight.

# 9 NOVEMBER

## UNIT Defends the Earth

Originally the United Nations Intelligence Taskforce, but later renamed the Unified Intelligence Taskforce, UNIT is an international military organisation charged with dealing with the odd and the unexplained – including alien threats to planet Earth. With its headquarters in Geneva, each nation's UNIT forces are seconded from that nation's regular military forces.

The Second Doctor first worked with UNIT against the Cybermen in *The Invasion* (1968). But he had met UNIT's commanding officer in the UK, Brigadier Lethbridge-Stewart, before – when Lethbridge-Stewart was a colonel. Together they battled against the Great Intelligence and its robot Yeti in *The Web of Fear* (1968).

When the Third Doctor was exiled to Earth by the Time Lords, he worked for UNIT as the organisation's scientific adviser. He gradually severed his ties to the organisation after the Time Lords lifted his exile, and even more so after regenerating into his fourth incarnation. But the Seventh Doctor worked with UNIT again – and with the retired Lethbridge-Stewart – in *Battlefield* (1989).

UNIT played a major role helping the Tenth Doctor in opposing the Sycorax in *The Christmas Invasion* (2005), and the Sontarans in *The Sontaran Stratagem* and *The Poison Sky* (2008). The Eleventh and Twelfth Doctors also worked with UNIT several times, and in particular with Lethbridge-Stewart's daughter Kate Stewart, who was UNIT's Chief Scientific Officer.

**1968** UNIT first appears as a full organisation in Episode 2 of *The Invasion*.

**1987** *Delta and the Bannermen* Part 2

**1988** *The Happiness Patrol* Part 2

## 10 NOVEMBER

# The Family of Blood Finds the Doctor

A short-lived species, the Family of Blood wanted to absorb the Doctor's Time Lord essence so that they could live for ever. Father, Mother, Son and Daughter, they hunted using a strong sense of smell, and kept in contact with each other telepathically. Having traced the Tenth Doctor to Earth in *Human Nature* and *The Family of Blood* (2007), they stole bodies from local people so they were disguised while they hunted for the Doctor – as they had no idea what he looked like. Their spaceship was invisible so that it would not attract attention.

Realising he was being chased by the Family, the Doctor had used a Chameleon Arch in the TARDIS to 'hide' his real personality inside a pocket watch. He travelled to Earth with Martha Jones, where he became John Smith, a history teacher at Farringham School in 1913.

The Family used molecular fringe animation to create an army of deadly scarecrows that they used to attack the school where they believed the Doctor was hiding – even though John Smith had no idea who he really was. When the Family was defeated by the recovered Doctor, the scarecrows ceased to have any life of their own.

As the Family discovered to their cost, the Doctor was hiding not because he was scared, but to protect *them*. If the Family of Blood found him, the Doctor knew he would have to take drastic action – and eventually he imprisoned them all for ever. Father of Mine was confined underground, bound with unbreakable dwarf-star chains. Mother of Mine was thrown into the event horizon of a collapsing black hole. Son of Mine was trapped in the form of a scarecrow, and Daughter of Mine was hidden inside every mirror for all eternity…

**1913 The main events of** *Human Nature* **and** *The Family of Blood* **take place.**

**1979** *The Creature from the Pit* Part 3

## 11 NOVEMBER

# John Smith *is* the Doctor

In *Human Nature* and *The Family of Blood* (2007), the Tenth Doctor used a Chameleon Arch to escape from the Family of Blood. The Time Lord device in the TARDIS allowed him to store his real personality inside a pocket watch and, in effect, to become someone else. The someone else he became was John Smith. He hid on Earth in 1913 at Farringham School, where he worked as a history teacher. Martha Jones, keeping watch over the oblivious Smith, also worked at the school as a maid.

Despite dreams of his real life, John Smith believed he was human, and even kept a diary of his strange dreams of time and space travel – 'A Journal of Impossible Things'. He met and – to Martha's horror – fell in love with the school matron, Joan Redfern. But when the Family of Blood found Smith, Martha tried to explain to him that he needed to turn back into the Doctor.

For a while, neither Joan Redfern nor John Smith believed that the Doctor existed. But as the Family of Blood went on the rampage in its increasingly desperate hunt for the Doctor, Joan and John were forced to accept the truth of Martha's story. They both desperately wanted the Doctor to stay as John Smith – and live the long, fulfilling lives they were sure they would have together. But, perhaps inevitably, despite his love and his new life, John Smith gave it up to become the Doctor again and defeat the Family of Blood.

**1913 John Smith becomes the Doctor again in *The Family of Blood*.**

**1967** *The Ice Warriors* first appear in Episode 1 of *The Ice Warriors*.

**1978** *The Stones of Blood* Part 3

## 12 NOVEMBER

# The Daleks Become Servants... Or Do They?

One of the biggest challenges the newly regenerated Second Doctor faced in *The Power of the Daleks* (1966) was convincing the human colonists on the planet Vulcan that Daleks are dangerous. The colony's chief scientist Lesterson had revived one of three dormant Daleks found inside a space capsule discovered in the mercury swamp close to the colony. Although the revived Dalek immediately exterminated one of Lesterson's colleagues, the scientist was convinced the 'robots' could make ideal servants. At his first demonstration of the Dalek, the Doctor struggled in vain to warn of the creature's true nature while the Dalek continually intoned: 'I am your servant...'

Of course, the Doctor was eventually proved right. While the Daleks appeared servile and cooperative, they set up a production line inside their capsule to create more Daleks. Finally, they emerged in force to exterminate the colonists.

In *Victory of the Daleks* (2010) the Eleventh Doctor found a similar situation. Winston Churchill was convinced that the Daleks were actually 'Ironsides' – a secret weapon invented by the scientist Bracewell. But Bracewell was really a robot created by the Daleks, and the Daleks' apparent servitude was a ruse to get the Doctor to acknowledge they were Daleks so they could reactivate a Progenitor device and create the New Dalek Paradigm...

By contrast, the three test Daleks that the Second Doctor imbues with the Human Factor in *The Evil of the Daleks* (1967) really do become helpful and friendly. Initially childlike, they play trains with the Doctor, and

**1964** The very first *Doctor Who* novel is published. A hardback book from Frederick Muller Ltd, it is a retelling of the first Dalek story and titled *Doctor Who in an Exciting Adventure with the Daleks*.

**1966** *The Power of the Daleks* Episode 2

**1977** *Image of the Fendahl* Part 3

he names them Alpha, Beta and Omega. Later, the Doctor infects more Daleks with the Human Factor, provoking a civil war on the Daleks' planet Skaro between the humanised Daleks and the others.

# 13 NOVEMBER

## The Master Tries to Harness the Power of the Eye of Harmony

According to the Fourth Doctor in *The Deadly Assassin* (1976), all the power of the Time Lords devolves from the Eye of Harmony. Most Time Lords by this time, however, believe it is a myth. But the Eye of Harmony is the nucleus of a black hole. Aeons earlier, Rassilon suspended a star in a permanent state of decay just as it collapsed into a black hole – an event triggered by the Time Lord Omega using a remote stellar manipulator. Rassilon then harnessed the potential energy of the collapse.

Bringing the nucleus to Gallifrey, Rassilon stabilised all the elements of the black hole and set them in an eternally dynamic equation against the mass of the planet. The Eye of Harmony – or Rassilon's Star as it was also sometimes known – was concealed beneath the floor of the Panopticon. But in *The Deadly Assassin*, the Master intends to use the energy to give himself new life, destroying Gallifrey and many other worlds in the process.

In the *Doctor Who* TV movie (1996), the Eighth Doctor had an Eye of Harmony inside the TARDIS, beneath a protective dome. Possibly this is a link to the actual Eye of Harmony, or an aspect of it. Again, the Master tried to use its power to renew himself, also stealing the Doctor's remaining regenerations. The Eleventh Doctor also made use of the Eye of Harmony to enter a pocket universe in *Hide* (2013), while in *Journey to the Centre of the TARDIS* (2013) it had the appearance of a collapsing star.

ON THIS DAY

**1965** *The Nightmare Begins* is the opening episode of the epic 12-part story *The Daleks' Master Plan*.

**1965 The Fifth and Sixth Doctors' companion Perpugilliam Brown – Peri for short – is born.**

**1976** *The Deadly Assassin* Part 3

**2003** *Scream of the Shalka* begins. It is an animated webcast produced by BBCi featuring Richard E. Grant as the Doctor.

# 14 NOVEMBER

## The Daleks Follow the TARDIS to Aridius

Pursued by the Daleks, although they don't yet know it, the First Doctor and his friends land on the planet Aridius in *The Chase* (1965). The planet has two suns, and the days and nights are very short. Whether the whole planet is desert is unclear, but the seas have dried up as the planet moved closer to the suns.

The Daleks describe the area where the TARDIS lands as the Sagaro Desert. There are strange sculptures in the sand. Vicki and Ian remark on one that looks like a man and Vicki suggests it might be made from frozen seaweed (though the heat of the suns must discount this).

The desert was once a vast ocean where the native Aridians lived in a city beneath the sea. When the ocean dried up, all the creatures that lived in the water perished and the Aridians were forced to live underground. The Aridians are humanoid amphibians with gills for ears, spines on their backs, and scaly bodies.

The Mire Beasts are the only other creatures to have survived. They lived in the slime at the bottom of the ocean and have also moved underground, attacking and invading the Aridian city. Now they are multiplying, and they feed on flesh. The only way the Aridians can control the Mire Beast numbers is by blowing up those sections of their city that the Beasts have overrun. The Mire Beasts apparently hunt at night and have a main body, glowing eyes, and many tentacles.

With the arrival of the Daleks in their own time/space machine, the Aridians have another threat to

**1959** Paul McGann, who played the Eighth Doctor, was born.

**1964** *Crisis* – the third and final episode of *Planet of Giants*

**1964** The Doctor makes his first comic-strip appearance, in *TV Comic*.

**2013** Paul McGann returns for his final appearance as the Eighth Doctor in *The Night of the Doctor*, a mini-episode released online as part of the series' fiftieth-anniversary celebrations.

**2015** *Sleep No More*

contend with. Having forced a group of Aridians to dig the TARDIS out of the desert after it was buried in a sandstorm, the Daleks decide they are 'worthless inferior creatures' and exterminate them.

# 15 NOVEMBER

# Fenric Returns from the Shadow Dimension

In *The Curse of Fenric* (1989), the Seventh Doctor describes Fenric as: 'Evil since the dawn of time… The beginning of all beginnings. Two forces, only good and evil. Then chaos. Time is born. Matter, space. The universe cries out like a newborn. The forces shatter as the universe explodes outwards. Only echoes remain, and yet somehow – somehow – the evil force survives. An intelligence, pure evil…'

At some time in the distant past, the Doctor challenged Fenric to solve a chess puzzle. He carved chess pieces from bones pulled from the desert sands, and when Fenric failed he was trapped in the Shadow Dimension for seventeen centuries. His essence was somehow imprisoned within a flask.

The flask was bought by a merchant in Constantinople, and then stolen by Viking pirates and buried. But the 'Wolves' of Fenric have unwittingly worked to bring about Fenric's reappearance. They are all descendants of Joseph Sundvik, the Viking who buried the flask.

At the military base where he again encounters Fenric during the Second World War, the Doctor reveals that he realised Fenric was involved when he saw a chess game set up in Lady Peinforte's house in *Silver Nemesis* (1988). Fenric plays games with time, allowing Ace to save her own mother, whom she hates, and bringing the Ancient One – the last survivor of a future polluted Earth – back in time to create its own poisoned future world. But once the Doctor has explained this to the Ancient One, it kills both itself and Fenric with the poison Fenric intended to use to destroy the human race.

# 16 NOVEMBER

## International Electromatics Prepares to Conquer the World

International Electromatics is the world's biggest electronics manufacturer, making its breakthrough in micro-monolithic circuit designs. In *The Invasion* (1968), the TARDIS lands inside the compound of International Electromatics' main facility. All the local people have been bought out, most of them joining the company. UNIT has been unable to trace those who did not.

The head of IE, Tobias Vaughn, has been working with the Cybermen for five years. He believes the world is weak, vulnerable, and a mass of uncoordinated and impossible ideals. It needs a strong leader – which Vaughn believes will be him after the Cybermen invade.

The micro-monolithic circuits built into IE equipment all round the world form an artificial nervous system. Once activated they produce a Cyber-hypnotic force. One hour before the invasion, the Cyber-transmitter units are launched into orbit around Earth, and their transmissions penetrate all areas – paralysing the human race. Vaughn and his team are protected by implanted audio rejection capsules. The Cybermen have already arrived in force. Dormant Cybermen have been delivered in spaceships – some of which have been spotted by UNIT – at the IE facility. Revived, the Cybermen wait in the sewers beneath London. But once the signal is transmitted, more Cybermen will land and select suitable humans for cybernetic conversion to Cybermen – unsuitable humans will be destroyed.

The Second Doctor, Jamie and Zoe get involved while looking for Professor Watkins – an associate of their friend Professor Travers, who they met in *The*

**1968** *The Invasion* Episode 3

**1987** *Delta and the Bannermen* Part 3

**1988** *The Happiness Patrol* Part 3

**2007** Peter Davison returns as the Fifth Doctor in *Time Crash* with David Tennant, a mini-episode written by Steven Moffat and shown on BBC One as part of the BBC's Children in Need appeal.

*Abominable Snowmen* (1967) and *The Web of Fear* (1968). Vaughn has Watkins working on the Cerebratron Mentor – a machine that produces excessively powerful emotional pulses as an aid to learning. Vaughn sees this as a weapon he can mass produce to use against the Cybermen after the invasion to avoid being totally converted into a Cyberman. In fact, his body is already cybernetic, but he insists that his brain will remain his own.

Having met the Doctor, Vaughn believes that even if this plan fails, he will have an escape route – the TARDIS…

# 17 NOVEMBER

# The Doctor Marries Queen Elizabeth

The Doctor's association with Queen Elizabeth I goes back longer than she knows. In *The Chase* (1965), the First Doctor saw her on the Time-Space Visualiser he got from the Moroks' Space Museum on the planet Xeros; he watched as the Queen asked William Shakespeare to write a play about Falstaff in love. At some point in one of his first two incarnations, the Doctor was locked in the Tower of London during Elizabeth's reign – the Third Doctor tells Jo Grant in *The Mind of Evil* (1971) how he shared a cell with Sir Walter Raleigh.

But it was the Tenth Doctor who actually met Queen Elizabeth. Believing her to be a Zygon in disguise, he proposed marriage to her while on a picnic in *The Day of the Doctor* (2013) to see how she reacted. But he was actually talking to the real Queen – who accepted. The Zygon was disguised as her horse. Later, a Zygon did disguise itself as the Queen, but she got the better of her double. For a while, Elizabeth pretended to be the Zygon imposter and learned of their plan to hide inside Time Lord paintings until Earth was ready for conquest.

With the Zygons trapped inside the paintings, Elizabeth had them locked away in the secret Under Gallery beneath the National Gallery. She left instructions that the Doctor was to be appointed Curator of the Under Gallery. She also insisted that the Tenth Doctor go through with his promise of marriage.

Years later, Elizabeth saw the Tenth Doctor again – although earlier in his own timeline – at the Globe Theatre in *The Shakespeare Code* (2007). Having been abandoned by him after their wedding, she ordered his death.

**1558 Elizabeth I becomes Queen.**

**1979** *The Creature from the Pit* Part 4

**Late twenty-ninth or early thirtieth century:** *Revenge of the Cybemen* takes place on Day 3, Week 47, which puts it in mid-November…

## 18 NOVEMBER

# The Krotons Enslave the Gonds

The planet that the Second Doctor, Jamie and Zoe arrive on in *The Krotons* (1968–1969) has twin suns, normal gravity, and air that is a mixture of ozone and sulphur. The native inhabitants are the humanoid Gonds, who worship the Krotons – creatures that never leave their Dynatrope machine. No one has ever seen the Krotons, but Gond legends tell of silver men who fell from the sky and caused poisonous rain to fall when the Gonds attacked them.

It is the law of the Krotons that everyone uses the Teaching Machines when young. The Gonds are therefore dependent on the Krotons for their patchy knowledge. Every so often, the two best students are sent into the Dynatrope to join the Krotons.

The Krotons' Dynatrope is a spaceship, part of a battle fleet, which operates through mental power. Four 'high brains' are needed in relay to operate it, but two Krotons were exhausted by enemy fire. So the Dynatrope was set in perpetual stability to preserve power and the systems instructed to educate the primitive Gonds to the level needed to reanimate the surviving Krotons. The mental energy of the Gonds who enter the Dynatrope is absorbed into the active circuits before the 'waste matter' (the Gonds themselves) is rejected and dispersed.

The Krotons, like the Dynatrope, are crystalline, based on tellurium. Krotons cannot die, but function permanently until they 'exhaust'. The exhaust procedure is merely a reversion to basic molecules, and the matter can be reanimated.

ON THIS DAY

**1967** *The Ice Warriors* Episode 2

**1978** *The Stones of Blood* Part 4

**2005** David Tennant and Billie Piper star in a short prequel to *The Christmas Invasion*, shown on BBC One as part of the BBC's Children in Need appeal.

But while the Krotons have ensured that their teaching machines impart no knowledge to the Gonds that might be used against them, they did not anticipate the arrival of the Doctor. He tells the Gonds how to create a version of sulphuric acid which dissolves the Dynatrope.

# 19 NOVEMBER

# The Doctor Diagnoses the Problems of Solos

Earth has ruled the planet Solos for five hundred years before the Third Doctor is sent there by the Time Lords in *The Mutants* (1972). The humans initially came for thaesium, one of the richest fuel sources in the galaxy, but now the supply has been exhausted. The atmosphere of Solos is unbreathable during daylight by humans without an oxymask, as the soil contains a nitrogen isotope released by the ultraviolet rays of the sun, causing a kind of poisonous mist.

Solos is ruled by the Marshal from Skybase One in orbit around the planet. The Marshal has had a visiting Administrator assassinated before the Administrator could publicly reveal that Solos is about to be granted independence from Earth's Empire. When the Doctor arrives, the Marshal is planning to change the atmosphere of Solos to be breathable by humans, but not the native Solonians.

The Solonian people are mutating into huge insectoid creatures. They think this is a result of the Marshal's experiments with the atmosphere. But the Doctor realises that the change is an accelerated genetic metamorphosis, an 'adaptive' change as the environment alters with the incredibly long seasons of the planet, albeit hastened and confused by the Marshal's work. The Mutts are merely an interim stage. Crystal from a thaesium cave is essential for the change – a bio-catalytic agent that hastens the mutations – which explains why the mutant creatures have converged on the area. The final mutation is a glowing humanoid creature that communicates by thought transference and glows with radioactive energy.

**1924** William Russell, who played the First Doctor's companion Ian Chesterton, was born.

**1966** *The Power of the Daleks* Episode 3

**1977** *Image of the Fendahl* Part 4

## 20 NOVEMBER

# Rassilon and the Old Time

First mentioned in *The Deadly Assassin* (1976), Rassilon is regarded as the founder of Time Lord civilisation, though in his own day he was seen mainly as an engineer and an architect. Early Time Lord history is chronicled in *The Book of the Old Time*, which tells how Rassilon travelled into the black void with a great fleet.

'Within the void, no light would shine, and nothing of that outer nature continue in being except that which existed within the Sash of Rassilon,' says the account, which the Fourth Doctor takes to mean that Rassilon was inside a black hole. This was where he found the Eye of Harmony, 'which balances all things that they may neither flux, not wither, nor change their state in any measure'. Rassilon brought the Eye of Harmony back to Gallifrey, where it has been a powerful energy source for the Time Lords ever since.

A great leader, Rassilon also led the Time Lords against the Great Vampires. He ordered the construction of Bow Ships, which fired a huge bolt of steel that transfixed the creatures through the heart. But the King Vampire escaped into E-Space, where the Fourth Doctor found – and destroyed – it in *State of Decay* (1980).

In *The Five Doctors* (1983), the First, Second, Third and Fifth Doctors travel to Rassilon's tomb – beneath a great tower in the Death Zone on Gallifrey. They communicate with the disembodied essence of Rassilon himself, and

watch as President Borusa is granted the eternal life he seeks – but not in the way he expected.

Whether the Rassilon first seen in *The End of Time* (2009–2010) who led the Time Lords during the Great Time War against the Daleks is a reincarnation of the same ancient and revered figure is not explicitly stated. If not, then he is simply another Time Lord President with the same name.

**1965** *Day of Armageddon* – the second episode of *The Daleks' Master Plan*

**1976** Rassilon, the founder of Time Lord society, is first mentioned in *The Deadly Assassin* Part 4.

# 21 NOVEMBER

## The Flood Infects the Crew of Bowie Base One

The planet Mars, the fourth planet from the Sun and the second smallest in the Solar System (after Mercury) was once home to the race of intelligent reptiles the Doctor calls the Ice Warriors. When the Second Doctor first meets them, in *The Ice Warriors* (1967), they believe their home planet is dead. But in *The Monster of Peladon* (1974), Federation Ambassador Alpha Centauri describes the Ice Warriors as 'natives of the planet Mars', so it possible that they have by then returned to their ancient home.

Being relatively close to Earth, Mars was the first planet that humans sought to explore. The British Mars Probe missions landed on the planet, and it was here that General Carrington met a group of aliens also exploring Mars. The aliens were unaware that their touch was fatal, and Carrington's fellow astronaut was accidentally killed by them. In *The Ambassadors of Death* (1970), Carrington sought to prove that the aliens were hostile, forcing kidnapped alien ambassadors to rob and kill.

Mars was eventually the location of the first off-world human colony. Bowie Base One was located in the Gusev Crater. When the Tenth Doctor visited the base in *The Waters of Mars* (2009), its occupants were being infected and possessed by the Flood – a virus life form that lived in water. The Doctor speculated that the Ice Warriors had also encountered the Flood, and managed to freeze it into a glacier. If one drop of infected water had got back to Earth, all of humanity could have been infected.

**1964** The Daleks return for the first time in the first part of *The Dalek Invasion of Earth*. The episode – titled *World's End* – is the first to enter the top 10 ratings chart.

**1990** Although *Doctor Who* is no longer being made by the BBC, *Search Out Science* on BBC 2 features the Seventh Doctor (Sylvester McCoy) and Ace (Sophie Aldred), alongside K-9, voiced by John Leeson.

**2009** The animated adventure *Dreamland* begins on the BBC website and 'Red Button' TV service.

**2013** *An Adventure in Space and Time*, a dramatised account of the origins and early years of *Doctor Who* written by Mark Gatiss, is broadcast on BBC Two.

**2015** *Face the Raven*

**2059** The events of *The Waters of Mars* take place.

Centuries later, as planet's Earth's resources were exhausted, the Usurians shipped the entire population to Mars as they exploited them for commercial profit.

**2119 The crew of the Drum, an underwater base near Caithness in Scotland, find an alien spaceship.**

# 22 NOVEMBER

## The Doctor Finds the Last of the Great Vampires

According to Time Lord legend, in the misty dawn of history when even Rassilon was young, a race of Giant Vampires swarmed throughout the universe. One Vampire could suck the life out of an entire planet and the vampires of legend on many planets are pale imitations of these creatures.

The Time Lords hunted down the giant vampires across the universe in a war so long and so bloody they were sickened of violence for ever. According to the *Record of Rassilon*: 'So powerful were the bodies of these great creatures and so fiercely did they cling to life, that they were impossible to kill save by the use of Bow Ships … Yet slain they were all were and to the last one by the Lords of Time – the Lords of Time destroying them utterly … However, when the bodies were counted, the King Vampire – mightiest and most malevolent of all – had vanished, even to his shadow, from time and space…'

As the Fourth Doctor found out in *State of Decay* (1980), the King Vampire had escaped into another universe known as E-Space. It mentally summoned the officers of the spaceship *Hydrax* – which was on an exploration mission to Beta Two in the Perigellis sector – to be his servants. Known as the Three Who Rule, King Zargo, Queen Camilla, and Councillor Aukon lived in the Tower, which was in fact the *Hydrax* itself. They were the original officers, while the local peasants were descended from the crew. Over time their names became corrupted – the officers were Captain Miles Sharkey (Zargo), Navigation Officer Lauren MacMillan

**ON THIS DAY**

**1963** The Ninth Doctor watches John F. Kennedy's motorcade travel through Dallas, and witnesses JFK's assassination. He is caught in a photograph that Clive shows Rose Tyler in *Rose*.

**1963** The second episode of the first Dalek story, *The Daleks*, is rehearsed and recorded at Lime Grove – the first time the Dalek props are used in a TV studio.

**1975** *The Android Invasion* Part 1

**1980** *State of Decay* Part 1

**1986** *The Trial of a Time Lord* Part 12

**1989** *Survival* Part 1

(Camilla) and Science Officer Anthony O'Connor
(Aukon). They served the Great Vampire, working to
nourish and revitalise it until it awakened. In return it
had given them immortality. When the Doctor arrived,
the Great Vampire was ready to rise again…

## 23 NOVEMBER

# Meet the First Doctor

Right from the start, the First Doctor is an enigma. Is he really Susan Foreman's grandfather, her teachers Ian Chesterton and Barbara Wright wonder? And what is he doing with a police box in a junkyard?

Two things that are immediately apparent are the Doctor's attachment to the TARDIS, and his love of his granddaughter, Susan. Rather than risk her leaving him, the Doctor transports himself together with Susan and the intruders Ian and Barbara away from 1963 London. It is this same love that drives him to lock Susan out of the TARDIS in *The Dalek invasion of Earth* (1964) when he realises that she has reached the place that will be her ideal home – that she has found someone to love her and look after her in the way the Doctor has done up till now.

The First Doctor is abrasive and brash. He tells Ian: 'Your arrogance is nearly as great as your ignorance.' Even after they have together faced death both in the Stone Age in *An Unearthly Child* (1963) and on the planet Skaro in *The Daleks* (1963–1964), the Doctor still accuses Ian and Barbara of sabotaging the TARDIS when it malfunctions in *The Edge of Destruction* (1964). But particularly from the point where he realises that the TARDIS has not been sabotaged, but is trying to send him a warning, the Doctor's attitude to Ian and Barbara mellows and he begins to treat them more as companions and less as unwelcome stowaways.

The First Doctor's relationship with later companions continues in this more mellow vein. He can still be irascible and never suffers fools gladly. But he does seem to have learned the value of friendship and how to appreciate what others have to offer. He is upset when

**1638 The Doctor launches the Nemesis statue into orbit from the field outside Lady Peinforte's house in Windsor.**

**1866 Clara Oswin Oswald, who the Eleventh Doctor met in** *The Snowmen* **(2012), was born.**

**1963** The first ever episode of *Doctor Who* – titled *An Unearthly Child* – is broadcast. It is the first episode of a four-part story also usually referred to as *An Unearthly Child*.

**1968** *The Invasion* Episode 4

**1983** The first broadcast of the twentieth-anniversary story *The Five Doctors* is on the US public broadcaster PBS in the USA (albeit slightly edited). It is broadcast in the UK on BBC 1 two days later, on 25 November, as part of the BBC's Children in Need appeal programming.

Dodo does not say goodbye to him in person in *The War Machines* (1966), sending a message with Ben and Polly.

But throughout, perhaps more than any other incarnation, the First Doctor remains a mystery to his companions. A mystery compounded when, in *The Tenth Planet* (1966) he collapses in the TARDIS and turns into a totally different and much younger man...

**1986 The Eleventh and Twelfth Doctors' companion Clara Oswald was born in Blackpool.**

**1987** Ace first appears in *Dragonfire* Part 1.

**1988 The Nemesis statue crashes back to Earth near Windsor, where the Cybermen are waiting to retrieve it.**

**1988** The first episode of the twenty-fifth-anniversary story *Silver Nemesis* is transmitted.

**2013** The fiftieth-anniversary story *The Day of the Doctor* is transmitted. It is the largest ever TV drama simulcast, broadcast simultaneously in 98 countries across six continents at 1950 GMT. Faith Penhale joins Steven Moffat as Executive Producer for this one story.

## 24 NOVEMBER

# The Doctor Discovers the Secret of Eden

The space liner *Empress* is en route from Station Nine to Azure with 900 passengers on board when it comes out of warp and collides with another, smaller ship, the *Hecate*. The two ships are locked together, the *Hecate* sticking through the *Empress* and creating dimensional instabilities as the two ships try to reject each other.

The effects of these instabilities are exacerbated by the presence of a Continuous Event Transmuter owned by the zoologist Tryst. The Continuous Event Transmuter – or CET Machine – takes sample areas and life from a planet and stores them as electromagnetic signals on a laser crystal inside the machine. The samples continue to live and evolve in this environment. When played back, the environment is reconstituted as an intra-dimensional matrix.

The CET Machine is basically a crude form of matter transfer by dimensional control and, without a dimensional osmosis damper, the sample environments become unstable when the *Empress* crashes into the *Hecate*. When the Fourth Doctor, Romana and K-9 arrive on board in *Nightmare of Eden* (1979), aggressive creatures from the planet Eden called Mandrels, have escaped into the ship and are killing passengers and crew.

The Doctor discovers that the Mandrels, when electrocuted, decompose into vraxoin powder. Vraxoin, or XYP, is an addictive drug. It induces complacency, then apathy and, ultimately, it kills. The only known source of vraxoin was destroyed – the planet incinerated. But Tryst has discovered a new source – the

**ON THIS DAY**

**1979** *Nightmare of Eden* Part 1

**2119 The Twelfth Doctor and Clara Oswald arrive at the Drum in *Under the Lake*.**

Mandrels on Eden – and he is using the CET Machine to smuggle the drug. It is up to the Doctor to deal with the rampaging Mandrels, separate the two spaceships, and capture the drugs smugglers.

# 25 NOVEMBER

# The Doctor Explores the Death Zone

The Death Zone registers on the TARDIS instruments as being no place in no time, but it is actually on the Time Lord planet Gallifrey. The Death Zone was an ancient arena used in Gallifrey's dark days. Alien beings were collected with a time scoop and made to fight for the amusement of the watching Time Lords. Certain life forms, including the Daleks and Cybermen, were never selected to do battle in the Death Zone as they played the so-called Game of Rassilon too well. Towering over the barren wastelands of the Death Zone is the Dark Tower – which is actually Rassilon's tomb.

The Death Zone has been unused and inactive for thousands of years when, in *The Five Doctors* (1983), President Borusa reactivates it. He plans to use the various incarnations of the Doctor to get to Rassilon's tomb and activate a transmat there so that he can travel to the tomb and gain the secret of immortality from Rassilon himself.

When his first incarnation is taken out of time, the Fifth Doctor experiences a twinge of what he describes as 'cosmic angst'. The effect worsens as more of his past selves are taken – he feels weak, 'diminished', and eventually starts to fade away. He stabilises once he arrives in the Death Zone, where all his previous incarnations have been transported. The only exception is the Fourth Doctor, who is trapped in a time eddy and never arrives.

Enemies gathered by Borusa to play the game against the Doctor include a lone Dalek, a number of Cybermen, a Yeti, and a Raston Warrior Robot. He also sends the Master and some of the Doctor's past companions to help him, including Sarah Jane Smith, Susan and the Brigadier. Conjured as obstructive illusions are Jamie, Zoe, Mike Yates and Liz Shaw.

**1963** The first newspaper review of *Doctor Who* is by Michael Gowers in the *Daily Mail*.

**1967** *The Ice Warriors* Episode 3

**1974 The events of** *Hide* **take place, centred on Caliburn House.**

**1978** *The Androids of Tara* Part 1

**1983** *The Five Doctors* – a feature-length twentieth-anniversary special – is broadcast in the UK.

## 26 NOVEMBER

# The Human Race Abandons Planet Earth

At various points in its history, the human race has left its home planet, Earth. In *The Ark in Space* (1975), the Fourth Doctor, Sarah Jane Smith and Harry Sullivan arrived on Space Station Nerva where humans were sleeping in cryogenic suspension. They had left Earth when the planet was about to be ravaged by solar flares, intending to return once it was habitable again.

The Doctor and his friends used the station's transmat system to travel down to Earth in *The Sontaran Experiment* (1975). They found that the area where London had been was now a grassy wilderness, the planet uninhabited. But a Sontaran – Field Major Styre – had lured a group of human colonists to the planet in order to assess human strengths and weaknesses ahead of a proposed attack on the galaxy. The colonists were descendants of people who left Earth centuries earlier to avoid the solar flares and colonise other planets.

At some point, presumably after Earth had then been repopulated, the planet's resources began to run out and humanity entered into a business deal with the Usurians to move the entire population to Mars. When the resources of Mars were also used up, the population was again moved, this time to Pluto, where six artificial suns were positioned above the planet to make it habitable. When the Fourth Doctor and Leela arrived in *The Sun Makers* (1977), they found the humans in effect enslaved by the immense taxes imposed by the Usurian Collector.

Whether humanity returned to Earth again is unclear. But the Doctor has twice witnessed the end of the world as the Sun expanded and destroyed the Earth. In *The Ark* (1966), the First Doctor was on a giant spaceship taking

**ON THIS DAY**

**1966** *The Power of the Daleks* Episode 4

**1977** *The Sun Makers* Part 1

**1993** The first part of the thirtieth-anniversary special *Dimensions in Time* is broadcast on BBC 1 as part of the BBC's Children in Need appeal. It is shot in 3-D.

the remains of the human race on a 700-year journey to settle on the planet Refusis II. In *The End of the World* (2005), the Ninth Doctor and Rose Tyler watched the Sun expand and engulf the Earth from Platform One.

# 27 NOVEMBER

## Sutekh Escapes from the Eye of Horus

Seven thousand years ago, the Osiran Sutekh (also known as Set) destroyed his own planet, Phaester Osiris, and left a trail of havoc across half the galaxy. Horus and 740 other Osirans finally cornered Sutekh in Egypt where their conflict brought about the Egyptian myths. Horus imprisoned Sutekh beneath a pyramid, powerless to move. The Osirans did not destroy him as that would have meant they were no better than he. So they imprisoned him using a force field controlled from a power source within a pyramid on Mars.

But in 1911, Professor Marcus Scarman found Sutekh's tomb. Sutekh killed Scarman, reanimating his corpse to do his bidding and help him escape. The opening of the tomb, however, triggered a distress signal from the pyramid on Mars, which the Fourth Doctor was able to decode as 'Beware Sutekh'.

Using Osiran Service Robots wrapped in protective bandages – and similar in appearance to Egyptian mummies – Sutekh had Scarman build a missile to destroy the Eye of Horus on Mars, which held him captive. After the Doctor destroyed the missile, Sutekh used the TARDIS to send Scarman to the Pyramid of Mars to get past Horus's traps and destroy the Eye. With the Eye of Horus destroyed, the Doctor and Sarah faced a race against time to stop Sutekh from escaping and destroying the world.

**ON THIS DAY**

**1965** *Devil's Planet* – the third episode of *The Daleks' Master Plan*

**1976** An edited compilation repeat of *Pyramids of Mars* is shown on BBC 1 – it runs for 62 minutes.

**1993** The second and final part of the thirtieth-anniversary special *Dimensions in Time* is broadcast on BBC 1 as part of *Noel's House Party*. It is shot in 3-D and feature's Jon Pertwee's last televised appearance as the Third Doctor.

## 28 NOVEMBER

# The Daleks Turn Humans into Robomen

About ten years before the First Doctor, Susan, Ian and Barbara arrived in *The Dalek Invasion of Earth* (1964), the Earth was bombarded with meteorites, which scientists called a 'cosmic storm'. Then people began to die of a new plague. Whole continents of people were wiped out, including Asia, Africa and South America. The plague split the world into small communities, too far apart to combine and fight, and too small individually to stand any chance when the invading Daleks arrived. Some cities were razed to the ground, others were simply occupied. Anyone who resisted was exterminated.

Because there were relatively few Daleks on Earth, they operated on some prisoners and turned them into living robots – Robomen. The 'transfer' operation took over the human brain. The Daleks passed orders to their Robomen through headpieces that picked up high-frequency radio waves. The helmets flashed when receiving instructions, and the Daleks could tell when a Roboman was attacked.

But the Dalek control was only temporary. After a while, the Robomen suffered a breakdown, going insane. Some smashed their heads against walls, while others they threw themselves off buildings or into the River Thames.

**1964** *The Daleks* – the second episode of The *Dalek Invasion of Earth*

**1987** Karen Gillan, who played the Eleventh Doctor's companion Amy Pond, was born.

**2015** *Heaven Sent*

# 29 NOVEMBER

## The Valeyard is the Doctor

The Prosecutor at the Doctor's trial in *The Trial of a Time Lord* (1986) was the Valeyard. As prosecutor, he could include any testimony he deemed relevant provided he could justify it to the court. In his opening evidence – the events in the segment usually called *The Mysterious Planet* – he maintained that the Doctor initiated the disastrous chain of events on Ravalox by his mere presence. The Valeyard claimed to have calculated that, based on a random sample, the Doctor's companions had been placed in danger twice as often as the Doctor himself. The Doctor pointed out that he'd had many companions but there was only one of him.

As the Master later revealed, the Valeyard was in fact a 'version' of the Doctor distilled from his dark side. As the Master explained: 'There is some evil in all of us, Doctor – even you. The Valeyard is an amalgamation of the darker sides of your nature, somewhere between your twelfth and final incarnation. And I may say, you do not improve with age.'

Although he seemed to be concerned primarily with having the Doctor executed and 'inheriting' his regenerations (having done a deal with the High Council of Time Lords), the Valeyard actually wanted to kill the Time Lords involved in the trial – the supreme guardians of the law. He had a MASER – a Microwave Amplification and Stimulated Emission of Radiation – which would act as a subatomic particle disseminator. It would kill all Time Lords at the Doctor's trial when the particles were disseminated through the main view-screen.

**ON THIS DAY**

**1942** Michael Craze, who played the First and Second Doctors' companion Ben Jackson, was born.

**1975** *The Android Invasion* Part 2

**1980** *State of Decay* Part 2

**1986** Part 13 is the first of the two-part final segment of *The Trial of a Time Lord*. It is usually referred to as *The Ultimate Foe*, or sometimes *Time Inc*, although in fact *The Ultimate Foe* was the original title for the Vervoids segment comprising Parts 9–12.

**1989** *Survival* Part 2

Although he was apparently destroyed by the ray phase shift triggered by the Doctor when he sabotaged the MASER, the Valeyard either took over as Keeper of the Matrix or was somehow always the Keeper in disguise.

# 30 NOVEMBER

# Ace is Caught in a Time Storm

Ace is working as a waitress in the café on Iceworld when the Seventh Doctor first meets her in *Dragonfire* (1987). Despite being able to mix up explosive Nitro-Nine – a derivative of nitro-glycerine – and store it in used deodorant cans, Ace is young and naïve. She does not disguise her feelings, be they enthusiasm at the prospect of a real-life treasure hunt, boredom and annoyance at her job, or dislike for her parents, in particular her mother. In many ways, Ace is a typical, rebellious teenager. She lies about her age, her room is a tip, she hates her job and she believes her parents cannot be her real mum and dad as they gave her such a naff name – her real name being Dorothy.

Back in her home of Perivale, it is unlikely Ace would stand out much from the crowd, except that she does everything with such a determination born of enthusiasm. She has been suspended from school for blowing up the Art Room (as a creative act). She reached Iceworld having been whisked through time and space by what she describes as a 'time storm'. As revealed in *The Curse of Fenric* (1989), however, this was no coincidence, but an element of Fenric's grand design – part of which involves Ace being brought face to face with her own mother as a baby. As one of the Wolves of Fenric, she carries his evil within her – and perhaps this really is why the Doctor agrees to take her with him.

Ace never really loses her 'obvious' nature. But by *Silver Nemesis* (1988) she has matured under the Doctor's influence enough to admit when she is frightened (but not enough to agree to his suggestion

**1874 Winston Churchill was born.**

**1963** *Doctor Who* gets its first ever repeat broadcast. *An Unearthly Child*, the opening episode, is shown again immediately before the second episode, titled *The Cave of Skulls*. This is because people may have missed it the previous week, following President Kennedy's assassination the day before, and a widespread power failure.

**1968** *The Invasion* Episode 5

**1987** *Dragonfire* Part 2

**1988** *Silver Nemesis* Part 2

she return to the TARDIS). Perhaps this is why he feels she is now able to cope with the trauma of returning to Gabriel Chase – the haunted house she burned down when she was 13 – in *Ghost Light* (1989).

# 1 DECEMBER

## Let It Snow

The Doctor has visited more than his fair share of cold and snowy environments – from the Plateau of the Pamir in *Marco Polo* (1964) to the snowy wastes of the Ood-Sphere in *Planet of the Ood* (2008); from the snowy planet of Necros when the Sixth Doctor visited Tranquil Repose in *Revelation of the Daleks* (1985) to the centuries he spent in the snowy town of Christmas on Trenzalore in *The Time of the Doctor* (2013).

The First Doctor regenerated after the exertions of fighting the Cybermen at Snowcap Base at the South Pole in *The Tenth Planet* (1966), whereas the Fourth Doctor barely seemed to notice the Antarctic cold in *The Seeds of Doom* (1976).

It was in the snowy wastes of a future ice age that the Second Doctor first met the Ice Warriors in *The Ice Warriors* (1967). Immediately before that he encountered the Great Intelligence in the foothills of the Himalayas in *The Abominable Snowmen* (1967). It would not be the Doctor's last encounter with the Great Intelligence. In *The Snowmen* (2012), the disembodied force not only took over Doctor Simeon but also attacked the Eleventh Doctor with snow it had imbued with life, and also with a homicidal governess made from ice…

ON THIS DAY

**1979** *Nightmare of Eden* Part 2

**1986 A calendar on the wall at Snowcap Base gives the date as December 1986, although on which day in December the events of *The Tenth Planet* actually take place is unknown.**

## 2 DECEMBER

# Double Trouble for the Doctor

**1967** *The Ice Warriors* Episode 4

**1978** *The Androids of Tara* Part 2

Travelling as much as he does and for so long, it is perhaps inevitable that the Doctor has occasionally met people that look very similar either to himself or to his companions. Sometimes this happens by chance. The fact that the Abbot of Amboise looked rather like the First Doctor in *The Massacre* (1966) was just such a coincidence – as was his similarity to the Roman lyre player Maximus Petullian in *The Romans* (1965). Also coincidental was the Second Doctor's similarity to the dictator Salamander in *The Enemy of the World* (1967–1968). In *Black Orchid* (1982), the Fifth Doctor's companion Nyssa met Ann Talbot – who looked just like her. Romana's similarity to the Princess Strella in *The Androids of Tara* (1978) landed her and the Fourth Doctor in trouble – not least when Count Grendel sent an android copy of Romana to kill the Doctor.

But sometimes meeting a double is not random at all. In *The Chase* (1965), the Daleks constructed a robot double of the First Doctor to infiltrate the TARDIS. The Daleks also created duplicates of the Fifth Doctor, Tegan and Turlough to assassinate the Time Lord High Council in *Resurrection of the Daleks* (1984). Omega took on the Fifth Doctor's form in *Arc of Infinity* (1983), just as Meglos tried to make himself into a copy of the Fourth Doctor in *Meglos* (1980). A copy of the Eleventh Doctor was made from the substance Flesh in *The Rebel Flesh* and *The Almost People* (2011). In *The Android Invasion* (1975), the Kraals created android copies of both Sarah Jane Smith and the Fourth Doctor – as well as Harry Sullivan, RSM Benton and many others.

Regeneration gives rise to other duplications. It seems unlikely that the Sixth Doctor's resemblance to Commander Maxil of the Chancellery Guard who appeared in *Arc of Infinity* was deliberate. But in *Destiny of the Daleks* (1979), Romana chose to regenerate into the form of Princess Astra, who she'd recently met in *The Armageddon Factor* (1979). Similarly, the Twelfth Doctor took on the form of Caecilius, having met him in *The Fires of Pompeii* (2008) – although this seems to have been a subconscious decision, a subliminal message to himself that he only understood in *The Girl Who Died* (2015).

# 3 DECEMBER

## Agatha Christie Helps the Doctor Solve a Mystery

The Tenth Doctor and Donna Noble arrived at Lady Eddison's house in 1926, where they met the young Agatha Christie in *The Unicorn and the Wasp* (2008). She was near the start of her writing career, but despite having had just six books published, was already becoming well known as a crime novelist.

Before long, guests and staff at the house party were murdered – all in the manner of an Agatha Christie whodunit. While investigating, Donna was menaced by a giant wasp and the Doctor poisoned with cyanide. With the help of Agatha Christie, whose keen powers of observation were well in evidence, the Doctor uncovered the villain – the Reverend Arnold Golightly. But Golightly was actually a Vespiform – an alien creature very similar to a huge wasp. Agatha Christie managed to lure the creature away by taking its Telepathic Recorder.

Dame Agatha Christie went on to became the most successful novelist in history. She wrote over 80 books, and her play *The Mousetrap* opened in London in 1952 and is still running. As the Doctor knew, she really did disappear for ten days in 1926. She was finally found staying in a hotel in Harrogate. The exact circumstances of her disappearance remain a mystery…

ON THIS DAY

**1926 The crime novelist Agatha Christie disappears. Despite a huge search involving over a thousand police officers and 15,000 volunteers, she is not found until 14 December.**

**1966** *The Power of the Daleks* Episode 5

**1977** *The Sun Makers* Part 2

# 4 DECEMBER

# Katarina Kills Herself to Save the Doctor

In *The Myth Makers* (1965), Katarina is barely more than a slave when she first encounters the First Doctor and his companions Vicki and Steven. She is the handmaiden to Cassandra, Princess of Troy. Katarina also believes she is doomed to die, as the auguries have foretold it.

Sent by Cassandra to spy on Vicki, Katarina helps the wounded Steven back to the TARDIS. With her home city of Troy overrun by the attacking Greeks, she leaves with Steven and the Doctor. Katarina never really understands what has happened to her or where she is. She believes that the Doctor is a god despite his protestations to the contrary, and she sees the TARDIS as his temple. She believes she is on a divine journey to her 'place of perfection' – and perhaps she is.

In *The Daleks' Master Plan* (1965–1966), Katarina is taken hostage inside the airlock of a spaceship by a homicidal prisoner named Kirksen from the planet Desperus. Always loyal to her new 'master' the Doctor, she uses what little knowledge she has acquired to open the airlock door rather than allow herself to be used by Kirksen, who is demanding the Doctor return the ship to the planet Kembel – where the Daleks are waiting. Together with Kirksen, she is ejected into the vacuum of space.

'She wanted to save our lives,' the Doctor tells Steven. 'And perhaps the lives of all other beings of the Solar System. I hope she found Perfection.'

**1872** The ship the *Mary Celeste* is discovered abandoned and adrift off the Azores.

**1965** The First Doctor's companion Katarina is killed in the fourth episode of *The Daleks' Master Plan*, titled *The Traitors*. Also killed is Bret Vyon – played by Nicholas Courtney, who later played Brigadier Lethbridge-Stewart. Sara Kingdom is introduced as a short-lived new companion.

**1976** An edited compilation repeat of *The Brain of Morbius* is shown on BBC 1. It runs for 60 minutes.

# 5 DECEMBER

## Things Get Timey-Wimey for Sally Sparrow

In *Blink* (2007), Sally Sparrow finds a message scrawled beneath the wallpaper in an old, deserted house called Wester Drumlins. It is a warning from the Tenth Doctor, who, together with Martha Jones, has been attacked by a Weeping Angel and sent back in time. Now he is stranded in the 1960s without the TARDIS. Intrigued by the message, Sally goes to see her friend Kathy Nightingale. Together they return to Wester Drumlins. Looking around, Kathy is attacked by a Weeping Angel, and finds herself transported back to 1920.

Just moments later, Kathy's grandson arrives with a letter for Sally – who thinks it is some sort of trick. But she soon realises the severity of the situation she is in. Together with Kathy's brother Larry Nightingale, Sally finds the Doctor has also left a message for her hidden as an 'Easter Egg' on each of the DVDs she owns – warning her about the Weeping Angels. Following the Doctor's clues, Sally and Larry manage to evade the Weeping Angels and send the TARDIS back to rescue the Doctor and Martha.

Sally and Larry later go into business together, selling old books and rare DVDs. When Sally eventually meets the Doctor in person, it is before he and Martha are sent back in time by the Angel. So Sally is able to warn the Doctor of what will happen and what messages to leave for her…

ON THIS DAY

**1920 Kathy Nightingale** is sent back to this day by a Weeping Angel in *Blink*.

**1964** *Day of Reckoning* – the third episode of *The Dalek Invasion of Earth*

**2009** The animated web series *Dreamland* is broadcast as a single compilation episode on BBC Two and BBC HD.

**2015** *Hell Bent*

# 6 DECEMBER

## The Cheetah People Hunt Down Humans

The people who created the now ruined buildings on the planet the Seventh Doctor and Ace are transported to in *Survival* (1989) thought they could control the planet. They also bred the Kitlings – which resemble black cats. These were creatures whose minds they could talk to and through whose eyes they could see – as the Master, trapped on the planet, now can. The Doctor describes the Kitlings as feline vultures. They have the power of teleportation, able to jump from world to world hunting for carrion – including people.

The Cheetah People that now inhabit the planet are also like cats. But they are the size of a person, walk upright on two legs and ride horses. The Cheetah people are hunters that can see in the dark and take their prey home. They also seem to return home to hunt. The Doctor realises he can return to Earth if he is hunted by an animal whose home is Earth.

Some at least of the other humanoid life forms that have been brought to the planet of the Cheetah People are from other worlds. The planet affects the people brought to it, mutating them into Cheetah People themselves. This is what is happening to the Master, and Ace is also affected to an extent. When one of the Cheetah People, named Karra, dies she turns back into human form, and her trip 'home' brings her to Earth.

The planet has only a short time left, as it is disintegrating. The Doctor describes it as 'an old planet,

**1975** Noel Clarke, who played Rose Tyler's boyfriend Mickey Smith, was born.

**1975** *The Android Invasion* Part 3

**1980** *State of Decay* Part 3

**1986** *The Trial of a Time Lord* Part 14 is Colin Baker's last episode as the Sixth Doctor and closes Season 23. While Script Editor Eric Saward worked on Episode 13, he has no involvement on this episode.

**1989** *Survival* Part 3 is the last full episode starring Sylvester McCoy as the Seventh Doctor and the final episode of the classic series, closing Season 26.

a bit frayed at the edges'. The Master says the planet is
alive, and that the animals are part of it – when they
fight each other they trigger explosions that hasten the
planet's destruction.

# 7 DECEMBER

# The Doctor Meets His Nemesis

Validium is a living metal created back in early times by Omega and Rassilon as the ultimate defence for Gallifrey, and none of it should ever have left Gallifrey. In 1638 a large lump of validium fell in the meadow behind the house owned by Lady Peinforte in Windsor. Lady Peinforte had the validium made into a statue in her own likeness holding a bow and arrow – the Nemesis. The Doctor launched the statue into space, leaving the bow and arrow on Earth so the metal could never attain critical mass. For this the statue needed to be reunited with its bow and arrow.

But the Doctor miscalculated and, rather than travelling deep into space, the Nemesis 'comet' circles the world until it crashes back to Earth at the point where it left on 23 November 1988 in *Silver Nemesis* (1988). The Seventh Doctor tells Ace that 'the Nemesis generates destruction, it affects everything around it'. Its orbit brings it back to Earth every 25 years and he implies its appearances coincided with: 1913 – the eve of the First World War; 1938 – when Hitler annexed Austria; 1963 – when President Kennedy was assassinated. The statue tells Ace that it has had other forms 'that would horrify you'. Lady Peinforte called her Nemesis, 'so I am retribution'.

Knowing of its legendary power, various parties are after the Nemesis. Lady Peinforte paid (then killed) a mathematician to calculate when it would return to Earth. Then she travelled through time using the power of the Nemesis arrow and a magic potion – an ingredient of which is the mathematician's blood. The

ON THIS DAY

**1947** Wendy Padbury, who played the Second Doctor's companion Zoe, was born.

**1963** *The Forest of Fear* – the third episode of *An Unearthly Child*

**1968** *The Invasion* Episode 6

**1987** Mel's last episode as the Sixth and Seventh Doctors' companion is the third and final part of *Dragonfire*, which closes Season 24.

**1988** *Silver Nemesis* Part 3

**1998** Michael Craze, who played the First and Second Doctors' companion Ben Jackson, died.

neo-Nazi De Flores has the bow, which was in Windsor Castle until it mysteriously disappeared in 1788. The Cybermen also want the Nemesis, which they know is a powerful weapon. Ultimately, the Doctor must decide which – if any – of them should have it…

# 8 DECEMBER

# Parasitic Seaweed Threatens the World

In *Fury from the Deep* (1968), the Second Doctor, Jamie and Victoria arrive at Euro Sea Gas Headquarters where a strange heartbeat noise is being heard from the gas pipeline, and contact has been lost with several gas rigs out at sea. The people on the rigs have been infected by a parasitic sea weed that takes over the people it touches.

The creature is part of a colony that derives its intelligence parasitically from the human brains of its hosts, and lives in vast quantities of sea foam. The Doctor believes that the Weed Creature has been documented before – by sailors in the North Sea in the middle of the eighteenth century. The Creature plans to absorb all human life into its collective colony. It infects and takes over humans through contact, and emits a toxic gas. Infected victims begin to grow weed over their skin – unnoticeable at first, but ultimately they will be consumed by the weed…

Oak and Quill were the engineers sent to clear the blockage caused by the Weed Creature's first contact – drawn up into the drilling pipes of one of the rigs. They were probably the first people to be infected by the Weed when they came into direct contact with it while clearing the pipe. The Weed Creature uses the two engineers in its plan to control the Euro Sea Gas complex. They take people over by breathing out toxic gas from their mouths. Weed grows down their arms and is visible on their hands and at their cuffs.

Robson, the chief of Euro Sea Gas, under the control of the Creature, tells the Doctor that its aim is 'the

ON THIS DAY

conquest of the human planet… The mind does not exist. It is tired. It is dead. It is obsolete. Only our new masters can offer us life … The body does not exist. Soon we shall all be one.'

# 9 DECEMBER

## The Ice Warriors Attack Britannicus Base

**1967** *The Ice Warriors* Episode 5

**1978** *The Androids of Tara* Part 3

Arriving in what turns out to be a future ice age in *The Ice Warriors* (1967), when the whole of Europe has been inundated by glaciers, the Second Doctor, Jamie and Victoria make their way to Britannicus Base. The base is a converted Victorian mansion preserved inside a protective plastic bubble, spared from redevelopment because it was classified as being of historic interest.

It is from Britannicus Base that the Ionisation Programme for this part of the world is run by Leader Clent, who explains that it is a lack of carbon dioxide that has caused the new ice age. He tells the Doctor that 'the amount of growing plants on the planet was reduced to an absolute minimum … Then suddenly, one year, there was no spring.'

Ionisation is a method of intensifying the Sun's heat onto the Earth, but into particular areas. The Doctor likens it to a magnifying glass. Clent's assistant Miss Garrett says that ionisation can produce temperatures intense enough to melt rock. But the programme is under threat as Clent has fallen out with his chief scientist, Penley, who has left the base. The root of their problems is that Clent trusts the main computer implicitly, whereas Penley believes that human innovation and discovery are more important than slavish adherence to the computer's directions.

But ultimately, as the Ice Warriors who have been thawed from the glacier attack the base, Clent realises that he cannot rely solely on the computer and comes to appreciate Penley's point of view.

# 10 DECEMBER

## Sharaz Jek Wants to Preserve Peri's Beauty

**1966** *The Power of the Daleks* Episode 6

**1977** *The Sun Makers* Part 3

Sharaz Jek was a doctor on the planet Androzani Major until the study of androids took his interest. When the ruthless industrialist Morgus needed androids to collect and refine the toxic raw spectrox on Androzani Minor, he entered into a partnership with Sharaz Jek. Jek would supply the androids, while Jek and Morgus would share the profits. As spectrox was a substance that greatly increased longevity, it was incredibly valuable.

But Morgus decided to kill Jek, and supplied him with faulty detection instruments when a lethal mudburst was imminent on Androzani Minor. Jek was almost killed by the scalding mud that exploded from the core of the planet. Badly burned, he saved himself by reaching a baking chamber. Vowing revenge, and hiding his scarred face behind a mask, Jek took control of vital stores of the refined spectrox with an android army.

When the Fifth Doctor and Peri arrived on Androzani Minor in *The Caves of Androzani* (1984), Jek's androids were holding their own against an attack by government troops led by General Chellak. Jek himself was immediately attracted to Peri's youthful beauty. By feeding her spectrox, he believed he could preserve her beauty for ever. Jek also saw the Doctor initially as a potential companion, with a mind Jek considered almost his equal – until the Doctor's apparent flippancy and obstructive nature made him expendable.

But what Jek did not realise was that both the Doctor and Peri had touched raw spectrox and contracted spectrox toxaemia. They were both dying, and the only cure was the milk of a queen bat from deep in the caves of Androzani Minor.

## 11 DECEMBER

# The SSS Struggles to Keep Earth Safe from the Daleks

The SSS is Earth's elite defence and security force in *Mission to the Unknown* (1965) and *The Daleks' Master Plan* (1965–1966). It was SSS Agent Marc Cory who discovered the Daleks on the planet Kembel as they and delegates from other alien races plotted to invade the Solar System in *Mission to the Unknown*. SSS may stand for *Space Security Service* (as stated on Cory's ID) or *Special Security Service* (as Cory identifies himself in his recorded report).

In *The Daleks' Master Plan*, the First Doctor met another SSS agent on Kembel – Bret Vyon. Vyon was bred on Mars Colony 16. He joined the Space Security Service in AD 3990. He gained First Rank in 3995 and Second Rank in 3998. The Doctor also met Agent Sara Kingdom of the SSS, who was a loyal agent of Mavic Chen – the Guardian of the Solar System. Bret Vyon was Kingdom's brother (perhaps they had different fathers, or Kingdom may be her married name).

But Sara Kingdom was tricked by Chen into killing her brother. Once convinced that Mavic Chen was actually a traitor and working for the Daleks, Sara helped the

Doctor and Steven Taylor to destroy the Daleks. But it cost her dearly. Sara Kingdom aged to death on the planet Kembel when the Daleks' Time Destructor was activated.

**1965** *Counter Plot* – the fifth episode of *The Daleks' Master Plan*

# 12 DECEMBER

## The Slyther Guards the Daleks' Mining Operations

In *The Dalek Invasion of Earth* (1964), the First Doctor and his companions find themselves in a London devastated after Earth has been invaded by the Daleks. The Doctor discovers that the Daleks' main operations centre on a mining project in Bedfordshire, and he makes his way there. Here he finds that the Daleks plan to drill through the Earth's crust and blow out the planet's core with a special penetration explosive. Their plan is then to install a guidance system so as to pilot the Earth like a giant spaceship.

The mine is worked by slave labour – groups of humans working in shifts and kept under control by Robomen acting as guards. The whole operation is under the control of the Black Dalek, who is also referred to as the Supreme Controller.

There is a strict curfew at night, enforced not just by the Daleks and Robomen, but also by the Slyther. This revolting creature is a 'pet' of the Black Dalek. It roams the mine area at night in search of food – humans. The Slyther's horrific, screaming cries strike terror into the mine workers. The Slyther attacks Ian Chesterton as he tries to get into the mine at night, but he manages to engineer the creature's fall down a mine shaft.

**1961** Sarah Sutton, who played the Fourth and Fifth Doctors' companion Nyssa, was born.

**1962** Sydney Newman, who was instrumental in creating *Doctor Who*, starts work as Head of Drama at the BBC.

**1964** *The End of Tomorrow* – the fourth episode of *The Dalek Invasion of Earth*

# 13 DECEMBER

# Ranks of the Daleks

The exact hierarchy of Dalek ranks has never been fully deciphered. In *The Daleks* (1963–1964), there is no obvious distinction between the different Daleks, but when the First Doctor encounters them again in *The Dalek Invasion of Earth* (1964), they are led by the Black Dalek, sometimes referred to as the Supreme Controller, while the commander of the Dalek saucer has alternating black lower panels.

In *The Chase* (1965) and *The Daleks' Master Plan* (1965–1966), the Daleks are commanded by the Dalek Supreme, which is predominantly black. Dalek Sec, leader of the Cult of Skaro first seen in *Army of Ghosts* and *Doomsday* (2006) also has a black casing. In *The Evil of the Daleks* (1967), the Second Doctor meets the Emperor Dalek guarded by its black-domed section leaders. The Ninth Doctor meets another Emperor Dalek in *The Parting of the Ways* (2005), while the Emperor the Seventh Doctor meets in *Remembrance of the Daleks* (1988) is in fact Davros.

Invading Earth again in *Day of the Daleks* (1972), most Daleks are now grey in colour, their leader being mainly gold – as is the case in *Frontier in Space* (1973). In *Planet of the Daleks* (1973), the Thal Codal describes the black and gold Dalek Supreme as being 'one of the Supreme Council', suggesting there may be more than one Supreme Dalek. The Dalek Supreme of *Resurrection of the Daleks* (1984) also has a predominantly black casing, while the New Paradigm version that first appears in *Victory of the Daleks* (2010) is mainly white.

A red Dalek Supreme appears in both *The Stolen Earth / Journey's End* (2008) and *The Magician's Apprentice / The*

ON THIS DAY

**1975** *The Android Invasion* Part 4 is the last episode to feature RSM – formerly Sergeant – Benton and Harry Sullivan.

**1980** *State of Decay* Part 4

*Witch's Familiar* (2015), while *Asylum of the Daleks* (2012)
features a Dalek Parliament presided over by the Dalek
Prime Minister – who seems to be superior to the Dalek
Supreme.

# 14 DECEMBER

## The Doctor Takes Ace to See the Greatest Show in the Galaxy

**1926 Agatha Christie is found at the Swan Hydropathic Hotel in Harrogate.**

**1963** *The Firemaker* – the fourth episode of *An Unearthly Child*

**1968** *The Invasion* Episode 7

**1988** *The Greatest Show in the Galaxy* Part 1

The Psychic Circus bills itself as The Greatest Show in the Galaxy, but it is apparently no longer as good as it used to be. By the time the Seventh Doctor takes Ace to see it in *The Greatest Show in the Galaxy* (1988–1989),it has settled on the planet Segonax. But things are not what they seem at the circus. The clowns are robots, and the performers are under a malign influence.

When the circus came to Segonax, one of the performers, Kingpin, found the power of the Gods of Ragnarok. But he was unable to control it, and his mind broke. Now he is called Deadbeat and does odd jobs like sweeping up, while mumbling to himself. Since then, the Circus has been slaved to the Gods of Ragnarok, who demand constant entertainment from the acts – when they tire of a performer, they kill them…

The Gods of Ragnarok exist in two times concurrently – the past of their temple (the Dark Circus) and the present-day Psychic Circus. They need to be entertained, and so long as the Doctor (and others) entertain them, they are allowed to live.

Their power seems to be represented by a huge eye at the bottom of an abyss. The symbol is also used on the kites Flowerchild makes and appears within Morgana's crystal ball. It is on Deadbeat's amulet – which he first used (as Kingpin) to summon the Gods of Ragnarok. Once he has worked out what is happening, the Doctor is able to use the amulet to reflect back their destructive energy and destroy the Gods and the Dark Circus.

## 15 DECEMBER

# Sarah Jane Smith Takes the Place of her Aunt

When she is introduced in *The Time Warrior* (1973–1974), Sarah Jane Smith is a 23-year-old investigative journalist. She works, at least some of the time, for *Metropolitan* magazine. Intelligent and determined, Sarah never misses an opportunity for a good story and is not afraid to take risks. Sarah first meets the Third Doctor at a research centre where top scientists have been asked to stay by UNIT in the hope of thwarting a series of kidnappings. The culprit is a Sontaran warrior, Linx, who is taking scientists back to the Middle Ages to help him repair his crashed spacecraft. Sarah has taken the place of her aunt, the famous virologist Lavinia Smith who is on a lecture tour in America, and Sarah sees the invitation as a chance to get a good story. Convinced that the Doctor is somehow involved, Sarah sneaks into the TARDIS…

The Doctor soon comes to admire Sarah's intelligence, determination, loyalty and conviction. In his fourth incarnation, he describes her not only as his friend – a rare admission for the Doctor – but as his *best* friend. When they are forced to part company as the Doctor is summoned back to Gallifrey at the end of *The Hand of Fear* (1976) both are saddened by Sarah's departure.

But they meet again – in both *The Five Doctors* (1983) and the Tenth Doctor story *School Reunion* (2006). The Doctor has also appeared in *The Sarah Jane Adventures*, a series featuring Sarah, her adopted son Luke, and K-9 Mark IV – given to her by the Doctor at the end of *School Reunion* to replace the Mark III model the Fourth Doctor left for her ahead of the spin-off *K-9 & Company* (1981).

**37 Nero, later to become Roman Emperor, was born.**

**1973** Sarah Jane Smith's first episode is Part 1 of *The Time Warrior*, which opens Season 11 and also introduces the Sontarans and a new title sequence.

**1979** *Nightmare of Eden* Part 4

# 16 DECEMBER

## The Chameleons Need New Identities

The Chameleons are an alien race that have suffered a catastrophe – a giant explosion – on their own planet. It has left them without identities and dying out. But their scientists have devised a process whereby they can take on the physical characterises of another being. When the Second Doctor comes into contact with the Chameleons in *The Faceless Ones* (1967), they are using a holiday company called Chameleon Tours to steal the identities of humans travelling from Gatwick Airport – kidnapping whole plane-loads of people.

Armbands maintain the link between the 'donor' and the Chameleon; removing the band or changing the controls on it can break the connection. The controls can also modify the Chameleon's speech – a Chameleon version of Jamie, for example, lacks his Scottish accent.

The Chameleons plan to abduct 50,000 young people this time. While the real versions of the Chameleon team at Gatwick are kept unconscious in cars in the airport car park, the majority of kidnapped humans are held miniaturised on a space station. The Chameleon Tours planes are themselves miniaturisation chambers that can turn into spacecraft that fly up into space and dock with the station.

An arrogant race, the Chameleons believe themselves to be superior to the people they are using who are 'only human beings'. In their native form, the Chameleons are humanoids with dark, scarred, globby faces and bodies. In this form they would soon suffocate in Earth's atmosphere.

**1773** The Ninth Doctor told Rose Tyler in *The Unquiet Dead* that he 'pushed boxes at the Boston Tea Party', which took place on this day.

**1929** Nicholas Courtney, who played the long-running character of Brigadier Lethbridge-Stewart was born. He also played SSS Agent Bret Vyon in *The Daleks' Master Plan*.

**1967** *The Ice Warriors* Episode 6

**1974** The premiere of the *Doctor Who* stage play *Seven Keys to Doomsday* takes place at the Adelphi Theatre on the Strand in London.

**1976** An updated version of *The Making of Doctor Who* (originally published by Piccolo) is published by W H Allen under the Target imprint.

**1978** *The Androids of Tara* Part 4

# 17 DECEMBER

## Jamie Macrimmon Meets the Doctor

James Robert Macrimmon first met the Second Doctor following the 1746 Battle of Culloden in *The Highlanders* (1966–1967). He is the son of Donald Macrimmon, and a piper like his father and his father's father. Because of his background, Jamie is simple and straightforward, but he is also intelligent and blessed with a good deal of common sense. When they examine his brain, the Dominators discover that he shows signs of recent rapid learning in *The Dominators* (1968). In many ways, Jamie's travels with the Doctor are a voyage of discovery. Almost everything is new to him, and while he struggles to understand he also enjoys the experience.

It is in his nature to accept things, and this helps Jamie to assimilate the worlds around him. He relates new experiences to his own world where he can – aeroplanes become flying beasts, a Cyberman is the legendary Phantom Piper that appears to members of his clan on their deathbeds. What he cannot find an analogy for he simply accepts with wonder but without worry.

Certainly Jamie is brave, never one to shirk a fight or run away. Despite knowing how dangerous and foolish the expedition is, he accompanies Zoe and Isobel into the London sewers to hunt for Cybermen in *The Invasion* (1968).

Ultimately, despite occasional reservations, Jamie sees the Doctor as a friend as well as a mentor. While he relishes the chance to travel and learn and have adventures, he also believes that the Doctor really does need his help. Although he feels betrayed by the Doctor's enforced cooperation with the Daleks and refusal to help rescue Victoria Waterfield in *The Evil*

**1929** Jacqueline Hill, who played the First Doctor's companion Barbara Wright, was born.

**1966** Jamie Macrimmon first appears in *The Highlanders* Episode 1.

**1977** *The Sun Makers* Part 4. It is Robert Holmes's last episode as Script Editor. He also wrote the story.

*of the Daleks* (1967), his anger does not last once he understands the true situation. If it were not for the intervention of the Time Lords in *The War Games* (1969), Jamie would have happily kept travelling in the TARDIS with the Doctor for many more years…

# 18 DECEMBER

## The Doctor Meets Splinters of an Impossible Girl

The Eleventh Doctor met two 'aspects' of Clara Oswald before he met the real woman in *The Bells of Saint John* (2013). Both were presumably created by Clara entering the Doctor's time stream as she followed Doctor Simeon in *The Name of the Doctor* (2013).

The first aspect of Clara he encountered was Oswin Oswald in *Asylum of the Daleks* (2012). She was the Junior Entertainment Manager on the starliner *Alaska*, which crashed into the planet where the Daleks had established their Asylum. She believed she had survived the crash and was safe but trapped in a secure area of the ship. However, as the Doctor found when Oswin guided him to her through the Asylum, Oswin had actually been converted into a Dalek.

In *The Snowmen* (2012), the Doctor met a barmaid called Clara Oswin Oswald in Victorian London. She also spent time masquerading as 'Miss Montague' and working as a governess for the Latimer family. Although Clara helped the Doctor and the Paternoster Gang against aggressive snowmen and an ice governess animated by the Great Intelligence, and the Doctor invited her to travel with him, Clara Oswin Oswald was killed. She died with the Doctor by her side.

**ON THIS DAY**

**1965** *Coronas of the Sun* – the sixth episode of *The Daleks' Master Plan*

**1981 The main events of the spin-off adventure *K-9 & Company: A Girl's Best Friend* starring Elisabeth Sladen as Sarah Jane Smith and John Leeson as the voice of K-9 take place from 18 to 22 December.**

# 19 DECEMBER

# Trying The Not-So-Miracle Diet

When their breeding planet was lost, the Adiposian First Family was forced to find another way to give birth to a new generation of Adipose children. Their solution was to create Adipose children on another planet. They chose Earth, knowing that they would have to operate in secret or they would be reported to the Shadow Proclamation for their illegal activities. The family hired 'Miss Foster' to take charge of the project.

As the Tenth Doctor and Donna Noble learned in *Partners in Crime* (2008), Miss Foster who set up Adipose Industries was actually Matron Cofelia of the Five-Straighten Classabindi Nursery Fleet (intergalactic class). The Adipose company seemed to offer a miraculous slimming treatment. Simply take a capsule every day, and you lose exactly one kilogramme of fat each night. 'The fat just walks away,' said the company advertising. And it was literally true – as the fat was converted into infant Adipose creatures.

The Adipose children created by Miss Foster were cute-looking creatures made from excess body fat. But the Adipose could also convert bone, organs, hair – converting a whole human body into Adipose material. A million of the infant Adipose creatures were created when Miss Foster was forced to activate her program early, because of the Doctor's intervention. When the Adiposians arrived to take their children, they also killed the one person who could implicate them in the crime – Miss Foster.

**1961** Matthew Waterhouse, who played the Fourth and Fifth Doctors' companion Adric, was born.

**1964** *The Waking Ally* – the fifth episode of *The Dalek Invasion of Earth*

**1981 The main events of the spin-off adventure** *K-9 & Company: A Girl's Best Friend* **starring Elisabeth Sladen as Sarah Jane Smith and John Leeson as the voice of K-9 take place from 18 to 22 December.**

## 20 DECEMBER

# Other Realities

As if the real universe were not dangerous and exciting enough for him, the Doctor has occasionally made trips *sideways* into other realities. In *The Space Museum* (1965), the TARDIS jumped a time track, arriving in its own future and giving the First Doctor and his companions a glimpse of what might happen to them on the planet Xeros. The First Doctor also travelled to the realm of the Toymaker in *The Celestial Toymaker* (1966) – a world where those who lost at the Toymaker's games became his playthings.

Forced to use the TARDIS's Emergency Unit in *The Mind Robber* (1968), the Second Doctor arrived in the Land of Fiction where he and his companions Jamie and Zoe met Gulliver, Rapunzel, and many other mythical and fictional characters.

Exiled to Earth, the Third Doctor managed to get the TARDIS console to take him sideways in time to a parallel Earth in *Inferno* (1970) – a distortion of the world where he was trapped inhabited by different versions of the same people. The Tenth Doctor also travelled to a parallel version of Earth in *Rise of the Cybermen* and *The Age of Steel* (2006), and met different versions of people he already knew – like Rose's parents Jackie and Pete Tyler.

The Doctor has also glimpsed alternative futures. As well as his own personal future in *The Space Museum*, he showed Sarah Jane Smith and Laurence Scarman a future Earth devastated by Sutekh if he managed to escape in *Pyramids of Mars* (1975). In *Day of the Daleks* (1972), the Third Doctor and Jo Grant visited a future where the Daleks had managed to change the history

**1981** The main events of the spin-off adventure *K-9 & Company: A Girl's Best Friend* starring Elisabeth Sladen as Sarah Jane Smith and John Leeson as the voice of K-9 take place from **18** to **22** December.

of Earth so they could invade. In *Turn Left* (2008), Donna Noble experienced a world in which she never met the Tenth Doctor – with disastrous consequences for the Doctor and for the world as a whole…

## 21 DECEMBER

# The Doctor Meets the Daleks

The Daleks are the most hated and feared life form in the universe. The mutated creatures live inside armoured casings and have a psychotic hatred of all other life forms. The mutated Dalek creatures are the end result of a thousand-year war between the Kaleds and the Thals on the planet Skaro. A Kaled scientist, Davros, experimented to discover the ultimate mutated form of his race, and designed the Dalek travel machine to enable the resultant creatures to survive. Now dependent on radiation, and powered by static electricity, the Daleks' only ambition is the conquest of all other life forms and the total extermination of their enemies. The Third Doctor once described the Dalek creature as 'a living, bubbling lump of hate'.

The First Doctor first visited Skaro in *The Daleks* (1963–1964), at a time when the Daleks were confined to their city, drawing the static electricity they needed through the metal floors. But since then he has encountered them on numerous occasions, across all of time and space. He has also met their creator Davros, and was on Skaro when the Daleks were originally created, sent there to prevent their creation by the Time Lords. Apart from failing in that mission for the Time Lords, the Doctor has always managed to defeat the Daleks – even provoking a civil war between the Daleks on Skaro – and he remains their most dangerous and hated enemy...

**ON THIS DAY**

**1963** The Daleks are introduced in the first episode of *The Daleks*, titled *The Dead Planet*. But all that appears of a Dalek in this episode is a sucker arm approaching Barbara in the cliffhanger...

**1965** The stage play *Curse of the Daleks* opens at Wyndham's Theatre in London.

**1968** *The Invasion* Episode 8

**1981 The main events of the spin-off adventure *K-9 & Company: A Girl's Best Friend* starring Elisabeth Sladen as Sarah Jane Smith and John Leeson as the voice of K-9 take place from 18 to 22 December.**

**1988** *The Greatest Show in the Galaxy* Part 2

## 22 DECEMBER

# The Doctor Names his Home Planet as Gallifrey

The planet Gallifrey, in the constellation of Kasterborous, is the home world of the Time Lords. The Doctor first reveals the name of the planet in *The Time Warrior* (1973–1974). Also called the Shining World of the Seven Systems, it is located at ten-zero-eleven zero-zero by zero-two from Galactic Zero Centre. The planet is ruled from the Capitol, with Arcadia being the second city. The fall of Arcadia to the Daleks was one of the final events of the Last Great Time War between the Time Lords and the Daleks.

With its two suns and orange sky, Gallifrey's grass was red and the trees had silver leaves. The Capitol was on the continent of Wild Endeavour, between the Mountains of Solace and Solitude. Much of the area round the Capitol at least was a sandy wasteland referred to as Outer Gallifrey. Somewhere in these wastelands was the Death Zone, where in ancient times the Time Lords brought other life forms to do battle for their entertainment and amusement. Also in the Death Zone is the Dark Tower – the tomb of Rassilon, the founder of Time Lord society.

The planet was protected by transduction barriers and a quantum force field while some cities – including Arcadia – also had sky trenches. Despite this, the Daleks penetrated the planet's defences at the end of the Time War. In the final conflict, the Dalek forces were apparently wiped out, and Gallifrey destroyed. But in fact, the Doctor had managed to move Gallifrey into a pocket universe where it existed in stasis, time locked and separated from the rest of the real universe.

**1973** Gallifrey is first mentioned by name in Part 2 of *The Time Warrior* – although the production office provided the name back in July in response to a letter in the comic *TV Action*.

**1979** *The Horns of Nimon* Part 1. This is the last story for which prolific composer Dudley Simpson composed the incidental music.

**1981 The main events of the spin-off adventure *K-9 & Company: A Girl's Best Friend* starring Elisabeth Sladen as Sarah Jane Smith and John Leeson as the voice of K-9 take place from 18 to 22 December.**

## 23 DECEMBER

# The Doctor Impersonates Salamander

Arriving in Australia in the near future in *The Enemy of the World* (1967–1968), the Second Doctor finds himself the target of an armed attack. His attackers are actually trying to assassinate Salamander – the world's leader. The Doctor looks almost exactly like him…

Although he obviously has enemies, Salamander is popular, since he has apparently saved the world from starvation by inventing a 'Sun Store'. This collects the rays from the Sun and stores them in concentrated form. The conserved energy can then be directed to areas lacking in sunlight.

Salamander himself is arrogant and assured. He is urbane – his wine is specially made in Alaska – and sophisticated. But he is also a cold-blooded, power-hungry killer who is determined to control the entire world. To this end he has kept a group of people captive in a secret bunker, lying to them that there has been a nuclear war. From the bunker he engineers massive 'natural' disasters in which thousands die.

He is also a master of initiative and improvisation. Having been defeated by the Doctor pretending to be him, Salamander learns from the mistake and turns that same trick back on itself – pretending to be the Doctor in order to make his escape.

**1892** The events of *The Snowmen* **begin.**

**1967** *The Enemy of the World* Episode 1 sees Patrick Troughton playing not only the Doctor but also the villain, Salamander.

**1978** *The Power of Kroll* Part 1

# 24 DECEMBER

# Jackson Lake is not the Doctor

When the Tenth Doctor arrives in London on Christmas Eve 1851, he finds that another Doctor is already there, battling against the Cybermen. At first he assumes this other Doctor must be a future incarnation of himself. But the other Doctor doesn't recognise him, and gradually the Doctor realises this is not the case. And when the Other Doctor shows him his TARDIS, it turns out to be a hot air balloon.

The man who thinks he is the Doctor is actually Jackson Lake. He has been traumatised by a chance encounter with the Cybermen, in which his wife was killed and his son abducted. Absorbing information from Cyber records stored on an infostamp device, Lake learns of the Doctor. His mind is so shocked by what has happened to him that Jackson Lake believes that he himself actually *is* the Doctor. With the help of his friend Rosita, Lake tries to live up to the Doctor's morals and courage.

With the real Doctor on the scene, the two join forces to fight the Cybermen and their deadly Cybershade creatures. The Doctor and Lake discover a huge work area where the Cybermen are using children as slave labourers to construct a massive CyberKing robot. With Lake finally realising who he actually is, and remembering his background, he is able to help the real Doctor defeat the Cybermen and save his own son.

## ON THIS DAY

**1851 Most of the events of** *The Next Doctor* **take place.**

**1869 The events of** *The Unquiet Dead* **take place.**

**1892 Clara Oswin Oswald dies in** *The Snowmen*.

**1941 Most of the events of** *The Doctor, The Widow and the Wardrobe* **take place.**

**1941** John Levene, who played Sergeant Benton throughout the Third Doctor's era, was born.

**1966** *The Highlanders* Episode 2

**2006 The events of** *The Christmas Invasion* **begin.**

**2007 Donna Noble's wedding never happens as she is transported into the TARDIS in** *The Runaway Bride*.

**2008 The events of** *Voyage of the Damned* **take place on 24 and 25 December.**

## 25 DECEMBER

# Santa Claus Saves the Doctor

The Pilot Fish Roboforms that track the newly regenerated Tenth Doctor to Earth for his regeneration energy in *The Christmas Invasion* (2005) and are later used by the Empress of the Racnoss in *The Runaway Bride* (2006) disguise themselves as versions of Father Christmas. But they are not the only Santa Claus that the Doctor has met.

In *Last Christmas* (2014), the Twelfth Doctor and Clara Oswald are helped by the real Santa Claus. Or are they? The Doctor believes that Santa actually represents the subconscious minds of the people attacked by Dream Crabs trying to break free. Assisted by his elves Ian and the Wolf, Santa takes the Doctor and the others affected by the Dream Crabs for a ride in his sleigh – pulled of course by flying reindeer. As they wake up, each of the dreamers disappears from the sleigh.

After the Doctor believes he has saved Clara, Santa appears again, telling him to wake up. Having finally rescued Clara from a Dream Crab, the Doctor confesses he was unsure who to thank for the second chance. Perhaps, after all, Santa Claus really was looking out for him. Certainly, someone left a tangerine on Clara's windowsill…

**1851 The Doctor has lunch with Jackson Lake after the events of** *The Next Doctor***.**

**1965** *The Feast of Steven*, the seventh episode of *The Daleks' Master Plan*, is the first episode of *Doctor Who* ever to be shown on Christmas Day. It ends with the First Doctor wishing 'a Happy Christmas to all of you at home'.

**1965 The 'contemporary' events of** *The Feast of Steven* **take place.**

**2005** *The Christmas Invasion* is David Tennant's first full episode as the Tenth Doctor. It is immediately followed, on the BBC's 'Red Button' service, by *Attack of the Graske*, an interactive adventure, also starring David Tennant, which offers viewers a chance to fly the TARDIS via their TV remote controls.

**2006 The second day of events of** *The Christmas Invasion* **take place.**

**2006** *The Runaway Bride* introduces the character of Donna Noble.

**2007 Most of the events of** *The Runaway Bride* **take place.**

**2007** *Voyage of the Damned* stars Kylie Minogue as Astrid.

**2008 The events of** *Voyage of the Damned* **take place on 24 and 25 December.**

**2008** *The Next Doctor*

**2009** Rassilon returns, played by Timothy Dalton, in *The End of Time, Part One*.

**2010** *A Christmas Carol*

**2011** *The Doctor, the Widow and the Wardrobe*. This is the first episode on which Caroline Skinner works as an Executive Producer, and the last for Piers Wenger.

**2012** A second 'aspect' of Clara appears in *The Snowmen*, which also introduces Doctor Simeon as the returning Great Intelligence.

**2013** *The Time of the Doctor* is Matt Smith's last full episode as the Doctor. It is also Brian Minchin's first as Executive Producer.

**2014** *Last Christmas*

**2015** Christmas Special – *The Husbands of River Song*

**5343 The events of** *The Husbands of River Song* **take place on Mendorax Dellora.**

## 26 DECEMBER

# The Doctor's Granddaughter Leaves the TARDIS

**1964** Susan leaves at end of the sixth and final episode of *The Dalek Invasion of Earth*, titled *Flashpoint*. It is David Whitaker's last episode as Story Editor.

'I was born in another world, another time,' Susan Foreman tells her teachers Ian Chesterton and Barbara Wright. The First Doctor says she is his granddaughter, and certainly there is a close bond between them and never any suggestion that this is not the case.

Susan looks and behaves like a typical 15-year-old girl. It is at her own insistence that she attends Coal Hill School, and it is here that her strange breadth of knowledge is noticed by Ian and Barbara. But Susan is not human. While she likes pop music, she can read a thick textbook in an evening and, in *The Sensorites* (1964), we discover she can communicate telepathically under certain circumstances.

Susan is an adventurer – she tells Ian and Barbara that she likes walking through the dark as it's mysterious. In *The Daleks* (1963–1964), she braves the dangers of the petrified jungle to retrieve the drugs her grandfather and friends desperately need. In *The Aztecs* (1964), she is headstrong enough to refuse to marry the Perfect Victim, who can demand anything of anyone.

When we first meet Susan, she is enjoying life as a 'normal' school girl on twentieth-century Earth. But Susan is growing up fast. She may have a bit of a crush on Ian and see Barbara as a mature confidante, but she falls completely in love with David Campbell in *The Dalek Invasion of Earth* (1964). Realising that she will never leave him, believing him to be dependent on her, the Doctor locks his granddaughter out of the TARDIS – putting her own future and happiness first.

# 27 DECEMBER

# The Vervoids Prove a Trial for the Doctor

The Vervoids encountered by the Sixth Doctor were a species of intelligent plant life created by the agronomist Professor Lasky and her team. In *The Trial of a Time Lord* (1986), they were transported in their pod form on board the luxury space liner *Hyperion III*. Infra-spectrum light did not affect the pods, but when they were exposed to high-intensity light, they hatched into humanoid plant creatures which broke out of the pods.

Professor Lasky's lab assistant, Ruth Baxter, was infected by a speck of Vervoid pollen that got into a scratch on her thumb while working on a cross-fertilisation procedure. Ruth started to mutate into a cross between a human and a Vervoid, and was confined to a cabin on the *Hyperion III*, hidden away from the passengers. Lasky hoped that Ruth could be treated when they got to Earth, but she was killed by the Vervoids.

The 'adult' Vervoids that emerged from the pods were carnivorous and highly intelligent. They attacked the ship's passengers – creating a compost heap from their dead bodies. Their intention was to travel to Earth and spread their seeds there, feeding on humanity. But their plans were thwarted by the Sixth Doctor, who was able to destroy the Vervoids with vionesium – an expensive metal found on the planet Mogar and stored in the ship's vault. Vionesium is similar to magnesium and emits intense light and carbon dioxide when exposed to oxygenated air.

**1972** An edited compilation repeat of *The Sea Devils* is shown on BBC 1 – it runs for 88 minutes.

**1973** An edited compilation repeat of *The Green Death* is shown on BBC 1 – it runs for 90 minutes.

**1974** An edited compilation repeat of *Planet of the Spiders* is shown on BBC 1 – it runs for 105 minutes.

**1975** An edited compilation repeat of *Genesis of the Daleks* is shown on BBC 1 – it runs for 86 minutes.

# 28 DECEMBER

# Meet the Fourth Doctor

In his fourth incarnation, the Doctor is more alien than ever. He is a constant surprise both to his enemies and to his companions. Less authoritarian and aristocratic than his predecessor, this Doctor is a rebel as well as a hero. He is Renaissance Man made real – a Jack of all trades and master of all of them.

It is not surprising that during his long tenure, this Doctor displays a gamut of emotions and attitudes. Yet he changes not from story to story but from moment to moment. Predominantly 'dark' in *The Seeds of Doom* (1976), he grins as he compares Scorby to a 'mindless' plant. Amused and jovial throughout *Nightmare of Eden* (1979), he cannot bring himself to speak to Tryst when the scientist tries to justify his actions.

For all his alien mutability and Olympian detachment, he is also at times the most 'human' of Doctors. He takes time in *The Ark in Space* (1975) to eulogise about humanity's indomitability. It is with almost human reluctance that he convinces Sorenson that the professor has only one way out of his dilemma in *Planet Of Evil* (1975) – to take his own life. For the first time he openly admits to having human friends and it becomes established that his favourite planet is Earth.

But, as with the Second Doctor, there is an air of superficiality to him and it is in the quieter, deeper moments we glimpse the darker and more 'genuine' Doctor. He is conscious always that he is essentially homeless, that he walks in eternity… It is ironic that this is the Doctor who is given an intimation of his own mortality in *Logopolis* (1981). In many ways, one gets the

**1963** The Daleks are seen fully for the first time in the second episode of *The Daleks*, titled *The Survivors*. The episode gets the highest ratings so far for the BBC in this timeslot.

**1968** *The Krotons* Episode 1

**1971** An edited compilation repeat of *The Dæmons* is shown on BBC 1 – it runs for 89 minutes.

**1974** *Robot* Part 1 is Tom Baker's first full episode as the Fourth Doctor and opens Season 12. Harry Sullivan appears for the first time in this episode, which is also Robert Holmes' first episode as Script Editor.

**1981** The spin-off *K-9 & Company: A Girl's Best Friend* is transmitted.

**1988** *The Greatest Show in the Galaxy* Part 3

impression that he has been aware of it right from the start, trying to live life to the full and cram in as many experiences, emotions, and journeys as possible into his all-too-brief long life.

# 29 DECEMBER

# The *Mary Celeste* is Abandoned

Having sailed from New York on 7 November 1872, the American merchant ship the *Mary Celeste* was found drifting off the Azores on 4 December 1872. There was no sign of the crew although the cargo and their possessions seemed undisturbed. What happened has remained one of the greatest unsolved sea mysteries of all time.

But in *The Chase* (1965), the First Doctor and his companions Ian, Barbara and Vicki arrive on the *Mary Celeste* – sometimes incorrectly referred to as the *Marie Celeste*, because that was how Arthur Conan Doyle misspelled the name in his fictional account, title 'J. Habakuk Jephson's Statement' and published in 1884. As well as altering the names of the captain and crew, Conan Doyle makes no mention of the Dalek time machine that materialises on board soon after the TARDIS.

Terrified by the sight of the Daleks as they emerge to hunt down the Doctor and his companions, the crew abandoned the ship, leaping overboard to escape the nightmare creatures. At least one Dalek was also lost overboard before the Doctor and his friends escaped and the Daleks returned to their own vessel and followed…

**1721 Jeanne-Antoinette Poisson,** also called Reinette, who later became Madame de Pompadour and who met the Tenth Doctor in *The Girl in the Fireplace,* **was born.**

**1928** Bernard Cribbins, who played Donna Noble's grandfather Wilfred Mott, was born. He also played Police Constable Tom Campbell in the second of the *Doctor Who* movies made in the mid-1960s, *Daleks – Invasion Earth, 2150AD*.

**1973** *The Time Warrior* Part 3

**1979** *The Horns of Nimon* Part 2

# 30 DECEMBER

# Multiple Doctors

According to the Time Lords in *The Three Doctors* (1972–1973), when they bring the first three incarnations of the Doctor together to defeat Omega, they must break the First Law of Time to enable the Doctor to meet himself. In fact, the Doctor had already met himself on several occasions. In *Day of the Daleks* (1972), the Third Doctor and Jo Grant briefly see versions of themselves from the future, and in *The Space Museum* (1965), the First Doctor and his companions see their future selves as exhibits…

It is rare for the Doctor to spend time with another of his incarnations. In *The Five Doctors* (1983), the Time Lord President Borusa attempts to bring together his first five incarnations – although the Fourth Doctor is trapped in a time eddy – in the Death Zone on Gallifrey. In *The Two Doctors* (1985), the Sixth Doctor follows the captured Second Doctor to Earth to rescue him from the Sontarans.

In *The Day of the Doctor* (2013) the Tenth and Eleventh Doctors meet the so-called War Doctor. Together with all of the Doctor's other incarnations up to and including the Twelfth Doctor, they manage to save Gallifrey from destruction…

While it does occasionally happen, it takes a crisis of epic proportions to bring multiple incarnations of the Doctor together.

ON THIS DAY

**1967** *The Enemy of the World* Episode 2

**1972** The first episode of *The Three Doctors* brings multiple Doctors together for the first time and opens Season 10.

**1978** *The Power of Kroll* Part 2

**1999 The Seventh Doctor arrives in San Francisco with the Master's remains, and is shot. He later regenerates into the Eighth Doctor in the morgue at the Walker General Hospital.**

## 31 DECEMBER

# An Adventure In Space And Time – The Doctor's Travels...

**1966** *The Highlanders* Episode 3

**1999 Most of the events of** *Doctor Who – The TV Movie* **take place on this day.**

When he first appeared out of the London fog in *An Unearthly Child* (1963), we knew almost nothing about the Doctor. Having witnessed his travels in the years since, we now know that he is a Time Lord from the planet Gallifrey. But we still know almost nothing about him – not even his real name. The Doctor has talked, occasionally, about his family. He has hinted at why he stole a TARDIS and left the Time Lords to travel through space and time. We have seen him angry, righteous, flippant, childish. We have seen him die and be reborn.

The Doctor is at once incredibly simple – demonstrating a well-defined moral stance and 'mission' – and yet also incredibly complex. His motivation and inner thoughts are a total mystery. The Doctor is a man who, by his own admission, walks for ever in eternity.

In *The Moonbase* (1967), the Second Doctor says: 'There are some corners of the universe which have bred the most terrible things. Things which act against everything that we believe in. They must be fought.' That must be as close to a mission statement for the Doctor as we are ever likely to get. One thing is for certain – the universe is a far better place with the Doctor in it…

# BBC

# DOCTOR WHO

## Royal Blood

### Una McCormack

ISBN 978 1 84990 992 1

*The Grail is a story, a myth! It didn't exist on your world! It can't exist here!*

The city-state of Varuz is failing. Duke Aurelian is the last
of his line, his capital is crumbling, and the armies of his enemy,
Duke Conrad, are poised beyond the mountains to invade.
Aurelian is preparing to gamble everything on one last battle.
So when a holy man, the Doctor, comes to Varuz from beyond
the mountains, Aurelian asks for his blessing in the war.

But all is not what it seems in Varuz. The city-guard have
lasers for swords, and the halls are lit by electric candlelight.
Aurelian's beloved wife, Guena, and his most trusted knight,
Bernhardt, seem to be plotting to overthrow their Duke,
and Clara finds herself drawn into their intrigue…

Will the Doctor stop Aurelian from going to war?
Will Clara's involvement in the plot against the Duke
be discovered? Why is Conrad's ambassador so nervous?
And who are the ancient and weary knights who arrive
in Varuz claiming to be on a quest for the Holy Grail…?

*An original novel featuring the Twelfth Doctor and Clara,
as played by Peter Capaldi and Jenna Coleman*

# BBC

# DOCTOR WHO

## Big Bang Generation

Gary Russell

ISBN 978 1 84990 991 4

*I'm an archaeologist, but probably not the one you were expecting.*

Christmas 2015, Sydney, New South Wales, Australia

Imagine everyone's surprise when a time portal opens up in
Sydney Cove. Imagine their shock as a massive pyramid now
sits beside the Harbour Bridge, inconveniently blocking Port
Jackson and glowing with energy. Imagine their fear as Cyrrus 'the
mobster' Globb, Professor Horace Jaanson and an alien assassin
called Kik arrive to claim the glowing pyramid. Finally imagine
everyone's dismay when they are followed by a bunch of con
artists out to spring their greatest grift yet.

This gang consists of Legs (the sexy comedian), Dog Boy
(providing protection and firepower), Shortie (handling logistics),
Da Trowel (in charge of excavation and history) and their leader,
Doc (busy making sure the universe isn't destroyed in an explosion
that makes the Big Bang look like a damp squib).

And when someone accidentally reawakens The Ancients of the
Universe – which, Doc reckons, wasn't the wisest or best-judged
of actions – things get a whole lot more complicated…

*An original novel featuring the Twelfth Doctor, as played by Peter Capaldi*

*Also available from BBC Books:*

**BBC**

# DOCTOR WHO

## Deep Time

Trevor Baxendale

ISBN 978 1 84990 990 7

*I do hope you're all ready to be terrified!*

The Phaeron disappeared from the universe over a million years ago. They travelled among the stars using roads made from time and space, but left only relics behind. But what actually happened to the Phaeron?

In the far future, humans discover the location of the last Phaeron road – and the Doctor and Clara join the mission to see where the road leads. Each member of the research team knows exactly what they're looking for – but only the Doctor knows exactly what they'll find.

Because only the Doctor knows the true secret of the Phaeron: a monstrous secret so terrible and powerful that it must be buried in the deepest grave imaginable…

*An original novel featuring the Twelfth Doctor and Clara, as played by Peter Capaldi and Jenna Coleman*

# BBC

# DOCTOR WHO

## The Legends of Ashildr

Justin Richards, James Goss, David Llewellyn
and Jenny T. Colgan

ISBN 978 1 78594 057 6

Ashildr, a young Viking girl, died helping the Doctor and Clara to
save the village she loved. And for her heroism, the Doctor used alien
technology to bring her back to life. Ashildr is now immortal – The
Woman Who Lived.

Since that day, Ashildr has kept journals to chronicle her
extraordinary life. *The Legends of Ashildr* is a glimpse of some of those
stories: the terrors she has faced, the battles she has won, and the
treasures she has found.

These are tales of a woman who lived longer than she should
ever have lived – and lost more than she can even remember.

*An original novel featuring the Twelfth Doctor as played by Peter Capaldi, and
Ashildr as played by Maisie Williams.*